D0055783

PROSECUTING WAR CRIMES
AND GENOCIDE

PROSECUTING WAR CRIMES AND GENOCIDE

THE TWENTIETH-CENTURY EXPERIENCE

Howard Ball

University Press of Kansas

© 1999 by the University Press of Kansas
All rights reserved

Published by the University Press of Kansas (Lawrence, Kansas 66049), which was
organized by the Kansas Board of Regents and is operated and funded by Emporia State
University, Fort Hays State University, Kansas State University, Pittsburg State University,
the University of Kansas, and Wichita State University.

Library of Congress Cataloging-in-Publication Data

Ball, Howard, 1937–
        Prosecuting war crimes and genocide : the twentieth-century
    experience / Howard Ball.
            p.   cm.
        Includes bibliographical references and index.
        ISBN 0-7006-0977-6 (cloth : alk. paper)
        1. International criminal courts—History. 2. War crime trials—
    History. 3. War crimes—History. 4. Genocide—History.
    I. Title.
    KZ6310.B35   1999
    341.7'7—dc21   99-22186

British Library Cataloguing in Publication Data is available.

Printed in the United States of America
10 9 8 7 6 5 4 3 2 1

The paper used in this publication meets the minimum requirements of the American
National Standard for Permanence of Paper for Printed Library Materials Z39.48-1984.

Dedicated to a caring human being,
Sidney B. Neidell

CONTENTS

ACKNOWLEDGMENTS

In writing this book, a number of people were helpful to me. Arthur Sweeny III was a regular source of data coming from nongovernmental organizations (NGOs) in the United States and elsewhere. Professor Gregory Gauss, a colleague of mine in the Department of Political Science at the University of Vermont (UVM), was also a useful resource on issues involving international laws of war. Excellent suggestions and words of encouragement were offered by Mike Briggs, the editor in chief of the University Press of Kansas. Last, a special thank you to Rabbi Joshua Chasan. His ideas about human nature presented in his sermons at Ohavi Zedek Synagogue in Burlington, Vermont, provided me with some Hebraic insights into the contemporary genocidal tragedies that played out in Bosnia-Herzegovina, Rwanda, and Kosovo province.

Like many researchers, I have come to appreciate the immense impact of the Internet on research. Much of the information I garnered and many of the documents used in the preparation of this book came from excellent Web sites, especially the United Nations' Web sites on the international criminal tribunals for the former Yugoslavia and Rwanda and on the Rome convention of June–July 1998. This technology has had an incalculable and positive impact on the way people—from elementary school students to Nobel Prize winners—discover knowledge.

My students at UVM and elsewhere have always provided me with new insights into these moral and realpolitik issues. I value their frank comments and the efforts of some of them to articulate the errors of my thinking about the possibility of an international criminal court (ICC). In particular, I'm appreciative of the comments and critiques made by Leon Smith, Sonja Eggert, and the uniquely gifted Robert Pontbriand.

My friend Phil Cooper, Gund Professor of Liberal Arts at UVM, disagrees with my conclusions and with my "Western" perspective. We have had a number of conversations on these matters that were of benefit to me in the writing of this book. There must be some process that keeps despotic leaders from committing crimes against humanity with *impunity*. Even if the process is imperfect, in a world with competing visions of who is to judge those who commit genocide, it is critical to take the first steps to apprehend and try such leaders—preferably in a nation-state, but if not, then in an international criminal tribunal. Phil has forced me to focus on these complex problems, and I thank him for his insights. However, he has not changed my mind on the values of universal jursidiction, complementarity, and comity.

As usual, my wife, Carol, has been a font of love and support. Her dad, Sid Neidell, the book's dedicatee, has always encouraged me to do my best, whether parenting, working, teaching, or doing research. He has been a loving father to me. His love is gratefully acknowledged, and returned.

Finally, my three daughters always deserve mention. Indeed, the first thing they do when a book of mine is published is to look at the dedication and the acknowledgments. Sue, Sheryl, and Melissa, you made it again—with all my love and appreciation.

And, for those who know me, there are Max and Maggie, the Chessies, Casey the Golden, and Stormin' Norman the quarterhorse to thank. These four lowered my blood pressure during the researching and writing of this book by being loving animals and friends.

INTRODUCTION

Prosecuting War Crimes and Genocide focuses on how a pained, shocked, and unbelieving civilized world community has struggled for a century to define the whats and understand the whys of war crimes, crimes against humanity, torture, and genocide. The question of what to do with the perpetrators has been a difficult, almost torturous one. A number of answers to this question have arisen out of the ashes of the genocidal tragedies of the twentieth century.

Amnesty. New national leaders may simply forgive, through grants of amnesty, the perpetrators of genocide in the belief that a societal reliving of the horrors will not enable the nation to get beyond its past. In the name of national reconciliation, criminal trials do not occur, and the past is forgotten. The accused war criminal is allowed to return as an ordinary citizen. In this clash between reconciliation and justice, mercy wins out and revenge is forsaken.

Is amnesty the correct answer for those former leaders clearly responsible for the tragedy of genocide? Khieu Samphan, who defected from the Khmer Rouge because of a promise of amnesty, said in December 1998, "We must forget the past in order to reach national reconciliation, peace and stability so we can rebuild our country." Hun Sen, the Cambodian leader who extended the amnesty, explained why he chose that alternative: "If we bring them to trial it will not benefit the nation, it will only mean a return to civil war. . . . If we put [them] in prison will this benefit society or lead to civil war?"[1]

Exile. Those responsible for war crimes may be exiled to a deserted island or subjected to a similar banishment. After World War I ended, should Kaiser Wilhelm II have been sent to the isle of Elba? This was the view of some of the Allies, including Great Britain, Belgium, and France, but it was rejected by the United States. Another version of this idea: In December 1998, a group

1

of U.S. senators, members of the Senate Foreign Relations Committee, sent a letter to President Bill Clinton about Slobodan Milosevic, leader of the Serbs and president of Yugoslavia. In order to bring about "a democratic government committed to the rule of law in Serbia and Yugoslavia," they urged Clinton to arrange a deal that would allow Milosevic and his wife, Mirjana Markovic, to take refuge in a third country in exchange for peacefully handing over power. "Absent fundamental change in Serbia and the leadership of Yugoslavia, the Balkans seem destined for perpetual crisis and successive Western interventions," they stated. They closed the letter by insisting on "an explicit statement that the U.S. seeks the replacement of the Milosevic regime."[2]

Vengeance. Some argue that vengeance is the answer to the "what to do" question. Should we just shoot the bastards who commit heinous offenses against civilians, prisoners of war (POWs), and belligerents on the field of battle? Certainly most of the Allied leaders in World War II, including Franklin D. Roosevelt but especially Winston Churchill (until the months preceding the Nuremberg trial), believed in the "bullet to the head" concept: summary capital punishment of the thousands of Nazi war criminals, without the benefit of trial.

Criminal trial. Others argue that a criminal trial, whether in a national or international criminal court, of political and military leaders charged with committing or ordering such crimes must take place. Defenders of this position argue that for peace to return to a society, those wronged in that society have to believe—and see—that wrongdoers are brought to justice in a court of law. Without justice for the perpetrators, there will be no peace. Someone must be held accountable. Further, those who survive the terror will continue to be "tormented by their past" until the guilty are brought before the bar of justice.[3]

Untold millions of civilians, POWs, and forces on the battlefield have lost their lives through the unmitigated cruelty of dictatorial political and military leaders. In the twentieth century, crimes against humanity and genocides took place in Europe, the Balkans, Turkey, China, Africa, Russia, and Southeast Asia. They occurred in civil wars, in regional clashes, and in the two world wars. They continue to take place as the world readies itself for the twenty-first century.

Kosovo, 1998

It is three years after the Dayton, Ohio, peace treaty ended the bloody, cruel fighting among Serbs, Muslims, and Croats in the former Yugoslavia. There is a 60,000-person multinational United Nations (UN) peacekeeping force in the region to protect the three ethnic groups as they go about the traumatic business of rebuilding shattered bodies and lives and communities.

A small band of insurgents in Kosovo, a once-autonomous province within Serbia,[4] seeks independence. The province's population is over 90 percent ethnic Albanian, with the remaining primarily Serb. Slobodan Milosevic, the president of Yugoslavia, cracks down on the ethnic Albanians, using the national army as well as special police forces. These special forces committed war crimes, crimes against humanity, and genocide in the 1991–1995 wars. In 1998, they were involved in the effort to end the rebellion, again using torture, killing, rape, and terror against civilian ethnic Albanians to end the rebels' efforts to attain independence. There is ample evidence that the Serb action against the ethnic Albanians is, according to former U.S. senator Robert Dole, a "human catastrophe in the making."[5]

A senior Clinton White House official said in September 1998 that the Kosovo "situation is awful and getting worse. If we don't want thousands of people to starve to death this winter, the White House will need to make a decision very quickly on whether to use firepower." There was continual shelling by the Serbs of villages populated by ethnic Albanians. Over 1,000 ethnic Albanians were killed by the Serb special forces and the bombardments. Almost 300,000 ethnic Albanian civilians were left homeless; some went to refugee camps, and others tried to cross over into Albania. And, most ominous, the Serb special forces rounded up boys and other male civilians from the villages for interrogation and, for many, cruel and inhuman death. John Shattuck, assistant U.S. secretary of state for human rights, cited evidence of "horrendous human rights violations, violations of humanitarian law and acts of punitive destruction on a massive scale."[6]

To place the situation in perspective, it is necessary to view the life and death of just one civilian in Kosovo, Rexhap Bislimi. His story illustrates the horrors of war crimes, crimes against humanity, and genocide and the importance of denying death squads and their leaders impunity for their actions.

Rexhap Bislimi was a thirty-three-year-old accountant who lived in Urosevac, Kosovo province, Serbia.[7] He was an ethnic Albanian, married with children, and not involved in the rebellion. He had been an active member of the Human Rights Council of Kosovo, founded in 1990 to seek a peaceful resolution of the status of Kosovars within the Serb Republic.

During the spring and summer of 1998, the Yugoslavian army swept into sections of Kosovo to beat down the uprising, followed by Serb "security police officers." The Milosevic-commanded military and security forces shelled cities and small towns in Kosovo, driving hundreds of thousands of civilians from their homes. "The crackdown has continued even though insurgents seeking independence for the ethnic Albanian majority in the Serbian province have ceased to be a fighting force."[8]

In early July 1998, the Serb security forces entered Rexhap's town, rounded up all the local civic and political leaders and professional persons, and systematically tortured and killed them in an effort to discover the whereabouts of the leaders of the rebellion and their arms caches—and to warn ethnic Albanian civilians "to stop supporting a separatist guerrilla force fighting for the independence of Serbia's Kosovo province."

On July 6, 1998, Rexhap was dragged to the local police station and beaten unmercifully by Serb special-unit men. The last time his mother, Hava Bislimi, saw her son was the following day, "his face battered with bruises." He was brought back to the family garden, given a shovel, and ordered to dig up the weapons that were allegedly buried there. "Reeling from beatings at the police station," Rexhap was "too weak to follow the orders," so neighbors were brought in to dig up the arms.

After failing to find any arms, the Serb security police told Rexhap to look at the house where he had been born. " 'This is the last time you will see it,' the Serbian officers were overheard saying as they marched him out of the gate." Six weeks later, on August 21, 1998, Rexhap Bislimi was dead.

Rexhap was never charged with committing any crime. He was not given an attorney to defend him. His family was denied the opportunity to visit him during his imprisonment. It was obvious that the Serbs did not want the family to see Rexhap because he was undergoing daily torture and beatings. Weekly, the family would try to see Rexhap, and weekly they would be prohibited from doing so.

On an official visiting day toward the end of August 1998, his mother noticed an ambulance pull up to the prison while she waited to see her son. Again she was told that she would not be able to see her son because he was being interrogated. Later, a sympathetic doctor at the hospital in Pristina, the capital, got word to Rexhap's family that he was in very bad condition. The family rushed to the hospital, but another friendly medic told them that Rexhap was in "such bad shape, you don't want to see him." They were also told that there was a chance to save Rexhap's life if they bought some medicine to stop the internal bleeding. The family spent 1,000 deutsche marks for the drugs and gathered blood donors from the family.

The next day, when they arrived with the medicine and the blood donors, the family was told that Rexhap Bislimi had died the preceding day. The official death certificate stated that death was caused "by [repeated] blows to the head and body." His belongings were returned to the family: "a watch, his identity card, his wallet with a dollar bill tucked inside."

Thousands of ethnic Albanians attended Rexhap Bislimi's funeral. The deceased accountant's children, wife, and mother led the march to the cemetery. Afterward, the grandmother recounted a conversation she had had with her granddaughter: "To console her son's oldest daughter, Ardita, 6, Mrs. Bislimi said she had told her he had gone to Germany. But the child had seen enough not to believe it. 'No,' Ardita replied, according to her grandmother, 'my father has gone to the graveyard.' "

"Will the killing ever stop? Will the scourge of genocide ever be eradicated? Will humanity ever be wise enough to prevent the deaths of potential genocide victims *before* they [become statistics]?"[9] These are some of the difficult questions raised by academicians, religious leaders, international nongovernmental organizations (NGOs) such as Amnesty International, and some national and international political leaders and agencies. These are some of the questions raised in this book.

Universal Jurisdiction, Complementarity, and Comity

Other significant questions ripple endlessly across the pages of this century's history. How does the world community respond to war crimes, crimes against humanity, and genocide? Kosovo 1998 is a repeat of the type of extreme brutality men inflict on other men, women, children, and the elderly. It occurs in civil as well as regional and world wars. War crimes were charged by the victorious Allies against the Germans and Turks after World War I. Since the end of the international military trials of Nazi and Japanese leaders of World War II, there have been dozens of regional military actions around the globe in which genocide, crimes against humanity, and war crimes were committed. Yet, with the exception of UN-created ad hoc international criminal courts for the former Yugoslavia (1993) and Rwanda (1994), little justice has been apportioned—by either domestic courts or international tribunals—to the killers and torturers of innocent civilians like Rexhap Bislimi. No justice has been meted out to those leaders responsible for untold thousands of rapes followed by execution.

As a consequence, there has emerged a culture of impunity, one that underscores the reality of an almost universal nonaccountability for war crimes and genocide. The Cambodian genocide is a glaring example of universally condemned actions by Pol Pot and his Khmer Rouge that went unpunished.

Pol Pot's radical regime led to the deaths of almost 2 million Cambodians between 1975 and 1979. He acted with impunity. Pol Pot and his lieutenants were never indicted under the criminal laws of Cambodia or in accordance with the body of international criminal law that has been in effect since 1899, especially the Nuremberg and Tokyo precedents. He died in 1998 without ever answering for his crimes. Two other Khmer Rouge leaders, upon being granted amnesty, surrendered to civilian authorities after his death. Cambodian prime minister Hun Sen welcomed them, in his own words, "with bouquets of flowers, not with prisons and handcuffs."[10]

Some argue for alternatives short of vengeance for national leaders responsible for crimes against humanity and genocide (including criminal trials, truth commissions such as South Africa's Truth and Reconciliation Commission, amnesty, exile, reparations, and political deals that lead to the abrogation of power),[11] but should forgiveness be one of these alternatives? Hun Sen's comment about the two Khmer Rouge defectors—that Cambodia "should dig a hole and bury the past and look ahead to the 21st century with a clean slate"—suggests such a choice.[12] Is his evidently benign choice going to work when millions of Cambodians who lost parents, brothers, sisters, and grandparents at the hands of the Khmer Rouge remain angry at the clear absence of justice? Commenting on the amnesty extended to the two Khmer Rouge, Son Chhay, a member of the parliament, said: "This is wrong. Every Cambodian who lost relatives during the Pol Pot regime cannot forget and is still suffering."

Should one's compassion for the victims and their surviving families outweigh "geopolitical or legal questions"?[13] Or should realpolitik trump the solemn cries for utopian justice?

The culture of impunity must end. If Cambodian leaders cannot or will not bring to justice—in Cambodian courts—those responsible for the 1970s "killing fields," then the 1998 Rome statute may be the answer.[14] The establishment of an international criminal tribunal with an independent prosecutor is—short of individual, unofficial assassinations of Khmer Rouge leaders[15]—the probable remedy when the national courts cannot act.

Nuremberg and Tokyo were watershed precedents in the "effort to establish an effective system of international criminal justice."[16] But they were only the *molecular* beginning of the internationalization of certain war crimes and the creation of the prosecutorial mechanisms to apprehend, try, and punish individuals guilty of war crimes and genocide. The unfinished legacy of the Nuremberg and Tokyo International Military Tribunals is the creation of a permanent international criminal court (ICC) that is effective and has the support of the world's major powers. Drexel Sprecher, one of the Nuremberg tribunal's prosecutors, said:

> [A] major part of the legacy would be the need to have a permanent establishment that is ready to go and hunt war crimes and develop materials on war crimes very early, and not to have to put together a last minute group of people. . . . Had we a permanent [criminal] tribunal ready to go with trained people, of high stature, we'd have been a lot further down the road [to minimizing genocide as a state policy] than we are today.[17]

Such an ICC, to be successful, must have the jurisdiction to address the war crimes committed, for example, by the Serb military and special forces in Kosovo in 1998, unless the Serb government conducts military courts-martial to punish the offenders (highly unlikely). If the domestic law cannot or will not be applied by a nation-state against those accused of war crimes and genocide, a permanent ICC must have jurisdiction to act. Without such a permanent international institution, the cruel, wanton, brutal murder of civilians such as Rexhap Bislimi will continue to go unpunished. And if there is no justice meted out, people will remember, and there will be no peace.

An international criminal tribunal is needed to provide justice for the victims and to end the culture of impunity that has emerged since 1950 and has immunized the perpetrators of genocide, war crimes, and crimes against humanity. As Hans Corell, a UN official, said:

> The very reason that certain armed conflicts occur, entailing crimes against international humanitarian law, is, in my view, that the international community has so far been unable to demonstrate that those responsible would be brought to justice—sooner or later.[18]

There are loud critics of this movement in international law. They argue that international law is very different from domestic law (the laws and justice systems of nation-states). In the international setting, there is no viable constitutional framework defining the general limitations of national governmental authority. There is, in international law, no equivalent to the limits on governmental power contained in the first ten amendments to the U.S. Constitution (the Bill of Rights). Nor is there any international mechanism for punishing those national leaders who act in inhumane ways to control their populations.[19]

However, even the critics have to admit that some crimes are *universally* recognized as abominable—criminal actions that shock the conscience of all civilized societies, whether in Asia, Africa, Europe, North or South America. Potter Stewart, the late associate justice of the U.S. Supreme Court, had some difficulty defining pornography, "but," he said, "I know it when I see it!" The actions described in this book, the war crimes, crimes against humanity, the use of torture, and genocide, *are known when seen*. A quick glance at photos of the heads of seven Chinese lying neatly in a row, one with a cigarette in the mouth; the ovens at Auschwitz, with a mostly charred body of a victim still inside, smoldering; human skulls littering Cambodia's killing fields, popping up from their watery graves; emaciated Bosnians captured by Serbs, placed in concentration camps, and then executed and dumped into Bosnia's killing fields; the consequence of a machete blow to the head of a young girl, and one *knows*, universally, what constitutes war crimes, crimes against humanity, torture, and genocide. There is a universal shock to the world's conscience.

During the twentieth century, the world has been witness to these universally condemned crimes, from the German destruction of the Herero in Africa at the turn of the century to the Serbian slaughter of Kosovars at its end. As a consequence of man's inhumanity to man, there has developed the equivalent of a written international bill of rights in the form of a catalog of horrors rightly condemned by Americans, Russians, Nigerians, Chileans, and others around the globe. This litany of crimes, because universally condemned, can be considered crimes of "universal jurisdiction."

Perpetrators of these universally condemned crimes should not be allowed to act with naked impunity; there must be some form of justice for those who rob others of peace and of life itself. Even the critics of international law agree that such human demons should be prosecuted and punished for their crimes against humanity—but "domestically," that is, only in a nation's criminal justice system.[20] Those who argue for an ICC do not disagree with this assessment but add an important caveat: complementarity.

Inherent in the 1998 Rome Treaty, in which the first permanent ICC was created by UN member states, is the concept of complementarity. Political and military leaders who commit actions that are universally condemned as war crimes or genocide must, when captured, face trial for their actions in a national court. If this does not occur, for whatever reason, then the accused must be brought before an international criminal tribunal.

Complementarity clearly suggests a functional form of comity, or respect, between domestic and international justice systems. Specifically, there is deference by the international community to a national legal response to acts of genocide committed in that country. However, complementarity also clearly suggests that if no action is taken by a nation's leaders to achieve justice, the international criminal tribunal can fill the vacuum by trying the alleged violators of universally condemned criminal acts.

Prosecuting War Crimes and Genocide examines these many questions and the answers they have engendered by tracing events since the Geneva Accords were signed in 1899. Most of the chapters focus on the world community's post–World War I efforts to address the general issue of defining crimes of universal jurisdiction and ensuring trial and punishment of those found guilty of committing war crimes, crimes against humanity, torture, or genocide.

The Rome statute of 1998 created such a court that would have the jurisdiction, the power, and the authority to provide justice to groups that have been the targets of war crimes and genocide. It is operational only when and if a national criminal justice system cannot or will not seek justice by bringing to trial the perpetrators of these crimes. Such an ICC will have an impact only if—and this is a very big if—powerful nation-states, the United States in particular, support the general concept, accept the court's jurisdiction, and assist in the apprehension of persons indicted for crimes against humanity.

Driving the supporters of a permanent ICC is the need to punish those who have committed war crimes in order to deter other despots from acting in a similar manner. Also driving the advocates is the somber and tragic reality voiced by a six-year-old in Kosovo: "My father has gone to the graveyard." Such wanton killings of innocent men, women, and children must be stopped; the world community, given the history of genocide in the twentieth century, is surely wise enough to demand that the nations' leaders act to prevent the deaths of future victims.

Opponents of such an international criminal tribunal argued that it would infringe on national sovereignty and place their leaders, both political and military, and their military forces in jeopardy of being indicted for war crimes. Since the 1919 Versailles conference, the Americans have consistently opposed an ICC because of the alleged inroads it would make on national sovereignty. This unwillingness to accept and act on the concept of comity accounted for the international community's failure to ratify a permanent court until 1998.

Prosecuting War Crimes and Genocide also examines the clash between two important and seemingly contradictory values: nation-state realpolitik versus justice for the victims and survivors of genocide, war crimes, or crimes against humanity. Clearly, as early as 1919 there was a perceived need for such an ICC; the post-Nuremberg quest to create it was muted during the decades of the cold war and, after 1989, by American insistence that the UN Security Council have a veto over cases that such a tribunal would hear. As the world enters the new millennium, there has been created, in the 1998 Rome treaty, both the form and the substance of such a permanent ICC. It emphasizes two general propositions: the need to hold accountable those who order and commit these universally scorned crimes, and the need to end the insidious culture of impunity that is presently the norm.

1

WAR CRIMES AND GENOCIDE: 1899–1939

War crimes and genocide are not new twentieth-century realities. Whether it was the poisoning of springs and wells to kill the enemy, showing no quarter to a defeated enemy in the field, mistreating prisoners of war, laying siege to undefended towns populated by civilians, or intentionally killing groups of people, young and old alike, because of race, color, religion, or ethnicity, the world has for centuries experienced war, war crimes, and acts of brutality that violated the customs and conventions of war and the "conscience" of humanity.

Throughout history, conduct-of-war issues have remained the same; only the specific customs and the conventions of warfare have changed. What constraints are there on the behavior of belligerents in battle on land? on sea? What about the treatment of prisoners? of civilians? What actions on the field of battle are permitted? prohibited? What about the introduction of new weapons systems? And what about enforcement of these constraints on the conduct of warfare and punishment for violators of these norms of war?[1] These questions have plagued society's leaders—political, military, and religious—for centuries, but there is in history slow movement toward their resolution.

Constraints on the conduct of war have been imposed by the international community—ironically, most manifestly in the twentieth century, the era of total war and genocidal atrocities. As the horrors of war were brought into the lives of people across the world, as the atomic bomb's mushroom cloud became the awesome signature, the century's metaphor, there developed a global consensus that limits had to be placed on actions before and during war. Nations have collectively sought to prevent war altogether, to ensure more humane treatment of belligerents (combatants, wounded, and prisoners) and civilians during war. Since 1945, the international community has enforced these laws of war through the creation of four ad hoc international criminal tribunals: Nuremberg, Tokyo, Yugoslavia, and Rwanda.

These limits on the conduct of war and on the imperative to punish violators of the laws of war, introduced by European powers, "grew out of the cultures of the[ir] war-making societies, . . . largely shaped by [the] Christian ethic. . . . At the root of the Christian humanist attempts to constrain war has been the recognition of the adversary as a human being possessing certain fundamental rights."[2] When a national leader determines that an adversary, residing in the nation or beyond its borders, does not possess those essential "human" rights, the treatment of that class of *untermensch* (underbeing) is not constrained. Sadly, in the past eight decades, the world has witnessed the consequences of unrestrained cruelty and bestiality toward those seen as less than human: Armenians in Turkey in 1915, Jews and Gypsies in Europe in the 1930s and 1940s, Chinese in 1937, Cambodians in the 1970s, Bosnian Muslims and ethnic Albanians in Kosovo, and Tutsi in Rwanda in the 1990s.

The Hague Era: Codifying the Conduct of Warfare

Laws of war were created to provide constraints, in the form of customary law and then treaties, governing the relations between nation-states in times of international tension. Treaty-based laws were the extension of customary law and were manifested in nineteenth-century bilateral and multilateral agreements among nations.[3] Until the twentieth century, the dominant focus of international law was the nation-state, and the concept of sovereign immunity was the paramount principle. War was viewed by the sovereign as an unfortunate but necessary characteristic of state sovereignty. There was no question that powerful nation-states—Germany, Great Britain, the United States, and France—determined the fate and security of their citizens and used their military and economic might to ensure the continued vitality of the state. Except for the International Red Cross and Red Crescent Movement[4] and the Catholic Church, there were no international organs on the world scene until the first decades of the twentieth century.

Until the twentieth century, wars were "conflicts over political power rather than ideology." They were small wars waged between professional armies "so far as possible with humanity."[5] They did not involve civilians, unless a town was under attack, nor were the economies of the warring nations adversely affected. They were generally over quickly, settled by an armistice and negotiated peace terms.

Customs and treaties concerning the conduct of war moderated the nastiness of battles and governed the use of force during war: They served as the "cultural regulation of violence."[6] Sacred truces were declared so that belligerents could participate in the Olympic Games in ancient Greece. In the Middle Ages, customs differentiated Bellum Romanum, or wars against pagans in which no quarter was given in battle, from Bellum Hostile, or wars fought between Christians in which civilians were spared (the Peace of God), wars were limited to certain days of the week (the Truce of God), quarter was given, and prisoners were paroled.

By the middle of the nineteenth century, nation-states began to codify the customs of war and to create treaty-based laws of war. In Paris in 1856, for example, a maritime convention met to address the status of neutral ships during wartime.

On June 24, 1859, Henry Dunant, a Swiss businessman, visited the battlefield at Solferino, Italy, where, in one day, over 40,000 French and Italian soldiers had been killed or wounded and left to die. Appalled at the slaughter of so many and that so few persons were caring for the wounded, he used his own money to buy medical supplies. At home in Geneva, he wrote a book, *A Memory of Solferino* (1862), about his experience on the battlefield. In it, he asked whether it would be "possible in time of peace and quiet to form relief societies for the purpose of having care given to the wounded in wartime by zealous, devoted, and thoroughly qualified volunteers?"[7] The book was widely read and had an impact on its readers.

At the call of another Swiss humanist, Gustave Moynier, president of Geneva's Welfare Society, sixteen European nations met in August 1864, and twelve signed the Geneva Convention for the Amelioration of the Wounded and Sick of Armies in the Field. The treaty created the International Committee of the Red Cross. It provided "inviolability" for medical staff and volunteers to care for wounded in the field, called for humane treatment of the wounded and prisoners of war, and created an emblem for those who treated the wounded: the red cross on a white background, "the reverse colors of the Swiss flag." (By 1900, there were Red Cross Societies in thirty-seven nations, including, in 1882, the United States, which was a reluctant signer because it was "suspicious of European politics [and] disdain[ed] . . . any entangling treaty dealing with war.")[8]

In 1868 in St. Petersburg, Russia, a treaty was signed that banned the use of explosive bullets in battle. The declaration produced by the nations reflected the war ethics of the era. The explosive bullets were prohibited because of the perceived need to "alleviate as much as possible the calamities of war." The use of those bullets "uselessly aggravate[d] the sufferings of disabled men [and were] contrary to the laws of humanity."[9]

During America's Civil War, President Abraham Lincoln asked a Columbia

University law professor, Francis Lieber, to draft a manual for the behavior of Union troops in the field. Promulgated as General Order No. 100, Adjutant General's Office, on April 24, 1863, it was distributed to every commander in the Union *and* Confederate armies, was followed by the belligerents, and remains the core of the latest manual for the conduct of war by American forces in the field. Lieber's code of behavior, entitled *Instructions for the Government of Armies of the United States in the Field*, covered the use of private property of the enemy; the protection of persons, "and especially of women, of religion, the arts and sciences, [and] the punishment of crimes against the inhabitants of hostile countries"; deserters, prisoners of war ("who shall be fed upon plain and wholesome food, whenever practicable, and treated with humanity"), partisan fighters, spies, and captured messengers; abuse of the flag of truce; exchange of prisoners; parole, armistice, and capitulation; and, in Section X, guidelines on "Insurrection—Civil War—Rebellion." (The manual became a model for other nations in the decades after it was published.)

So long as the warring sides observed "the requisite formalities, [the rules of conduct that] limited those uses of force,"[10] there was no talk of war crimes. War crimes were committed by persons, under the command of a sovereign, in violation of these rules of engagement. Punishment after a conflict ended was, until World War I, rare and was handled by a nation's military courts.

Many of these norms were further codified at the Hague conferences of 1899 and 1907. A fundamental principle was born at these meetings: the individual, irrespective of nationality, had rights and duties inherent in human nature and was both a subject and a member of an international community. The first treaty of the modern era that addressed "the illegality of aggressive force [and its effects on civilians] was embodied in the 1899 Hague Conventions for the Pacific Settlement of International Disputes" and was amplified at the 1907 meeting.[11] (Whether as a member of a belligerent force or as a citizen living in an area occupied by enemy forces, the human rights of individuals in international law have expanded since then, especially after World War II.)[13]

The 1899 conference at the Hague, attended by twenty-six nation-states at the invitation of Czar Nicholas II of Russia, focused on the arms race then taking place. Disarmament and the need for arbitration and mediation forums as an alternative to war were the foci of the conference. For the treaty signers, international arbitration was "recognized . . . as the most effective, and at the same time, the most equitable, means of settling disputes which diplomacy has failed to settle."[13]

Since 1899, "there have been many attempts to form an effective body of international criminal law to eradicate aggressive war as a method of international decision making and to secure humane treatment for persons during both war and peacetime."[14] At the 1907 meeting in the Hague, this time at the call of American President Theodore Roosevelt, a treaty was signed with annexes that dealt with the laws and customs of war on land.

The general thrust of both conferences was to "serve the interests of humanity and the ever progressive needs of civilization" by "diminish[ing] the evils of war." This was to be accomplished by revising "the general laws and customs of war, either with a view to defining them with greater precision or to confining them within such limits as would mitigate their severity as far as possible." Because the treaties entered into could not cover "all of the circumstances which arise in [war]," the Martens clause (named for Russian jurist Feodor Martens, who insisted on including such a general statement of principle) was added to the preamble of the 1907 treaty:

> Until a more complete code of the laws of war has been issued, the High Contracting Parties deem it expedient to declare that, in cases not included in the Regulations adopted by them, the inhabitants and the belligerents *remain under the protection and the rule of the principles of the laws of nations, as they result from the usages established among civilized peoples, from the laws of humanity, and the dictates of the public conscience.*[15]

The 1907 annex contained a list of regulations agreed to by the signatory powers. The restrictions underscored the principle "that the right of belligerents to fight war is not unlimited." It prohibited certain methods of fighting war, and the implicit assumption was that persons could be prosecuted for violating these new laws of war if they:

Attacked or bombarded undefended towns, villages, or dwellings

Used poison or other weapons that caused "superfluous" injuries

Declared "no quarter"

Improperly used the flag of truce

"Wantonly" destroyed enemy cities or towns or caused "devastation not justified by military necessity"

"Willfully damaged institutions dedicated to religion, charity, and education, the arts and sciences, historic monuments, and works of art and science"

Abused lawful authority over enemy civilians when occupying an enemy's territory

Mistreated prisoners of war

Attacked soldiers who had laid down their arms

Used dumdum bullets

Used projectiles containing asphyxiating gases, "calculated to cause unnecessary suffering"

Used aerial bombs

Violated a nation's neutrality[16]

Both the 1899 and the 1907 conventions raised a new issue regarding the conduct of war: "the duty owed by a belligerent occupant to citizens of the overrun nation." That "duty" meant that the occupier "shall take all the measures in his power to restore and ensure, as far as possible, public order and safety, while respecting, unless absolutely prevented, the law in force in the country."[17] This was a major issue at the conclusion of both world wars, given the allegations of war crimes, crimes against humanity, and genocide committed by the occupying authority.

Although there was agreement on the cataloging of specific war crimes, there was little willingness by the twenty-six sovereign nations to "submit to the jurisdiction of an international court" tasked to try alleged war criminals.[18] The conferences failed to get agreement on the creation of a permanent international criminal court "with compulsory jurisdiction that would transcend national boundaries." Sovereign nations, with the United States the principal outspoken opponent, were unwilling to be bound by the judgments of an impartial international judicial authority. The United States continually claimed that it "reserved the right to resolve any purely American issue."[19] (This argument against granting substantive jurisdiction to international legal tribunals is still being used as the world enters the twenty-first century.)

Consequently, the 1907 treaty was mostly silent regarding punishment of war crimes on the battlefied as well as collateral war crimes against unarmed civilians.[20] There was no enforcement mechanism agreed to by the parties to the treaty, and only one of the articles addressed the consequences of violating the regulations. Article III stated, in its entirety, that "a belligerent party which violates the provisions of the said Regulations shall, if the case demands, be liable to pay compensation. It shall be responsible for all acts committed by persons forming part of its armed forces."

These two Hague treaties codified certain actions in wartime as war crimes. They were the "critically significant . . . beginnings of substantive international criminal law"—laws of war that became the basis "for the substantive law that an international criminal court would apply" decades later.[21] These treaty restraints on the conduct of war were visited less than a decade later, with the outbreak of the First World War.

World War I: War Crimes and Punishment

The First World War (1914–1918) was a watershed conflagration for a number of reasons. It was the first major conflict after the Hague Conventions of 1899 and 1907, and, during and after the war, the question of how to deal with the perpetrators of war crimes was openly discussed and debated by the Allied and Associated Powers. It was the world's first total war, with over 65 million men from thirty-two nations involved in the four-year conflict (the four Central Powers—Germany, Austria-Hungary, Bulgaria, and Turkey—arrayed against twenty-eight Allied and Associated Powers—including the United States, Great Britain, Italy, France, Russia, and Japan). Battles raged on the European continent, as well as in the Balkans, Africa, the Middle East, the Pacific and Atlantic Oceans, and the North Sea. Over 21 million belligerents were wounded, and almost 9 million military personnel were killed in once unimaginable ways.

Administratively, the war exhibited significant changes in the ways armies were organized and transported to battle. Conscription had become a basic element in the creation of most armies. Those few powers that did not conscript young men into the military, such as Great Britain, quickly had to adopt such a method to provide the necessary military forces to fight the war. The mobilization of the military, especially of the reserves, was speedy and logistically well-coordinated.

The war also saw new technological developments, from improved battlefield communications and transport to new weapons of war, including the machine gun, powerful explosives, barbed wire, zeppelins, poison gases, and long-range artillery (which heaved shells six to thirty kilometers), as well as the introduction of the tank, airplane, and submarine. New weapons research and development was done by large industrial firms working closely with the military. This new symbiotic military-industrial complex included industrial behemoths such as Krupp in Germany, Vickers in Great Britain, DuPont in the United States, and Creusot in France.

Finally, the world war had an ideological dimension that had not been

World War I. Allied poster, "A Good Month's Business," depicting German war crimes against innocent civilians, circa 1918. (Library of Congress)

evidenced in earlier conflicts between nation-states. Propaganda developed by the warring nations to incite their populations cast the enemy in a purely evil way. Enemy armies and their leaders were evil "beasts" or "Huns"; the artwork (films, posters) and news stories created during the war were essential parts of the propaganda campaign. Their goal was to objectify and dehumanize the enemy and, in so doing, generate a passionate hatred of the enemy.

From the outbreak of the war, the Central Powers, especially Germany and Turkey, were charged with gross violations of the laws of war. Germany invaded a neutral nation, Belgium, in order to outflank the French, move rapidly on Paris, force the French to surrender, and then move its armies by train to the eastern front in time to defeat the Russians. Invading Belgium, however, was a violation of a nineteenth-century treaty of neutrality between Belgium and other signatories, including Germany. During the course of the long war, Germany and Turkey were accused by the Allies of, among other war crimes:

Treating Belgian citizens harshly during the German occupation of that nation

Deporting Belgian civilians to Germany for slave labor

Executing civilians who opposed the German advance

Taking civilians hostage, and shooting many of them

Sacking Louvain, Belgium, killing hundreds of civilians and destroying the old town

Using poison gas at the battle of Ypres

Sinking the passenger ship *Lusitania,* resulting in over 2,000 deaths

Executing Edith Cavell, a British nurse working in Brussels who was accused of aiding Allied soldiers

Killing of over a million ethnic Armenians by the Turkish government and military beginning in April 1915[22]

Given the heavy and continuous propaganda barrage by the Allies concerning the "rape" of Belgium by the German "Huns," almost immediately in France, Belgium, and Great Britain there was a passionate cry for the punishment of those who committed atrocities against civilians. The public was outraged by the alleged war crimes committed by the Germans and the Turks.

During the war, both the Allies and the Central Powers tried military prisoners before their courts-martial for war crimes. The French held courts-martial for German soldiers who plundered Rheims Cathedral and who gave no quarter to French soldiers during battle. The British tried captured U-boat (submarine) sailors and officers as war criminals and did not treat them as prisoners of war (POWs). The Germans reciprocated by holding many French and British POWs in prison cells and conducting trials that led to the deaths of Allied personnel, including nurse Cavell.

World War I saw the Allied victors attempt to create an international court of criminal justice to punish governmental and military leaders of the Central Powers and other individuals for war crimes. The demand for war crimes trials grew out of alleged German and other Central Powers' violations of the Hague Conventions of 1899 and 1907. The British and French strongly believed that Germany's head of state, Kaiser Wilhelm II, "was responsible for international crimes and that superior orders might not serve as a defense in every case; [these views] added a new dimension to legal developments in international penal law."[23]

Consequently, some of the victorious Allies (France, Great Britain, and Belgium), full of hatred toward Germany and its Central Power allies for their cruel behavior during the war (especially Turkey, whose Young Turk leaders ordered the mass deportation and genocide of over a million Turkish-Armenian Christians), included the demand for war crimes tribunals in the postwar diplomatic discussions that would lead to peace treaties formally ending the hostilities. These demands marked the initiation of a new phase in the development of individual criminal responsibility for war crimes.

However, the creation of an international tribunal to address alleged war

World War I. Allied poster, "Remember Belgium," depicting German war crimes against innocent civilians. German soldier, leading girl by hand, with city burning in background. (Library of Congress)

crimes committed by the Germans and Turks did not come to pass, owing primarily to the intransigence of the Americans. The United States categorically objected to such an international criminal tribunal. Secretary of State Robert Lansing believed that the punishment of war criminals must be left to each nation's military tribunals. Lansing opposed the establishment of a war crimes tribunal precedent. (This would be one of the arguments made by representatives of the Clinton administration in 1998 as 161 nations met in Rome to discuss the possibility of creating a permanent international criminal court.)

Furthermore, Lansing opposed trying Kaiser Wilhelm II of Germany because of the all-powerful principle of sovereign immunity, that is, that the civil and military leaders of a sovereign nation could not be tried for war crimes committed while they were in power. Lansing also opposed the concept of "negative criminality" put forward by France and Great Britain, which would enable the Allies to try military leaders because they had *failed* to prevent war crimes committed by their subordinates in the field. Finally, Lansing and his staff opposed the use of the Martens clause as the basis for indicting and trying the defeated military and civilian leaders in an international war crimes tribunal.

Interestingly, President Woodrow Wilson greatly distrusted the State Department and disagreed with Lansing's views on this and other key postwar issues, including creation of the League of Nations. Although Wilson believed that Lansing was "too cautious and legalistic," he did not replace him or countermand his secretary's views on the punishment of war criminals.[24]

The British and French public clamor for such a tribunal, unprecedented in world history, forced the issue into the peace settlement discussions among the Allies. Indeed, it became one of the primary issues at Versailles, with the French demanding the establishment of a permanent international criminal tribunal with jurisdiction to adjudicate allegations of war crimes. Although confronted by American opposition, in 1919, the Allies created a Committee of Enquiry into the Breaches of the Laws of War, consisting of fifteen international law jurists from the victorious Allied nations. It was charged with examining and then reporting back to the delegates at the peace conference on the following matters:

1. The facts regarding the start of the world war and the culpability for it;
2. Whether there were offenses by the Central Powers against the laws and customs of law in their conduct of the war; and
3. A process by which accused war criminals could be tried.[25]

In 1919, the Commission on Responsibility produced its findings. Its report urged the creation of an international criminal court composed of Allied judges to try all heads of state and top military leaders accused of war crimes (setting aside the notion of sovereign immunity) because they had ordered illegal acts or failed to prevent them, thus violating the laws of war and the laws of humanity (as defined in the preamble to the Hague Convention of 1907).[26]

The final report, detailing hundreds of war crimes and identifying many hundreds of German, Turkish, and Bulgarian war criminals, led to the inclusion of Sections 227 to 230 in the Versailles Peace Treaty mandating the establishment of an international war crimes tribunal. After intense and lengthy wrangling among themselves without total resolution, the Allies included war crimes clauses in the peace treaties foisted on the defeated nations—but they also let it be known, especially to the Dutch (who had granted Kaiser Wilhelm II political asylum at the end of the war), that they would not enforce these sections of the peace treaties. "Ultimately, the Dutch government refused to extradite the exiled Kaiser, citing as a ground for refusal the absence of an international statute defining the specific offenses alleged to have been committed."[27]

However, for the first time in history, these clauses in the peace treaty established the principle that punishment of some sort for war crimes was a proper conclusion of a war, rather than the traditional amnesty that had followed earlier wars. Although not enforced, Sections 227 to 230 were precedent setting in international law. Section 227 "publicly arraign[ed] William II of Hohenzollern, formerly German Emperor, for a supreme offence against international morality and the sanctity of treaties."

> A special tribunal [consisting of five judges, one each from the United States, Great Britain, France, Italy, and Japan] will be constituted to try the accused, thereby assuring him the guarantees essential to the right of defence, . . . [and] to fix the punishment which it considers should be imposed.

Germany and the other defeated Central Powers were required, in Section 228, to "recognize the right of the Allied and Associated Powers to bring before military tribunals persons accused of having committed acts in violation of the laws and customs of war. Such persons shall, if found guilty, be sentenced to punishments laid down by law." They were required to "hand over" to the victors "all persons accused of having committed an act in violation of the laws and customs of war." Section 229 outlined the process accused war criminals would face:

> [They] will be brought before the military tribunals of that Power. [Those guilty of crimes] against the nationals of more than one [of the Powers] will be brought before military tribunals composed of members of the military tribunals of the Powers concerned. In every case the accused will be entitled to name his counsel.

Finally, in Section 230, Germany and the other defeated nations were required to "furnish all documents and information of every kind, the production of which may be considered necessary to ensure the full knowledge of the incriminating acts, the discovery of offenders and the just appreciation of responsibility."

These war crimes sections of the Versailles Treaty were immediately referred to as the *schmachparagraphen*, the "shame paragraphs." Attempts to implement them by postwar German governmental leaders led to violence and serious political unrest until 1922.

Based on the research conducted and the findings submitted by the special committee established by the Allied Powers at Versailles, almost 1,000 Germans were identified as war criminals by the Allies, and plans were drawn up for Great Britain, France, Italy, Belgium, Poland, Romania, and Yugoslavia to prosecute them before military tribunals in accordance with Section 229 of the treaty. Because of American unwillingness to force Germany to hand over the indicted men to the Allies, these trials did not take place.

Because of clashes between the United States and its allies regarding this "unchartered area of international law," there was no unanimity among the victors regarding the establishment of the war crimes tribunal process and precedent.[28] Without unanimity, the will to enforce the *schmachparagraphen* was absent.

The American objection, as reflected in Secretary of State Lansing's official comments at the treaty talks in Versailles, was that the proposed international war crimes tribunal was a direct attack on the concept of state sovereignty, as well as a reflection of a total "lack of precedent, precept, practice, or procedure" about such processes.[29] Lansing's remedy was to democratize the defeated nations and to have their own legal and military authorities provide justice for their nationals who had committed war crimes.[30]

Reluctantly, the Allies allowed Germany to try its alleged war criminals in the Reichgericht, Germany's Supreme Court, in Leipzig. Of the 900

Germans identified by the Allies, 888 were acquitted or had the charges dismissed without trial. Only twelve trials ever took place: six men were acquitted by the court—primarily due to the successful employment of the "military necessity" or "following superior orders" defenses—and six were convicted, given light sentences, and pardoned within a few years.[31]

The *Llandover Castle* case illustrates the character of the "justice" rendered by the German judges. A U-boat commander and his two junior officers were charged with sinking the hospital ship *Llandover Castle*. The ship was returning empty from Canada, but the Germans believed that it was transporting American pilots to Europe. The ship was sunk, with the few survivors afloat in three small lifeboats. After determining that there were no pilots on board, the Germans sank the lifeboats so that there would be no witnesses. However, one of the sailors survived and gave testimony against the German officers. Two of the three were convicted, and one was acquitted. The convicted officers were pardoned by the German authorities.[32]

The trials were shameful mockeries of justice. Great Britain called them a "scandalous failure of justice." (During discussions in the early 1940s that led to the Nuremberg trials of Nazi leaders, the Allies concluded that major war criminals could not be tried in German courts.) French military courts continued to try and convict Germans who had been POWs, as did the Belgians. The trials took place through 1925, and more than 1,200 Germans were found guilty and sentenced to prison terms.

Because of the United States' unwillingness to support the creation of a postwar international war crimes tribunal, there was ultimately a lack of will on the part of England, France, and Italy to push for the strict enforcement of those sections in the peace treaties. The fact that there were no international military trials of the more than 1,200 alleged war criminals identified by the Allies after World War I "showed the extent to which international justice can be compromised for the sake of political expedience."[33] When, in late 1920, the Dutch refused to extradite the kaiser to face trial, the victorious Allies walked away from the reality of an international war crimes tribunal.[34]

However, there were positive consequences of what was seen as a negative action by the United States:

A major international peace treaty had established the principle in international law that war crimes punishment was a proper conclusion of peace, that the termination of war did not bring a general amnesty as a matter of course. The culpable acts for which men might be held personally responsible did not include initiation of aggressive war, but, nonetheless, the penalty clauses were clear evidence of changes in moral, political, and legal attitudes toward international violence. But for American opposition, the Europeans probably would have provided for an international tribunal to judge war criminals.[35]

Germany in the Treaty of Versailles (June 28, 1919), Austria in the Treaty of Saint-Germain-en-Laye (September 10, 1919); Bulgaria in the Treaty of Neuilly-sur-Seine (November 27, 1919); Hungary in the Treaty of Trianon (June 4, 1920); and Turkey in the Treaty of Sèvres (August 10, 1920), were all forced to accept unforgiving peace terms, reflecting the Allies' deep hatred of Germany. In Section 231 of the Versailles Treaty, Germany was judged to be the nation solely responsible for initiating war. It was forced to pay reparations. Germany also saw France occupy the Ruhr in 1924 because of its failure to pay reparations; had to disarm and destroy its weapons; could not maintain any military aircraft or possess any submarines; was limited to 100,000 men in the army and had to do away with its military general staff; lost all its colonies; was forced to cede Alsace-Lorraine to France; saw the Saar become a protectorate of the League of Nations, until a plebiscite held in 1935 led to its return; saw northern Schleswig ceded to Denmark and West Prussia and Silesia ceded to Poland; and saw Danzig made an open port city.[36]

The harshness of the victors' peace terms led to the emergence in Germany of tens of thousands of nationalist, right-wing militants, among them a disaffected, virulently anti-Semitic World War I corporal, Adolf Hitler.

Genocide

Some historians have labeled the twentieth century "the century of genocide."[37] Coming from the Greek *genos* (race, tribe) and the Latin *cide* (killing),[38] the term *genocide* has been defined by its originator Raphael Lemkin, a Polish Jew who immigrated to the United States in the 1930s, as an *intentional*,

coordinated plan of different actions aiming at the destruction of essential foundations of the life of national groups with the aim of annihilating the groups themselves. The objectives of such a plan would be the disintegration of the political and social institutions of culture, language, national feelings, religion, economic existence, of national groups and the destruction of the personal security, liberty, health, dignity and even the lives of the individuals belonging to such groups, . . . the actions involved are directed against individuals, not in their individual capacity, but as members of the national group.[39]

Many acts of genocide have been committed in the twentieth century: the attempted destruction of the native Herero in 1904 in South-West Africa (now central Namibia), where, in over two years, 10,000 German soldiers killed 70,000 of the 80,000 members of that Bantu tribe;[40] the Nazi slaughter of over 6 million European Jews, as well as the Nazi genocide committed against Gypsies, Poles, and Russians in 1939–1945; the Cambodian "killing fields" genocide, when between 1975 and 1979, almost 2 million of the 8 million people in Cambodia were killed by the Khmer Rouge under the leadership of Pol Pot; the events that took place in Bosnia in the early to mid-1990s, where state leaders "operat[ed] within the vortex of the fiercest ethnic war in Europe in the second half of the 20th century";[41] the machete genocide of the Tutsi in Rwanda, where over 800,000 Tutsi were slaughtered by the Hutu *in three months* in 1994; and Serbia's efforts to destroy or force out of Kosovo province millions of ethnic Albanians, who constitute 90 percent of the population of Kosovo.

The twentieth century's first major genocide, referred to as the "forgotten genocide" by many,[42] was the slaughter of an estimated 1 million Turkish Armenians by Turkish forces during and after World War I. There had been decades of cruel persecution by the Muslim Turks against the Christian Armenian minority, one of several large minorities residing for centuries in the Ottoman Empire. There were massacres of Armenians by Turks in 1894–1896 and 1909 (with more than 200,000 killed). Between 1915 and 1923, "the Armenian population of Anatolia and historic West Armenia was eliminated."[43]

The Armenians, who were Christian (Catholic and Protestant), had lived in the area for over 3,000 years, under the domination of Islamic Turkish dynasties. Periodically, they felt the oppression of the Turkish majority. They were seen as infidels and less than human by the Muslim Turks. A Turkish soldier engaged in the killing of Armenians in the 1895 massacres wrote to his family, "We killed 1,200 Armenians, *all of them food for the dogs.*"[44]

After the disastrous (for the Ottoman Empire) Balkan war of 1912, the Armenians and the Arabs were the only minority populations left in Turkey. By 1913, the others—Bosnians (1878), Romanians (1878), Serbs (1878), Albanians (1913), Bulgarians (1908), and Greeks (1913)—had broken away from the empire. The Turks felt that the Armenians had to be dealt with, for

World War I. Turkish Armenian orphans being sent to Greece, circa 1915. (Library of Congress)

a number of reasons: their religious faith; their acceptance of the Western notion of "progress"; their habit of sending their children to schools run by American and European missionaries and sending them to Europe for university training; their association with European powers, especially Russia (where Armenian brigades fought alongside Russians on the eastern front in 1914); and their insistent demands for some kind of autonomy within the empire.

Turkey entered the First World War on the side of the Germans (who had been the sole European power to support Turkey, providing the Turks with military advisers who dramatically improved the quality of the Turkish military) to "resolve once and for all certain lingering domestic conflicts": the "Armenian question." Turkey signed a mutual assistance pact with Germany on July 30, 1914. Within months of entering the war, in August 1914, Turkey targeted its "internal foe—the Armenians."[45] The Ittihadists, called the Young Turks, had assumed power in 1908 and believed that the empire could be saved only by eliminating its last remaining Christian population. The Young Turk leaders were Talat Bey, the minister of the interior; Enver Pasha, the minister of war; and Djemal Pasha, the navy minister.

Beginning in April 1915, under the guise of national security and "military necessity," the Turks forcibly deported the Armenians to the Syrian and

Mesopotamian deserts, allegedly to keep them from engaging in espionage and treason. Starvation and privation of all kinds were the realities for these unfortunates as they trekked on foot to their final destinations. Massacres by special Turkish killing units greeted them. Due to starvation, exposure, and cold-blooded murder, only about a quarter of the deportees ever arrived at their final destinations. Once there, they were left to die from exposure to the elements or at the hands of marauding bands of Kurds.

This genocide of over a million Armenians was the national policy of the Young Turks, openly implemented with a bureaucratic organization and centralized planning to ensure that the deportations and executions went smoothly. (The Nazi genocide of more than 6 million European Jews before and during the Second World War shared these same characteristics.) The first step in the genocide was the emasculation, the total dehumanization, of the Armenian population in Turkey.[46] Armenian soldiers in the army were removed from the ranks, stripped of all weapons (as were all Armenian civilians), and used as road laborers and "pack animals" until they died or were killed. They were often used as bayonet target practice for Turkish soldiers. Said one weeping Turkish soldier, decades after the events, "an officer in [my] company walked over and told [me] and [my] companions to go into the group and bayonet some of them for practice, since they were going to die anyway. 'God help me, I did.'"[47]

The U.S. ambassador noted in his diary:

> The punishment inflicted upon [the Armenians] forms one of the most hideous chapters in modern history. Many of us believe that torture has long ceased to be an administrative and judicial measure, yet I do not believe that the darkest ages ever presented scenes more horrible than those which took place all over Turkey. Nothing was sacred.[48]

Desecration of Armenian churches was common, including the burning of dozens of these structures—with Armenians locked inside them. In all cities and towns in the empire, culling of the Armenian community's social, political, legal, and professional leaders and their summary executions by Turkish soldiers occurred. Historian Arnold Toynbee prepared a report for the British government on the genocide. He observed the horrors that befell Armenian women and their children. After the mothers were raped and killed, "their babies were left on the ground or dashed against the stones."[49]

The second step in the planned genocide was the forced deportation, countrywide, of the rest of the ethnoreligious Turkish minority. It was done not for relocation but for extermination. They were deported to destroy the Armenian community in the empire. No provisions were made to feed and house them. As U.S. ambassador Henry Morganthau, Sr., noted in his diary: "When the Turkish authorities gave the orders for these deportations, they were merely giving a death warrant to a whole race; they understood this well, and in their conversations with me, they made no particular attempt to conceal the fact."[50]

The third step was the "death caravans," the forced marches of unarmed, unprotected Armenians across Turkey. Minister Talat established, with the full knowledge of the parliament and the military authorities, a special killing unit called the Special Organization. Made up of convicts in military uniforms, the unit's task was to ambush and destroy the convoys of Armenian deportees.[51] The final step, for those few unfortunates who survived the death marches, was death by exposure and starvation.

Dehumanization, deportation, execution, and death by starvation constituted the plan that was developed and successfully implemented by the Young Turks to solve the ethnoreligious "Armenian question." As Talat said to a German diplomat: "The Question is settled. There are no more Armenians."[52]

Talat even had the audacity to request of Ambassador Morganthau that two insurance companies that had issued life insurance policies to thousands of Armenians (New York Life and Equitable Life) turn over the cash to the Young Turk government:

> I request that you would get the American life insurance companies to send us a complete list of their Armenian policy holders. They are practically all dead now and have left no heirs to collect the money. It of course all escheats to the State. The Government is the beneficiary now. Will you do so?

Shocked and angry, Morganthau refused and walked out.[53]

The Allied Powers, a month after the genocide began, condemned the Young Turks "for their connivance and often assistance" in the genocide. Publicly, the Allied governments warned the Ottoman cabinet ministers of the dire consequences of such inhuman acts. On May 24, 1915, they stated:

> In view of these new *crimes* of Turkey *against humanity* and civilization, the Allied governments announce publicly . . . that they will hold personally accountable . . . all members of the Ottoman government and those of their agents who are implicated in such massacres.[54]

However, after the First World War ended, the Allied governments did not follow through with their commitment to prosecute the government and military leaders responsible for killing the Armenians. In March 1919, the new Turkish government, "eager to mollify the Allies had arrested a huge group of prominent wartime Ottoman leaders. . . . They went on trial in April 1919 before a special Turkish court martial. But the Court's first death sentence brought mobs into the streets" and quickly ended any further prosecutions of the indicted Turks.[55]

Much like the Leipzig trials of German war criminals held in 1921–1922, there was no justice meted out to those who had planned and carried out crimes against humanity. This example of political expediency by the victors was not lost on the future leader of Germany, Adolf Hitler, who in 1942 said derisively: "Who, after all, speaks today of the annihilation of the Armenians?"[56] As the world found out in the Second World War, the genocide of the Armenians was "a terrible harbinger of worse things to come."[57]

Creation of the League of Nations: A Revolutionary Act in International Relations

Beyond condemning the "aggressive war" initiated by the Germans, Article I of the Versailles Treaty created the League of Nations in an effort to prevent war from occurring again. The purpose of the league, its covenant stated, was to "promote international cooperation and to achieve international peace and security by the acceptance of obligations not to resort to war . . . by establishment of international law as the actual rule of conduct among Governments, and by the maintenance of Justice."[58]

Although it failed to prevent the Second World War, the league was an "extraordinary event" in international relations and law.[59] President Woodrow Wilson was its parent. In May 1916, he stated that there was a need to establish a "universal association of nations" to maintain the security of the seas and to "prevent war begun either contrary to treaty covenants or without warning and full submission of the causes to the opinion of the world—a virtual guarantee of territorial integrity and political independence."[60]

This was radical rhetoric at the time because of the dominance in international relations of the powerful nation-states. Also, there were no precedents in the world's history of international relations for this "universal association" of nation-states. Its creation was not the conclusion of some evolutionary process; it was sui generis. Its essential purpose was the radical notion of providing collective security to its member states, "great and small alike," by offering "mutual guarantees of political independence and territorial integrity."[61]

The league's charter called on member nations to enter mediation and to have a three-month "cooling-off period" before taking any military action. Aggressive war was to be prevented by an open diplomacy that would manage emergent crises by mediation, conciliation, and arbitration through the league's council (made up of the great powers); through the intervention of the Permanent Court of International Justice created in 1921; and through the mutual disarmament of land and naval forces by the major world powers.

Originally, only the Allied and Associated nations were members of the League of Nations. By the 1930s, almost two dozen other nations had become members, including Germany in 1926 and the Soviet Union in 1934. The United States refused to join the league, although on occasion it sent visiting delegations to observe its actions. (Germany withdrew in 1933, as did Japan that same year. Italy withdrew in 1937. In 1939, the Soviet Union was expelled because it initiated aggressive war against Finland.)

Unfortunately, the league came into existence in an era of unrestrained and conservative nationalism, with accompanying aggressive wars. In the fall of 1922, the politics of the streets saw Benito Mussolini and his nationalistic *fascisti* successfully march on Rome, forcing out the moderate government. Mussolini was invited to assume power by King Victor Emmanuel III, and he became the first of the major dictators in postwar Europe. A few years later, in Russia in 1924, Joseph Stalin seized the reins of power in the new Soviet dictatorship.

At the same time, Adolf Hitler, another street politician and hater of popular democracy,[62] was imprisoned in March 1924 for participating in an abortive *putsch* in Munich. While jailed, he wrote *Mein Kampf.* He and millions of Germans seethed with anger at what they claimed was "a stab in the back," a national betrayal by Jews and other enemies of Germany that forced the Germans to agree to the armistice ending the war. After his release in 1925, he formed the National Socialist (Nazi) Party, and by 1932 the Nazis were the most popular party in Germany, winning 37 percent of the popular vote (with the Communists a close second). In 1933 he was appointed chancellor, and in short order Hitler quickly ended the Weimar Republic; destroyed democracy in Germany by killing or imprisoning leaders of other political parties in concentration camps; began the rearmament of the German military; introduced domestic policies that, by the beginning of the war in 1939 emasculated Germany's 660,000 Jewish citizens legally, politically, and socially; won the plebiscite victory in the Saar region in 1935; remilitarized the Rhineland in 1936; led the *anschluss* (union) with Austria in 1938 (forbidden in the Versailles Treaty); seized, with the approval of France and Great Britain, the Sudetenland (where ethnic Germans lived) in Czechoslovakia in 1938; occupied Prague, transformed Bohemia and Moravia into German "protectorates," and made Slovakia a puppet state of Nazi Germany; and, in 1939, declared war on Poland, thus beginning the European segment of the Second World War.[63]

In the 1930s, Japan, Germany, and Italy rejected the league's principles by asserting a fundamental right to wage aggressive war. When they went to war—in Manchuria in 1931 (Japan), China in 1937 (Japan), Ethiopia in 1935 (Italy), Spain in 1936–1939 (with Germany and Italy supporting the rebel generals led by future dictator General Francisco Franco, and the Soviet Union supporting the Spanish government's armed forces), Finland in 1939 (Russia), and Poland in 1939 (Germany)—they showed an "indifference to the Laws of War."[64] The ominous fact was that these dictatorships "were quite deliberately renouncing their traditional cultural values"[65] that emphasized constraint in warfare as well as recognition of the enemy as men who shared a common humanity.

There were a number of events and attitudes that mitigated against an effective League of Nations. There was the emergence of these dictatorships in a chaotic, economically depressed world. The "collective security" concept was new and unprecedented, and the dictators relied on an aggressive resort to war to achieve national goals. Finally, there was the absence of the United States as a member nation and the unwillingness of Great Britain and France to use the offices and potential power of the league to curb violations of international law by these rogue nations. Consequently, it was not surprising that the league was unable to preserve the peace. Similar to the *schmachparagraphen* of the Versailles Treaty, however, the league was a revolutionary attempt to abolish aggressive war, and its failures were taken into account when the world, once again prodded by an American president, Franklin D. Roosevelt, created the United Nations during the Second World War.

Other Postwar Efforts to Prevent War

In addition to the creation of the League of Nations, modest efforts were made in the two decades following the cessation of hostilities in 1919 to reduce armaments, to modify the laws of war, to find ways to enforce the laws of war and create a process for punishing violators, and to establish a

Permanent Court of International Justice to peacefully resolve conflicts between states. The hope of the war-exhausted victors was expressed in another way in the first article of the 1919 Versailles Treaty: "Maintaining peace requires the reduction of national armaments to the lowest point consistent with national safety."

There were halting steps to reduce armaments and to reexamine the laws of war in light of the horrors of the First World War and the Allies' inaction in response to demands for justice after the war ended. In 1922 in Washington, D.C., the five-nation (United States, France, Japan, Great Britain, and Italy) Conference Establishing a Commission of Jurists to Consider the Laws of War met and agreed to create a ten-jurist commission to consider two questions: Do the existing laws of war adequately cover new methods of attack and defense in light of the new techniques and technologies of warfare? If they do not, what changes in the laws of war ought to be proposed by the international community?

That same year, the same five nations met in Washington to consider a treaty regarding the use of submarines and noxious gases in warfare. They proposed that violators of the laws "shall be liable for trial and punishment—brought to trial before civil or military authorities." In addition, a naval conference by the Allied Powers sought to reduce the number of warships each had on line.

A ban on "aggressive war" was included in the general covenant of the League of Nations and was further embedded in international law with the signing of the Kellogg-Briand Pact of 1928, referred to by its critics as "toothless" rhetoric.[66] It specifically renounced the aggressive use of military force as an instrument of a nation's foreign policy,[67] asserting in Article I that:

> The High Contracting Parties solemnly declare in the names of their respective peoples that they condemn recourse to war for the solution of international controversies, and renounce it as an instrument of national policy in their relations with one another.

There were conventions held in Geneva in the 1920s to draft documents prohibiting the "first use," but not limiting the possession, of poison gases and bacteriological methods of warfare (1925) and ameliorating the terrible conditions that wounded and sick belligerents in the field had experienced (1929). Also drawn up in Geneva in 1929 was a new convention on the treatment of POWs. As finally approved, the treaty prohibited reprisals and collective penalties against POWs; indicated that POWs had to provide the enemy only with name, rank, and regimental number; and called for POW camps to provide work, recreation, decent food, packages and mail from home, and repatriation. It did not make the escape effort a capital crime and called for the immediate removal of all POWs from the war zone unless they were seriously wounded and hospitalized.

During the 1930s, as the world confronted the ravages of economic depression and the brutality of the absolute dictatorships in Russia, Germany, Japan, and Italy, international efforts to formulate treaties to reduce armaments and to settle territorial disputes peacefully were halted. There was the sad recognition of the futility of these efforts to resolve international disputes without resort to war.

In 1937 in Asia and in 1939 in Europe, less than two decades after the end of the First World War—one fought "to end all wars"—the Second World War began. The Asian war was a consequence of the dominance of an ultraconservative military clique that came to power in Japan in the mid-1930s. Japan left the League of Nations in 1933 and in 1935 repudiated the 1922 Washington Naval Treaty, quickly building a modern naval fleet that would be capable of going to war with the United States seven years later.

The European war was seen by many as a resumption of the Great War of 1914–1918, "caused by the revival of military power and territorial ambitions of Germany."[68] These two regional wars became a global one when Japan attacked the United States on December 7, 1941, and Hitler declared war on the United States a few days later. It was to be a far more terrible, far more violent, far more genocidal conflagration than the Great War. But the Second World War's closure was quite different from the events that followed the end of the First World War.

2

WORLD WAR II IN EUROPE
AND THE NUREMBERG TRIBUNAL

The post–World War I abortive efforts by the Allies to give legal significance to the concepts of universal rights of individuals and individualized war guilt[1] set the background for the events that occurred after World War II ended in 1945. The First World War introduced the world to new technology in the air and under the sea, let loose on the various battlefields, as well as the Turkish genocide of its Armenian minority. The Second World War exposed the world to an even more technologically proficient, brutally inhumane, and aggressive warfare against combatants and civilians alike.

Both in Europe and in Asia, World War II was a total war. Absent was the trench warfare of the Great War; consequently, there was less wholesale destruction of ground forces of the belligerents. It was the first war to exhibit the terror and destructiveness of mass bombings from the air. There was unprecedented destruction of undefended towns and cities, and the accompanying deaths of millions of civilians far behind the battle lines. No major city in Europe was spared the bombing terror, in daylight and at night. After 1943, when the Allies gained air superiority over the Germans, British and American bombers devastated Germany and killed enormous numbers of noncombatants. Airpower in the Second World War destroyed the distinction between belligerent and civilian. "Collateral damage" was the ubiquitous euphemism for the killing of noncombatants during air strikes. It became a phrase both sides used when describing the effects of bombing the enemy.

The scale of military and economic mobilization for fighting a global war was unprecedented. All the major nations engaged in the war—Germany, Japan, Russia, Great Britain, and the United States—used their citizens in the war effort and called up tens of millions of combatants through conscription. Russia alone saw 7 million combatants lose their lives in the war (including 3.7 million of the 5.7 million Russian soldiers who were POWs in Nazi

Axis control in Europe, 1942. (From *In Pursuit of Justice*, United States Holocaust Memorial Council, Washington, D.C., 1996)

camps), with uncounted millions of civilians killed during the Nazi occupation of Russia. Germany lost 3.5 million soldiers. Over 300,000 civilians were killed by Allied bombs and by the Allied invasion of Germany. Japan lost over 1.2 million of its soldiers and over 500,000 civilians to Allied bombings, including the two atomic bombs dropped on Hiroshima and Nagasaki (killing almost 200,000 Japanese) that brought the Asian war to a sudden end in August 1945. Great Britain lost 250,000 military personnel and more than 60,000 civilians from Luftwaffe bombing raids over English cities and towns. The United States lost 300,000 servicemen during the Second World War.[2]

The Second World War exhibited shocking, unbelievable crimes against humanity in the form of cruelty toward captured POWs and civilians in the territories occupied by Nazi Germany and Japan. The terror of invasion preceded a harsh occupation. In these occupied nations, partisan resistance began against the oppressors, which led to bloody reprisals by the Nazi and Japanese occupiers.

The war also exposed the world to the unrelieved horrors of the Nazi concentration camps, the mass extermination "killing centers," the consequences of an intentional Nazi policy of genocide that swept across all of occupied

Europe. Of all the events that occurred in Europe between 1933 and 1945, the Nazi persecution of Europe's 10 million Jews stands out as the most grotesque feature of the war in Europe.

So terrible were the evil deeds of the Nazis during the European war (1939–1945) and of the Japanese during the Asian war (1937–1945) that there was a universal demand for some kind of punishment of those who engaged in the planning and execution of war crimes and genocide. Additionally, when the scope of the Nazi terror was fully realized, all the Allies believed that the international community must take some action to deter national leaders from acting so viciously and without restraint in future wars or from taking actions against their own nationals in peacetime (as Hitler did to Germany's Jews between 1933 and 1939).

For all the victorious Allies, however, there were some major ethical dilemmas, predicaments that were not publicly addressed at the war crimes tribunals of the defeated Nazi and Japanese leaders. Some of the victors' actions during the war would truly shock the consciences of many observers. In the United States, over 120,000 Japanese American citizens and Japanese resident aliens were forcibly removed from their homes on the West Coast and placed in internment centers in isolated areas of the American West. There they remained until the end of the war because of fears that they were disloyal to the United States. They were not charged with any crime and could not use the habeas corpus legal protection to leave what one U.S. Supreme Court justice labeled America's "concentration camps."[3] At the same time, the British government interned, also without hearings, aliens and British citizens suspected of supporting the Nazis.[4]

Moreover, the Russians were allies of Nazi Germany until attacked in 1941. In 1939, the Soviet Union had plundered Poland no less wantonly than did its Nazi ally. Russia's military treated prisoners brutally, and one infamous incident in Poland—the Katyn Forest massacre, where hundreds of Polish military personnel were summarily executed—was actually committed by the Russians, not the Nazis. Great Britain and America's air war against Nazi Germany, consisting of daily bombing raids, lay waste to many nonmilitary targets, killing tens of thousands of Germans and destroying historic cultural monuments and old cities.

In the final analysis, although war brings out the bestiality of combatants on all sides, it is manifestly clear that both the Nazis and the Japanese committed egregious war crimes, both in the number of innocent people exterminated and in the organization of the slaughters, that far surpassed any war crimes committed by the Allies. In the United States, the 120,000 Japanese

Americans and resident Japanese aliens were not led to gas chambers and to crematoria. Clearly, they were denied due process of law during the war, and in 1991, legislation was passed and signed by the president that formally apologized for the internment and provided financial remediation for the survivors of the internment camps.

The point is that there were significant differences between the behavior of the Nazis and the Japanese and, with the exception of the Russians, the behavior of the rest of the world during the war.

Nazism, Aggressive War, and Genocide: 1933–1945

The Jews of Europe, like the Armenians living in the Ottoman Empire a generation earlier, became the target for mass extermination by the Nazis.[5] For Adolf Hitler, the Jews were a mortal threat to the racial purity of the German Aryan race. As he wrote in *Mein Kampf,* the Jew was "less than nothing." Jews were a race of "vermin, rodents"; they were a "deadly bacillus," the "carriers of disease" that had to be eliminated to protect the Aryan racial stock. Jews were not human, they were "a parasite in the body of other peoples," they were the "people's vampire." The history of the world was the fight of good versus evil. It was the clash between the pure Aryan, the creators of culture and civilization, and the Jew enemy. The enemy had to be destroyed, concluded Hitler, for the Aryan to survive.[6]

Hitler's ascent to power in 1933 immediately led to the destruction of democratic institutions and processes in Germany. After rival political parties were destroyed by the Nazis (with their leaders either killed or sent to concentration camps such as Dachau, built a few miles northwest of Munich), the Jew quickly became the primary target for Hitler's minions. The Nazis introduced a series of discriminatory laws that prohibited all Jews from holding civil service jobs, serving as judges, practicing medicine or law, teaching at universities, serving in the military, or owning businesses and places of public accommodation.[7] "Aryanization" of Jewish property began in 1933, with homes and businesses seized by the Nazis and turned over, "voluntarily" until 1938, to German Aryans.

For the more than 600,000 German Jews—almost 1 percent of Germany's population of 62 million[8]—these actions of the Nazis flew in the face of everyday life in Germany over the past century. Most of Germany's Jews froze in disbelief at the growing crescendo of hatred directed against them. All Germans who were born of Jewish parents were subject to these new Nazi restrictions, even those who had converted to Christianity. Victor

Klemperer, a distinguished professor of French Enlightenment history, was a Dresden Jew who had converted to Protestantism, had fought in the Great War and received the Distinguished Service Medal, and had married a non-Jew. On January 10, 1939, in frustration and anger, he wrote in his diary:

> Until 1933, and for a good century before that, the German Jews were entirely German and nothing else. Proof: the thousands upon thousands of "half" and "quarter" Jews. Jews and Germans lived and worked together without friction in all spheres of life. The German Jews were part of the German nation; they had their place in German life, and were in no way a burden on the whole society. They were and remain (even if they no longer wish to remain so) Germans—mostly intellectuals and educated people.[9]

Racially restrictive Nuremberg laws (for Hitler saw Jews as members of a subhuman racial group, not a religious group) were promulgated in 1935, limiting Jews even more by depriving them of German citizenship and prohibiting marriages between Jews and non-Jews. The horrors of Kristallnacht came three years later. Kristallnacht was the infamous "Night of the Broken Glass" when, on November 9–10, 1938, 191 synagogues in Germany were destroyed (synagogues in Austria and the Sudetenland were also destroyed); 7,500 Jewish-owned businesses in Germany and Austria were burned down; almost 100 Jews were killed; and over 30,000 Jewish men over the age of sixteen were sent to Dachau, Buchenwald, Sachsenhausen, and other concentration camps for short periods of time (hoping to scare them into emigrating).[10] Hermann Göring, the Nazi government's reichsmarshall (one of twenty-two leading Nazis brought to trial at Nuremberg in 1945–1946), then forced Germany's Jews to pay for the ensuing insurance claims through the levy of a fine of over 1 billion deutsche marks (in the form of an additional property tax on the Jewish community).[11]

Jews in Germany lost all civil rights. They could not even possess radios or driver's licenses. A Jew driving a car "offended the German traffic community, especially as they have presumptuously made use of Reich highways built by German workers' hands."[12] Identity cards were a necessity, with "Israel" and "Sarah" the designated names for all Jews. Stars of David were required to be worn by all Jews, and curfews for Jews were instituted. A version of American Jim Crowism socially segregated German Jews, as well as deprived them of all rights of citizenship. After Kristallnacht, "organized Jewish life in Germany [was] rendered impossible."[13]

World War II. Smiling Nazis cut off the beard of an orthodox Jew, Warsaw, Poland, circa 1941. (Library of Congress)

By 1937, Nazi Germany was rapidly remilitarizing, contrary to Versailles Treaty constraints. With the silent acquiescence of the British and French governments, slave labor was introduced and continued throughout the war, ending only with Germany's unconditional surrender in May 1945. Jews, Gypsies, Socialists, Communists, intellectual opponents of Nazism, and, after 1939, Poles and Russian POWs were used by German industry. Typically, the slave laborers worked sixteen hours a day in facilities built by German industrial giants such as I. G. Farben and Krupp, adjacent to the network of over 100 concentration camps that sprang up across Germany after 1933.

After 1939, male civilians from the nine German-occupied nations were brought into Germany to supply the labor needed to produce the materials of war. When the war ended, there were over 7 million of these laborers, more than 40 percent of the labor force in Germany.

Once war began and Germany occupied large areas of Europe, mass executions of civilians and military personnel occurred. Targeted by the Nazis were those groups who were "unworthy of life"[14]—Jews, Gypsies, Russians, and Poles, as well as mentally and physically defective persons. Four mobile, battalion-sized *Einsatzgruppen*, Nazi special killing units totaling about 3,000 men, were created in 1941. Their task, much like that of Turkey's Special Organization during World War I, was to follow the advancing

Wehrmacht into Poland and Russia and kill those unworthy of life. These four units killed between 1 million and 2 million Polish and Russian Jews and other *untermenschen* between 1941 and 1944.[15]

The *Einsatzgruppen* were part of the dreaded Nazi SS, the *Schutzstaffel*, the "protection squad." This organization of black-shirted troops was formed in 1925 to be Hitler's personal bodyguard. After 1929, they were the elite military unit of the Nazi Party. During the war, the SS provided personnel for police and *Totenkopf* to run the concentration camps and the killing centers. Commenting about the task of the *Einsatzgruppen*, SS General Bach-Zelewski testified at Nuremberg that their actions in Poland and Russia were the outcome of decades of Nazi indoctrination that "the slavic race is an inferior race and Jews are not even human."[16]

By 1940, German Nazi leaders had begun implementing the "final solution," *die Endlösung*, to the "Jewish problem": the mass systematic killing of more than 6 million Jews who were deported from the concentration camps to ghettos in Polish cities such as Cracow and Warsaw, and then, for those who survived to that point, transportation to the killing centers in Germany's Polish "general government." Sent to these massive killing centers, with their gas chambers and crematoria, were Jews from the occupied nations, from Germany's allies (Italy, Hungary, Romania), and from Germany itself.

In addition, Gypsies, Jehovah's Witnesses, homosexuals, Poles, Russians (including Russian POWs), and physically and mentally handicapped persons residing in the occupied countries of Europe met their end in the camps and killing centers. Between 1941 and 1945, the six killing centers located in Poland (Auschwitz, Treblinka, Chelmno, Sobibor, Belzec, and Majdenek) and operated by SS battalions gassed and cremated over 3.5 million Jews (as well as others) from across conquered and occupied Europe.[17]

The European war began in September 1939 with Germany's duplicitous attack on Poland. Rapidly, the Nazi *blitzkrieg*, the "lightning war," crushed and occupied nation after nation. Germany's mechanized armies were mobile, its *Luftwaffe* frightening; its submarines terrorized shipping in the Atlantic Ocean and the Mediterranean Sea. The Nazis swept east, capturing Poland, and west and north, defeating Belgium, France, Luxembourg, and the Netherlands in May and June 1940; Norway and Denmark fell soon afterward. By 1941, the German armies were in southern Europe, conquering and occupying Yugoslavia and Greece; finally, they went east again, attacking the Soviet Union (a former ally) in June 1941.

After their swift victories, the German occupying forces brutally ruled these nations. Underlying their inhuman rule, especially in Poland and Russia, was

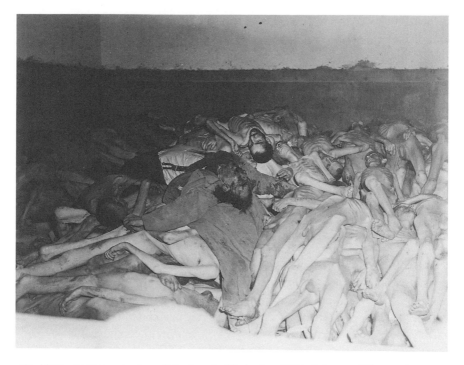

World War II. Extermination of the Jews by Nazis, circa 1945. (Library of Congress)

a basic premise voiced by another Nuremberg defendant, General Keitel: "[Slav and Jewish] life has absolutely no value" for the occupiers.[18] Just as quickly as they conquered these nations, the Nazis instituted harsh regulations that jeopardized the civilians, especially those groups targeted by the Nazis for the *Endlösung*. Soon, horror stories came to Great Britain (where the occupied nations established their governments in exile) and to the United States, alleging war crimes, crimes against humanity, and violations of international treaties.

During his prison detention while the Nuremberg tribunal heard the case against him, Hermann Göring told one of his captors that "just between us, I considered your [international] treaties so much toilet paper."[19] The Nazis had violated international treaties signed by German diplomats at the Hague, Paris, and Geneva. Contrary to the laws of war and the standards of civilized nations, the Nazi military executed captured Allied commandos, downed Allied airmen, and Allied POWs who had escaped and been recaptured.

Russian POWs were horribly mistreated, in violation of international law and the laws of humanity, and there were grisly stories of Nazis murdering American POWs who had surrendered on the field of battle. From the beginning of Nazi Germany's occupation of Europe, innocent civilian hostages were shot in reprisal after partisan attacks, towns and cities such as Lidice and Warsaw were destroyed, and art treasures and other valuables were plundered from these occupied territories.[20]

By November 1940, Polish and Czech leaders in exile had begun receiving information from their occupied nations about the war crimes and crimes against humanity committed by the Nazis. (Czechoslovakia had been carved up by Germany in 1938 when Hitler's troops seized the Sudetenland, an area populated by ethnic Germans, with the acquiescence of the British and the French.)

In October 1941, after hearing about the execution of French civilian hostages, Winston Churchill, Britain's prime minister, and President Franklin D. Roosevelt issued warnings to Hitler about the "fearful retribution" he and his leaders would face at war's end because of the war crimes committed by the Nazis. A month later, the Russians warned of punishment for the wanton killing of Russian civilians and Russian POWs.

In January 1942, the leaders in exile of the nine occupied nations (Belgium, France, Czechoslovakia, Greece, Luxembourg, Norway, the Netherlands, Poland, and Yugoslavia) issued the St. James Palace Declaration, which announced that postwar criminal trials would take place because of Nazi war crimes and violations of the Hague and Geneva treaties. (That same month, senior Nazi leaders attended the Wannsee Conference in Berlin to coordinate plans to implement the "final solution.")

In October 1942, Roosevelt and Churchill called for the creation of a United Nations War Crimes Commission to investigate the accusations. A year later, the commission was investigating the data coming out of occupied Europe, examining the laws of war with regard to the punishment of war criminals.

In Moscow in November 1943, Stalin, Churchill, and Roosevelt announced that war criminals would be punished where the crimes had been committed; crimes committed by Nazi leaders, including the military, that went beyond the territory of one nation would be punished by an international tribunal. In the spring of 1944, prior to the Normandy invasion, Roosevelt again openly warned the enemy about retribution for their crimes against humanity.

Clearly, between 1940 and 1944, the air was rife with stories about the Nazis' cruelty toward enemy civilians, especially those unfortunates living in

World War II. In Poland, GIs find the ovens in the camps and killing centers used to cremate victims of genocide. (Library of Congress)

Central and Eastern Europe—Jews, Poles, and Russians in particular. After the Wannsee Conference in 1942, horror stories emerged about the destruction of whole towns full of Jews and of the deportation of millions of Jews from across occupied Europe to the killing centers in Poland. Although the Nazis were publicly warned by Allied leaders, it was not until the end of the war in Europe that the victorious Allies settled on a plan to punish those responsible for the war, the war crimes, and the crimes against humanity.

The Path to Nuremberg: 1944–1945

There is a common wisdom about Allied punishment of Nazi leaders after the war ended. Because of the brutal actions taken by Nazi Germany against belligerents, prisoners of war, civilians in occupied nations, and especially targeted-for-extermination *untermenschen* such as Jews, Gypsies, Poles, and Russians, the victors would quickly create an ad hoc international criminal justice tribunal to bring to trial and punish the Nazis found guilty of waging aggressive war, war crimes, crimes against humanity, and genocide. In actuality, the decision to try the major Nazi leaders in a courtroom was finally reached only after the war in Europe ended in May 1945.

Although it is correct to say that the "punishment of war criminals came to be regarded among the most urgent problems to be solved after the war,"[21] it is somewhat misleading because of what it leaves out. Until the spring of 1945, to the British and the Americans, "punishment" of Nazis for war crimes meant *summary execution after capture—without a trial.* Ironically, as early as November 1942, it was the Russians who suggested and continually pushed for the establishment of a postwar tribunal.[22] As late as the winter of 1945, the British and Americans were in agreement on a plan that called for summary execution, and these two nations fruitlessly tried to convince the Russians to go along.

For the Allies, until May 1945, the promised "stern justice" for the Nazi war criminals was not spelled out. There were essentially two choices: judicial proceedings (like those enumerated in the Versailles Treaty) or executive action. The British were strongly in favor of executive action, that is, summary executions of Nazi leaders without trial. An aide-mémoire from Great Britain, sent to Roosevelt on April 23, 1945, stated Churchill's views:

> [His Majesty's Government is] deeply impressed with the dangers and difficulties of this course [judicial proceedings], and they think that execution without trial is the preferable course. [A trial] would be exceedingly long and elaborate, [many of the Nazis' deeds] are not war crimes in the ordinary sense, nor is it at all clear that they can properly be described as crimes under international law.[23]

In the United States, no fewer than seven federal agencies were working on plans for a defeated postwar Germany (the Departments of State, War, Navy, Treasury, and Justice; the Office of Strategic Services; and the White House staff). The most influential person through early 1945 was "the president's old friend,"[24] Secretary of the Treasury Henry Morganthau, Jr. (whose father, as U.S. ambassador to the Ottoman Empire, had observed firsthand the Turkish genocide of the Armenians in 1915). Roosevelt asked Secretary of War Henry Stimson and Secretary of State Cordell Hull to prepare recommendations as to how the Nazi leaders should be punished after the war, but Morganthau also gave the president his thoughts and a plan. Morganthau, a member of one of New York's old Jewish families,[25] agreed with the British and recommended a "tough peace" for Germany. On his return from a visit to France in the summer of 1944, he quickly prepared and sent to Roosevelt a vengeful plan in opposition to a War Department plan that he thought would "coddle the defeated Nazis."[26]

Morganthau called for the deindustrialization of the Ruhr and Saar Valleys and for Germany to be turned "into a country primarily agricultural and pastoral."[27] He also called for the use of German POWs to rebuild Europe, the banishment of all SS storm troopers and their families from Germany to "remote places,"[28] and the distribution to the advancing Allied armies of a list of 2,500 top Nazi war criminals—generals, admirals, party leaders, gestapos, and industrialists—to be shot upon capture.[29]

Churchill approved Morganthau's plan, as did Roosevelt, and the two leaders sought to convince the Russians to accept it. But there were Americans in the Roosevelt administration, in particular Stimson and his assistant secretary, John McCloy (with behind-the-scenes support from U.S. Supreme Court Justice Felix Frankfurter, a friend of Stimson's and McCloy's mentor), along with Hull and the Army Judge Advocate Group, who were dead set against the tough summary justice plan—the Old Testament's "eye for an eye" punishment.[30] However, through December 1944, the Morganthau plan was on "the front burner."[31]

Stimson and Hull had always believed that some kind of international judicial proceeding for the punishment of the Nazi leaders was required. The task of developing such a plan was given, in September 1944, to a Jewish lawyer in the War Department's three-man Special Project Branch, Lieutenant Colonel Murray Bernays. He addressed the problem of punishment by asking two questions: how to punish Nazi leaders for prewar crimes against German Jews and others, and how to deal with the millions of Germans who were members of the SS, the gestapo, and other Nazi organizations responsible for the murder of millions of persons during the war.[32]

His answer was one found in American and British jurisprudence: the law of criminal conspiracy. (He noted some precedents: the Smith Act in America, passed in 1938, and the British India Act of 1836.[33]) Nevertheless, a big problem existed for Bernays and the Americans if this plan were adopted: Conspiracy was essentially an American and British concept. It did not exist in French, Russian, and German jurisprudence or in their criminal law.[34]

If a Nazi organization—political, military, or police—"contemplate[d] illegal methods or illegal ends," each member of the organization was liable for the acts of all other knowing members. Collective criminality, the crime of membership, was at the core of the Bernays plan. As developed by the international military tribunal (IMT) at Nuremberg, there were five questions that had to asked by prosecutors before indicting a detainee:

1. Did the Nazi organization have a common plan of criminal action?
2. Was a group's actions criminal?
3. Was a person's membership in such a group voluntary?
4. Was a person's membership a knowing one, that is, did the person have some knowledge of the criminal aims of the organization?
5. Was there evidence that the person was such a member and that he or she acted to achieve the organization's criminal goals?[35]

The strategy was to indict and try the Nazi leaders for conspiring to commit criminal acts; charge them with committing the actual violations themselves; then quickly try other low-ranking Nazi war criminals under this "guilt by knowing association" charge inherent in the criminal conspiracy–criminal organization strategy.

Within weeks, Bernays devised a plan that would be implemented at the IMT at Nuremberg. From the time Hitler came to power in 1933, reasoned Bernays, the Nazi dictatorship had been a gigantic criminal conspiracy to wage aggressive war and to commit war crimes and crimes against humanity.

> The whole movement had been a deliberate, concerted effort to arm for war, forcibly seize the lands of other nations, steal their wealth, enslave and exploit their populations, and exterminate the . . . Jews of Europe.[36]

Bernays sent the plan to Stimson, and in the fall of 1944, the secretary of war began lobbying for its adoption, rather than the vindictive Morganthau plan. It was, until January 1945, a "mission impossible." Most of Roosevelt's advisers were against the Bernays plan; instead of indictments and trials for conspiracy, there was comfort in the security of Morganthau's summary execution proposal. There was little chance that Roosevelt would opt for the War Department proposal for dealing with Nazi war criminals.

The turning point came in January 1945, when Americans woke up to read and hear about German atrocities committed against American soldiers who had surrendered at a place in Belgium called Malmédy. During the December 1944 battle of the Bulge (a futile German effort to breech the Allied forces in Belgium and turn the war around), over seventy Americans were captured by the fanatical Waffen SS First Panzer Division, tied up, machinegunned to death, and buried under the snow in the Malmédy battlefield. The "emotional impact in America was unbelievable."[37] Stimson quickly argued that Malmédy was not an isolated war crime: it was part of a general Nazi plan to wage a brutal, criminal war against military and civilians alike. The tragedy at Malmédy violated the Geneva Accords regarding the treatment of prisoners of war. Malmédy was a small part of a "purposeful and systematic conspiracy to achieve domination of other nations and peoples by deliberate violations of the rules of war as they have been accepted and adhered to by the nations of the world."[38]

In a joint memorandum sent to Roosevelt by Stimson and Hull on January 22, 1945, they forcefully restated their views:

> While [executive action] has the advantage of a sure and swift disposition, it would be violative of the most fundamental principles of justice, common to all the United Nations. This would encourage the Germans to turn these criminals into martyrs and, in any event, only a few individuals could be reached in this way. Consequently [although there are serious legal difficulties involved in a judicial proceeding], we think that the just and effective solution lies in the use of the judicial method. Condemnation of these criminals after a trial, moreover, would command maximum public support in our own times and receive the respect of history. The use of the judicial method will, in addition, make available for all mankind to study in future years an authentic record of Nazi crimes and criminality.[39]

Roosevelt was finally persuaded by their arguments and took the Bernays plan with him for his meeting at Yalta in February 1945 with Churchill and Stalin. Bernays's plan met stiff resistance from the British. Churchill still insisted on a Morganthau-type plan that would summarily execute the top Nazi political and military leaders. In April 1945, he was still calling for death without trial for the Nazi leaders.[40] (France, a late participant in these conversations, agreed with Russia and the United States on the necessity of war crimes trials.)

However, in late April 1945, the British and American armies came across the concentration camps at Belsen, Buchenwald, and Dachau, and the Russian armies discovered the killing center at Auschwitz. The shock of discovering the Holocaust moved the Allies to adopt a postwar plan that would show the world the horrors of a bureaucratically planned and implemented genocide of unimaginable magnitude. In May 1945, the plan was finally, though grudgingly, accepted by Great Britain,[41] and the Allied quartet prepared to ask the recently formed United Nations to adopt the plan at its first meeting in San Francisco, California, later that summer.

At this time, another problem surfaced. It was "the most nettlesome one that would face the judges."[42] And it is still controversial more than fifty years after Nuremberg: the "victors' justice" label placed on the work of the Nuremberg tribunal.[43]

The Roman adage *nullum crimen et nulla poena sine lege*, "no crime and no punishment without law," was a criticism heard by the jurists who drafted and the prosecutors and judges who were involved in the trial of the major Nazi war criminals at Nuremberg. German actions, however horrible and violative of the basic values of civilized communities, were committed in the absence of a specific set of international criminal laws. Furthermore, other than the *schmachparagraphen* of the 1919 Versailles Treaty, which were never enforced by the Allies, there was a near total absence in international law of punishment meted out to violators of the norms, nor were there any guides as to who would determine the verdict and pronounce sentence on those found guilty of violating international criminal law.

The criticism of the Bernays plan was that it *had* to lead, *after the fact*, to the establishment of a set of specific international criminal laws. These newly crafted criminal laws would be used, ex post facto, to indict and then punish the defeated Nazi leaders. Underscoring this controversial issue, Göring wrote on the front of his indictment (issued in late October 1945): "The victor will always be the judge and the vanquished the accused."[44]

However, Justice Robert H. Jackson, America's chief prosecutor, responded to the ex post facto criticism of the trial in a manner that reflected the views of all who participated when he said: "Let's not be derailed by legal hair-splitters. Aren't murder, torture, and enslavement crimes recognized by all civilized people? What we propose is to punish acts which have been regarded as criminal since the time of Cain and have been so written in every civilized code."[45] In effect, Jackson was applying the Martens clause in the 1907 Hague Convention to justify the jurisdiction and justiciability of the Nuremberg tribunal.

The London Charter: August 1945

In June 1945, the legal representatives of the four victorious Allies met in London to establish guidelines and procedures for the international military trial of the major Nazi war criminals.[46] Representing the United States was its chief prosecutor, Justice Robert H. Jackson, on leave from the U.S. Supreme Court. Great Britain had its attorney general, Sir David Maxwell-Fyfe, heading the delegation. Russia's representative was its chief prosecutor, Lieutenant General Roman Rudenko, assisted by Major General of Jurisprudence Ion Timifeevich Nikitchenko. The French delegation was led by Robert Falco.

There would be an international criminal tribunal created to try all Nazis charged with war crimes that went beyond the territory of a single occupied nation. (Many thousands of Nazis were put on trial in Polish courts.) There were more than six weeks of discussions and debates over jurisdiction of the international tribunal, trial procedures, and the nature of the indictments against the Nazis.

These were complex negotiations, because the Russians and the French followed Continental criminal procedures, where judges play a major inquisitorial role in the trial itself and lawyers have only a limited role in the criminal proceedings; the Americans and the British followed the adversarial criminal justice process, where prosecutors and defense attorneys engage in examination and cross-examination of witnesses in an effort to find the truth. The two systems were quite different, and some Allied jurists were clearly uncomfortable. Telford Taylor, one of the young American assistant prosecutors at Nuremberg, remembers the Russian prosecutor Nikitchenko asking: "What is meant in the English by 'cross-examine?'"[47]

Compromises were developed in the trial procedures so that the four Allies could comfortably and effectively prosecute the defendants. Included in the negotiations was the question of who would be brought to Nuremberg to stand trial. In the end, twenty-two were tried, including one, Martin Bormann, in absentia. These were some of the major leaders of Nazi Germany who had survived the war, had been captured, and, unlike Hitler, Heinrich Himmler (who ran the extermination programs), and Joseph Goebbels (Nazi minister of propaganda), had not committed suicide. One of the major Nazi leaders arrested and brought to Nuremberg to stand trial was Robert Ley, the head of labor in the Nazi dictatorship. In late October 1945, after he was indicted, he took his own life in his prison cell.[48] Gustav Krupp, head of Germany's leading industrial and arms maker, escaped trial before the IMT because of his mental deterioration. His son, Alfred Krupp, was subsequently tried and convicted in a U.S. sector court. The defendant list follows, showing the charges against them and the judgment of the IMT. Most of them had been captured and detained in military prisons by the advancing American forces. All were flown to Nuremberg in late

Name/Position	Counts*	Verdict†
Generals and Admirals from the German General Staff		
General Jodl, former chief of staff, Wehrmacht	1–4	D
General Keitel, chief of staff, Wehrmacht	1–4	D
Admiral Raeder, former commander, Navy	2, 4	L
Admiral Doenitz, commander, Navy	2, 3	10
Nazi Party and Government Leaders		
Göring, Reichsmarshall	1–4	D
Bormann, Nazi Party leader	3, 4	D
Frank, governor, occupied territory, Poland	2, 4	D
Frick, governor, Bohemia-Moravia	1–4	D
von Ribbentrop, foreign minister	1–4	D
Rosenberg, head, occupied territories	1–4	D
Seyss-Inquart, head, occupied Netherlands	1–4	D
Hess, Nazi Party leader, deputy to Hitler	1, 2	L
Neurath, minister, foreign affairs	1–4	15
von Papen, vice-chancellor, Nazi government	1, 2	A
von Schirach, head, Hitler Youth	4	20
Streicher, publisher, *Der Sturmer*	4	D
Fritzsche, head, Radio Division, Ministry of Propaganda	1, 2	A
Saukel, head, labor mobilization	2, 4	D
Bankers and Industrialists		
Funk, president, Reichsbank	2, 4	L
Speer, minister, armaments and war production	3, 4	20
Schacht, minister, economics	1, 2	A
Secret Police		
Kaltenbrunner, head, Reich Central Security Office‡	3, 4	D

*1: planning and conspiring to wage aggressive war, a crime against the peace; 2: waging aggressive war; 3: war crimes; 4: crimes against humanity.
†D: death; L: life imprisonment; A: acquitted; 10, 15, 20: years of imprisonment
‡This agency included the gestapo, or *Geheime Staatspolizei,* the secret state police established in 1933 to interrogate, torture, and kill "enemies" of the Reich; and the SD, or *Sicherheitsdienst,* the security and intelligence service.

summer 1945 to await the beginning of the IMT's actions, scheduled to start in November 1945.

On August 8, 1945, the London agreement was signed by the four Allied legal representatives. Immediately, it became the basis for the international war crimes trials of Nazi and Japanese leaders, as well as the foundation for subsequent actions by the international community in the area of international law.

The agreement consisted of seven general articles and an important annex: the Charter of the International Military Tribunal, which contained seven parts and thirty articles. After describing how the IMT was to be constituted (four members, each with an alternate, representing the four Allies: Russia, the United States, Great Britain, and France), the core of the IMT's jurisdiction was laid out in Article VI:

> [The IMT] shall have the power to try and punish persons who, acting in the interests of the European Axis countries, whether as individuals or as members of organizations, committed any of the following crimes [which fall under the jurisdiction of the IMT and] for which there shall be individual responsibility:
>
> (a) *Crimes against peace:* namely, planning, preparation, initiation or waging a war of aggression, or a war in violation of international treaties, agreements or assurances, or participation in a common plan or conspiracy for the accomplishment of any of the foregoing.
>
> (b) *War crimes:* namely, violations of the laws or customs of war. Such violations shall include, but not be limited to, murder, ill-treatment or deportation to slave labor or for any other purpose of civilian population of or in occupied territory, murder or ill-treatment of prisoners of war or persons on the seas, killing of hostages, plunder of public or private property, wanton destruction of cities, towns, or villages, or devastation not justified by military necessity.
>
> (c) *Crimes against humanity:* namely, murder, extermination, enslavement, deportation, and other inhumane acts committed against any civilian populations, before or during the war; or persecution on political, racial, or religious grounds in execution of or in connection with any crime within the jurisdiction of the tribunal, whether or not in violation of the domestic law of the country where perpetrated.

Article VII rejected the sovereign immunity, "head of State" defense, and Article VIII stated that "the fact that a defendant acted pursuant to [an] order of his Government or of a superior shall not free him from responsibility, but may be considered in mitigation of punishment if the Tribunal determines that justice so requires."

The concept of criminal conspiracy was embedded in Articles IX and X: "At the trial of any individual member of any group or organization the Tribunal may declare (in connection with any act of which the individual may be convicted) that the group or organization of which the individual was a member was a criminal organization." Once the IMT declared a Nazi organization criminal, at any subsequent trial of individual members of that organization, "the criminal nature of the group or organization is considered proved and shall not be questioned."

The four nations' chief prosecutors (and staff) were responsible for investigations, collection of data, examination of all witnesses, preparation and lodging of indictments against the Nazi defendants, and prosecution of the defendants. The defendants were promised, in Article IV, a fair trial, which meant the right to conduct their own defense or to have the assistance of counsel (half of the defense attorneys selected by the defendants had been members of the Nazi Party); to have full particulars of the charges, including documents, enumerated in their indictments; and to present evidence at trial "in support of [their] defense, and to cross examine any witnesses called by the prosecution."

Article XXIV laid out the process followed by the IMT: the reading of the indictment, followed by the plea (guilty or not guilty) of each defendant; prosecutors' opening statements; tribunal determination of admissibility of evidence submitted by prosecution and defense; witnesses for prosecution; cross-examination; witnesses for defense; cross-examination; rebutting evidence; tribunal questioning of witnesses and defendants (allowable at any time); defense addresses to the tribunal; prosecution addresses to the tribunal; defendant statements to the tribunal; delivering of judgment and pronouncement of sentence.

The IMT's judgment "shall be final and not subject to review" (Article XXVI). Finally, upon conviction, imposition of the death sentence "or such other punishment as shall be determined by it to be just" was declared a basic "right" of the IMT (Article XXVII).

The International Military Tribunal at Nuremberg: 1945–1946

The IMTs at Nuremberg and Tokyo took place in the months immediately following the conclusion of hostilities and the unconditional surrender of

Nazi Germany and Japan. The IMT at Nuremberg was precedent setting; it was history's first international criminal tribunal. The purpose of the trial was evident: punish those major figures in the defeated nations who were responsible for war crimes and the mass extermination of millions of civilians and prisoners of war. Inherent was the belief that "superior orders," "acts of state," and "sovereign immunity" were not defenses and that the concept of "individual responsibility" was the prominent characteristic of the post–World War II trials.

The trial was also a lesson for future military rulers. Newly written and internationally agreed-upon (in the UN in 1946 and 1948, and in Geneva in 1949) international criminal laws became part of international law. The international community's willingness to create an ad hoc (and afterward, as contemplated in 1946, a permanent) international criminal court to try and punish those found guilty of war crimes or genocide was another key outcome of Nuremberg.

There were 403 open sessions of the IMT at Nuremberg between November 1945 and October 1946. Thirty-three witnesses were called by the prosecution, and sixty-one witnesses for the defendants appeared in court. There were an additional 143 written depositions presented to the tribunal by defense counsel. Due to the ingenuity of IBM engineers, working feverishly in the United States in the months preceding the opening of the trial, there was simultaneous translation of the proceedings into four languages: German, French, Russian, and English.[49]

There were gaffes and clashes among the four Allies at Nuremberg. With hundreds of staff, including military personnel, lawyers, translators, researchers, investigators, and secretaries, there was bound to be some friction and jealousy. The Americans were the most populous group at the IMT, with over 700 persons. (The next largest Allied staff was the British group, numbering about 170.) The Americans' salaries were seen as outrageously high compared with the salaries of other Allied personnel working in Nuremberg. An American lawyer (and many hundreds of them moved between Nuremberg and the United States) received a salary of over $7,000. The president of the tribunal, Great Britain's Sir Geoffrey Lawrence, received about $2,800 annually, "roughly at the level of an American translator."[50]

The prosecution presented its case against the twenty-two defendants from November 1945 to March 1946, followed by defense arguments from March to July 1946. In July, the defense summarized its case, followed by the prosecution's closing arguments.

In July and part of August 1946, the tribunal heard arguments by the prosecution charging seven Nazi organizations with criminal conspiracy: Nazi Party leaders; the Reich cabinet; Nazi government ministers; the SS; the gestapo; the SD; the Sturmabteilung (SA), the storm troopers; and the military high command, consisting of German army, navy, and air force commanders in chief, both former chiefs and those in command at war's end.[51]

In August 1946, there were fifteen-minute statements by each defendant to the tribunal. The tribunal adjourned for deliberation in September 1946, and on September 30–October 1, 1946, it rendered its judgments in open court.

At the start of the trial, in November 1945, defense counsel jointly objected to the core juristic foundations of the IMT itself. This plea was summarily rejected by the tribunal, and the trial began.

Justice Jackson made the opening remarks for the combined prosecution team, thus beginning the first international war crimes tribunal. His words have remained benchmark values for those who seek to bring to justice persons who have violated the laws of war and the conscience of the international community.

> The wrongs which we seek to condemn and punish have been so calculated, so malignant, and so devastating that civilization cannot tolerate their being ignored because it cannot survive their being repeated. That four great nations, flushed with victory and stung with injury, stay the hand of vengeance and voluntarily submit their captive enemies to the judgment of the law is one of the most significant tributes that power has ever paid to reason. . . . Either the victors must judge the vanquished, or we must leave the defeated to judge themselves. After the First World War, we saw the futility of the latter course.

Over the next few days, the four Allies took turns reading the general indictment against the defendants. There were four counts in the indictment. Counts one and two—planning, conspiring, and carrying out an aggressive war, that is, conspiring to commit "crimes against the peace"—were presented to the tribunal by the Americans and the British. Jackson presented the charge that twelve of the defendants were involved in the development of the common plan or conspiracy to wage aggressive war, in violation of the 1928 Kellogg-Briand Treaty signed by Germany and sixty-odd nations, and Sir Hartley Shawcross charged most of the defendants with the actual waging of aggressive war.

The French presented the third count of the indictment, maintaining that thirteen defendants had committed a variety of war crimes in violation of the Hague and Geneva treaties. These war crimes—such as massive use of slave labor, Luftwaffe medical experiments with human brains, the wanton killing of captured Allied aircrews and prisoners who tried to escape, the looting of art treasures, the killing of civilian hostages in the occupied territories of Europe—said the French prosecutor, "spring from a crime against the spirit, [one] which denied all spiritual, rational, and moral values by which nations have tried, for thousands of years, to improve the human condition."[52]

The Russian prosecutor, Rudenko, presented the final count, claiming that seventeen of the defendants had committed "crimes against persons and humanity" in occupied Europe "and against Slav countries first of all." Millions of civilians, he stated, "were subjected to merciless persecutions, atrocities, and mass extermination."[53]

Over the course of five months, the prosecution presented the case against the defendants, using over 2,500 Nazi documents from among the more than 1,700 tons of documents, records, photographs, and movies seized by the Allies. By September 1945, there were thirteen Allied document collection centers operating in Germany and Austria, where all documents were "cataloged, photographed, translated into English, and given a unique document number."[54] These documents were also used by prosecutors in the trials of thousands of lesser Nazis in the four occupation zones controlled by the French, Russians, British, and Americans in the years following the IMT at Nuremberg.

In addition to the showpiece trial of the major Nazi leaders at Nuremberg, in the four Allied occupation zones, controlled by the Americans, Russians, British, and French, trials of thousands of Nazis took place during and after the conclusion of the IMT at Nuremberg. By 1950, in the American zone, 570 Nazis had been confined and 185 indictments had been handed down. American civilians, both judges and lawyers, were brought to Germany to form six three-judge tribunals to hear twelve sets of cases against these lower-tier Nazi leaders. In the end, 177 were tried and 142 were convicted (with twenty-five executed after trial).

The twelve separate trials in the American sector included the doctors' trial, in which doctors were charged with conducting medical experiments on Jews and others; the jurists' trial, in which fourteen Nazi judges were charged with participating in the enforcement of Nazi edicts; the I. G. Farben trial, in which twenty-three German industrialists were charged with exploiting slave labor; the Krupp trial, in which twelve leaders of the arms manufacturing firm were charged with using slave labor and POWs in its factories; the hostages' trial; the *Einsatzgruppen* trial, in which twenty-two members of the SS were tried and convicted for their role in the extermination of Jews and others; and the SS Office for Race and Resettlement trial, in which fourteen SS members were charged with mass extermination of Jews and others at the killing centers.

In addition, British military courts heard almost 1,000 cases involving war crimes, with about 700 Nazis convicted and 230 sentenced to death. French military tribunals tried over 2,100 Nazis, with over 1,700 convicted and 104 sentenced to death. German courts conducted over 2,100 trials. About 900 of the Nazi defendants (or 40 percent) were *acquitted* in these courts (and only four were sentenced to death). There are no records of the number of Nazis tried, convicted, and executed in the Soviet zone military tribunals. (Other trials took place in Poland and the Netherlands.) Between 1947 and 1953, the British, French, and Americans tried 10,400 accused Nazi war criminals, and 5,025 were convicted and sentenced, including 506 who were sentenced to die by hanging.[55]

Beginning on March 8, 1946, for a second time, the Nazi defense attorneys tried to counter the mass of evidence presented by the prosecution. It was an impossible task, given the enormous volume of Nazi documents used to show, in their own words, how the defendants had planned, conspired, and acted to wage aggressive war and commit war crimes and crimes against humanity. The German lawyers, many of whom were former Nazi Party members themselves, were given great latitude, but given the evidence amassed against the defendants and given their lack of experience with adversarial criminal proceedings, they did not fare well. The witnesses and depositions introduced on behalf of the Nazi defendants tried to present mitigating and extenuating explanations for some of the accusations, but they did not stand up well to prosecutorial cross-examination.

Challenges to the tribunal's jurisdiction having been set aside on the first day, the defense argued the *Führerprinzip,* that is, that Hitler was responsible for all the crimes. All the defendants had done, as "good, loyal Germans," was show obedience to their leader by following his orders.[56] Beyond this defense, shot down in cross-examination by the prosecutors (who demonstrated the defendants' complicity in these crimes), the defense tried to explain, for example, that the Luftwaffe had flown defensive sorties only; that the invasion of the Netherlands and Norway and the alleged war crimes of the Wehrmacht had been acts of "military necessity"; that the defendants, especially the military leaders, had merely been following the orders of their superiors; and that the navy captains had always followed the customs and laws of sea warfare (in Admiral Doenitz's case, using a deposition from U.S. Admiral Chester Nimitz stating that German U-boat actions during the war had been no different from the actions of American submariners). Russian POWs had been treated differently from other Allied prisoners, the defense argued, because Russia had not signed the 1929 Geneva Accord on the treatment of prisoners of war.

For contemporary observers, it was ludicrous to argue, for example, that the Hitler Youth, which prepared young German males for war, was analogous to America's Boy Scouts. Allied prosecutors quickly pointed out, in cross-examination, that the Hitler Youth was a training ground for the Wehrmacht; that the Hitler Youth were kept busy with small-caliber weapons training and glider piloting; and that von Schirach, head of the organization, had an agreement with SS leader Heinrich Himmler that those Hitler Youth "who meet SS standards would be considered as the primary source of replacements for the SS."[57]

Equally comical amidst the tragedy of the trial was Göring's argument that his massive looting of the art treasures of occupied Europe was done to protect the art and to open a massive people's art museum after the war. And so on. Even before the defense concluded their arguments, four American lawyers on Jackson's staff, including Herbert Wechsler and James Rowe (who were to become highly respected figures in U.S. jurisprudence and politics) began drafting guilty verdicts for the tribunal to use in reaching its final judgments.[58]

Justice Jackson began his closing arguments after the defense rested with an apt quote from Shakespeare.

> These defendants now ask the tribunal to say that they are not guilty of planning, executing, or conspiring to commit this long list of crimes and wrongs. They stand before the record of this trial as blood-stained Gloucester stood by the body of his slain king. He begged of the widow, as they beg of you: "Say I slew them not." And the Queen replied, "Then say they are not slain. But dead they are. . . ." If you were to say of these men that they are not guilty, it would be as true to say that there has been no war, there are no slain, there has been no crime.[59]

In the face of damning "tested evidence" showing the defendants' participation in waging aggressive war and committing war crimes and crimes against humanity, Jackson ridiculed the "flimsy excuses" offered by way of defense. The British prosecutor maintained that the mass of evidence presented by the prosecution—not successfully rebutted by the defense—clearly showed that the defendants were guilty of "crimes so frightful that the imagination staggers and reels back."[60]

The judgment of the tribunal was announced on September 30 and October 1, 1946. Read over the two days, the lengthy judgment noted the importance of the documents introduced by the prosecution. "The case against the defendants rests in a large measure on documents of their own making, the authenticity of which has not been challenged except in one or two cases." The tribunal next carefully considered the four charges against the defendants: planning and waging aggressive wars and committing war crimes and crimes against humanity.

Were the first two charges violations of international treaties promulgated in 1899, 1907, 1919, 1925, 1928, and 1929 and signed by Germany? The tribunal noted that the actions taken by the Nazi government since 1937 were both illegal and criminal "crimes against the peace." The defense's use of the ex post facto "no punishment without law" maxim, the judges concluded, "has no application to the present facts." Hitler, the judges determined, "could not make aggressive war by himself. He had to have the cooperation of statesmen, military leaders, diplomats, and businessmen." By supporting the Nazi dictator, "they made themselves parties to the plan."

Regarding the third charge in the indictment, commission of war crimes in violation of international treaties signed in 1907 and 1929, the tribunal concluded that the "evidence has been overwhelming in its volume and its detail" that the Nazis committed war crimes "on a vast scale never before seen in the history of war." These war crimes included the murder and ill treatment of POWs, civilian populations, and slave laborers.

Finally, the tribunal took judicial notice of the mass of data that illuminated the Nazis' "crimes against humanity," especially their persecution of European Jewry, where, the tribunal noted, the Nazi "record of consistent and systematic inhumanity [was] on the greatest scale."

The IMT judges then ruled that four of the seven Nazi groups charged by the prosecution with being "criminal organizations" were criminal: the Nazi Party leadership, the gestapo, the SS, and the SD. The three others—the military high command, the Reich cabinet, and the SA—were not. The tribunal noted that individual members of Hitler's cabinet and military would be tried by the Allies. The SA, the brown shirts, were "ruffians and bullies," but since the group was in disfavor by 1935, it was not involved in planning or conspiring to wage war and did not, as a group, engage in war crimes or crimes against humanity; thus it could not be labeled a criminal organization.

The tribunal then came to the question of guilt or innocence of the twenty-two defendants. It found nineteen of them guilty of some or all of the charges leveled against them. The other three were acquitted because of a two-to-two deadlock among the judges; conviction required three judges to vote guilty. Finally, each defendant was brought before the tribunal to hear the sentence read by the chief judge. Twelve were sentenced to death by hanging, three received life imprisonment, and four were sentenced to prison terms ranging from ten to twenty years. The death sentences were carried out within fifteen days of the tribunal's pronouncements. (Just before his scheduled execution, Hermann Göring committed suicide by taking cyanide.)

The Russian judge announced three dissents from the decisions of the IMT: the not-guilty verdicts for Schacht, von Papen, and Fritzsche; the judgment that the military high command and the Reich cabinet were not criminal groups; and the sentencing of Hess to life imprisonment, arguing that he should have been executed along with the others.

The tribunal completed its work on October 1, 1946, and adjourned. By then, trials of other Nazis were beginning in the four Allied occupation zones of Germany. And in Tokyo, Japan, that IMT was in the middle of hearing criminal cases against twenty-eight Japanese leaders, most of them military.

Both IMTs were ad hoc international courts created by the victors to try their defeated enemies and punish the guilty. The victorious participants in both trials had to address the charge, voiced by jurists from both victorious and defeated nations, that the tribunals were ex post facto "victors' justice." One response to this criticism was the argument for the creation of a permanent international criminal court composed of jurists from states that were party to the treaty creating the international criminal tribunal, with authority to hear cases involving grave violations of the Nuremberg principles.

The unfulfilled legacy of Nuremberg has been the creation of such a permanent tribunal. Nuremberg crafted principles that the international community agreed on; individual rights, individual responsibility for war crimes, and international criminal laws of war were the major outcomes of Nuremberg. The world community was beginning to discuss the creation of such a tribunal when the cold war began just months after the IMT at Nuremberg ended. The discussions would not be revived for another forty years.

There have been over 100 revolutionary and regional wars since 1945. As an upcoming chapter notes, war crimes, crimes against humanity, and genocide occurred in many of these conflicts, but without a permanent international tribunal to hear charges against those accused of violating international criminal laws, and without a worldwide sense of outrage to lead to another ad hoc international tribunal, the perpetrators have gone unpunished. Until the 1990s, no international criminal tribunals were convened other than those at Nuremberg and Tokyo.

The August 1945 London Charter also became the jurisprudential foundation for the trial presented by the eleven victorious Allies against the leaders of Japan before the IMT of the Far East. However, the Tokyo war crimes tribunal was in many ways very different from and much more controversial than the European IMT.

3

WORLD WAR II IN ASIA, THE FAR EAST TRIBUNAL, AND POSTWAR DEVELOPMENTS IN INTERNATIONAL LAW

The war in the Far East, Gavan Daws wrote, "was a clash of armies, a clash of cultures and—most brutally—a clash of races": the white man against the yellow man in a "race war on both sides and the [Allied] prisoners of war suffered for it."[1] It was also a clash between "yellow men," between the Japanese and the Chinese, that led to the deaths of millions of Chinese, mostly civilians, between 1937 and 1945.[2] It was, finally, a clash of arms in which the Japanese exhibited unbelievable cruelty toward their captives, whether military or civilian.

Unlike the Nazi slaughter of millions of Jews and other *untermenschen,* the monstrous Japanese behavior toward the Chinese and other national groups was public. Newspapers across the world covered the events taking place in the Far East in the 1930s. Commercial newsreel camera crews captured the slaughter of Chinese by the Japanese. Embassy officials in Peking, Nanking, Shanghai, and other cities across Asia dutifully recorded the Japanese cruelties and sent these reports to their home offices in Washington, D.C., London, Berlin, and Moscow. The shock experienced by the world when the Allied troops came upon Dachau and the other concentration camps and killing centers did not occur when Japan surrendered to the Allies in September 1945. The world had known of the atrocities and war crimes committed by the Japanese for over a decade. When, in late 1944, the Americans liberated some Allied POWs held in the Phillipines, the world found out about the brutal treatment of these prisoners by the Japanese military.[3]

The Second World War in Asia: 1937–1945

The war began in Asia for some of the same reasons that led to war in Europe: (1) seizure of governmental power by ultranationalists who glorified militarism and who believed that Japan's economic and defense problems could be solved only by territorial expansion through aggressive warfare. (2) the need to seize territory to provide "living space" for the Japanese people and to make the Japanese Empire economically self-sufficient, and (3) the belief that Japan's enemies, especially the Chinese, were inferior races.

The view that the Chinese were subhuman mirrored that of the Nazis about the Jews, Gypsies, and Russians and that of the Turks regarding the Armenians. For the Japanese, Chinese were not human; they were animals held in

virulent contempt [as] subhuman beings whose murder would carry no greater moral weight than squashing a bug or butchering a hog. . . . A Japanese General told a correspondent: "you regard the Chinese as human beings while I regard the Chinese as pigs." . . . [A Japanese soldier's 1938 diary entry read]: "A pig is more valuable now than the life of a Chinese. That's because a pig is edible."[4]

Like their Nazi and Turkish colleagues, Japanese soldiers were "hardened for the task of murdering Chinese combatants and noncombatants alike."[5] Quickly desensitized, the officers and soldiers of the Japanese armies killed Chinese for sport and for bayonet practice. "Soldiers impaled [Chinese] babies on bayonets and tossed them still alive into pots of boiling water," a medical doctor, Nagatomi Hakudo, recalled fifty years after his participation in Nanking's desecration in 1937. He recalled the first test of his courage on the streets of Nanking when a superior officer gave him a sword and instructed him to kill bound Chinese captives. "I remember smiling proudly as I took his sword and began killing people."[6]

The Empire of Japan initiated the war in Asia in July 1937 when its armies invaded northern China in response to an "incident" near the Marco Polo Bridge outside the city of Tientsin. Japan alleged that one of its regiments on night maneuvers had been shot at by Chinese and that one of its soldiers was missing. The Japanese demanded that a Chinese garrison be opened so that they could search for the missing soldier. When the Chinese refused, the Japanese armies attacked Shanghai in August.

Earlier, at least going back to 1928, the Japanese military had begun its successful effort to control the government of Japan with its actions in northern China and, in 1931, Manchuria, which was occupied by the Japanese after a crafted incident at Mukden.[7] At the time, Japan's empire included Formosa, Korea, Manchuria (occupied in 1931), and the Marshall, Caroline, and Mariana Islands in the Pacific Ocean. By 1936, Japan's military leaders had effectively taken over the reins of government from the political leaders. What struggles there were regarding the direction of Japan's expansionist plans took place between the leaders of Japan's army and navy. Army leaders wanted the nation to expand into China, and the navy sought economic self-sufficiency through the conquest of Dutch, British, French, and American possessions in the Far East.[8]

When Japan attacked China in 1937, its navy planners were engaged in a crash program to rapidly build up the empire's fleet in order to dominate the Pacific Ocean from Australia to the Japanese islands. Admiral Yamamoto had already withdrawn Japan from the terms of the 1922 Washington Naval Treaty. More than 150,000 Japanese soldiers were involved in the initial battles against the Chinese. By November 1937, Shanghai was captured, and in December 1937, Nanking fell to the Japanese (which led to the infamous Rape of Nanking, where over 350,000 Chinese civilians and soldiers were raped, tortured, and murdered by the Japanese occupiers over a period of six to eight weeks).

By September 1938, Japan occupied 700,000 square miles with a population of 170 million Chinese—at a cost of over 70,000 dead Japanese soldiers. In that month, twelve Japanese army divisions moved south in an effort to conquer the rest of China. It was to be a frustrating effort, lasting until the war's end in 1945. It was one in which Japan's imperial armies were continually confronted by the guerrilla warfare of the Chinese communists led by Mao Tse Tung. In August 1940, the Chinese launched the "100 regiments" offensive against the occupiers. Japan's response was much like that of the Nazi occupiers: implementation of a "three all" policy of terror: "Take all, burn all, kill all."[9]

In an effort to cut China's supply routes, Japanese leaders planned the occupation of French Indochina (which consisted of Vietnam, Cambodia, and Laos), British Burma, and Dutch Malaysia. The empire had begun to implement this plan when, in May and June 1940, its new Axis ally, Germany, attacked and occupied the low countries of Europe, including Belgium, the Netherlands, and France. In September 1940, the collaborationist Vichy government of France granted Japan the right to occupy northern Indochina. By July 1941, all of Indochina was occupied by the Japanese.

After the seizure of Indochina by the Japanese, President Franklin Roosevelt froze all Japan's assets in the United States and, joined by Great Britain and the Netherlands, placed an embargo on Japan's oil supply. These countries accounted for 80 percent of Japan's oil imports, and the embargo had a major impact on the war policy of the Japanese government. The

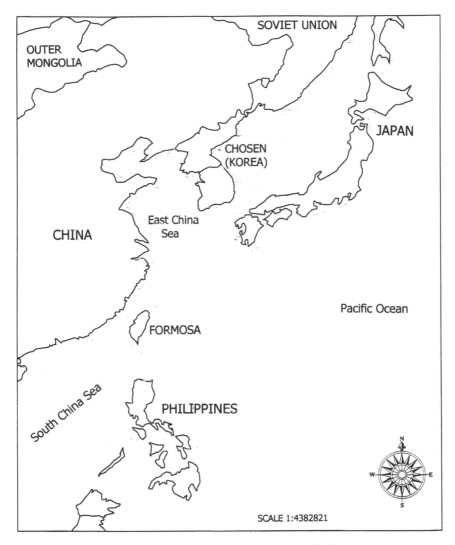

Japanese control of Asia, 1942. (UVM Geography Department: Professor Lesley Ann Dupigny-Giroux and Patrick Keane)

United States demanded that Japan end its occupation of China and In-dochina before these sanctions would be rescinded. But this action was not unforeseen by the Japanese military and government.

Japan's military leaders, from the beginning of their reign of terror in the occupied territories, saw the United States as their primary opponent in the

Pacific. Friction between the two nations had begun in the 1930s, especially with regard to naval dominance of the area. Admiral Yamamoto and others projected that even with Japan's rapid expansion of its navy, the U.S. Navy would dominate the area by 1943. If no actions were taken by Japan, its fleet would be "consigned to inferiority forever."[10] Japan had until then to take aggressive military action in the Pacific. The United States responded by cutting off aid to Japan and threatening to break off diplomatic relations unless the empire withdrew its military forces from China and Indochina.

In October 1941, General Tojo Hideki formed a war government and began the final plans for the attack on the United States at Pearl Harbor on December 7, 1941. Admiral Yamamoto led the naval attack on the U.S. Fleet. Six Japanese aircraft carriers, with 360 planes, stealthily moved to within striking range of the Hawaiian Islands and attacked on Sunday morning. Eight American battleships were sunk and over 300 American planes were destroyed, with a loss of over 8,000 lives. At the same time, Japan struck against the British at Hong Kong, Thailand, Malaya, and Burma, as well as against Dutch Indonesia, attacking the Shanghei bund, Kota Bharu (Malaya), Sigora and Patani (Thailand), Singapore, Guam, and Hong Kong.

By Christmas 1941, Guam, Wake Island, and Hong Kong had fallen to the Japanese armies. Malaya fell in January 1942. In February 1942, as American and Filipino troops surrendered to the Japanese at Bataan and Corregidor, more than 130,000 British troops surrendered to 50,000 Japanese troops at Singapore.

By April 1942, Japan had won smashing victories against the American and British forces and occupied vast new territories in the Pacific. The Japanese Empire became the hub of what its leaders now called the Greater East Asia Co-Prosperity Sphere. When Japan formally surrendered to the Allies on September 2, 1945, millions of its soldiers still occupied vast sectors of the Asian mainland.

Following the military successes came the Japanese occupation and the atrocities committed against civilians and prisoners of war in the conquered lands. Horror stories about Japanese cruelty began to appear after 1937. Hardly a Chinese town or city in the areas occupied by Japan escaped the brutality.

The code of conduct for the Japanese military was the *bushido* ethic, that is, the "way of the warrior." The fundamental tenet was that it was more honorable to die in battle for the emperor than to lay down arms and surrender to the enemy.[11] The Japanese soldiers and officers "were the products of a stern and coercive society and of a hard and brutal military system."[12] In the eyes of the Japanese military, "white men who allowed themselves to be captured in war were despicable. They deserved to die."[13] No Allied POWs held by the Japanese escaped the cruel treatment randomly meted out by their captors. Furthermore, Allied fliers were not considered POWs and were tortured, starved, and then executed. Chinese soldiers were considered "bandits" by the Japanese and were not afforded the protections of the Geneva Accords of 1929.

Dreaded incidents abound. The more notorious of these cruelties included infamous Rape of Nanking by the Japanese in December 1937 where, over a period of six to eight weeks, over 350,000 Chinese were slaughtered by the Japanese and more than 20,000 Chinese women were raped, tortured, and then executed. The Nazi chargé d'affaires in Nanking was so horrified at the brutality of the marauding Japanese soldiers that he wrote to Berlin: "The Japanese Imperial Army is nothing but a beastly machine."[14] (In its final judgment, the Far East IMT noted that Japanese troops were "let loose like a barbarian horde to desecrate the city.") The general in charge of the Japanese forces who committed the atrocities, Matsui Iwane (one of the twenty-eight leaders indicted, tried, and convicted after the war), noted, while the events were still taking place, "My men have done something very wrong and extremely regrettable."[15]

There was also the tragedy surrounding American and Filipino military personnel who, after bravely fighting for five months against overwhelming Japanese army and navy forces, surrendered on April 9, 1942, thus beginning the infamous Bataan Death March. This was, in the eyes of all historians, "a tragic nightmare, without form, reason, or mercy."[16] More than 76,000 American (12,000) and Filipino (64,000) POWs started the seventy-mile march from Mariveles to their prison camp. Only 54,000 reached the camp alive. The Japanese comments about the death march were brief and shocking to the Allies: the Bataan Death March was a "regrettable aberration."[17] Civilians in the Philippines suffered as well; between 1942 and 1945, almost 150,000 of them were massacred by the Japanese.

In Korea, between 100,000 and 200,000 women were enslaved as "comfort women," or prostitutes, for Japanese soldiers at the front.

Chinese POWs and civilians endured ghastly treatment by the occupying power. Tens of thousands were used for bayonet practice by Japanese soldiers. Killings were done in a number of grisly ways, including drowning, shooting, live burial, death by ice (with victims forced to strip and then "go fishing" by jumping into holes chopped in frozen lakes), decapitation, hanging by the tongue, impalement of the vagina, and being burned alive. There

World War II. Chungking, China. Bodies of Chinese civilians stacked in piles, victims of Japanese war crimes, circa 1938. (Library of Congress)

was also the infamous Unit 731 in Harbin, China, where over 3,600 Japanese soldiers, medical doctors, and scientists conducted biological testing, including vivisections, on thousands of POW and civilian guinea pigs.[18] Between 6 million and 19 million Chinese were killed by the Japanese between 1937 and 1945. For many observers, this treatment of the Chinese was the Second World War's "forgotten holocaust."[19]

The Japanese used poison gas in China from the beginning of the war in 1937. Japanese soldiers were ordered to pick up "expended cannisters and [they] removed all traces of its use from the battlefield."[20]

Between 1942 and 1943, over 250,000 civilian laborers and 5,000 POWs used by the Japanese to build the Siam-Burma Railway died due to inhuman working conditions, torture, neglect, and lack of medical care..

Torture inflicted by the Japanese on POWs and civilians stretched the human imagination to infinity. The water treatment, burning with lighted cigarettes, electric shock, suspension, the knee spread, kneeling on sharp instruments, and removal of finger- and toenails were some of the more popular methods employed with relish by the Japanese. Other inhumane treatment included cannibalism, mutilation before death, and impaling infants on swords and bayonets.

The infamous "hellships" were freighters used by the Japanese to transport Allied POWs to prison camps in Japan after the Allies began their successful invasion of the Japanese-held Philippines in July 1944. The Japanese took desperate measures to get the Allied POWs to Japan before they could be liberated by American troops. Between September and December 1944, "too many men were put on too few freighters."[21] More than 5,000 Allied POWs died on board these vessels in the four-month period, due to illness, the atrocities committed by their Japanese guards, or, ironically, when the unmarked vessels were torpedoed by American submarines or bombed by Allied planes.

The Japanese occupiers were primitively brutal compared with their more efficient, more technologically proficient Teutonic partners. (Nazi diplomats in Nanking in 1937, repulsed by the killing orgy of the Japanese occupiers, provided safe haven for many Chinese as well as vigorously complaining to their government about Japanese cruelties.[22]) The Japanese were especially cruel toward Chinese and Korean civilians and toward all enemy POWs. At the Far East tribunal, the prosecution identified at least sixteen different types of killing committed by the Japanese on POWs.[23] These atrocities and crimes against humanity clearly shocked the conscience of the world when they were first revealed in the 1930s and again at the war crimes trials that took place in Tokyo and elsewhere from 1945 to 1951.

The Tokyo Tribunal: 1946–1948

Given the worldwide coverage of Japanese atrocities committed against Chinese military personnel and civilians in the late 1930s, the Americans were gravely concerned about the treatment of U.S. POWs. Within weeks of the Japanese attack on Pearl Harbor, U.S. representatives began sending messages through Swiss emissaries, voicing their concern about the treatment of American POWs. In 1943, Secretary of State Cordell Hull warned the Japanese government that if American POWs were mistreated, abused, or treated in ways contrary to the laws and customs of war, the "American government would visit upon the officers of the Japanese government responsible for such uncivilized and inhumane acts the punishment they deserve."[24]

On July 26, 1945, the United States, Great Britain, and China issued the Potsdam Proclamation. It defined the terms for Japan's unconditional surrender to the three Allies. It basically stated that the Japanese Empire must surrender or face utter destruction. The combined armies were "poised to strike the final blows upon Japan."

> The full application of our military power, backed by our resolve, will mean the inevitable and complete destruction of the Japanese armed forces and just as inevitably the utter devastation of the Japanese homeland.

The terms of surrender followed. They included the following basic demands:

> (6) There must be eliminated for all time the authority and influence of those who have deceived and misled the people of Japan into embarking on world conquest . . .
> (7) . . . Points in Japanese territory to be designated by the Allies shall be occupied to secure the achievement of the basic objectives we are here setting forth . . .
> (9) The Japanese military forces, after being completely disarmed, shall be permitted to return to their homes with the opportunity to lead peaceful and productive lives,
> (10) . . . Stern justice shall be meted out to all war criminals, including those who have visited cruelties upon our prisoners.

The formal Japanese response was ominous silence. On August 1, 1945, a massive air raid (involving 836 B-29 "Superfortresses") bombed the Japanese cities of Jyushu and Honshu. On August 6 and 9, 1945, a single American B-29 dropped atomic bombs over Hiroshima and Nagasaki, respectively. The massive devastation of these two cities—with the accompanying loss of life—led Emperor Hirohito (the titular head of the Japanese government) to go on national radio on August 15, 1945, to tell his people that Japan would surrender unconditionally to the Allies. It was the first time the nation had actually heard the emperor's voice.

The decision by the United States to use atomic weapons against the Japanese has always been controversial. Many have argued, and continue to argue, that the American action was a war crime as well as a crime against humanity. By and large, nonmilitary targets and civilians took the overwhelming brunt of the devastating effect of the bombs. Most of the 200,000 killed were civilians. However, President Harry Truman wanted to end the conflagration before many more tens of thousands of civilians and combatants on both sides were killed during the invasion of Japan planned for 1946. When the Japanese failed to respond to the Potsdam Proclamation, Truman reluctantly gave his approval for the use of the new military weapon against the Japanese.

On August 28, 1945, the first American forces landed in Japan, and on September 2, 1945, the instrument of surrender was signed by the Japanese and by General Douglas MacArthur, the Supreme Commander of the Allied Powers (SCAP), on board the USS *Missouri* in Tokyo Bay.

During the month of August, the hiatus between the Japanese surrender and the Allied occupation of Japan, Japanese military leaders either falsified documents or destroyed incriminating evidence of their wrongdoing "by the warehouseful. . . . Tons of records were burned" in Japan and across the territories occupied by the Japanese.[25] Cables were sent to commanders of Japanese garrisons in the Philippines, Indochina, China, and elsewhere ordering that decisive actions be taken before the formal surrender. One such cable read:

> Personnel who mistreated POWs and civilian internees are permitted to take care of it by immediately transferring or by fleeing without a trace. . . . Documents which would be unfavorable for us in the hands of the enemy are to be treated in the same way as secret documents, and destroyed.[26]

Also in August 1945, before the occupying forces arrived, over 1,000 Japanese government officials and military officers committed suicide rather

World War II. Beheading of Allied airmen by the Japanese, circa 1945. (Alliance for Preserving the Truth of Sino-Japanese War)

than face the shame of being tried as war criminals. One of the major Japanese leaders subsequently tried and hung, former premier Tojo Hideki, was unsuccessful. He explained why he had tried to commit suicide: "I should not like to be judged before a conqueror's court."[27]

During that same month, the report and recommendations of the United Nations War Crimes Commission (UNWCC) were given to the Allies. In 1944, in Chungking, China (the wartime capital after the fall of Nanking), the Subcommittee for Far East and Pacific War Crimes had begun its work. Less than a year later, its findings and recommendations were ready. The report read, in part, that civilians in the countries overrun by the Japanese armies were "ruthlessly tortured, murdered, and massacred in cold blood; rape, torture, pillage, and other barbarities have occurred. . . . Despite the laws and customs of war, and their own assurances, POWs and other nationals of the UN have been systematically subjected to brutal treatment and horrible outrages calculated to exterminate them." It concluded that many international treaties dealing with the laws of war had been violated. Specifically, the report noted that a number of articles of the 1907 Hague Convention had clearly been violated by the Japanese. These included Article XXII, which stated that "the rights of the belligerents are not unlimited as regards the adoption of means of injuring the enemy"; Article XXIII, which forbade the killing or wounding of an enemy "who, having laid down his arms, or no longer having means of defense, has surrendered"; and Article XXVIII, which stated that "the giving over to pillage of a town or place, even when taken by assault, is forbidden."

The subcommittee's recommendation was trial of the wrongdoers, including leaders in government, the military, and financial and economic affairs, before an international military tribunal.[28] Its recommendation was subsequently accepted, and months later, preparations for an international war crimes trial were under way.

MacArthur established his headquarters in Tokyo on September 8, 1945. On September 22, 1945, the U.S. Joint Chiefs of Staff forwarded detailed instructions to SCAP to establish the international military tribunal. There would be three classes of war criminals: class A, those who planned, initiated, and waged aggressive war in violation of international treaties; class B, those who violated the laws and customs of war; and class C, those who carried out torture and murder on orders of their superiors.

Furthermore, MacArthur was instructed by the policy makers not to take any action against the emperor, not even to call him as a witness in the trials of the Japanese war criminals. These instructions did not displease the general, for he feared the outbreak of guerrilla warfare in Japan if Hirohito were punished or dethroned. Many thousands of American forces would be needed to quell the uprising and enforce the occupation of Japan.[29] The prosecutors, MacArthur, the U.S. State Deaprtment, and the Joint Chiefs "were convinced that the Japanese public, although willing to blame the Emperor's underlings, would not tolerate punishment and consequent dethronement of Hirohito himself."[30]

Finally, not known for decades was the fact the American policy makers granted immunity to over 3,600 military personnel, medical doctors, and scientists who had conducted ghastly experiments on thousands of Allied prisoners in Harbin, China, in northern Manchuria. Chinese, Koreans, Mongolians, Americans, and other Allied POWs were used as human guinea pigs in bacteriological experiments by Special Military Medical Group 731. More than 3,000 POWs met horrible deaths during the experiments (1941–1945). POWs and civilians were injected with bubonic plague and cholera; some received horse blood transfusions. Women were injected with syphilis to make vaccines. Vivisections, without anesthetics, were common. Some POWs were infected with gangrene to see how long it took to die; others were exposed to high levels of x-rays.[31] The quid pro quo: the Japanese handed over to the Americans the carefully recorded and documented results of their germ and biological testing.

The decision was made, soon after MacArthur began his rule as SCAP, to identify and try a small number of class A Japanese officials before the IMT. Long before that major trial began in May 1946, trials and executions of class B and class C accused war criminals took place in Japan and other territories formerly occupied by the Japanese Empire's armies. Accused class B and C war criminals were brought to trial before U.S. military tribunals in Yokohama, Japan; Manila and Luzon in the Philippines; Nanking, China; and other locales across the Pacific.

By the end of 1946, while the Far East IMT was muddling along, American military courts had convicted 845 Japanese military personnel, executing 51 of them. Included in this number were two class B criminals: General Homma, whose troops had been involved in the Bataan Death March, and General Yamashita, leader of the Japanese armies in the Philippines when, between October 1944 and September 1945, over 35,000 unarmed civilians were killed.

For the first time, in the *Homma* and *Yamashita* cases, a commanding officer was charged with "failure to exercise adequately his command responsibility *when no conclusive evidence* directly linked him to the violations."[32]

World War II. Biochemical experimentation by Japanese on live civilians and POWs, circa 1943. (Alliance for Preserving the Truth of Sino-Japanese War)

The prosecutor's argument in both cases was that Homma and Yamashita, even if they did not actually order the actions of their subordinates, should have known about the atrocities committed by troops under their command and should have taken action to effectively end such acts.

The military court in *Yamashita* concluded that the war crimes committed by Japanese forces were so widespread, so "extensive," and so "methodically supervised" by lower-ranking Japanese officers that they had to be either "wilfully permitted" by General Yamashita or "secretly ordered" by him. Yamashita's attorneys appealed to the U.S. Supreme Court, arguing that because he had been charged with a crime not recognized in international law, Yamashita had been denied due process of law, a right guaranteed to "any person" facing loss of liberty or life in an American court. After hearing the case, the Court, by a six-to-two vote (with Justice Jackson not participating), dismissed the case as beyond its jurisdiction to hear and resolve. Chief Justice Harlan Stone wrote that the case was "utterly devoid of constitutional protection." Justices Frank Murphy and Wiley Rutledge wrote strong dissents, maintaining that Yamashita had the protection of the Fifth Amendment's guarantee against loss of life, liberty, or property without due process of law.

Both jurists were labeled "Jap coddlers" by the press because of their dissents. Wrote Murphy, Yamashita "was entitled, as an individual protected by the due process clause of the Fifth Amendment, to be treated fairly and justly. . . . He was also entitled to a fair trial . . . and to be free from charges of legally unrecognized crimes that would serve only to permit his accusers to satisfy their desires for revenge." Rutledge wrote: "With all deference to the opposing views of my brethren, I cannot believe in the face of this record that the petitioner has had the fair trial our Constitution and laws command."[33] A few months later, in a short per curiam opinion, the U.S. Supreme Court denied General Homma's request for a writ of habeas corpus.[34] Again, Murphy and Rutledge were the dissenters.

The trials of Homma and Yamashita occurred in October 1945. They were executed after appeals to the U.S. Supreme Court were denied and General MacArthur, not finding any mitigating circumstances in the trial record, confirmed their sentences.

In the Philippines, 133 were convicted and 17 were executed. Chinese courts convicted 504, including, in a courtroom in Nanking, the officer directly in charge of the Rape of Nanking.[35] French courts (in Indochina) convicted 198 Japanese, Dutch courts convicted 969, British courts-martial convicted 811, and Australians convicted 644 Japanese.[36] In total, over 5,600 class B and C Japanese defendants were tried in 2,200 Allied military tribunals. Over 4,400 were convicted, and almost 1,000 of those were sentenced to death and hung within weeks of their convictions.[37]

The Allies were committed to a very public, very visible trial of the major Japanese leaders who had conspired to wage aggressive war against them. It was to be the Far East's version of the Nuremberg trial of the twenty-two major Nazi leaders. The United States was the prime mover in the creation and implementation of the IMT. On November 30, 1945, President Truman appointed a loyal New Dealer, Joseph Berry Keenan, to serve as the Allies' chief prosecutor at the Tokyo war crimes trial. Ten other associate prosecutors were nominated by their nations and then appointed by SCAP to serve alongside the American chief prosecutor.

In early December 1945, the International Prosecution Section (IPS) was created by SCAP. Very quickly a prosecuting team of fifty attorneys, half of them Americans, was created, with a staff of over a hundred. "Prosecuting and defense attorneys came and went like waves at sea," observed a young reporter covering the trial for a news service.[38] By December 1945, Sugamo Prison in Tokyo held over 1,200 suspects, including more than 80 class A suspects. In April 1946, shortly before the trial began, a Defense Division was created, consisting of Japanese and American defense counsel for the accused. Prosecutors in the IPS, from the beginning of their work,

> tailored their legal approaches in light of what they thought would make a more persuasive story, on account of popular understandings of the period. Most notably, the chief prosecutor at Tokyo, Joseph Keenan, was ordered not to indict Emperor Hirohito. Prosecutors also encouraged some witnesses to mention the Emperor's role and presence at key meetings as little as possible, if at all.[39]

On January 19, 1946, by proclamation of SCAP, the charter establishing the International Military Tribunal for the Far East (IMTFE) was announced, followed by the apprehension of those suspected of being war criminals. In many respects, the charter of the IMTFE was a copy of the London Charter for the Nuremberg IMT. Unlike the latter, the IMTFE Charter was promulgated by SCAP and handed to the other Allied nations participating in the trial. In its final format, the IMTFE Charter called for eleven judges to be appointed by MacArthur, who also appointed the president of the tribunal. The eleven chosen were nominated by their respective governments and represented the nations that had fought the Japanese: the United States, Great Britain, Australia, New Zealand, Canada, France, Russia, China, the Netherlands, India, and the Philippines.

The SCAP named an Australian jurist, Sir William Webb, to serve as the tribunal's presiding judge, or president. A quorum for the tribunal was six judges sitting, and voting was by majority vote. A vote of six was also sufficient for issuing a judgment and verdicts. Absences were allowed, and during their lengthy two-and-a-half-year trial, many judges were absent from the court proceedings. Like in the Nuremberg Charter, the defendants were guaranteed a fair trial.

The powers and jurisdiction of the tribunal were identical to those of the Nuremberg IMT. Article V described the tribunal's jurisdiction: to hear cases involving crimes against the peace ("the planning, preparation, initiation or waging of a declared or undeclared war of aggression, or a law in violation of international law, treaties, agreements or assurances, or participation in a common plan or conspiracy for the accomplishment of any of the foregoing"), conventional war crimes, and crimes against humanity ("murder, extermination, enslavement, deportations, and other inhumane acts committed before or during the war, or persecutions on political or racial grounds"). Article VI, like its Nuremberg counterpart, stated that "neither the official position, at any time, of an accused, nor the fact than an accused acted pursuant to order of his government or of a superior shall, of itself, be sufficient to free such accused from responsibility for any crime with which he is charged."

By late April 1946, after reviewing over eighty class A suspects held in Sugamo Prison, twenty-eight major Japanese leaders, mostly military personnel, were indicted by the IPS. (The more than forty major class A suspects who were held at Sugamo Prison but not indicted by the IPS that April were released and never faced court proceedings for their actions.[40]) By the end of the trial, two of the twenty-eight indicted men had died, and one had a nervous breakdown; twenty-five were convicted of war crimes. Nineteen were military leaders, and nine were leaders of the Japanese government. There were four former premiers, three former foreign ministers, four former war ministers, two former navy ministers, six former generals, two former ambassadors, three former economic and financial leaders, one imperial adviser, one theoretician, one former colonel, and one former admiral.

They were charged with fifty-five counts involving five separate crimes[41]: thirty-six counts of crimes against the peace, sixteen counts of war crimes, and three counts of crimes against humanity. The indictment accused the defendants

> of promoting a scheme of conquest that contemplated and carried out murdering, maiming, and ill-treating prisoners of war and civilian internees. [The Japanese forced] them to labor under inhumane conditions, plunder[ed] public and private property, wantonly destroying cities, towns, and villages beyond any justification of military necessity. . . . [The Japanese perpetrated] mass murder, rape, pillage, brigandage, torture, and other barbaric cruelties upon the helpless civilian population of the over-run countries.[42]

Notably missing from the list of those indicted, besides the emperor, were the leaders of Japan's Kempeitai (Japan's gestapo), the leaders of Japan's Zaibatsu (Japan's financial and industrial combines), and the leaders of Japan's ultrapatriotic secret societies.[43]

Finally, on May 3, 1946, the IMTFE began its work. The indictments were formally read in court on May 3 and 4, and on May 6, all the defendants pled not guilty. The tribunal then adjourned until June 3, 1946, at which time the prosecution presented its complex case against the defendants.

The core of the IPS's case against the major military and governmental leaders was their extended conspiracy to wage aggressive war in order to exploit and dominate the Far East. These actions were in violation of international law and the customs and law of war. It began its work six months after the Nuremberg tribunal began (November 1945); the events taking place at Nuremberg were followed closely by the accused, the prosecutors, the defense attorneys, and the members of the tribunal. It was, as one critic wrote, "the Nuremberg of the Pacific."[44]

When the IMTFE ended in November 1948, two years and ninety-eight days later (not counting time off for adjournments), there had been 818 court sessions (on 417 days), 419 witnesses for the prosecution and defense, and 779 affidavits and depositions. The final transcript ran over 49,000 pages and contained 10 million words. The judges took seven months to develop their judgment and verdict. Three of the eleven judges dissented from the judgment in its entirety, and two others wrote concurring opinions. The dissenting judges were the representatives from France, who dissented in part because the emperor had not been indicted; India, who maintained that there was no criminal conspiracy, nor was aggressive war a crime in international law; and the Netherlands, who maintained that civilians could not be held responsible for the actions of the military in the field.[45]

The IMTFE followed Nuremberg's format, procedurally and substantively. The indictment was followed by the defense's challenges to the legality of the IMTFE and to the authority of SCAP, as well as by its claims that aggressive war was not a crime under international law, that there is no such thing as "individual responsibility" in wartime, that "negative criminality" is not found in international law, and that the defendants were being subjected to ex post facto victors' justice.

From June 1946 through January 1947, the prosecution presented its case against the defendants. There were seven wars of aggression planned and implemented by the Japanese Empire between 1931 and 1945: China, Mongolia, the United States, Great Britain, the Netherlands, France, and Russia. The prosecutors maintained that the defendants were personally and individually liable for the planning and the commission of crimes against the peace and war crimes in the name of the Empire of Japan.

The IPS showed the tribunal how Japanese intrigues on the Asian mainland—from their instigation of the 1928 assassination of Chang Tso-lin, a northern Chinese warlord, to the 1931 Mukden incident, to the 1937 incident at the Marco Polo Bridge that led to the commencement of war against China—were part and parcel of a long-range plan by these defendants to have Japan dominate Asia. By 1940, Japan was isolated from the West (due to its clashes with the British, Dutch, and Americans) and entered into the Tripartite Alliance with the Italian Fascists and the Nazis. In the spring of 1941, Japan entered Indochina, and in December 1941, the empire simultaneously attacked American, British, and Dutch forces throughout the Pacific.

The prosecution's first phase was to establish, using diaries, witnesses (both Japanese and Allied), and documents that had not been destroyed by the Japanese, the existence of a police-state mentality in Japan where the ultranationalistic military quickly controlled the civilian government (the reverse of the Nazi Germany experience, where civilians took control of the military command structure). The terroristic actions of the notorious Kempeitai were presented to show one example of the Japanese police state. Additionally, the prosecutors tried to show how the military had staged incident after incident, much like the Nazis in the 1930s, to seize and consolidate power in Japan and on the Asian mainland, and how the specific defendants had been involved in the conspiracy to plan and wage these aggressive wars.[46]

Then the prosecutors went, methodically, from general condemnations to more specific examples of crimes against the peace and crimes against humanity. These included exhibits, documents, diaries, and witnesses that showed how the accused's planning led to:

The 1931 Manchurian intrigues and use of military force

The 1937 war against China and the Nanking holocaust[47]

The organization, in 1932, of a Japanese opium monopoly to finance the occupation of China

The surprise attack on Pearl Harbor and other Allied possessions in December 1941

The occupation atrocities from Manchuria to Malaya, from Bataan to the Siam-Burma Railway, from Harbin to Manila

The "negative criminality" concept—that is, the "failure to act" charge—was linked by the prosecution with the commission of crimes against humanity in count 55, which charged a number of the defendants with "deliberately and recklessly disregarding their duty to take adequate steps to prevent atrocities."

The prosecutors did not, however, indict the emperor (who had been involved in all the key decisions of the Japanese military and government). They also did not present the biological warfare case against the Japanese, nor address the Japanese use of Korean "comfort women" during the war.

The defense arguments began in February 1947 and ended in January 1948. According to contemporary observers, it was a very "weak case" that was presented to the tribunal,[48] one that led to titters from the audience and, infrequently, laughter at the absurdity of the defense allegations. The defense strategy evolved into a five-part division of the arguments: general comments, Manchuria, China, Soviet Union, and Pacific. After this, individual defendants would take the stand to refute the charges leveled against them by the IPS. (Ultimately, fifteen of the twenty-five defendants took the stand.)

In addition to the general arguments that the IMTFE lacked the authority and the jurisdiction to hear the case against the twenty-eight defendants, the defense argued that Japan had not engaged in aggressive wars but had acted in response to devastating economic and military pressures from the Allied nations, especially Great Britain and the United States. Japan, the lawyers claimed, was not out to rule the world; the wars were wars of self-defense, not aggressive wars. Besides, "aggressive war" and "crimes against the peace" were not crimes in international law until the IMTFE Charter made them crimes. Consequently, the defendants were charged with violating ex post facto laws. Further, in wartime, there is no individual responsibility for acts taken—or not taken—by government and military leaders.

Although the atrocities were admittedly "most regrettable," the men in the dock were not aware of these cruelties and should not be punished because of "defective communications" between field commanders and the government in Tokyo. Further, there were no crimes against humanity, no genocide, because there was no equivalent to the "Jewish problem" in Asia (ignoring the Japanese attitudes about Chinese persons).

The Manchurian defense was based on the claim that the Japanese Empire had special rights and interests in that territory. It was the buffer between Japan's captive colony Korea and the Chinese and the Russians. Furthermore, the Chinese people welcomed the creation of the puppet state of Manchuko by the Japanese. To the claim that the Japanese indiscriminately killed Chinese soldiers and civilians, the defense maintained that there were no Chinese POWs because they either fell on the battlefield or peacefully accepted the Japanese occupation and were allowed to go home. The defense attorneys could not rebut the prosecution's evidence showing POW camps and the cruelties inflicted on captured Chinese by their captors.

China was responsible for the enlargement of the war with Japan, claimed the defense. The lawyers maintained that the general message from Tokyo regarding the occupation of China was: "Love the people. Don't burn. Don't violate. Don't loot."[49] The millions of deaths and the brutalities committed by Japanese forces against Chinese civilians, such as the Rape of Nanking, were realities unexplained by the lawyers and the defendants. Finally, the defense claimed that the Japanese war with China was to stem the tide of international communism.

The defense was equally inept in its efforts to show that Japan had not planned an invasion of the Soviet Union as early as 1941–1942, when Russia's fortunes in war were at a low ebb and Japan had yet to taste defeat in the Asian wars. Regarding the Pacific war, the defense maintained, to the annoyance of the tribunal, that the Japanese Empire had been "provoked" by the United States, that it had been "lured" into striking first at Pearl Harbor. This elicited laughter in the courtroom.

Contrary to the evidence presented by the IPS, the defense argued, without documentation to substantiate its claim, that the bombing of Pearl Harbor and the surprise attacks on British, Dutch, and American bases elsewhere in Asia were "not premeditated acts indicating aggressive war." It was American duplicity and trickery that caused the wider Pacific war, the defense claimed.

In addition, the Pacific war was not for domination of the region; rather it was for "defensive purposes."[50] Addressing the barbaric treatment of POWs, the defense maintained that the treatment was poor and inadequate because the lines of communication were cut by the Allies. Food and medical shipments for the prisoners and civilian internees were erratic and beyond the Japanese high command's control.

From September 1947 to January 1948, individual defenses were presented by fifteen of the accused. The testimony presented was much like that in the preceding five segments: self-effacing, without data to buttress their claims. The defendants were vigorously cross-examined by the IPS, and they all were caught in outright lies and forced to resort, on many occasions, to the weak "I don't recall/remember" response. It was a weak defense because there was no way to minimize the charges brought forth by the prosecution.

Rebuttal evidence was presented by both sides between February and April 1948. On April 6, 1948, the IMTFE adjourned for deliberations. Finally, on November 4–12, 1948, the judgment of the tribunal was read in court. All the defendants were found guilty. Seven of the twenty-five were sentenced to death by hanging, and the sentences were carried out on December 23, 1948. By 1958, the other eighteen defendants had been paroled or pardoned from Sugamo Prison.

The tribunal concluded that Japan, under the leadership of the defendants and others, had waged a series of aggressive wars in violation of existing international treaties, including the Hague Treaties of 1899 and 1907, the Geneva Accords of 1929, and the Kellogg-Briand Pact of 1928. Further, between 1931 and 1945, the Japanese had freely practiced torture, murder, and rape as a matter of state policy. "Atrocities were either secretly ordered or willfully permitted by the Japanese government or individual members thereof and by the leaders of the armed forces."

Although forty-five of the fifty-five counts against the defendants were thrown out by the tribunal, the judges found all the defendants guilty of one or more of the following:

Being leaders, organizers, instigators, or accomplices in the formulation or execution of a common plan or conspiracy to wage wars of aggression or wars in violation of international law (count 1)

Waging unprovoked wars against China (count 27)

Waging aggressive war against the United States (count 29)

Waging aggressive war against the British Commonwealth (count 31)

Waging aggressive war against the Netherlands (count 32)

Waging aggressive war against France—Indochina (count 33)

Waging aggressive war against the USSR (counts 35 and 36),

Ordering, authorizing, and permitting inhumane treatment of POWs and others, and committing crimes against humanity (count 54)

Deliberately and recklessly disregarding their duty to take adequate steps to prevent atrocities (count 55)

The judgment of the IMTFE was over 1,200 pages long. There were 207 verdicts, all guilty, handed down by the tribunal over the eight-day period of November 4–12, 1948. The judgment rejected all the legal defenses proffered by the defendants. There were sufficent data to show planning and conspiracy to wage aggressive wars. Page after page described the scope and extent of the savage actions of the Japanese that "were either secretly ordered or wilfully permitted by the Japanese government and its military leaders," the tribunal concluded.

Furthermore, government and military leaders had a "duty to secure proper treatment" of POWs and civilian internees. Each of the defendants has a duty to ascertain that the system [established to provide for POWs and internees] is working and if he neglects to do so he is responsible. He does not discharge his duty by merely instituting an appropriate system and thereafter neglecting to learn of its application. [Those charged with count 55 were found guilty because] they had knowledge that crimes were committed, or they failed to acquire such knowledge.

The waging of aggressive wars and the actions of the Japanese toward civilians and POWs violated existing international laws and customs of war, concluded the tribunal. The Hague Conventions of 1907, the 1929 Geneva Conventions on the treatment of POWs, and the Red Cross Convention of 1929 were cited by the tribunal.

The tribunal noted that of 353,475 Allied POWs in Nazi and Italian camps, 9,300, or 2.6 percent, died in captivity. However, the Asian war produced very different statistics: of 132,134 Allied POWs in Japanese camps, 35,756, or 27 percent, died in captivity.[51] Put another way, one in forty American and British POWs died while in German prison camps, while more than one in four died while in Japanese camps.[52]

Sixteen defendants were sentenced to life imprisonment, and two were sentenced to lesser prison terms. Seven of the defendants were sentenced to death by hanging. These were Generals Doihara Kenji (commander in Singapore, 1944–1945; commandant of POW camps in Malaya, Sumatra, Java, and Borneo), guilty of counts 1, 27, 29, 31, 32, 35, 36, 54; Kimura Heitaro (chief of staff, Japanese Army in China; army commander in Burma; helped plan surprise attacks in 1941; approved brutalization of Allied POWs; field commander in Burma when POWs and civilians were used to build the Siam-Burma Railway), guilty of counts 1, 27, 29, 31, 32, 54, 55; Itagaki Seishiro (chief of staff, Japanese Army in China; chief, army general staff; commandant, Korea; responsible for running POW camps in Java, Malaya, Borneo), guilty of counts 1, 27, 29, 31, 32, 35, 36, 54; Matsui Iwane (commander, China Expeditionary Force, 1937–1938; commander of troops that committed the atrocities during the Rape of Nanking), guilty of count 55; Muto Akira (vice chief, China Expeditionary Force; army chief of staff, Philippines, 1944–1945; troops under his command committed atrocities known as Rapes of Nanking [1937] and Manila [1944–1945]), guilty of counts 1, 27, 29, 31, 32, 54, 55; Tojo Hideki (chief, Manchurian secret police; minister of war, 1940–1944; premier, 1941–1944; the major Japanese war leader), guilty of counts 1, 27, 29, 31, 33, 54; and former premier Hirota Baron Koki (ambassador to Russia, foreign minister during Rape of Nanking, premier during planning of invasions of Southeast Asia and Pacific Islands; member of the Black Dragon secret society), guilty of counts 1, 27, 55.[53]

Four of the defendants appealed their convictions to the U.S. Supreme Court, arguing that MacArthur had exceeded his authority when he established the tribunal. Although the Court took the case, it ruled, six to one (with Justice Robert Jackson not participating and Justice Wiley Rutledge reserving his opinion) that no U.S. court has the legitimate authority and jurisdictional power to review the judgment and verdict of an international tribunal.[54] On December 23, 1948, the seven convicted Japanese leaders were executed in Sugamo Prison. Clearly, looking at the results of the IMTFE, "stern justice" had been meted out.

A postscript: In May 1998, on a formal visit to Great Britain, Japanese Emperor Akihito, the son of Hirohito, was roundly booed by British survivors of the Japanese prison camps, who turned their backs to him as he passed. All the survivors wore white sashes saying "POW Japan, 1941–1945," and many wore red gloves "to symbolize the blood they said was on Japan's hands." Later in the day, Akihito said: "The Empress and I can never forget the many kinds of suffering so many people have undergone because of that war. Our hearts are filled with deep sorrow and pain."[55]

The Moral Issue Revisited: Victors' Justice

Nullum crimen et nulla poena sine lege (no crime; and no punishment without law) was the cry of defense counsel for the Japanese defendants—as it was for the Nazi defendants and their lawyers. In Tokyo as in Nuremberg, the argument was rejected by the judges, but fifty or more years after these tribunals handed down their verdicts, the debate continues.

At the time, the IMTFE itself addressed this claim of the defendants. *Nullem crimen* "is not a limitation on sovereignty but is in general a principle of justice," intoned President Webb in open court in November 1948. The defendants, said the president, echoing the words spoken by prosecutor Robert Jackson at Nuremberg, "knew that they were doing wrong," and no general principle can prevent practical justice from being carried out. The Allies set aside the criticism that the international war crimes tribunals were a form of victors' justice. As Jackson observed:

Unfortunately, both prosecution and judgment must be by victorious nations over vanquished foes. . . . Either the victors must judge the vanquished or we must leave the defeated to judge themselves. After the First World War, we learned the futility of the latter course. . . . The real complaining party at your bar is civilization [which] asks whether law is so laggard as to be utterly helpless to deal with crimes of this magnitude by criminals of this order of importance.

He concluded his opening presentation to the Nuremberg tribunal's judges by observing that "the wrongs which we seek to condemn and punish have been so calculated, so malignant, and so devastating that civilization cannot tolerate their being ignored because it cannot survive their being repeated."

Accepting the victors' justice argument presented by the defense at Tokyo (and at Nuremberg) would have "easily become a way of forgetting Nanking, Bataan, the Burma-Siam Railway, Manila, and the countless Japanese atrocities."[56] As Jackson noted, there were few choices available to the Allies after the wars ended.

What was critical in these first two international war crimes tribunals was the firm establishment in international law of the principle of individual responsibility for the commission of egregious crimes that violated the laws and customs of war.

UN Codification of the Nuremberg Principles

In August 1945, the victorious Allies signed the London Charter. Article VI of the charter created three categories of international war crimes for which individuals, including the leaders of defeated nations, could be tried before the international bar of justice. These were, in December 1946, codified and made part of international law by the UN's General Assembly. As Principle VI of the Nuremberg Principles," the three categories were:

1. *Crimes against the peace:* planning, preparing, participating in, or conspiring to wage a war of aggression or a war in violation of international treaties.
2. *War crimes:* violations of the laws and customs of war, including murder, ill treatment, or deportation to slave labor or for any other purpose of the civilian population of or in an occupied territory; murder or ill treatment of prisoners of war or persons on the seas; killing of hostages; plunder of public or private property; wanton destruction of cities, towns, or villages; or devastations not justified by military necessity.
3. *Crimes against humanity:* murder, extermination, enslavement, or deportation before or during the war, or persecutions based on political,

racial, or religious grounds in execution of or in connection with any crime within the jurisdiction of the tribunal, whether or not in violation of the domestic law of the country where perpetrated.

The codification of the Nuremberg Principles was, in effect, the codification of segments of the charter that had created the IMT. There were seven principles incorporated into international law in December 1946. In addition to Principle VI, the others were:

Principle I: There is individual responsibility for war crimes.

Principle II: Individual responsibility lies in international law, regardless of whether domestic law has no such prohibition.

Principle III: "Head of state" is no longer an immunizing defense against war crimes charges.

Principle IV: "Superior orders" is no longer a defense against war crimes charges, "provided a moral choice was in fact impossible."

Principle V: A person charged with war crimes has "the right to a fair trial on the facts and the law."

Principle VII: Complicity in the commission of the above war crimes is a crime in international law.

These Nuremberg Principles ushered in a new era of international laws of war. They stated that, even in wartime, there are limits "to what governments may use as means of killing and what they may do even to their own citizens; such issues may appropriately be judged by an international tribunal and, most important, those who gave the orders and those who carried them out both bear full responsibility."

Crimes such as those committed by the Nazis and the Japanese "are never anonymous," said Soviet ambassador Valentin Falin. "They are always committed by people. And all crimes must be punished." These principles were indeed revolutionary ones in international law. After these war crimes trials, it was clear that "all individuals, regardless of military rank or governmental position, are answerable to international law for their conduct in initiating and waging war."[57]

The 1948 Genocide Convention

Making genocide an international crime came up after the war. In December 1946, the UN passed Resolution 96 (1), which defined the crime of genocide and "elaborated basic standards that were to be incorporated into the more important convention on genocide that the General Assembly resolved to conclude."[58] The resolution stated:

> Genocide is a denial of the right of existence of entire human groups, as homicide is the denial of the right to live of individual human beings; such denial of the right of existence shocks the conscience of mankind, results in great losses to humanity in the form of cultural and other contributions represented by these groups, and is contrary to moral law and to the spirit and aims of the United Nations. Many instances of such crimes of genocide have occurred when racial, religious, political or other groups have been destroyed, entirely or in part. The punishment of the crime of genocide is a matter of international concern. The General Assembly therefore, affirms that genocide is a crime under international law which the civilized world condemns, and for the commission of which principals and accomplices—whether private individuals, public officials or statesmen, and whether the crime is committed on religious, racial, political or any other grounds—are punishable.[59]

In December 1948, after the war crimes trials of the German and Japanese leaders had concluded, the international community, under the auspices of the United Nations, drafted and signed a convention that formally defined genocide and made it, "whether committed in time of peace or in time of war" (Article I), an international crime alongside the original trio of war crimes noted in London in 1945 and codified by the UN in December 1946. Passed unanimously, the new international law defined genocide (Article II) as follows:

> Genocide means any of the following acts committed with intent to destroy, *in whole or in part, a national, ethnical, racial, or religious group* [but not a *political* group], such as killing members of the group; causing serious bodily harm to members of the group; deliberately inflicting on the group conditions of life calculated to bring about its physical destruction in whole or in part; imposing measures to prevent births within the group; forcibly transferring children of the group to another group.[60]

Article III of the convention enumerated the acts that were punishable: "genocide; conspiracy to commit genocide; direct and public incitement to commit genocide; attempt to commit genocide, and complicity in genocide." Article IV stated that "persons committing genocide [or those acts listed in Article III] shall be punished, whether they are constitutionally responsible rulers, public officials or private individuals." Furthermore, one accused of the crime of genocide could not seek extradiction to avoid trial. Article VII stated that the crimes of genocide "shall not be considered as political crimes for the purpose of extradiction."

Genocide was thus made an international crime, imposing responsibility on an individual—someone who cannot claim the defense of "superior orders" or an immunized "act of state."[61] It also freed the concept of genocide "from its association with war and render[ed] it applicable to the crimes of governments against their own nationals, whether committed in time of war or in time of peace."[62]

One major debate that raged during the discussion of the genocide convention was whether a state's efforts to destroy a *political* group fell within the definition of genocide. Because of the growing specter of the cold war, the Soviets vigorously and successfully blocked attempts to include political groups in the definition of genocide in the final language of the convention. Even though the 1946 resolution passed by the General Assembly specifically included political groups, two years later, that category was removed from the document.

Over 100 nations have ratified the genocide treaty since 1948. The United States, however, took almost forty years to ratify it. The inordinate delay was because of the continuing opposition of conservative groups and U.S. senators. They argued that application of the terms of the genocide treaty would replace domestic laws with international law, thereby violating the essence of American constitutionalism. Sovereignty inheres in the citizens of the United States, and the legislature acts in their name. Americans, they argued, must not be placed in jeopardy of losing their rights to an international entity and international laws of war unless the U.S. government gives its consent to such an international intervention. (In June 1949, President Truman asked the Senate to give its advice and consent to the treaty; in November 1988, President Ronald Reagan deposited the signed treaty, with reservations, in the United Nations.[63])

In August 1949, the world community met and formally adopted the Geneva Conventions. These four conventions "contributed to the development of the modern law of war" by obligating individuals engaged in war to observe some fundamental humanitarian rules of war. The first three conventions expanded on the 1907 Hague Convention principles involving (1) the wounded and sick armed forces in the field; (2) the wounded, sick, ship-wrecked members of a nation's naval forces; and (3) the humane treatment of prisoners of war. The fourth convention, the only new one, focused on the need to protect civilians in time of war.[64]

Thus, by the time the cold war grew hot with the outbreak of hostilities in Korea in June 1950, the international criminal laws of war had changed dramatically. By 1950, given the existence of the Nuremberg Principles, the 1948 Genocide Convention, and the 1949 Geneva Conventions, the once exalted concept of "sovereign immunity" was thoroughly discarded, displaced by the notion of war guilt and individual responsibility for war crimes, no matter the rank and office of the alleged war criminal (unless, as in the case of Hirohito, the head of state is immunized from prosecution by political fiat).

By 1950, then, there was the beginning of a much expanded codification of international criminal law through treaty, convention, and customary law. Because of the gross horrors that took place during the Nazi-Japanese era, the molecular move from nation-state to international community picked up a little speed.

Post–1950: The Emergence of International Human Rights Law

The Nuremberg and Tokyo war crimes trials condemned official actions by military and civilian men and women that denied persons fundamental human rights. The Allies rejected the "immunity," the "just following orders," and the "military necessity" defenses of the Nazis and Japanese in the dock. Individual responsibility for inhumane actions against other human beings was one of the major outcomes of the two trials. If one was found guilty in a court—national or international—of inhumanity against other persons (i.e., war crimes and crimes against humanity and, after 1948, genocide), one suffered the consequences of the guilty verdict.

From 1950 to 1999, there were nearly two dozen major international treaties crafted and ratified that focused on the protection of all persons from a variety of governmental actions deemed by the treaty makers to be violative of human rights and human dignity. Included in this group of human rights conventions were the protection of refugees (1951), the protection of the political rights of women (1952), the protection of stateless persons (1954), abolition of slavery (1956), abolition of forced labor (1957), the suppression of apartheid (1973), and the protection of the rights of children (1989).

The 1987 Convention against Torture and Other Cruel, Inhuman or De-grading Treatment or Punishment, for example, called on states to prevent torture in their jurisdictions and to ensure that torture and other related in-humane actions were included in the nation's criminal code as major of-fenses against other persons. The Convention against Torture was an effort to provide persons around the globe with freedom from torture. Torture, by definition, is

> any act by which severe pain or suffering, whether physical or mental, is intentionally inflicted on a person for such purposes as obtaining from him or a third person information or a confession, . . . when such pain is inflicted by or at the instigation of or with the consent or ac-quiescence of a public official or other person acting in an official ca-pacity.[65]

Political leaders and their regimes that violate these human rights con-ventions, in war or in peace, or that commit war crimes against humanity, or genocide are *hostis humani generis* (an enemy of all humankind). These are crimes of "universal jurisdiction," and under this concept, any country has the right to try any perpetrator, no matter where the crime was committed or by whom.

These human rights conventions reflected the world community's grow-ing commitment to the UN's Universal Declaration of Human Rights, a watershed document ratified by the UN General Assembly in December 1948. The declaration was a clear defense of the integrity and rights of all persons, regardless of race, color, gender, or political persuasion. Article I is its cardinal tenet: "All human beings are born free in dignity and rights. They are endowed with reason and conscience and should act towards one another in a spirit of brotherhood."

The Universal Declaration established two basic sets of rights possessed by all persons: civil and political rights, and economic, social, and cultural rights. The former included prohibitions against slavery, torture, arbitrary arrest, and discrimination based on race, gender, religion, language, political views, nationality, and ethnicity. It also sought to protect civil and political rights such as fair trial; marriage; property; political asylum; freedom of religion, expression, assembly, association, and travel; and the right to vote. The latter set of rights sought to ensure that all persons had social security, employ-ment, fair work environment, quality education, health care, and a decent standard of living. Both sets of rights promulgated in 1948 were codified by the UN when, in 1966, the International Covenant on Civil and Political Rights and the International Covenant on Economic, Social, and Cultural Rights were ratified by the international community.

Human rights law has become "the conscience of mankind."[66] All individuals, as members of the group *Homo sapiens,* have basic cultural, economic, social, civil, and political rights that must not be abridged by government. Since 1948, "there is no immunity for perpetrators of serious human rights abuses—no matter where those crimes were committed. . . . [The world has come far] from the days when tyrants could terrorize their own populations, secure in the knowledge that at worst they might face a tranquil exile on the world's golf courses."[67]

Nuremberg's Principles

"The lasting contribution of Nuremberg was to make individuals responsible" for their actions, said Jutta Limbach, president of Germany's Supreme Court. As Richard Goldstone, the South African constitutional court judge who served as chief prosecutor in the international criminal tribunal for the former Yugoslavia in the early 1990s, said recently:

> Interethnic violence usually gets stoked by specific individuals intent on immediate political or material advantage, who then call forth the legacies of earlier and previously unaddressed grievances. But the guilt for the violence that results does not adhere to the entire group. Specific individuals bear the major share of the responsibility, and it is they, not the group as a whole, who need to be held to account, through a fair and meticulously detailed presentation and evaluation of the evidence, precisely so that the next time around no one will be able to claim that all Serbs did this, or all Croats or all Hutus—so that people are able to see how it is specific individuals in their communities who are continuously endeavoring to manipulate them in that fashion.[68]

However, since 1945, there have been over 100 international wars (classic invasions, wars for independence, as well as wars to sustain spheres of influence) and civil wars fought around the globe.[69] In many of these armed conflicts, war crimes, crimes against the peace, crimes against humanity, and genocide have been committed by some of the warring parties. Yet, until the creation of the ad hoc international criminal tribunals for the former Yugoslavia, which began its work in 1993, and for Rwanda, which began its work in 1994, none of the alleged war criminals had been indicted for violating these international criminal laws. Nuremberg and Tokyo were watershed precedents in the "effort to establish an effective system of international criminal justice."[70] However, until 1993, they stood alone in history as efforts to apply principles of practical justice to those accused of major war crimes.

There were many examples of war crimes and genocide prior to 1993. Since the Nuremberg and Tokyo tribunals, genocide itself has been "alleged to have occurred in various regions of the world: in Africa, against tribal groups in various countries, including Burundi, Rwanda, and Uganda; in Latin America, against primitive Indian tribes in Paraguay and Brazil; in Asia, during the breakup of India in the late 1940s, the creation of Bangladesh in the early 1970s, the struggle for control of Cambodia (formerly Democratic Kampuchea) by the Khmer Rouge in the 1970s, and the suppression of Tamil separatists in Sri Lanka during the 1980s."[71]

One reason for so many wars and so much brutality and bestiality is that there is, as yet, no permanent international criminal court where offended and persecuted groups, those who have been targeted for cruel destruction by their enemies, can seek justice through the application of the new rules of international law. These post–World War II violations of international treaties and customary laws of war may underscore a disdain for the codified laws of war because there is no permanent international criminal court to punish those who violate the norms of behavior in wartime.

Pol Pot, leader of the victorious Khmer Rouge forces (recently deceased before he could be brought to trial on charges of genocide), ordered his troops to commit genocide against nearly 2 million Cambodians—various ethnic, intellectual, and professional groups of "enemies" of the agrarian communist revolution. He reflected Hitler's views before the start of World War II. In late August 1939, Hitler remarked to a group of soldiers just before Germany's unprovoked invasion of Poland: "I have put my death-head formations in place with the command recklessly and without compassion to send into death many women and children of Polish origin and language. Only thus can we gain the living space that we need. *Who after all is today speaking about the destruction of the Armenians?*"[72]

The tragedy that befell Cambodia between 1975 and 1979 is one of the more horrid examples of crimes against humanity and genocide that has thus far gone unpunished by the international community.[73] The following chapter examines the history surrounding the events that took place in that nation.

4

THE CAMBODIAN GENOCIDE

Headlines across the world blared the news on April 15, 1998: Pol Pot, "the Butcher of Cambodia," was dead.[1] Born Saloth Sar seventy-three years earlier, the son of prosperous Cambodian landowners, he was educated in France from 1949 to 1953 and became a Communist at that time. Pol Pot led the Khmer Rouge, Cambodia's radical Communist Party, and took power in mid-April 1975, vowing "to turn back the clock [in Cambodia] to 'Year Zero.' In the name of a bizarre blend of peasant romanticism and radical Maoism, the Khmer Rouge conducted a reign of terror to give birth to an agrarian utopia."[2]

Pol Pot's "primitivist ideology"[3] was a merging of Chinese Communist Party leader Mao Tse-tung's Great Leap Forward and Cultural Revolution models with the brutal totalitarianism of Russia's dictator Joseph Stalin. It had been born in his mind when, as a university student in Paris in 1949, ostensibly studying radio technology, he joined the Stalinist Marxist Study Group.

Back in Cambodia in 1953, he married and took a job (along with his Paris friends Ieng Sary—who married Pol Pot's wife's sister—and Hou Yuon) as a teacher of French, history, geography, and civics at a private high school in Phnom Penh. He was also a member of the underground "Vietnamese-sponsored anti-French resistance, at that time under Communist China's direct influence."[4] In 1963, Pol Pot left the capital to establish the Khmer Rouge's military arm, the Revolutionary Army of Kampuchea (RAK), in northeastern Cambodia. He did not return to Phnom Penh until his victory over Lon Nol in April 1975.

Pol Pot helped form (in 1960) and then assumed control of the Khmer Rouge. He led his armies to victory over the Cambodian government of Lon Nol (who was supported by the Americans and the French) in April

1975. April 17, 1975, the day the Khmer Rouge marched into Phnom Penh, began Year Zero of Pol Pot's fanatical new agrarian Cambodian society, newly renamed Democratic Kampuchea.

From the beginning of the movement in 1960, the Cambodian Communist Party's appeals were directed to the peasants, not to the proletarian workers in the cities. Like the Chinese Communists, Pol Pot's target was not the cohort that Marx and Engels had targeted, the working class, but was instead the peasantry.

Within days of his victory, Pol Pot began to take drastic steps to accomplish his Marxist-Stalinist, agrarian, totally classless society. Under his crazed, paranoid leadership, money was abolished, cities were forcefully emptied, and everyone was ordered to "return to the villages." The urban population—including the sick (who were forcefully evacuated from hospitals), the elderly, the blind, and infants—was sent to the countryside to work and to die on state-run agrarian communes. Religion, prayer, and formal education were barred, and professionals (doctors, teachers, lawyers), and intellectuals were killed because they were threats to the new society. The Khmer Rouge were largely successful in reorganizing Cambodia's traditional kinship system into a communistic communal order.

Political indoctrination and coercion occurred daily. The most important cohort of pupils were Cambodia's children. They were immediately separated from their families to work in mobile agricultural groups or as soldiers; they received indoctrination daily. Those youngsters who "did not bend to the political mania were buried alive, or tossed into the air and speared on bayonets. Some were fed to crocodiles."[5] At the agricultural communes, "holidays, music, romance and entertainment were banned."[6] Thousands upon thousands of Cambodians were tortured and executed by Pol Pot's minions in places such as Tuol Sleng, a Phnom Penh schoolhouse turned into a prison and torture chamber.[7]

In almost four years (1975–1979), the Khmer Rouge slaughtered close to 2 million Cambodians in Pol Pot's manic effort to create a "collectivist society of peasant slaves, watched over by [Pol Pot's army of] gun-toting illiterates."[8] Especially targeted for persecution, torture, and execution were Cambodia's ethnic minorities: Chinese, Muslim Chams, Vietnamese, Laos, and Thais who had lived in Cambodia for many generations. After continued border clashes between the Khmer Rouge forces and Vietnam, Vietnam invaded Cambodia on December 25, 1978. Within two weeks, on January 7, 1979, Vietnamese forces entered Phnom Penh, proclaimed the end of Democratic Kampuchea, and drove Pol Pot from power. For another nineteen years he moved about in the jungles of northern Cambodia and Thailand, with the remnants of his Khmer Rouge army forming a ragtag guerrilla movement, continually evading capture.

In Paris in 1991, a settlement that called for UN-supervised elections was signed. After the 1992 elections, the new government offered amnesty to the Khmer Rouge, and within a few years, Pol Pot's Khmer Rouge ranks numbered only in the hundreds. In July 1997, some of his former Khmer Rouge followers seized him and, in their jungle lair, held a trial in which he was denounced for committing crimes against humanity and put under house arrest for life. Less than a year later, in April 1998, Pol Pot died—evidently, "just as [the Khmer Rouge] prepared to hand him over to Western justice."[9]

His horror-filled legacy is the Cambodian genocide that occurred between 1975 and 1978: a bequest of fanaticism and of "killing fields" where millions of Cambodians were slaughtered, for example, for wearing "glasses . . . because it was assumed that they could read."[10] It is a part of Cambodian history, yet it is so different from all that had gone on before in this area of Southeast Asia.

From French Protectorate to Independence: 1863–1954

The Khmer Empire, Cambodia, reached its zenith in the thirteenth century. At that time, its territory extended from present-day South Vietnam to Myanmar (formerly Burma), from the Malay Peninsula in the south to Laos in the north. By the sixteenth century, Siam (now Thailand) and Vietnam had conquered a great deal of Khmer territory, and the Khmer Kingdom sought peace and security by ceding Siam and Vietnam more territory.[11]

In 1864, the French, after colonizing Cochin China (South Vietnam), pressured the Khmer Kingdom's King Norodom to sign a treaty that effectively created the French Protectorate of Cambodia.[12] Although there were occasional rebellions prior to World War II, the French had no difficulty managing them. In 1940, the Japanese signed an agreement with France (under Nazi pressure) that permitted the movement of Japanese troops throughout Indonesia (Vietnam and Cambodia).

By 1941, there was an 8,000-man Japanese military garrison stationed in Cambodia, although the occupiers allowed the Vichy French police force to continue to maintain law and order in Cambodia. In April 1941, the Cambodian king died, and nineteen-year-old Norodom Sihanouk was chosen by the French to succeed him. (From 1941 to the present, Sihanouk has been a leading figure in Cambodian politics, including the Pol Pot era.)

On March 9, 1945, Japanese forces in Cambodia and Indochina threw out the French colonial administration and encouraged these two nations' indigenous nationalists to declare independence and join Japan's Greater East Asia Co-Prosperity Sphere. Four days later, Sihanouk announced the existence of an independent Kampuchea (the traditional Khmer word for Cambodia). This independence lasted until France, at the conclusion of the Second World War in Asia, resumed colonial control over Cambodia in October 1945.

For almost a decade, until 1954, Cambodia retained its status as a French protectorate. Cambodian nationalists, the Khmer Issarak, operated in the border region between Cambodia and Vietnam; by 1954, with the assistance of the Vietminh (the Vietnamese Communist insurgents), they controlled over half of Cambodia's territory. In the meantime, the French allowed free elections and the drafting of a Cambodian Constitution, modeled after the French Fourth Republic's fundamental law. Sihanouk had also managed, by September 1949, to wrangle independence from France, with Cambodia becoming a member of the French Union. By July 1953, France granted full independence to the three states of Vietnam, Laos, and Cambodia, and independence day was celebrated in Cambodia on November 9, 1953.

From Independence to Control by the Khmer Rouge: 1954–1975

Since 1945, France had been engaged in military clashes with nationalists and Communists in Vietnam, and a major goal of the 1954 peace conference was to end the fighting in Indochina. In the spring of 1954, the Geneva Conference began, attended by representatives from Cambodia, North Vietnam, South Vietnam, Laos, the People's Republic of China, the Soviet Union, France, Great Britain, and the United States. It ended the French-Vietnamese wars. Vietnam was split into Communist North Vietnam and non-Communist South Vietnam. Cambodia also saw its traditional enemy, the Vietnamese, forced to withdraw from its eastern provinces. Between 1955 and 1963, Sihanouk's neutralist Cambodia received security assistance and military aid from the United States (along with American military advisers). During this period, Cambodia saw continuing border clashes with its traditional enemy to the east, Vietnam, as well as border skirmishes with its western neighbor, Thailand.

In addition, Sihanouk's security forces had to deal with an internal threat, the antimonarchist Khmer Serei forces, which Sihanouk believed was supported by both Vietnam and Thailand. Military clashes in the late 1950s were typically followed by amnesties, surrenders, trials, prison sentences, and executions. Believing that the Khmer Serei forces were being assisted by the United States, Sihanouk ended the American economic and military assistance program in November 1963. This was followed by Sihanouk's successful request for aid from the Soviet bloc, especially the Soviet Union and China.

It was at this time that the second Indochina war, between the United States and South Vietnam and the Vietcong (the South Vietnamese Communist military forces) and their allies the North Vietnamese began in earnest. It was a conflagration that engulfed Cambodia from the beginning of the war (1963), even though by 1965 Sihanouk had ended all diplomatic relations with the United States. Inexorably, due to Cambodia's military weakness, it was drawn into the conflict raging in Vietnam.

"It was the agonies of the Indochina conflict, particularly the secret attacks on Cambodia conducted by the U.S. and South Vietnam, that helped build grassroots support for the Khmer Rouge."[13] The Vietnamese Communists used eastern Cambodia as a sanctuary from American military forces. Sihanouk also allowed transshipments of military aid from Communist countries to the Vietminh and the North Vietnamese military through a major seaport, Sihanoukville, across Cambodia to the Communist forces in eastern Cambodia and Vietnam. This led to secret retaliatory military actions in eastern Cambodia by the United States and South Vietnamese military after 1965. Tragically for Cambodian civilians, between 1969 and 1973, the United States regularly dropped bombs on northeastern Cambodia in a futile effort to curtail the North Vietnamese use of the Cambodian forests to move supplies and military personnel from the north into the fighting zones in South Vietnam.

By 1967, Pol Pot and his followers had moved back into the eastern Cambodian jungles (from a self-imposed exile that had taken him to North Vietnam and China) and led a number of peasant uprisings against the Sihanouk government. Sihanouk's forces put down the uprising, attributed correctly to the Khmer Vietminh, or, as Sihanouk called them, the Khmer Rouge (i.e., Red, or Communist, Cambodians). In January 1968, Pol Pot announced the creation of the RAK. Through 1970, it was a small, ragtag band (between 500 and 2,000 young men and boys) using captured weapons, without any support from other Communist movements or nations, and facing a Cambodian population not too eager to wage revolutionary war against Sihanouk.

The first extensive—and secret—U.S. bombing operation took place in 1969 against North Vietnamese and Vietcong targets along the Cambodian border, and it changed the picture dramatically. The bombings forced the Vietnamese Communist forces deeper into Cambodia—which meant new clashes between them and Sihanouk's forces. The bombings also killed tens of thousands of innocent Cambodian civilians, enabling Pol Pot to seize the opportunity to find new recruits for the RAK. This widening of the war in Vietnam "fueled the Communist movement in Cambodia and [in 1967] Pol Pot began his move into armed rebellion. By 1970, he had 3,000 fighters under arms."[14]

In March 1970, while in France, Sihanouk was ousted by his own Cambodian National Assembly. His former prime minister and leading general of the Cambodian forces, Lon Nol, was granted emergency powers and named head of state of the newly named Khmer Republic. It was a bloodless coup. A few months after the coup, in a major expansion of the Vietnam War, U.S. ground forces entered Cambodia to engage the Vietnamese Communists in battles and destroy them if possible. For Lon Nol's government, these U.S. military actions on Cambodian soil were devastating. As the Vietnamese Communists kept retreating westward, they overran the Cambodian military and were quickly in control of all of northwestern Cambodia. As soon as the Vietnamese Communists gained the upper hand in a province, they turned the captured areas over to Pol Pot and his RAK.

Further compounding the dilemma for non-Communist Cambodians was the fact that Lon Nol had entered into a military and economic assistance pact with the United States. By the end of 1970, Lon Nol had declared martial law and called for total mobilization of the armed forces in order to end Pol Pot's Khmer Rouge from taking over the reins of government. Thus began the civil war between Lon Nol's government forces (assisted by the United States) and Pol Pot's Khmer Rouge (assisted by the Chinese). Given the presence of their Vietnamese Communist allies, when the civil war began, Pol Pot's legions had control of almost half of Cambodia. Lon Nol's forces in the field had to contend with military attacks from the Khmer Rouge as well as from the North Vietnamese. In such a struggle, Lon Nol's forces were unable to hold on to the territory they had been ordered to protect.

Sihanouk, in exile in Beijing, China, and furious about his fate at the hands of Lon Nol and the Americans, made a radio appeal to all Cambodians to turn out the usurpers and gave his support to the Khmer Rouge. Sihanouk saw it as essentially a national liberation group bent on overturning Lon Nol's "puppet" government, controlled by the United States.

With Sihanouk on board, recruitment of volunteers, mostly from among the uneducated peasants who saw Sihanouk as a demigod, became very successful, and Pol Pot changed the name from the RAK to the Cambodian People's National Liberation Armed Forces. Pol Pot's military force grew dramatically, and by 1973, there were only a few thousand North Vietnamese soldiers left in Cambodia. That year saw the signing of the Paris agreement by the United States and North Vietnam, which called for the end of all military action in Cambodia, including the devastating bombing.[15] By 1973, Pol Pot's forces controlled 60 percent of Cambodia, containing a quarter of the nation's population. Also in 1973, Pol Pot purged all Sihanouk supporters from the ranks of the Khmer Rouge's military and civil forces.

In January 1973, the United States contributed to the victory of Pol Pot when it began its second secret and extensive carpet bombing campaign—in direct violation of the Paris peace agreement it had just signed. It lasted over eight months and was named Operation Arclight. The massive bombings involved 79,959 sorties flown by U.S. B-52 bombers and F-111 fighters over Cambodia, with the B-52s dropping a total of 539,129 tons of bombs—about 350 percent of the tonnage dropped on Japan in all of World War II.[16] Between 30,000 and 500,000 Cambodian civilians as well as Vietnamese military forces were killed by the American bombing raids, until the U.S. Congress forced President Nixon to halt Operation Arclight in August 1973. According to Ben Kiernan, an eminent scholar of the recent Cambodian civil wars, at least 150,000 civilians were killed as a result of the American bombing raids over Cambodia.[17]

The anger, pain, and frustration felt by the Cambodians toward the U.S. bombings increased the size of Pol Pot's army—as well as its will to defeat the Lon Nol government. Inexorably, the Khmer Rouge successfuly battled the Khmer Republic's military forces. On January 1, 1975, Pol Pot's final offensive against Lon Nol's forces in the capital of Phnom Penh began. By early April 1975, the capital was surrounded on all sides by the Khmer Rouge, and it fell on April 17, 1975, to Pol Pot's forces. "Year Zero" of Pol Pot's agrarian revolution began within days of the fall of the Lon Nol government.

The Radical Transformation
of Cambodian Society: 1975–1979

With the defeat of Lon Nol, the Angkar Loeu (the "high organization")—in actuality, Pol Pot's Communist Party—was the dictatorial authority in Democratic Kampuchea. (It was not until 1977 that Cambodians were told that the Angkar Loeu was the Kampuchean Communist Party and that Pol

Pot was the leader of the party.[18]) A basic lesson was quickly learned by the Cambodians: "Anyone who disobeys the Angkar will be killed," read posters and blackboards across Democratic Kampuchea.[19] The Angkar grimly and ruthlessly controlled all of Cambodia, from the seven zones into which Cambodia was divided down to the local communal society, the village hamlet. Pol Pot exclaimed that 1975 was "Year Zero" and that "more than 2,000 years of Cambodian history came to an end." Pol Pot, through the Angkar, immediately sought to exercise total control in order to "preside over the destruction of Cambodia's past."[20]

Even before it took over fully in 1975, Pol Pot's Khmer Rouge had shown what Cambodians could expect from the Angkar. In March 1974, for example, Pol Pot's forces captured the city of Odungk (population over 20,000), located north of Phnom Penh. Pol Pot immediately ordered all the city's inhabitants into the countryside and summarily executed its teachers, professionals, and civil servants.

However, unlike other totalitarian Communist systems such as China and the Soviet Union, Pol Pot's was able to dramatically, and tragically, refashion Cambodian society "with extraordinary speed and intensity."[21] Within a week, the radical foundations for the transformation to an egalitarian, communal society had been put into place. By May 1975, less than a month after his victory, Pol Pot had structured an eight-point agenda for the Angkar to force on Cambodia's population:

1. Evacuate the people (over 3 million of Cambodia's 8 million) from the cities
2. Abolish all markets
3. Abolish currency
4. Defrock all Buddhist monks
5. Execute the leaders of Lon Nol's government and army
6. Establish cooperatives across Cambodia, with communal eating
7. Expel the entire ethnic Vietnamese population
8. Dispatch Khmer Rouge troops to the Thai and Vietnamese borders to secure the integrity of the revolution from encroachment from Cambodia's traditional rivals[22]

For three years, eight months, and twenty-one days, it was "Pol Pot time" in a horribly transformed Cambodia, for he and his followers succeeded in implementing all eight items. Cities were emptied of their inhabitants, hospitals were cleared, schools closed, factories purged of workers, currency abolished, monastaries burned down, books destroyed. When the Khmer

Rouge entered the capital in April 1975, Phnom Penh had over 2.5 million civilians (including about 1.5 million war refugees) within its environs. It had grown phenomenally because of refugee movement away from American bombings and away from the sweeping terror of Pol Pot's forces—and it emptied out in less than a week.

Economically, Cambodia under Pol Pot became one "gigantic workshop of indentured agrarian labor."[23]

> To own a watch or a clock during this period was to engage in the sort of recidivist individualism that every Cambodian soon learned could be corrected only by execution. [Those not executed] lived—or, rather, tried to evade death—in a state of temporal oblivion that they speak of today [1998] as "Pol Pot's time." [During this period, one Cambodian recalled] we never knew the day. We never have Tuesday. Never have Wednesday. We have a kind of saying: "Every day we call Monday. Monday is always a workday. We have Monday only—Monday, Monday. Nobody hope. Hundred percent nobody hope that everything will change."[24]

Kiernan noted that with the start of Year Zero, "a whole nation was kidnapped and then besieged from within." Human communication in the Democratic Kampuchea run by Pol Pot almost disappeared. The new radical society "was a prison camp state and the eight million prisoners served most of their time in solitary confinement."[25]

Executed immediately after the fall of the capital were the leaders of the Lon Nol government, the generals as well as the soldiers, police, bureaucrats, merchants, intellectuals, "parasites," and others believed undesirable. The "undesirables" list was a long one and included doctors, lawyers, monks, nuns, teachers, landlords, rich farmers, students, poets, "people who wore glasses," the rebellious, the kindhearted, the brave, the clever, individualists, complainers, popular persons, the lazy, the talented, and those with "soft hands."[26] Evacuation of Phnom Penh and all the other cities in Cambodia took place abruptly after the civil war ended in April 1975. Although some were aware of Pol Pot's plans because of his earlier actions, most residents of Phnom Penh were shocked when the evacuation orders were issued.

There were no exceptions. Patients from hospitals were included in the exodus from Phnom Penh. Sydney Schanberg recalled that "it was like something obviously none of us had ever seen—two million people being forced to leave their homes and marched into the countryside, hospitals

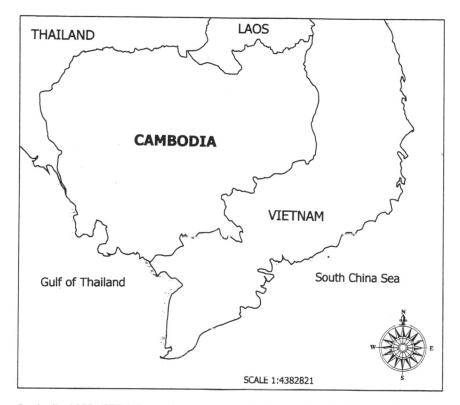

THAILAND   LAOS

CAMBODIA

VIETNAM

Gulf of Thailand   South China Sea

SCALE 1:4382821

Cambodia, 1975. (UVM Geography Department: Professor Lesley Ann Dupigny-Giroux and Patrick Keane)

emptied, patients severely wounded being pushed up the avenues on their beds with serum bottles dripping into their arms. It was a truly mad sight."[27]

In Cambodia before 1975, there were, according to Pol Pot, five classes of citizens: peasants, workers, bourgeoisie, capitalists, and feudalists. Pol Pot's revolution aimed to reconstruct society so that there were only two classes: workers and peasants. For Pol Pot, there were two basic social divisions in the transformed Democratic Kampuchea: the "new people," or "depositees," that is, those who resided in Cambodia's cities under Lon Nol's rule during the 1970–1975 civil war (about 30 percent of the population); and the peasant majority, those Cambodians who were "liberated" by the Khmer Rouge and had lived in the insurgent jungle areas, called the "base" or "old people." The latter, the peasantry, remained in their villages during Pol Pot time; the former, the workers, were forcibly removed from the cities and became the slave laborers in Pol Pot's new classless society.

There was a fundamental mistrust and hatred of the city folk by the young, uneducated, peasant-class Khmer Rouge cadres and the masses of old people. In the second phase of the revolution—that is, the "Socialist Revolution" (the first phase had been "War Communism," the 1970–1975 period)—they came down very hard on the new people. Pol Pot "stirred up the insane and lethal hatred" of his minions toward the new people; the Khmer Rouge and the old people had "an implacable hatred of the 'new' people [for they had led] 'American' lives of luxury while those under Khmer Rouge control [the old people] suffered not only complete deprivation but also American and, to a lesser extent, Cambodian bombing."[28]

One survivor recalled a tense conversation between the Khmer Rouge leader and three new people from Phnom Penh—a policeman, a medical doctor, and a schoolteacher:

> How do you bourgeoisie feel now? Where were you when we were suffering, living in the jungle, fighting the Americans and their puppet regime? You were home sleeping with wives on comfortable beds and making a mockery of us who were trying to liberate our country from French, Japanese, and American imperialism. We didn't then, and we certainly don't need you now. To keep you is no benefit and to destroy you is no loss.[29]

"To keep you is no benefit [or profit] and to destroy you is no loss" became the mantra of the Khmer Rouge cadres who guarded and controlled the lives and destinies of the Cambodians, both old and new. Across Democratic Kampuchea, this was the threat uttered by Pol Pot's soldiers to people who had acted incorrectly. It was a threat that everyone knew was all too real. It was the phrase that "everyone dreaded—it was used throughout Democratic Kampuchea as the ritualized threat of death."[30]

For the urban dwellers and their families who walked into the jungles in April 1975, survival was precarious. As one of the younger new people said, "We were civilized people. We had never lived in the jungle without houses and electricity and running water. [There was] no medicine, no doctors, never any food, [but always] malaria, and exhaustion."[31] The almost 3 million new people were effectively the slave labor for the Khmer Rouge. They were assigned the heavy, labor-intensive work in remote collectives, and they never had enough food, supplies, or housing. And when they made mistakes, they heard the mantra and felt the fear of death constantly.

The second phase of the revolution lasted until Pol Pot's forces were defeated by the Vietnamese army in January 1979. Pol Pot and his surrogates constantly indoctrinated both the Khmer Rouge cadres and the Cambodians, especially the petit bourgeois new people, that the new Cambodia "would be a classless society of absolute egalitarianism." Individualism was a personal characteristic that was anathema to Pol Pot's regime and was never tolerated. It was "outlawed" socially and economically by the Angkar. The Khmer Rouge cadres who ran the collectives "told people who they were to marry and how to live."[32] The punishment for showing signs of counterrevolutionary individualism and disobedience to the orders of the young military cadres was quick execution in the dark of night, without trial, without fairness.[33]

Pol Pot's agrarian revolution was a "unique, murderous experiment in social engineering,"[34] where everyone was called "friend" or "comrade." It was a revolution carried out in all its horror by Pol Pot's Khmer Rouge minions, children ten to twelve years of age dressed in black guerrilla uniforms and sandals made of old tires, armed with machine guns and hand grenades, and full of hatred toward the new people and all other counterrevolutionaries identified for them by the Angkar. The Khmer Rouge "used children as cadres—the future of the revolution was with the 12 year olds taken from parents and indoctrinated and trained as military cadres." They ran the collectives, took care of the youngsters separated from their families, and were in complete charge of the Cambodian population living in the collectives that sprang up after April 17, 1975.[35]

Pol Pot had lived among the old people in the Cambodian jungles for over twenty years, and these peasants "found him very kind—I mean the poor people," said one of Pol Pot's bodyguards many years later.[36] After his death in 1998, some of his peasant followers recalled with fondness his contacts with them during the early phases of the battle. Said one to a journalist:

This is where he would come and sit in the evening. When he was depressed he would call me, and I would come sit with him. He drank expensive ginseng tea, and he kept a bottle of Thai whiskey, and he would talk about developing the country for the poor people.[37]

However, although many peasants thought kindly of Pol Pot, once he assumed power they were treated only a little better than their uprooted urban "comrades." They were not immune to counterrevolutionary accusations by the Khmer Rouge and the terror-filled consequences. By the end of Pol

Pot's time, 15 percent of the 4.5 million old people, or 675,000, had been executed by the Khmer Rouge. This was a smaller proportion than the 21 percent of new people killed by the Khmer Rouge (650,000 of 3.1 million), but that was little consolation to the peasantry who survived these mass executions in the nearly four-year rule of the Khmer Rouge.[38]

Very quickly, in order to survive the killing fields, Cambodians adapted to the new routine of life in the classless agrarian society, which was divided into seven zones.[39] The routine reflected Pol Pot's hatred of traditional Cambodian society's reverence for family, land, and religion. Pre-Khmer Cambodia had been dominated by subsistence rice cultivation, and the nuclear family had been its social core.[40] Family life as it existed for centuries had to end. The Angkar had to quickly destroy the traditional authority of the family if the radical experiment in social engineering was to succeed.[41]

Therefore, the labor camp collective became the basic framework for life. Each collective consisted of about twenty families, but the family unit itself was broken up. All the new people were divided into five groups: small children, older children, single men and women, married men and women, and elderly men and women. For Pol Pot, the "children belonged not to their parents but to Angkar, Democratic Kampuchea's ruling organization."[42] To further this goal of separating children from parents, the Khmer Rouge created mobile youth groups consisting of young boys and girls who would be sent to live and work far from the forced labor camps where their parents lived and worked.

Except for the small children, each group was given a different task and worked in a different field. All worked long days with little food or protection from the elements. And these units were not permanent; every few months, everyone in a family group would be sent to another collective, often hundreds of miles away.[43]

Hunger was always present. "Hunger led people to eat their own pets and other creatures, including mice, bats, and insects. We ate grass like animals," observed another youthful survivor of Pol Pot time.[44] Since paper currency was without value, having been outlawed, gold and silver were the means of purchasing anything in the black markets that sprang up across Cambodia after 1975. Some new people had taken the precious metals with them when they left their urban residences, and for a while, until their gold ran out or they were caught by the Khmer Rouge, they were able to purchase food and modern medicine on the black market.[45]

They worked fourteen- to eighteen-hour days that began before dawn, usually between 4 and 5 A.M. People went off to the fields and worked until

11 A.M., when work stopped for half an hour for breakfast, the first of two meals each day. Breakfast was a thin, watery soup of rice, occasionally sprinkled with greens and salt. Work continued until 6 P.M., when a second bowl of watery rice was served. Labor then continued until 11 P.M. On moonless nights, the elderly would hold torches so that the workers could continue to labor.[46] The work was not only hard and long but also unsafe. The new people had to work in snake-infested lands with thousands of land mines that exploded, killing and maiming, when struck by their hoes, rakes, and shovels.

"Nothing exemplified the revolution's disdain for the traditional rural life of the vast majority of Cambodians more than the regime's destruction of the Buddhist way of life."[47] More than 80 percent of Cambodians were Buddhists, so Pol Pot immediately exterminated their religious leaders and places of worship. In 1975, there were about 70,000 Buddhist monks living in Cambodia, practicing their religion and serving as spiritual leaders for their communities. Less than four years later, fewer than 2,000 Buddhist monks had survived extermination by the Khmer Rouge. The Khmer Rouge eradicated Buddhism within a year of taking power. As a September 1975 Kampuchean Communist Party (CPK) document stated: "The monks have disappeared . . . 90 to 95 per cent [killed]."[48]

Terror was the Cambodian new people's constant companion. It was a terror associated with living without hope and with the threat of random death in the labor collectives. The Khmer Rouge cadres who ran the camps were mostly uneducated, very young, fully indoctrinated with Pol Pot's radical social engineering ideas, and full of hatred toward the new people; these fanatics possessed the power of life and death over all. If a laborer committed a mistake, for example, breaking his rake or hoe, there were essentially only two such incidents before he was extended an "invitation" by the cadre leader. This was the euphemism for execution. These people were of no benefit to the Angkar if kept alive, and certainly no loss if executed. Death from hunger, disease, and exhaustion, as well as violent death, "became a national phenomenon" in Democratic Kampuchea.[49]

Violent death, when it came, came at night. The victim was rousted by the young cadre, blindfolded, and, with hands tied behind the back, taken from the camp to a nearby killing field or execution pit that had already been dug. *Chap teuv* is the Cambodian phrase for "taken away, never to be seen again." There was the "recurrent abrupt disappearance of people, often without apparent reason, [which] created the fear of being 'taken away.'"[50] Terror-filled, sleepless nights were the result for those who woke up in the morning.

In the darkness, people couldn't sleep; "every night seemed to last forever," uttered one young survivor.

> Every night, I could hear the footsteps of the Khmer Rouge soldiers walking around. They were laughing and drinking, and enjoyed killing. They took the kids to kill. They walked them outside and said, "We want you to join your family." The kids were so happy and said good-by to us. "I am going to see my parents. See, Angka is very good." I would peek my head out of my bag and see them go. They never came back.[51]

Execution took many primitive forms, including being beaten to death by farm instruments such as ax handles, pickaxes, shovels, and hoes. Execution by suffocation in plastic bags occurred frequently, as did beheadings with machetes and drownings in barrels of water. Many were buried alive by the Khmer Rouge or boiled alive in huge pots.[52]

When parents were accused of counterrevolutionary thoughts, they and their families were executed, including the young children in other labor camps. Their teenaged children were executed by hanging them from their arms and disemboweling them, cutting out their livers and gallbladders. "Some Khmer Rouge ate the livers of their victims. The young boys moaned and shouted out in pain. They disfigured the bodies and slashed the throats of young children and babies. The Khmer Rouge tore the babies into pieces." When these slaughters took place in the killing fields adjacent to the labor camps, the Khmer Rouge used loudspeakers "because they didn't want the villagers to hear the shouts of pain and moaning. After a while, when the villagers heard the loudspeaker they knew that the Khmer Rouge were slaying people."[53]

These unfortunates were accused of antirevolutionary behavior, thoughts, and words, discovered by the pervasive Khmer Rouge spy system. Spying was endemic because of the Khmer Rouge's fundamental distrust (bordering on paranoia) and hatred of Cambodians, especially the new people. All felt the "pressure of spies daily [although they had no idea] who the appointed spies were in the collective."[54] The story of why the Khmer Rouge killed all the dogs is an apocryphal comment on the ubiquitousness of spying in the labor collectives. A survivor told the tale to a reporter:

> They kill all the dogs because they always spy, they always under your bed. [Two Cambodian brothers slept in the same room] on beds made of bamboo slats. One of the slats was broken, and he reached out in the

darkness to adjust it. "One of my hands touched a Khmer Rouge—under my bed," he said. "They want to spy when my brother comes, what he tells us, what we tell him." "But why kill all the dogs?" "Because," he said impatiently, "easy to come to your bed, come to your house, underneath your bed." I understood. Dogs like to sleep under beds, and the Khmer Rouge liked to sneak under beds for nighttime spying. The Khmer Rouge killed the dogs so they could take the dogs' place.[55]

In Pol Pot's Democratic Kampuchea, "fear dominated life, and immediate death was constantly at hand."

There was the deadly fear of falling ill, whether from hunger, overwork, or the three principal "natural" causes that plagued the "new people." These causes were malaria, long hours of diarrhea, and colds that quickly degenerated into grave respiratory illnesses.[56]

Death other than execution by the Khmer Rouge came from long days of hard work, from malnutrition and exhaustion brought on by overwork and a lack of sleep. There were no modern medicines available (except those bought on the black market), so the people had to make do with herbs, tree bark, and roots of questionable value. Death was the inevitable result, especially for the very young and the old. Those who were not executed were dying a slow death nonetheless.

The rules of behavior from the Angkar were posted on bulletin boards and written on blackboards in the communes across Cambodia: "No stealing. No drunkenness. No prostitution. No marriage outside the commune. No commerce without permission. No contact with outsiders. No listening to any radio station other than that of the Khmer Rouge. [And] 'anyone who disobeys the Angkar will be killed.'"[57] New people were killed, for example, because they failed to hide their education. One young survivor recalled seeing another man killed because "he was caught reading a letter from his poor mother."[58]

Pol Pot's Genocide: 1975–1979

With the victory over Lon Nol came immediate actions by Pol Pot and his Communist Party cadres, through the Angkar, to radically transform Cambodian society. This was accomplished with the use of terror and extermination of the class-, religion-, and ethnic-based enemies of the regime.

It is estimated that 25 to 30 percent of Cambodia's 1975 population of close to 8 million died or were killed in the four-year period 1975–1979.[59] "The violence escalated over time," said Professor Ben Kiernan, the head of Yale University's Cambodian Genocide Program. Pol Pot's "regime continued to go after increasingly broad categories of people; not only ethnic minorities, but specific political or religious groups in the Khmer majority."[60]

There was some form of order to the Khmer Rouge's final solution. As noted, a top priority were those Khmer who did not live in Cambodia's "liberated" zones prior to 1975. They were not pure Khmers; their crime was "that they lived in the enemy's zone, helping and supporting the enemy." They were, as one survivor said, "VOID. We were less than a grain of rice in a large pile."[61]

More than 20,000 mass grave sites, "killing fields," exist in Cambodia, as well as signed execution orders and many documents on the workings of the Khmer Rouge secret police, the Santebal.[62] In the Cambodia genocide, "the majority of the victims were Khmer—of the majority ethnic group—but the ethnic minorities suffered in much greater numbers proportionately."[63]

Although Cambodia was a mostly homogeneous society, because of its history as a French colony for over a century, there were substantial, unintegrated, minority populations in Cambodia, including Chinese (430,000) and Vietnamese (450,000) (both minorities dominated trade and commerce in the cities), Laos (10,000), Thais (20,000), a large Islamic Cham rural community (250,000), and sixteen other small tribal groups (totaling about 65,000).[64] Consequently, there were also "racial pogroms" during Pol Pot time. "The most desperate people in Democratic Kampuchea," Elizabeth Becker observed, "were those targeted for elimination because of their race, creed, or culture. Implicit in the Khmer Rouge drive to force everyone to lead the same narrow, isolated existence was the corollary requirement that everyone be the same. All citizens had to be proper Khmers, as defined by the revolution."[65] The new people, because of their urban lifestyle prior to Year Zero, were constantly suspected of not being "proper" Khmers—and hundreds of thousands of them disappeared in the killing fields. The ethnic minorities—the Chinese, Vietnamese, Thais, Laos, and Chams—also fared poorly because they were not seen as pure Khmer. The Khmer Rouge

> adopted a philosophy of racial superiority and purity that resembled that of Nazi Germany, including the use of pogroms to eliminate minorities. [It was, like the Nazi view of Aryan purity, unscientific because] the idea of a pure Khmer blood or a pure Khmer race is based

Cambodia. Young children at the Killing Fields Memorial, 1993. (UN PHOTO 159733/ J. Isaac, Doc. 1026L)

on superstition. . . . The Khmer Rouge confused the idea of race with that of culture, creed, language, and nation, as had the Nazis. They arbitrarily decided that Cambodia's minorities—the Chinese, Chams, the ethnic Thais and, on occasion, even the hill tribespeople—were a threat to the health and vitality of the Khmer nation.[66]

And, like the "final solution" decree that concluded the Wannsee Conference in Berlin, sealing the fate of European Jewry, Pol Pot issued a decree in 1976 stating, "There is one Kampuchean revolution. In Kampuchea there is one nation, and one language, the Khmer language. From now on the various nationalities do not exist any longer in Kampuchea."[67] This decree sealed the fate of the ethnic minorities in Cambodia.

Over the nearly four years of Pol Pot time, half the ethnic Chinese living in Cambodia, more than 225,000 men, women, and children, were executed by the Khmer Rouge. The ethnic Vietnamese living in Cambodia fared much worse—they were totally eradicated. By 1979, there were no ethnic Vietnamese living in Kampuchea. Of the 450,000 living in Cambodia in 1970, 225,000 had been forcibly expelled by Lon Nol's government. In 1975, Pol Pot's army expelled another 100,000 Vietnamese. The

125,000 that remained were simply murdered by the Khmer Rouge between 1976 and 1979.[68]

The Muslim Chams were twice doomed because of their "foreign race" (they were, hundreds of years earlier, originally from Vietnam) and their "reactionary faith" (Islam). For centuries they had lived apart from the Khmer in their own villages (there were 113 small villages in existence when Pol Pot came to power), where the mosque was the center of life. However, they were labeled counterrevolutionaries by Pol Pot and subject to brutal harassment, torture, and then execution (almost 100,000 Chams died between 1975 and 1979). Like the Nazi treatment of the Jews and the Japanese treatment of the Chinese, the Khmer Rouge forced these Muslims to eat pork and to cut their hair and beards and prohibited them from practicing their religion. After the 1976 decree, the attacks on them were "open and systematic," and by the end of Pol Pot time, more than half the Cham population had been executed by the Khmer Rouge.[69]

By the time Vietnamese forces seized power from the Khmer Rouge in January 1979, the Pol Pot genocide against the new people and the ethnic minorities in Cambodia had taken a devastating toll of human life:

Approximate Death Tolls in Democratic Kampuchea, 1975–1979[70]

Social Group	1975 Population	Number Who Perished	(%)
Urban Khmer	2,000,000	500,000	(25)
Rural Khmer	5,100,000	825,000	(16)
Chinese (all urban)	430,000	215,000	(50)
Vietnamese (urban)	100,000	100,000	(100)
Vietnamese (rural)	25,000	25,000	(100)
Thai (rural)	20,000	8,000	(40)
Lao (rural)	10,000	4,000	(40)
Cham (all rural)	250,000	90,000	(36)
Upland tribes (rural)	65,000	11,000	(17)

"Strings of Traitors" in the Khmer Rouge

Like all other tyrannies, Pol Pot's Khmer Rouge had its secret police, called the Santebal, and its torture and extermination camps. The Santebal was the office that plotted spying missions on suspected new people and was also "the nerve center of the Khmer Rouge purge apparatus."[71] For the most part, the camps were used to torture and execute members of Pol Pot's cadres who fell out of favor with the Angkar or who had plotted unsuccessful coups against Pol Pot. As he said, the Khmer Rouge had "strings of traitors" who had to be "burned out" of the party if the revolution was to succeed.[72]

The purges within the CPK began almost as soon as the party was created in 1960. Given Pol Pot's fears about Vietnamese Communist influence on his cadres, as early as 1962 there were executions of party figures who were "too close" to Vietnamese Communists. In the early 1970s, while the CPK was still battling Lon Nol's government forces, almost 900 Hanoi-trained Khmer Rouge party leaders were executed by Pol Pot's security forces. By 1978, the Pol Pot purges accounted for the deaths of half the CPK Central Committee.[73]

The "burning out" of the party "traitors" took place in interrogation camps such as Tuol Sleng prison. Becker wrote that "if a regime can be understood by the institutions it creates, Democratic Kampuchea should be remembered through Tuol Sleng" (a former high school located in a suburb of Phnom Penh).

> Tuol Sleng was the tip of the iceberg, the headquarters of the security police and the home of the Center's incarceration center. . . . There were countless other "Tuol Slengs" bloodying the country. There were prisons, execution sites, and pits. Work and murder, work and murder were the two certainties of Democratic Kampuchea.[74]

"Like the administrators of the Nazi death machines, the Khmer Rouge kept meticulous records of their victims and protocols of their interrogations [including photographs of everyone who entered Tuol Sleng]."[75] Tuol Sleng was Democratic Kampuchea's major "death factory," where, in less than four years, over 20,000 Khmer Rouge "enemies of the party"—men, women, and children—were taken, tortured for months to elicit confessions of treason and counterrevolutionary action, and then executed.

As Chandler notes correctly, the analogy is not to the Nazi death camps, where the *untermenschen* were executed, but to Stalin's purges of Russian Communist Party members, millions of peasant kulaks, and the Soviet Union's military leaders throughout the late 1920s and 1930s because of their either real or imagined counterrevolutionary actions and thoughts. Just as Stalin's secret police wrung "confessions" from the accused, the Santebal regularly spent months eliciting "confessions" from the Khmer

Rouge cadres accused of plotting against Pol Pot. The paranoia of Stalin was no greater than that of Pol Pot, and in both dictatorships, thousands of party cadres met death after horrific torture and "confessions" of anti-party behavior.

The End of the Pol Pot Genocide: 1977–1979

In January 1977, Pol Pot began the effort to regain Cambodian territory in South Vietnam through warfare. The beginning of the end of the Pol Pot regime came in December 1977, when he broke off diplomatic relations with a now-unified Communist Vietnam. Then, in January 1978, he ordered his guerrillas to "attack from behind the enemy's back."[76] Pol Pot accused the Vietnamese of aggression against Democratic Kampuchea, and for a year, military skirmishes took place along the Cambodia-Vietnam jungle borders, with Vietnam seizing territory from the Khmer Rouge.

In December 1978, Vietnam created the Kampuchean National Front for National Salvation (NFNS) in the territory it had taken from the Khmer Rouge. The NFNS consisted almost entirely of captured Khmer Rouge soldiers and purged leaders, as well as civilians, including Chams, who had fled from the killing fields. Within a month, the NFNS's three regiments, with the massive assistance of twelve to fourteen Vietnamese military divisions (a combined total of over 100,000 soldiers), marched into central Cambodia and captured Phnom Penh, forcing Pol Pot and his forces to flee to the jungle along the Thailand border. With a quick victory at hand, Vietnam established a puppet government consisting of former Khmer Rouge members and changed the name of the country to the People's Republic of Kampuchea.

Tragically and ironically, Pol Pot's tattered government in exile was now supported by Thailand, China, and the West, including the United States. "Most of the world considered Vietnam's invasion a greater evil than the Pol Pot regime it overthrew."[77] During the administration of President Jimmy Carter (1977–1981), the United States provided military aid to the Chinese Communists for transshipment to Pol Pot's Khmer Rouge. "'I encouraged the Chinese to support Pol Pot,' said Zbigniew Brzezinski, Carter's national security adviser. 'The question was how to help the Cambodian people. Pol Pot was an abomination. We could never support him, but China could.'"[78]

In 1979, the Carter administration "tacitly supported the rearmament of the Khmer Rouge and worked successfully to insure that it retained Cambodia's seat at the United Nations, as the country's legitimate government-in-exile."[79]

First Lady Rosalyn Carter even made a trip to the region to show U.S. support for Pol Pot. (Twenty years later, in 1998, Carter, in a sad and ironic about-face, said of the Khmer Rouge genocide that "there is a great disappointment that this kind of horrendous atrocity can go on—recognized by the world but with the perpetrator [Pol Pot] immune to any kind of punishment."[80])

The world community did nothing to bring Pol Pot to some kind of justice for his genocidal commands. After Pol Pot was forced from power by the invading Vietnamese, his government in jungle exile "retained the political recognition of the United States and much of the world through the 1980's while Vietnamese-occupied Cambodia was placed under severe international sanctions."[81]

Over the next decade, there were continued military skirmishes between the Pol Pot forces and Vietnamese troops, as well as clashes between Communist China and the Vietnamese military, with heavy casualties on both sides. By 1981, because of American and other Western pressure, Lon Nol supporters and Sihanouk joined in the newly formed opposition to the Vietnamese-created People's Republic of Kampuchea. These opposition forces were called the coalition government of Democratic Kampuchea.

In 1987, discussions began between Sihanouk, representing the coalition government, and Prime Minister Hun Sen of the People's Republic. These talks led, in 1989, to the renunciation of communism by the Phnom Penh government, to the changing of the country's name from the People's Republic of Kampuchea to the State of Cambodia, and to the Vietnamese withdrawal of occupation forces. Sihanouk was once again, in September 1990, named the head of the new entity.

In Paris, in October 1991, seventeen nations and all the warring Cambodian factions signed the "Agreement on a Comprehensive Political Settlement of the Cambodian Conflict." The United Nations was given the task of implementing its political (fair and free general elections) and military sections; a United Nations Transitional Authority (UNTAC) was established for this purpose, and over 20,000 civilian and military personnel were employed in the implementation of the 1991 Paris accords. To date, events in Cambodia have been a continuation of the old fighting and political maneuvering among the various factions.[82]

A Belated Call for an International Criminal Tribunal

Reports by fleeing refugees of the genocide occurring in Democratic Kampuchea, like the reports of refugees from Nazi Germany about the concentration camps, "were often met with disbelief" by the outside world.[83] Only after 1979, when Vietnam allowed foreign visitors into Cambodia, did the world begin to grasp the horrors of Cambodia's killing fields. Yet even then, because of the recently concluded wars in Indochina and the continuation of the cold war between Moscow and its surrogates and the United States, there was silence regarding trial and punishment of the men responsible for the genocide in Cambodia.

It was not until 1997, more than two decades after Pol Pot and his Khmer Rouge came into power, that the world community began to pursue "Brother No. 1" in order to bring him to trial for committing genocide. "By not having a trial and not punishing Pol Pot and the Khmer Rouge over the past two decades we have, in effect, told the Cambodians that what happened wasn't a crime. . . . If there was no punishment, there was no crime," said Diane Orentlicher, a law professor at American University.[84]

Throughout the 1980s, the Reagan administration (1981–1989) blocked attempts in the UN to characterize the events of 1975–1979 as genocide or to hold Pol Pot and his followers responsible for the mass murder of Cambodians that took place during their reign. Amazingly, until 1992, the Khmer Rouge, although out of power since 1979, occupied Cambodia's seat at the UN.

The Bush administration (1989–1993) addressed the question of punishment of those who had commited crimes against humanity and genocide when the president signed the 1991 peace accord. It was a less than proactive commitment, however, one based on what a future Cambodian government might do. Bush's secretary of state, James Baker, said, "Cambodia and the United States are both signatories to the Genocide Convention and we will support efforts to bring to justice those responsible for the mass murders of the 1970s *if the new Cambodian government chooses to pursue this path.*"[85]

For most Cambodians, there was a question that needed answering before justice could be realized in their country: "I want to know what happened, why Pol Pot killed so many people, why he killed my brothers,"[86] said Oum Bun Thoeun, a legal assistant in Siem Reap, Cambodia, after the world learned that Pol Pot had died. Toward achieving the answer, in 1994 the U.S. Congress passed and President Bill Clinton signed into law the Cambodian Genocide Justice Act.[87] It states:

> Consistent with international law, it is the policy of the United States to support efforts to bring to justice members of the Khmer Rouge for

their crimes against humanity committed in Cambodia between April 17, 1975 and January 7, 1979.

The legislation established the Office of Cambodian Genocide Investigation within the State Department's East Asia and Pacific Affairs Desk, requiring that office to contract with private "individuals and organizations" to make preparations to bring Cambodian war criminals to justice. The principal activities of such an organization were to:

(1) investigat[e] crimes against humanity committed by national Khmer Rouge leaders during that period,

(2) submit relevant data to a national or international penal tribunal that may be convened to formally hear and judge the genocidal acts committed by the Khmer Rouge, [and]

(3) develop the United States proposal for the establishment of an international criminal tribunal for the prosecution of those accused of genocide in Cambodia.

Yale University was selected as the organization to collect data on genocide in Cambodia and to prepare other information and reports for possible use by the government. It began its work in 1995 as the Yale Cambodian Genocide Program. It is presently building databases that include computerized maps of prison sites and victim graveyards, a list of the Cambodian elite at the time of the genocide, a list of the Khmer Rouge leadership, thousands of photographs of victims before their execution by the Khmer Rouge, and archives of original documents of the Pol Pot regime.

In 1995, two legal scholars, Professors Jason Abrams and Steven Ratner, prepared a report and recommended to the State Department, based on their research into Cambodian war crimes, that a "legal or quasi-legal body be established to provide some form of accountability for what happened in the Khmer Rouge period: There is a prima facie case that genocide, crimes against humanity, and war crimes were all committed by the Khmer Rouge."

The Khmer Rouge leadership "committed genocide against religious and ethnic groups (such as Chams, Vietnamese, and Buddhist religious leaders); massive offenses of crimes against humanity (including murder, extermination, forced labor, torture, rape, forced transfers of population, removal of children, forced wearing of distinctive clothing, closure of religious institutions); war crimes in connection with Cambodia's conflict with Vietnam; and breaches of other international treaties, including slavery and torture."

They proposed a number of possible scenarios for action: "creation of an ad hoc international tribunal; creating an international commission of inquiry or truth commission; or pursuing a trial under Cambodian domestic law." If an international criminal tribunal were created, the two recommended that "prosecutions or investigations or judgments should be restricted to the top leadership responsible for national policy (in those days); and to individuals at a lower level who are responsible for heinous crimes such as mass murders or running extermination centers."[88]

In the months preceding Pol Pot's death, Cambodia's two prime ministers asked the United Nations for help in establishing legal proceedings to hold the Khmer Rouge accountable for serious human rights violations committed between 1975 and 1979. The special representative of the secretary-general for human rights, Thomas Hammarberg, called on the international community to respond constructively to the request.

> It would be difficult to establish respect for human rights in Cambodia and to combat the *phenomenon of impunity* if nothing else were done. The phenomenon of impunity continued to be a problem in Cambodia. None was held accountable for criminal acts, in particular those related to human rights.[89]

Despite Pol Pot's death, "President Clinton indicated that the United States would continue to pursue Khmer Rouge leaders and try them as war criminals."[90] He said:

> Although the opportunity to hold Pol Pot accountable for his monstrous crimes appears to have passed, senior Khmer Rouge, who exercised leadership from 1975 to 1979, are still at large and share responsibility for the monstrous human rights abuses committed during this period. We must not permit the death of the most notorious of the Khmer Rouge leaders to deter us from the equally important task of bringing these others to justice.[91]

However, Professor Stephen Heder has pointed out the dilemma the United States faces in the unlikely event of such a war crimes trial. He said recently, "There's certainly a major American responsibility for this whole situation. A war crimes trial could have posed a problem for the U.S. because it could have raised questions about U.S. bombing from 1969 through 1973."[92]

Roger Rosenblatt cited Milan Kundera, who wrote, "The struggle of man against power is the struggle of memory over forgetting." That is why it is necessary, Rosenblatt continued, "for the West, America especially, . . . to call for another Nuremberg."[93] To date, other than reports and press conference rhetoric, there has been no concrete move toward the establishment of some kind of legal or quasi-legal forum to examine the Cambodian genocide. As another Cambodian scholar observed, "The charge of genocide remains hostage to political convenience."[94]

Dith Pran, the Cambodian news reporter whose life story was made into the film *The Killing Fields,* urged the world community to create an ad hoc tribunal to bring to justice the other Khmer Rouge leaders responsible for the four-year reign of terror who are still alive and living in Cambodia.

The Jewish people's search for justice did not end with the death of Hitler, and the Cambodian people's search for justice doesn't end with Pol Pot. I am hoping that the world will continue to help the Cambodian people bring Pol Pot's inner circle to trial. . . . I'm hoping the world will create an international tribunal to prosecute the surviving top Khmer Rouge leaders.[95]

Such cries from the heart, as well as editorials in major international papers calling for such legal action, have not yet moved the world community to act on the requests for justice.

In January 1999, new events in Cambodia reignited the possibility of a war crimes trial for top Khmer Rouge leaders—either in a Cambodian court or in an ad hoc ICC. On Christmas Day 1998, two Khmer Rouge leaders, given a pledge of amnesty by Cambodia's prime minister, walked out of their jungle hideout and arrived in Phnom Penh. They were Khieu Samphan, the Khmer Rouge head of state, and Nuon Chea, the chief ideologue of the Khmer Rouge. After a week of VIP treatment, including a trip to Cambodia's seaside resorts, Prime Minister Hun Sen reneged on the amnesty promise. On January 1, 1999, he said that the two men, and other Khmer Rouge leaders still living, would face justice. He announced his support for an investigation into the killing of almost 2 million Cambodians, after which the trial of the Khmer Rouge should proceed. Although he left open the questions of where such trials would take place and whether it would be a Cambodian court or an ICC that would convene, he assured the world that the trials would occur. In the meantime, the two Khmer Rouge leaders remain free until arrest warrants are issued by the jurisdiction that will hear the arguments. The two have since moved to the remote village of Pailin, home to other Khmer Rouge leaders who have recently come in from the jungle.

In March 1999, Hun Sen, Cambodia's unpredictable prime minister, announced that the Khmer Rouge leaders would be charged with genocide under a 1994 Cambodian law and tried in Cambodian courts. He ruled out an international court tribunal because, he told French reporters, "a trial should proceed without waiting for these foreign countries to spend money and waste time until [the defendants] die."[96]

However, the global nonresponse to the Cambodian genocide is somewhat different from the world community's reaction to the terrible bloodshed and cries of genocide—labeled "ethnic cleansing" by the press—that came out of the former Yugoslavia in the early 1990s. Unlike in Cambodia, the bloodshed and cruelty of the wars there led to formal action by the United Nations in 1993, after three years of inaction.

5

"ETHNIC CLEANSING" IN THE BALKANS AND THE INTERNATIONAL CRIMINAL TRIBUNAL FOR THE FORMER YUGOSLAVIA

Until 1993, the Nuremberg and Tokyo IMTs remained unique historical events. No such tribunals had existed prior to 1945–1946, and none had been created since. Although dozens of genocidal tragedies dotted the world's landscape after 1948, there were no loud cries for an international tribunal to provide a forum for justice for the victims until the early 1990s.

However, the world was shocked at the atrocities in the war-torn former Yugoslavia. In 1993, the United Nations created a prosecutorial protocol and process and an international court, the International Criminal Tribunal for the Former Yugoslavia (ICTY), to put on trial and to punish those individuals found guilty of violating the post-1945 international conventions and protocols, that is, the 1946 Nuremberg Principles and the Genocide Convention of 1948.

It is important to underscore that both in the Nuremberg and the Tokyo IMTs and in the ICTY, the prosecutorial focus was on the individuals who committed the atrocities and engaged in genocide, not on groups or nation-states.

Yugoslavian Diversity, Nationalism, and War

At the time of the Balkan wars of the early 1990s, Yugoslavia had a population of 15 million in a territory of 96,000 square miles. In this relatively small area, there was great diversity. For centuries, the territory and its people were dominated by two vastly different occupiers and cultures: in the north and west, there was the influence of the Austro-Hungarian Empire; in the east, south, and central areas, there was the impact of the Ottoman Empire.[1]

In Yugoslavia, there were at least six basic languages—Albanian, Hungarian, Serb, Croat, Slovenian, and Macedonian—as well as the languages of other minorities living there, including Italians, Slovaks, Romanians, Bulgarians, Turks, and Rom (Gypsies). There were three major religions in the area: Roman Catholicism in the north and west, Greek Orthodox Christianity in the east and south, and Islam in the center. Part of the tragedy of the wars in the area was the fact that the Republic of Bosnia-Herzegovina (BiH), the center of the disputed battle zone, was the geographical area where all three religions "met and mingle[d]."[2]

BiH was referred to as "Little Yugoslavia" because its 4.4 million people were divided among Muslims, "who were native Slavs who adopted the religion of the invading Turks centuries ago"[3] (44 percent); Serb–Greek Orthodox (31.5 percent); and Croat–Roman Catholics (17 percent). Furthermore, these three groups did not live in discrete sections of BiH. Unlike Switzerland's demographics, for example, only 3 of the 112 *opstinas* (districts) were ethnically homogeneous. Muslims had a majority in 37 *opstinas*; Serbs in 32, and Croats in 13; there were an additional 30 districts without a clear majority. Another part of the tragedy that was to overtake the country was that 16 percent of all the children in BiH were offspring from mixed marriages. It was the one republic in the federated Yugoslavia that was truly multiethnic, reflected in the cosmopolitan capital of Sarajevo, the host city for the 1984 Winter Olympics.[4]

Croatia, under Austro-Hungarian rule for centuries and heavily Roman Catholic, was one of the major participants in the wars of the 1990s. In 1990, it had a population of 4.8 million people. Seventy-eight percent of the people were Croat–Roman Catholic; 12 percent were Serb–Greek Orthodox, and only 1 percent were Muslim. The Serbs were concentrated in 13 of the 100 *opstinas* in Croatia and were greatly concerned about their freedom in a republic that had slaughtered almost half a million Serbs during World War II.

Serbia was the largest of the republics in Yugoslavia, with a population of 9.8 million. Serbs accounted for 66 percent of the population, 17 percent were ethnic Albanians, 3.5 percent were Hungarians, 2.4 percent were Muslims, and only 1.1. percent were Croats. Greek Orthodox Christianity was the religion of the majority who lived in Serbia. A critical factor that accounted for the bloody, cruel wars in Croatia and Bosnia triggered by the Serb Republic was that in 1990 there were 1.4 million Serbs living in BiH and almost 600,000 living in Croatia.

The nation-state called Yugoslavia was created in 1918 and was called the Kingdom of the Serbs, Croats, and Slovenes. In 1919, the United States was the first world power to recognize the new nation-state. Aided by Italian dictator Benito Mussolini, Croat secessionists in 1928 created the Ustasha (the "uprising") Party to create a separate and independent state. In response to these actions, King Alexander proclaimed a royal dictatorship; renamed the country Yugoslavia, the "Land of the South Slavs"; and, using his new powers, attacked the Ustasha, arresting many of its leaders. In 1934, Ustasha thugs assassinated King Alexander, creating chaos in Yugoslavia until World War II.[5]

World War II Genocide in Yugoslavia

In April 1941, Yugoslavia was invaded by the Nazi and Italian armies. Immediately the puppet state of the Ustasha Independent State of Croatia was established by the Axis powers. Croatia and BiH constituted this new state, and Ande Pavelic was its leader. In Serbia, occupied by Nazi Germany, bands of equally nationalistic and royalist Serb Chetniks, committed to the creation of a "Greater Serbia," roamed the land to cleanse the region of ethnic minorities (Jews, Gypsies, Muslims, and Croats). The only real partisan group that fought the Nazis were the Yugoslav Communists, led by General Josip Broz Tito, who was to rule post–World War II Yugoslavia until his death in 1980.

Both the Ustasha and the Chetniks took actions against ethnic and religious minorities. Using language common to dictators bent on genocide, Pavelic said that "Slavoserbs are the rubbish of the nation."His top deputy, Mile Budak, boldly proclaimed on July 22, 1941, that "we shall slay one third of the Serbian population, drive away another third, and the rest we shall convert to the Roman Catholic faith and thus assimilate them into Croatia."[6] The Ustasha regime "hurled [thousands] from mountain tops, others were beaten to death, entire villages were burned down, women raped, people sent on death marches in the middle of winter, still others starved to death."[7] Like its Nazi ally, the Ustasha established twenty-seven death camps where the Serbs were executed, including the infamous Jasenovac killing center, where over 85,000 persons were massacred. All told, over 500,000 were killed in the Ustasha death camps, and millions were forced to flee fascist Croatia.[8]

Many Croats "turned against the bloodthirsty Ustasha regime and fought bravely with Tito's partisans."[9] Tito's command post was centered in the mountains of BiH. His partisans warred successfully against the Nazi and fascist occupiers and the Ustasha's political and military leaders. By mid-1944, with Allied support, Tito controlled all of Yugoslavia and created the federal state of Yugoslavia, consisting of six republics (Slovenia, Croatia,

BiH, Serbia, Macedonia, and Montenegro) and two autonomous provinces (Kosovo and Vojvodina), both located in Serbia. He brought, as he said, enforced "brotherhood and unity" to Yugoslavia after the war ended.

At war's end in 1945, 60,000 Jews (there had been 69,000 Jews in Yugoslavia in 1940) and 27,000 Gypsies had died at the hands of Germans, Chetniks, and the Ustasha. But there were also 400,000 Serbian deaths at the hands of the Ustasha and about 100,000 Muslim and Croat deaths at the hands of the Chetniks. Additionally, Tito's victorious partisans, after May 1946, murdered over 100,000 Ustasha military prisoners.[10] (In the 1980s and 1990s, these World War II horrors were very much a part of the memory of Serbs in Croatia and Croats in Bosnia.)

The Rise of Nationalism and the Dissolution of Yugoslavia; 1980–1991

Tito's death in May 1980 ushered in the beginning of the end of Yugoslavia, a nation he had held together. Within ten years, Yugoslavian federalism was no more. In 1986, Serb intellectuals issued a manifesto that attacked Tito's discrimination against and suppression of Serb nationalism in Yugoslavia. This manifesto was used by Serb nationalists to claim what they felt was rightfully theirs because of Serbs' widespread presence across Yugoslavia.

By 1987, Slobodan Milosevic, a forty-five-year-old Serb nationalist, became the Serbian Communist Party leader and began calling for the creation of a "Greater Serbia," to the chagrin and fear of the non-Serb republics in Yugoslavia, especially the (Catholic) Croats and the (Islamic) Bosnians in BiH. Under his skilled leadership, the process of "national homogenization" took place.

Serb nationalism could not be contained within the boundaries of the Republic of Serbia, and a nationalistic wave swept across Yugoslavia. Milosevic led a popular, populist campaign in Serbia as well as in Croatia, BiH, and the autonomous province of Kosovo,[11] where he continually called for "Serbian unity." Clearly, his aggressive speech making "fired up the imagination of Serbs in other Republics."[12] As the world was soon to know firsthand via CNN and other media, it was Serb nationalism, led by Milosevic, that caused the tragedy that engulfed most of the former Yugoslavia after 1991. As Anthony Lewis commented at the time: "the hatred that astounded the world in Yugoslavia was engineered, not innate."[13]

In 1989, there was the trauma of the collapse of Russian and Eastern European communist systems. The death of Tito and the rapid end of communism "unleashed the long-festering centrifugal forces which would soon lead to Yugoslavia's dissolution."[14] The end of communism in adjacent nation-states led to the dissolution of the Yugoslav Communist Party and state secret police in 1990, when the other two "nationalistic" republics, Slovenia (with a population of about 2 million—90 percent Slovenes–Roman Catholics) and Croatia (where its Serb population of almost 600,000, recalling the horrors inflicted on them by the Ustasha in World War II, came down with the disease called "Croatomania"), walked out of a party meeting.

The rotating leadership of the nation fell apart as the two republics declared their sovereign independence from Yugoslavia in June 1991 and sought and received nation-state status (diplomatic recognition) from many nation-states in the international community, including the United States. (They were followed into independence almost a year later, in April 1992, by BiH. On May 22, 1992, these three republics were granted full membership in the UN.)

The Balkan Wars: 1991–1995

In June 1991, immediately after Slovenia and Croatia declared their independence, the Balkan wars of the 1990s began. These included clashes between Slovenia and Yugoslavia (June 1991), the Serb-Croat war (1991–1992), the Serb-BiH war (1992–1995), and clashes between BiH and the Croats (1993). All told, these wars accounted for over 300,000 deaths and the deportation of over 2 million civilians from the battle zones.[15] (Another war developed in 1998 between Serbia and its once autonomous province of Kosovo.)

Richard Holbrooke correctly enumerates five basic reasons for the ensuing tragedy in the former Yugoslavia. First of all, the tragedy was the "product of bad, even criminal political leaders who encouraged ethnic confrontations for personal, political, and financial gain." Then there was the collapse of communism and the end of the cold war, one waged tirelessly (in both "hot" and "cold" varieties) since 1946. By the time Yugoslavia was, in 1991, in its "final agony, momentous events elsewhere (including Desert Storm, the war fought between the Allies and Iraq) obscured what was happening in the Balkans."

A third factor was the fact that Tito had not "permitted the development" of a strong successor, so that after his death in 1980, there were unchecked, ultimately successful moves toward an "unbridled nationalism." A fourth factor was the United States' nonresponse to the growing war fever in the

Bosnia and Kosovo, 1991–1999. (UVM Geography Department: Professor Lesley Ann Dupigny-Giroux and Patrick Keane)

Balkans. President Bush and his cabinet were unwilling to use 100,000 American troops in Yugoslavia for an indefinite period in what they felt was an ethnic and religious quagmire, especially only a year before the 1992 presidential election. Finally, there was the false belief that the Balkan problem would be resolved by the European powers—without American support.[16]

Military organization in these states lacked the formal command and control structure found in the Western European and U.S. military. BiH, Slovenia, and Croatia did not have standing armies when they found themselves in battle. None had heavy armaments or airpower with which to defend their territories. The only standing army in the area was the Yugoslavian People's Army (JNA), which had lost its non-Serb officers and men when "their republics" declared independence. By 1992, therefore, the JNA was an almost all-Serb army, with a scattering of Montenegran soldiers and officers.

The three new sovereign entities had local—and independent—territorial defense forces, the militia, and local police forces, expanded during the wars with armed civilians. Additionally, the warring sovereignties, especially the Bosnian Serbs, had "special forces" under the command of a local leader who operated with a great deal of autonomy. Some of the more notorious of the forty-five special forces that operated in BiH were Arkan's Tigers[17] and e elj's White Eagles. These special forces were sent into captured towns to "ethnically cleanse" them and were charged with committing some of the worst crimes against humanity in the Balkan wars. A number of their leaders were indicted by the ICTY's prosecutor for war crimes and genocide.

When the wars began, then, the Bosnian Serbs, the Bosnian Muslims, and the Croats had essentially four kinds of military forces in the field, operating independently of the other forces. There were the regional army, the militia, the special forces, and the local police. In such a situation, command and control, and the ultimate responsibility for military actions taken against belligerents and civilians, were unclear.

The first of the Balkan wars commenced with the Yugoslavian army invading Slovenia days after its announcement of independence. Within ten days that war was over, and the Yugoslavian army was forced to withdraw from Slovenian territory. The new independent state of Slovenia had successfully resisted the military incursion and had actually defeated the Yugoslavian army in a number of small battles.

The following month, July 1991, ethnic Serb special forces in Croatia (where Croatomania had grown into a plague), with the help of the Yugoslavian army (now made up almost entirely of Serb officers and soldiers), began the second Balkan war (to acquire territory for a Greater Serbia) and seized 25 percent of Croatia's territory. Within weeks, the Serb victors instituted "ethnic cleansing" of Croats in the occupied territories, vicious actions that led to charges of genocide. (In Vukovar, one of the many Croatian towns seized by the Serbs, Serb soldiers massacred hundreds of patients in a local hospital, to the world's shock and dismay.)

At the same time, Croats were committing particularly horrendous crimes against ethnic Serbs living in Croatia. Miro Bajramovic, a forty-year-old ex-militiaman in Croatia who was not under indictment by the ICTY, described the actions taken by his paramilitary unit called "Autumn Rains," one of Croatia's death squads. The group ran a concentration camp that held ethnic Serbs at Pakracka Poljana and Medurici. Bajramovic himself confessed to torturing Serbs with electric shocks[18] and killing hosts of Serb men and women:

> I am responsible for the death of 86 people. I go to bed with this thought and, if I sleep at all, I wake up with the same thought. I killed 72 people with my own hands. Among them were nine women. We made no distinctions, asked no questions. They were Chetniks and our

enemies. The most difficult thing is to ignite a house or kill a man for the first time, but afterwards everything becomes routine. . . . *To be a Serb in Gospic [was] to mean that you did not exist any more.* The order was to perform ethnic cleansing, so we killed directors of post offices and hospitals, restaurant owners and many other Serbs.[19]

By 1992, after 10,000 deaths (most of them Croatian) and the arrival of UN troops, the conflict was brokered to an uneasy peace in which Serbia retained control over one-third of Croatia. (In May 1995, Croatia broke the peace with a successful counterattack that took back most of the land and, at the same time, forced more than 200,000 Croatian Serbs to flee to Serbheld areas of Bosnia and to Serbia itself. By the fall of 1995, after the general cease-fire, less than 3 percent of the population of Croatia was Serb.)

Ethnic Cleansing by the Serbs: 1991–1995

The battles among the Croats, the Muslims, and the Serbs were set pieces that illustrated the manner in which Serb forces—both the Serb army and the Serb irregulars—would do battle against the Croats and, a year later, in 1992, against the Bosnians. First, the regular Bosnian Serb forces and the Yugoslav People's Army troops, sent on orders from Belgrade, Serbia, would establish roadblocks that encircled the town or village they were planning to attack. They would ask all Serbs living in the attack zone to leave the area. Then a siege of the town commenced, involving artillery and mortar fire for hours to days, depending on the resistance put up by the defenders. The siege would also cut off all vital supplies, including water, medicine, and food. After the Muslims or Croats capitulated, the special forces, the "dreaded paramilitary groups," entered the town and "ethnically cleansed" it of Croats or Muslims.[20] After the executions and the deportation of women and very young children, the Serbs who had left town would return and occupy the homes and businesses of the former residents—a tactic repeated in Kosovo in 1998–1999.

The first objective, cleansing the towns of Croats or Muslims, led inexorably to the second goal: "minimizing future [Croat or] Muslim resistance" by making sure that all young males were executed. This was followed, as was the case in Pol Pot's Cambodia, by the cultural genocidal act of executing, in front of the townspeople, the Muslim clerics and other Muslim civic and political leaders.[21] Ethnic cleansing by the Serbs included what Peter Maas termed "eliticide." This is how it occurred in one small town, Korazac:

One of the Serbs who lived in the town stood on a balcony and pointed out every important Muslim—the mayor, police chief, doctors, lawyers, businessmen, even sports heroes. Most were shot on the spot by Serb soldiers[22] or taken to a nearby house where their throats were slit. . . . This was eliticide, the systematic killing of a community's political and economic leadership so that the community could not regenerate. At least 2,500 civilians were killed in Korazac in a seventy two hour period. The survivors were sent to the prison camps.[23]

Clearly, the Serbs especially and, to a lesser extent, the Slovenes and the Croats, given their leaders' commitment to nationalism, were the "combined disintegrative forces" that led to the collapse of Yugoslavia and the tragedy of the Balkan wars.[24] As the world would see, "ethnic cleansing" was a euphemism for genocide. It was first practiced on the Croats in 1991. A year later, the Muslims in BiH experienced the horrors of Serbian ethnic cleansing. As one Yugoslav diplomat wrote, "The common thread in all phases of the war was, tragically, the immense suffering of the innocent civilian population."[25]

Genocide in BiH: 1992–1995

Peter Maas, Laura Silber and Allan Little, Roy Gutman, Edward Vulliamy, Thomas Cushman and Stjepan Mestrovic, Michael Scharf, Mihailo Crnobrnja, Richard Holbrooke, Amnesty International, Human Rights Watch/Helsinki, and other reporters and numerous official reports, private as well as UN and U.S. State Department reports, have chronicled the shocking events that have taken place in BiH since 1991.[26] All these authors present clear evidence that the Muslims in BiH "endured four years of bloody and violent aggression" by the Serbs and their terroristic surrogates, the Bosnian Serbs.[27]

One of the ICTY's eleven judges, Fouad Riad, wrote that the events in BiH were "scenes of unimaginable savagery . . . truly scenes from hell." The judge was referring to a report indicating that hundreds of Muslims had been buried alive, children had been killed in front of their mothers' eyes, and a man had been forced to eat the liver of his own grandchild.[28] Ethnic cleansing, a new term for a policy of systematic genocide,[29] has ravaged Croatia and BiH since the beginning of the wars in 1991.

Ethnic cleansing is "the killing, rape, and forced removal of people from their homes on the basis of their ethnic background. Both Muslims and Croats were targets of [such] Serb brutality."[30] In Croatia and BiH, it has meant planned, violent, systematic—albeit (for tactical reasons) *seemingly* random—acts of murder, torture, beating, slave labor, and rape; forced prostitution and pregnancy; other types of sexual abuse; the general, brutal intimidation of civilians; and the destruction of private property after it has been plundered. These are but some of the horrors that the war in BiH has produced.

Maas noted that in 1992 the phrase ethnic cleansing "had not yet entered the American vocabulary."

> It was a learning process, and I was at the start of it. Like an infant trying to speak, you had to learn the building blocks of cleansing before you could understand its meaning. First the syllables, then the word; articles of speech, then grammar. So you had to learn about mass arrests, torture, rapes, and expulsions, and you needed to understand that it was a system rather than a series of random incidents. Then you could understand what cleansing meant. It took time. You digested the patterns reluctantly, rather than intuitively, because it made no sense that Europe was falling into madness again at the end of the twentieth century.[31]

Silber and Little, in their report on the Bosnian war, refer to the evil of the systematic ethnic cleansing by the Bosnian Serbs, *etnicko cis cenje*, as "a term that has proved the enduring lexicographical legacy of the Yugoslav war. . . . It had been practiced . . . in Croatia [in 1991]; in Bosnia it became the defining characteristic of the conflict." Expulsion of the Bosnian Muslims from their homes, after the wanton killing and rape of thousands of them by Bosnian Serb hit squads, "was the whole point of the war."[32]

In January 1991, Serb President Milosevic, the éminence grise behind these wars, told Western European diplomats that there would be a new Serbian state, the "Fatherland of all Serbs." Included in this Greater Serbia homeland envisioned by Milosevic were the existing Republic of Serbia and huge chunks of Croatia, Montenegro (which had a population of 600,000, including about 10 percent ethnic Serbs), and BiH (which had 1.4 million ethnic Serbs, about 32 percent of the population). Milosevic told them that the enemies of the Serbs were Slovenian and Croatian nationalists and "Bosnian Muslim Fundamentalists" and that the Serbs would act decisively to destroy them.[33]

In the autumn of 1991, Milosevic ordered the Yugoslav army, then essentially a Serb army, to redistribute weapons, including artillery, to the Serbian

Territorial Defense Forces in BiH. In October 1991, the BiH parliament adopted a resolution of sovereignty. Radovan Karadzic, the parliamentary leader of the Bosnian Serbs (and an indicted war crimes defendant) said that if this happened, "Bosnian Muslims will disappear off the face of the earth."[34] His speech in the parliament on the night of October 14–15, 1991, was seen as the issuance of a Serb "death sentence to the Muslim people."

> You want to take BiH down the same highway of hell and suffering that Slovenia and Croatia are travelling. Do not think that you will not lead BiH into hell, and do not think that you will not perhaps make the Muslim people disappear, because the Muslims cannot defend themselves if there is war—How will you prevent everyone from being killed in BiH?[35]

Immediately after the BiH declaration of independence in October 1991 and Karadzic's ominous speech in the parliament, Karadzic and the Bosnian Serb nationalists left Sarajevo and established their Bosnian Serb rump government in Banja Luka in northern, Serb-populated Bosnia. There, Karadzic declared himself the president of the newly created Republika Srpksa, which he claimed was "part of the territory of [Serbian] Yugoslavia."

At this time, with the war between Serbia and Croatia winding down, Belgrade "began sending [into Bosnia] every Serb officer and enlisted man born in Bosnia into the Yugoslavian People's Army (JNA) forces stationed in Bosnia. On March 6, 1992, after a February 1992 referendum on independence was passed by the overwhelming number of Bosnian Croats and Muslims (with the ethnic Serbs not participating in the vote), BiH declared its independence from Yugoslavia. The Serb war against BiH began a few weeks later.

"On May 4, 1992, . . . Belgrade ordered the JNA out of Bosnia—but allowed Bosnian Serb personnel to remain in the country, fully armed. The effect of this," according to a prosecution witness before the ICTY, "was to establish on the territory of an independent state of BiH a fully equipped army operating at the behest of a foreign power [Serbia]."[36] By May 1992, Serb forces occupied 60 percent of BiH (up from 50 percent before the war began). By the time of the Dayton Peace Treaty, November 1995, the Serbs controlled 70 percent of BiH.

After the parliamentary action, and due to European Community insistence, there was a February 1992 referendum in BiH in which those who voted (about two-thirds of the population, with the Bosnian Serbs largely boycotting the election) overwhelmingly (99.4 percent) approved independence. In April 1992, the new nation, led by President Alija Izetbegovic (elected in 1990), was recognized by the European Community, the United States, and almost eighty other members of the international community. A month later, Milosevic—fearing that the Bosnian Serb minority would be persecuted by the Muslims, and after placing fully armed Serb-born JNA troops in Bosnia—started formal military actions by advising the Bosnian militia and the semiautonomous special forces units, supported by the largely Serb-led and controlled JNA forces, to "beg[in] their campaign of cleansing and conquest."[37]

The war of Serbs and Bosnian Serbs against Muslims began in April 1992 with the Serb capture of the Muslim city of Bijeljina. On April 5, 1992, Sarajevo came under siege, one that would last until the peace agreement was signed in the fall of 1995. Croats and Muslims fought together in Sarajevo's defense throughout the siege, even though in other parts of BiH, especially the town of Mostar, Muslims fought Croats in 1993–1994.

By the end of May 1992, the front lines in this Balkan war had stabilized and would remain that way until the summer of 1995, when the BiH military went on the offense. By 1993, with the exception of Sarajevo, the Serbs "were cleansing and killing as a matter of policy rather than happenstance, racking up a huge lead in the atrocity sweepstakes."[38] Karadzic called repeatedly for the separation of Serbs from non-Serbs "and the taking of land without people, which . . . necessitated exterminating the people that inhabited the land."[39]

Entire villages—homes, mosques, schools, ball fields, hospitals—were destroyed by these paramilitary Serb units. They terrorized "residents with random killings, rapes, looting; local Serb 'crisis committees' took charge to detain, beat, and imprison anyone who did not flee, collecting them into camps where abuse and mass killing were routine. Finally the units would massacre any remaining ethnic rivals until no one was left but the Serbs."[40]

Prisoners in the concentration camps were forced to carry out horrible acts. In the notorious Omarska prison camp, one survivor was forced to "tear off [the] testicles [of three prisoners], with [his] teeth."[41] (The first Bosnian war crimes trial, which began hearing testimony in May 1996, heard these charges directed against Dusan Tadic, a minor Serb paramilitary leader who allegedly participated in this and other atrocities at the prison camp.)

As a May 1994 UN Report of the Commission of Experts to the Security Council indicated, "the Commission confirms its earlier view that 'ethnic cleansing' is a purposeful policy designed by one ethnic or religious group to remove by violent and terror-inspiring means the civilian population of another ethnic or religious group from a certain geographic area." The report concluded that, "with respect to the practices by Serbs in BiH and Croatia, 'ethnic cleansing' is commonly used as a term to describe a policy conducted in furtherance of political doctrines relating to 'Greater Serbia.' . . . [It is a policy] put into practice by Serbs in BiH and Croatia and their supporters in the Federal Republic of Yugoslavia [Serbia]."[42]

With the stabilization of the military lines in the spring–summer of 1992, the eastern Muslim enclaves in BiH, including Sarajevo and smaller towns to the east and south, such as Srebrenica, were vulnerable targets for the Serbs in the hills surrounding them. BiH leaders used their vulnerability "as pressure points on the international community" to have the UN intervene to save the Bosnian Muslims.[43]

In April 1993, the UN declared Sarajevo and the other Muslim enclaves "safe areas." Small detachments of UN military forces from Canada, the Netherlands, and other member nations were sent into these vulnerable areas to patrol them and to provide humanitarian aid. It was an impossible situation for the Muslims and the UN troops, for all these cities and towns were surrounded by hostile ethnic Serb forces and were constantly being shelled and attacked. Although the North Atlantic Treaty Organization (NATO) had offered to supply close air support to assist the UN forces on the ground, only a handful of NATO sorties were ever flown over the area.

During all this time (1992–1995), although declared a "safe area," Sarajevo was under constant artillery, mortar, and sniper fire from Bosnian Serbs in the hills surrounding the once-beautiful multiethnic city. Estimates of the number of artillery pieces ranged from 600 to 1,100. UN military in the city estimated that the daily shelling of Sarajevo ranged from 200 to 300 impacts on a quiet day to between 800 and 1,000 shells when the Serbs were active. Additionally, supplies were cut off, and the residents desperately sought food, medicine, and other necessities of life under the most difficult of circumstances.

Beyond the random daily shellings, the basic targets of the Serb gunners were the Kosovo Hospital, the radio and television stations, the newspaper building, public transportation buildings, the parliament and presidency facilities, the city brewery, the flour mill, the main bakery, the Olympic complex, the city's industrial area, railroad yards, various cemeteries, the city airport, large apartment complexes, public marketplaces, the old Muslim quarter of the city, and other cultural and religious places and public facilities. The Sarajevo siege was as terrible as any fourteenth-century blockade, and the citizens suffered greatly.

Bosnia. Bosnian refugees at UN safe haven, 1992. (UN PHOTO 159249 /J. Isaac DOC 1011L)

Zlata Filipovic, a preteen who lived in Sarajevo with her parents during the Serb onslaught, kept a diary of her life in the city under siege that vividly described the fears of its inhabitants. Her words follow:

May 23, 1992. Dear Diary: I'm not writing to you about me anymore. I'm writing to you about war, death, injuries, shells, sadness, and sorrow. Almost all my friends have left. Even if they were here, who knows whether we'd be able to see one another. The phones aren't working. . . . Lots of people Mommy and Daddy know have been killed. Oh, God, what is happening here??? . . . May 27, 1992. SLAUGHTER! MASSACRE! HORROR! CRIME! BLOOD! SCREAMS! TEARS! DESPAIR! That's what Vaso Miskin Street looks like today. Two shells exploded in the street and one in the market. . . . As Mommy came into the house she started shaking and crying. Through her tears she told us how she had seen dismembered bodies. . . . May 30, 1992. The City Maternity Hospital has burned down. I was born there. . . . The fire devoured everything. . . . God, people get killed here, they die here, they disappear, things go up in flames here. . . . October 17, 1993. Yesterday our friends in the hills reminded us of their presence and that they are now in control and can kill, wound, destroy. . . . Yesterday was a truly horrible day. Five hundred and ninety shells. From 4:30 in the morning on, throughout the day. Six dead and fifty six wounded. That is yesterday's toll. . . . We went down into the cellar. Into the cold, dark, stupid cellar which I hate. We were there for hours and hours. They kept pounding away. All the neighbors were with us. . . . They keep taking and burning all our hopes. . . . Why [do they want to destroy us]? Why? We haven't done anything. We're innocent. But helpless! . . .

I will try to get through all this, with your support [diary], hoping that it will all pass and that I will be a child again, living my childhood in peace.[44]

In February 1994, a Serb shell fell on a marketplace in Sarajevo, killing 68 Muslims and wounding 200 others. It was a bloody scene carried by television stations around the world, one that led NATO to threaten air strikes on Serb artillery emplacements if the Serbs refused to pull their weapons back seven miles. In April 1994, in one of the Muslim eastern enclaves, Gorazde, which was under heavy Bosnian Serb attack, NATO planes launched air strikes against the artillery batteries, relieving the pressure on the town briefly.

In January 1995, former U.S. president Jimmy Carter brokered a four-month cease-fire between BiH and the Bosnian Serbs. However, between March and August 1995, both the Bosnian and the Croatian armies launched offensives against Serb-held territories. (By the end of August 1995, Croatia had successfully retaken territory it had lost to the Serbs in 1992. In all, the Muslim-Croat offensive took back 1,500 square miles of territory, forcing more than 150,000 Serbs to flee to eastern Slavonia.)

In July 1995, while the shelling of Sarajevo continued, the Bosnian Serbs were ordered to attack Srebrenica and other small towns located smack in the middle of Serb-held BiH in order to "demilitarize" the areas. Thus began one of the last and one of the worst genocides that occurred in BiH. The ethnic cleansing that ensued was planned and "controlled, without doubt, by the Bosnian-Serb military and political leadership and, most likely, by the rump-Yugoslav military and political leadership as well."[45]

More than 30,000 Bosnian Muslims were victims of the ethnic cleansing in Srebrenica that July. After the shelling and shooting, which targeted the Dutch peacekeepers as well, the irregulars took over the town. Immediately, the women and young children were separated from the men and the older boys. The small town's two mosques were dynamited by the Serbs and the clerics executed. There was nightmarish chaos as these separations took place, much like the separations that occurred at the Nazi killing centers during World War II.

Terror, as two reporters noted, "was kept at a constant level."[46] The Muslim men and boys were told that they would be screened for possible "war crimes" activity; instead, they were taken into fields and to the soccer stadium and executed by the Bosnian Serb soldiers. The women and children were removed from Srebrenica and other towns and transported to Muslim areas. The best estimate of the number of dead at Srebrenica came from the International Committee of the Red Cross: 6,546 men and boys were missing and were never found—although there was evidence of freshly dug mass graves in the fields surrounding the town.[47]

"Everyone is the enemy in ethnic warfare," said one of the Serb leaders during these executions. A Dutch sergeant told of the attitude of the Bosnian Serb murderers:

> They bragged about how they had murdered people and raped women. They were proud of what they were doing. I didn't get the feeling that they were doing it out of anger or revenge, more for fun. They seemed pleased with themselves in a sort of professional, low-key way.[58]

"The destruction of Srebrenica was an enormous shock to the Western Alliance, and to the conscience of the West," wrote one American diplomat.[49] On August 28, 1995, another Serb shell landed in Sarajevo, killing thirty-eight Muslims. Within two days, NATO air strikes hit the Serb batteries surrounding the city. By the end of the summer, the ethnic cleansing finally ended. Through the intervention of U.S. President Bill Clinton, the Sarajevo siege was finally lifted in mid-September. A cease-fire was accepted and began on October 10, 1995. The warring parties also agreed to convene in Dayton, Ohio, to begin talks aimed at reaching a comprehensive agreement on ending the Balkan wars.

The Dayton, Ohio, Peace Treaty

The peace talks—brokered by President Clinton and his chief diplomat Richard Holbrooke, then the assistant secretary of state for European and Canadian affairs—began on October 21, 1995. Meeting in Dayton, Ohio, were Presidents Franjo Tudjman of Croatia, Alija Izetbegovic of BiH, and Slobodan Milosevic representing the Bosnian Serbs, along with diplomats from Russia, Great Britain, France, Germany, and the European Union, as well as President Clinton.

"After twenty days of torturous negotiations on a spartan American air base," the "extraordinary diplomatic ballet" skillfully coordinated by Holbrooke, led to a tentative peace, the Dayton, Ohio, agreement, initialed in November 1995 and signed in Paris on December 14, 1995.[50] The agreement called for the formation of a NATO implementation force (IFOR); a military group of up to 90,000 personnel, including 20,000 American troops; and a serpentine partition of BiH between the Bosnian Serbs on one side and the Confederation of Muslims and Croats on the other.

It was a peace arrangement that the Bosnian Serbs opposed. The president of the Bosnian Serb parliament, a delegate at the conference, "denounced the deal as 'an especially bad mistake. . . . No one has the right to give away territories that we defended with blood.' "[51] However, the Bosnian Serbs, including their leader Karadzic, unwillingly went along due to the pressure from Milosevic.

By the time of the December peace agreement, over 300,000 persons had died in the former Yugoslavia, and the UN High Commissioner for Refugees estimated that there were more than 3.9 million displaced persons and refugees within the six republics, including 500,000 in Serbia, 385,000 in Croatia, and more than 2.7 million in BiH.

The Dayton agreement created two entities in the former BiH: the Federation of Bosnia and Herzegovina, a Muslim-Croat federation; and a Bosnian Serb republic called Republika Srpska. Both of the warring forces had to cede territory they controlled. The BiH federation controlled a unified Sarajevo and a secure land corridor to the eastern enclave of Gorazde, and the Serbs gained control of some of the lands they had ethnically cleansed, including the former "safe areas" of Srebrenica and Zepa. Included in the agreement was a "right of return," whereby the millions of displaced persons would be allowed to return to their homes or receive compensation.

Prior to the war crimes trials themselves, evidence clearly suggested a carefully planned, cold-blooded Serb campaign to devastate the Bosnian Muslims, to effectively destroy their new nation and their culture, and to create what the Serbs called a "Greater Serbia." By 1993, the combination of government documentation,[52] UN reports, independent reports, and documented news accounts of the brutality of ethnic cleansing, with accompanying photographs and television tapes, was enough to call for some form of war crimes tribunal.

The 1995 Dayton agreement called on the warring parties to cooperate with the ICTY, which had begun its work a year earlier. All indicted war criminals were prohibited from holding elected office, and the IFOR was called on to arrest all indicted war criminals it encountered and to turn them over to the ICTY in the Hague.

Both the Bosnian Serb and Croat leaders at Dayton and the ICTY prosecutor, Judge Richard J. Goldstone, a South African, called for Milosevic's surrender of Radovan Karadzic, the Bosnian Serb political leader, and General Ratko Mladic, the military leader. Both were seen in Pale, the capital of the Republika Srpska, during the Dayton negotiations (and still remain at large, even though they were twice indicted for genocide and crimes against humanity for their roles in the ethnic cleansing of Srebrenica and other Bosnian Muslim cities and towns). Milosevic refused to turn the two men over to the ICTY, saying that "while he would like the two men out of the political picture, they should be allowed to leave office eventually through the electoral process."[53]

Goldstone, speaking privately to U.S. State Department officials and publicly to the press, argued that there could not be peace in the Balkans without justice, that is, without a successful prosecution of the indicted major war criminals, especially men like Mladic and Karadzic. He insisted, unsuccessfully, that the peace treaty call for their surrender. If they were not turned over to the ICTY, he said, "there will not be any peace. Any agreement will break down."

> There are just too many victims who can't be ignored. If you sweep it under the rug, you'll have a cancer in your society. If individuals are not brought to justice, then there is collective guilt. The victims and their survivors cry out for justice against a group.[54]

The ICTY deputy prosecutor, Graham Blewitt, echoed his boss: "It is necessary for any long-term peace that justice be administered."[55]

By the spring of 1998, according to reports from BiH, the "flamboyant wartime leader of the Bosnian Serbs, psychiatrist and amateur poet" Radovan Karadzic, often in disguise, was on the run in Republika Srpska, "hotly pursued by NATO [forces]."[56]

> [He] is moving daily from one location to the next, often just hours ahead of units intent on bringing him to trial at the [ICTY] at the Hague. . . . [He] frequently finds shelter in the monasteries, churches, and other properties of the Bosnian Serb Orthodox Church, [which] has set up . . . a very sophisticated system of electronic surveillance to monitor NATO communications.[57]

The probability is that Karadzic will eventually be brought to the ICTY to face charges of war crimes, crimes against humanity, and genocide. His comrade in arms, General Mladic, also under indictment by the ICTY, fled to Serbia. As a former officer in the Yugoslavian army before 1991, Mladic "has retired . . . with his Army pension, to Belgrade, in neighboring Yugoslavia, and is believed to be writing his memoirs for a Greek publishing house. NATO commanders concede that for the moment, General Mladic is beyond reach."[58]

The International Criminal Tribunal for the Former Yugoslavia

The events that led to the creation of the UN tribunal[59] in 1993 were very different from the events following World War II. In 1945, the world saw nations that had unconditionally defeated other nations conduct trials to prosecute and punish the vanquished. In 1993, there was no clear end to the war in Yugoslavia, nor were there unconditional victors and vanquished: "Nobody in the Balkans has been defeated."[60] However, in 1993 there was the daily diet of death and disfigurement shown in living color on CNN and other networks, and these images led to demands by people around the globe to do something to stop the violence and punish those responsible for the torture and the killings.

There also existed international authority—the Nuremberg Principles, the Genocide Convention, the 1949 Geneva Protocols, for example—to prosecute alleged war criminals, whereas in 1945, there were no such international conventions to legitimize the war crimes trials of the leaders of the vanquished nations. Also, the German and Japanese defendants were captured and in the dock; in 1996, many of the seventy-five indicted war criminals, mostly Serbians, were still in power (Karazdic and Mladic) or lounging in cafés in Belgrade or Pale.[61] The president of Serbia, Slobodan Milosevic, who "delivered the war in Bosnia through his sponsorship of the Bosnian Serbs,"[62] has not yet been indicted by the war crimes tribunal, although the other trials may produce enough hard evidence of his involvement to transform his "elliptical style" of command leadership into concrete actions that warrant indictment.[63]

In the summer of 1992, with the war against the Bosnian Muslims and ethnic cleansing by the Bosnian Serbs going full blast across 70 percent of BiH, the BiH government asked the UN to intervene. The country's ambassador to the UN, Muhammed Sacirbey, attached to the request a list of ninety-four prisons and concentration camps in BiH and eleven in Serbia and Montenegro run by the Bosnian Serbs. He accused them of holding captured Muslims and treating them in violation of the principles of international law.[64]

A preliminary report was prepared by the UN's Commission of Experts and presented to the Security Council at the end of August 1992. The commission had carefully examined and analyzed the data submitted and concluded that Bosnia was the "scene of massive and systematic violations of human rights, as well as serious grave violations of humanitarian law" and that harassment of Muslims, including torture and violence, was "commonplace" by the occupying power, the Bosnian Serbs.[65]

After repeated, unsuccessful attempts to halt the violence and warfare, the UN Security Council, in May 1993, adopted the Statute of the International Tribunal in order to prosecute individuals responsible for serious violations of international humanitarian law, specifically, violations of the Nuremberg Principles and the Geneva Accords adopted by the UN in 1949.[66] The Security Council established the ICTY because it was "convinced that the establishment . . . of an international tribunal and the prosecution of persons responsible for serious violations of international humanitarian law . . . would contribute to the restoration and maintenance of peace."[67] Although the UN and the Western allies (the members of NATO) were unwilling to use force to stop the bloodshed, creating a criminal tribunal was a different matter.

Holbrooke wrote that in 1993 the ICTY was "widely viewed as little more than a public relations device, . . . no mechanism existed for the arrest of indicted war criminals."[68] The UN and the major world actors took the politically convenient road in the Yugoslavian crisis: ignore the genocide. Although there was a formal opening ceremony in the Hague in November 1993, the ICTY immediately adjourned, for there were no judges, no chief prosecutor, and no prosecutorial staff. Rules of procedure had to be created by the tribunal's staff. No indictments could be issued until the personnel and the procedures had been appointed and developed. But Nuremberg and Tokyo had given the world a set of protocols and conventions for prosecutors to draw on. With the appointment of "a forceful and eloquent jurist, Richard Goldstone of South Africa, as its chief [prosecutor, and with the support of] Madeleine Albright, John Shattuck, . . . the Dutch hosts and the Germans, [the ICTY] emerged as a valuable instrument."[69]

As structured by the UN, the ICTY has three parts: the Chambers (about 435 persons), the Prosecutor's Office (about 211 persons), and the Registry (about 200 persons). People of fifty-six nationalities work at the ICTY. The Chambers are the eleven judges elected by the UN's General Assembly from a list submitted by the Security Council and hundreds of staff members. There are three judges from Asia, two from Europe, two from Africa, two from North America, and one each from Latin America and Australia. The president, or chief judge, of the tribunal is Judge Antonio Cassese of Italy. Two of the eleven judges are women, including former U.S. District Court (Texas) judge Gabrielle Kirk McDonald, an African American. There are two trial "panels," or courts, consisting of three-judge panels. The remaining five judges, including Cassese as head, serve as the appellate tribunal. There is no jury, and it takes a two-thirds vote to convict. The standard of proof in the ICTY trials is "guilt beyond a reasonable doubt."

The Prosecutor's Office was initially headed by the chief prosecutor, Richard Goldstone of South Africa. Goldstone was authorized by the ICTY's rules of procedure and evidence to conduct investigations and file indictments. He began serving in August 1994 and returned to South Africa's Constitutional Court in October 1996. He was replaced by Judge Louise Arbour from the Ontario, Canada, Court of Appeals.

The Prosecutor's Office, in 1997, had a staff of about 211 persons, including some 60 war crimes investigators on loan from national governments (twenty-two of these from the United States).[70] These investigators were divided into nine teams, including a team that has been focusing on the command and control activities of the leaders of the three nations involved in the warfare. Since 1994, these teams "have been working furiously to put together cases and indictments."[71] Their task, including travel to the former Yugoslavia "to depose witnesses and victims," is to assemble proof of the crimes committed by the suspects. "This included depositions, reports by military observers, press reports, photographs, maps, charts, autopsy reports, etc. Each team has a data analyst to organize and ensure the chain of custody of evidence."[72] Each investigating team also has a legal adviser working with one of the three senior prosecuting trial attorneys to determine which articles a suspect's alleged actions fall under.

The administrative and clerical responsibilities for the ICTY are handled by the 200 personnel in the tribunal's Registry, including about 40 translators and interpreters. It is the ICTY's repository for all filings and documents and will hold all evidence uncovered by the tribunal during the course of the trials of the seventy-five persons indicted.

The ICTY's rules of procedure and evidence were hashed out in two lengthy sessions in February 1994 and entered into force on March 14, 1994, with additional amendments approved in January 1996. They are a combination of common-law and civil-law systems, although they tilt toward the common-law, adversarial mode because so many of the judges come from that system.[73] There are over 300 personnel from thirty-seven nations involved in the operations of the ICTY.

The jurisdiction of the ICTY is limited to trying cases involving alleged war crimes in the former Yugoslavia.[74] The ICTY is empowered to hear cases involving (1) grave breaches of the (four) Geneva Conventions of 1949 (and the 1977 protocols), (2) violations of the laws and customs of war (the Nuremberg Charter) , (3) genocide (the 1948 Genocide Convention), and (4) crimes against humanity (the Nuremberg Charter).

The ICTY is not a permanent tribunal and is limited to addressing war crimes that were alleged to have taken place after 1991. It will cease to function when the trials and appeals of all those indicted have run their course and the guilty men have been incarcerated. Given the large number of persons indicted and the slow pace of the trials, the ICTY may well continue into the twenty-first century. It also has concurrent jurisdiction with nation-states, although there is the implicit understanding that the ICTY has preemption rights if there is a dispute. (The first trial, which began in May 1996 and ended in November 1997, came about because the ICTY asked Germany to defer jurisdiction so that the defendant, Dusko Tadic, could be tried in the ICTY.)

Unlike Nuremberg, there cannot be trials in absentia, and there is no death sentence. The maximum penalty is life imprisonment, with the convicted defendant sentenced to serve his term in a prison in one of eleven nations.[75] Once a convicted prisoner is transported to a national prison, the ICTY no longer has jurisdiction over that person. Conceivably, once a person arrives in one of these nations to serve his prison term, he could be pardoned immediately by the chief executive of that nation.

The ICTY's Trials and Tribulations

At one level, applying the Nuremberg Principles' three categories of crime (war crimes, crimes against the peace, and crimes against humanity) and the crime of genocide seems to be possible, although there is the need for proof of systematic planning by high government officials of the atrocities committed in Bosnia. However, there was a "political hurdle" at the peace discussions held in the United States in the fall of 1995 that may be impossible to overcome in the effort to dispense justice. Even though the Dayton Peace Agreement stipulated that all parties would support the actions of the ICTY, the chief engineer of the Serb atrocities, Slobodan Milosevic, was participating as a head of state.

Is "peace more precious than justice"?[76] This question has haunted and followed the ICTY since its creation in 1993. The Nuremberg and Tokyo trials "established the idea that peace without justice is an incomplete peace," said Yale University professor of international law, Harold Koh.[77] The presence of realpolitik surrounding and subsequent to the Dayton Peace Agreement suggests that peace must be made with leaders like Milosevic, who can deliver peace, even though the leader himself may be tainted with evil. There are many, including Richard Goldstone, who forcefully maintain that there can be no real peace without a commitment to do justice: no justice, no peace.[78] And no justice can come about without individual accountability for war crimes and crimes against humanity committed in BiH.

Are some of the cruel horrors of the Bosnian war simply beyond an amnesty that might eventually come about as a means of achieving long-lasting peace in Bosnia? "The burial grounds seem to be everywhere in Serbian-held parts of Bosnia. . . . Skulls and femurs turn up in the soggy earth;

empty warehouses bear witness to terrible doings. . . . [Estimates suggest] that there are some 200 to 300 mass graves scattered in Bosnia."[79] Must those who suffered grievously in Bosnia see justice deferred in order to bring peace to the region? This is the unanswered question that the ICTY implicitly addresses.

Indictments

The ICTY's first indictment was issued November 11, 1994. By the summer of 1999, the Prosecutor's Office had brought nineteen public indictments, involving a total of eighty-four individuals, including Karadzic and Mladic.[80] Most of those indicted are Bosnian Serbs, although eighteen are Bosnian Croats, and a smaller number are Bosnian Muslims. Twenty-seven defendants were in custody at the Hague as of the summer of 1998.

Three of the Bosnian Serbs indicted and held by the ICTY, Slavko Dokmanovic, General Djordje Djukic, and Milan Kovacevic, died prior to or during their trials. Dokmanovic committed suicide in his prison cell by hanging himself using two neckties, and Djukic died of cancer. Kovacevic's trial began in July 1998, and his death on August 1, 1998, led to controversy. His lawyer argued that he had bled to death in his cell because he did not get the proper medical treatment in the tribunal prison (a Dutch jail run by the UN at Scheveningen, a suburb of the Hague). The ICTY claimed that he had died of a heart attack.[81]

Kovacevic was a medical doctor, an anesthesiologist, and the director of the Prijedor Clinic before the wars.[82] He was a key Bosnian Serb leader who organized and ran three notorious prison camps—Omarska, Keraterm, and Trnopolje[83]—where thousands of Muslims were starved, tortured, and executed. He was arrested in his medical clinic by British troops in 1997 and was immediately flown to the Hague for trial. This action was significant, for it signaled a change in UN and NATO actions regarding indictees who were still in Bosnia. Prior to his arrest, NATO forces had done nothing to apprehend these wanted fugitives.

Kovacevic's trial was important because he was the first defendant in history to be charged with genocide in an international court, and the ICTY judges would have the opportunity to define the scope of the crime in an actual case. His death means that this groundbreaking legal examination will have to await other defendants charged with that crime; there are three others in custody and a number of men charged with genocide who are still at large, including Karadzic and Mladic.

The ICTY's twenty-one public indictments fell into seven broad categories:

1. Alleged offenses involving the massacre of 261 non-Serb patients forcibly removed from the Vukovar Hospital, after destruction of the Croatian city of Vukovar by JNA forces in November 1991.
2. Alleged offenses relating to the occupation of towns and villages in BiH in 1992 by Bosnian Serb forces and associated killings, rapes, and other inhumane actions, including the use of concentration camps at Omarska and Keraterm.
3. Alleged offenses committed in a concentration camp, Celebici, by Bosnian Serbs in 1992.
4. Alleged offenses committed during the 1993 war between Bosnian Croats and Muslims in which the Croats "ethnically cleansed" Muslims from parts of BiH, most notably the Lasva River Valley area and the village of Stupni Do.
5. Alleged offenses in the Serbian Krajina region of Croatia by Croatian Serbs—namely, the firing of rockets into the center of Zagreb in May 1995.
6. Alleged offenses ordered by Bosnian Serb leaders Karadzic and Mladic during the siege of Sarajevo (1994–1995).
7. Alleged offenses involving the fall of Srebrenica to Bosnian Serbs in July 1995, including genocide charges against the Bosnian Serb leaders Karadzic and Mladic.[84]

The First ICTY Trial

The trial of Dusko Tadic began on May 7, 1996,[85] a little more than two years after he was arrested in Munich, Germany, and three years after the Security Council created the ICTY. Pronouncement of judgment came exactly one year later, on May 7, 1997. (It took a long time to create the protocols and find the personnel to operate the machinery of justice at the Hague.) There were 115 witnesses, and the trial transcript was more than 6,000 pages long. Because Germany was a signatory to the post-Nuremberg international conventions, Tadic was indicted in Germany on charges of murder and torture for his actions in Bosnia. In accordance with the rules of the ICTY, however, prosecutors at a deferral hearing at the Hague asked Germany to allow the ICTY to try Tadic. In April 1994, Tadic was transferred to an ICTY detention facility in the Hague. A year later, in April 1995, Tadic pled not guilty to the charges against him. In July 1995, Tadic's lawyers presented a motion arguing that the ICTY lacked authority to prosecute Tadic. One month later, the ICTY rejected the argument. A trial date was set for November 1995, but the defense requested a delay, and it was reset for May 1996.

Dusko Tadic, a Serb café owner, was born in Bosnia in 1955; he was married with children. Tadic was formally charged by the ICTY prosecutors with 132 separate counts involving crimes against humanity, violations of the laws and customs of war, and grave breaches of the 1949 Geneva Conventions. Many of the alleged crimes were committed at the notorious Bosnian Serb–controlled Omarska prison camp in Prijedor province, in northwestern Bosnia. From all accounts, Omarska was the most brutal of the four major camps in that region. Using an open iron ore mine as the prison facility, the Bosnian Serbs committed unimaginable acts against their Bosnian Muslim and Croat prisoners—military personnel as well as high-placed local civilians who were caught fleeing their towns. These acts included beatings that led to death and sexual mutilations, such as the biting off of prisoners' testicles on Tadic's orders. He was also charged with pulling more than thirty prisoners out of a line marching to Omarska and pulling Muslims out of their homes in Sivci and Jaskici, beating them, and then having them executed.

The three-judge panel that heard the case included Gabrielle Kirk McDonald, who served as the presiding judge in the trial. She had been in private practice and was about to take a teaching position at the Thurgood Marshall School of Law at Texas Southern University when she was asked to be an ICTY judge. The other two judges were Datuk Lal Vohrah of Malaysia and Sir Ninian Stephen of Australia.

The ICTY's chief prosecutor in the Tadic trial was Grant Niemann of Australia, assisted by three Americans: Alan Tieger (on loan from and paid by the Justice Department's Civil Rights Division), Lieutenant Colonel Brenda Hollis (on loan from and paid by the U.S. Air Force Judge Advocate General [JAG]), and Major Michael Keegan (on loan from and paid by the U.S. Marine Corps JAG office). Tadic had three defense counsel appointed and paid by the ICTY: lead defense counsel Michail Wladimiroff of the Netherlands, assisted by Alphons Orie of the Netherlands and Steven Kay of the United Kingdom.

The strategic goal of the prosecutors was to show that Tadic's violent and inhumane actions were but a part of the larger plan, developed in Belgrade, to create, at the expense of a viable Muslim Bosnia, a Greater Serbia. As the ICTY prosecutors wrote in their application for deferral, the legal action presented to the German courts to bring Tadic under the jurisdiction of the ICTY:

> The case of Dusko Tadic is important to the prosecution of those persons responsible for committing the serious violations of international humanitarian law which occurred in the territory of the former Republic of Yugoslavia since January 1, 1991. . . . *The criminal acts allegedly committed by Dusko Tadic would provide a clear illustration of a plan for the widespread and systematic destructive persecution against the civilian population of the Prijedor region (commonly referred to as "ethnic cleansing").*[86]

Tadic was found guilty of eleven counts of crimes against humanity and violations of the laws and customs of war (persecution of non-Serbs and beatings of concentration camp inmates) and was sentenced to twenty years' imprisonment. The tribunal found, unanimously, that Tadic "was a willing executioner of the policy of persecution on religious, racial, and political grounds. . . . [Muslims were subjected to] a policy to terrorize [them], its implementation was widespread and systematic; [there was] horrendous treatment on the basis of religion and politics," concluded the court

> The accused's role in, inter alia, the attack on Kozarac and the surrounding areas, as well as the seizure, collection, segregation and forced transfer of civilians to camps, calling-out of civilians, beatings and killings of two Muslim policemen by cutting their throats, clearly constituted an infringement of the victims' enjoyment of their fundamental rights and these acts were taken against non-Serbs on the basis of religious and political discrimination.

Seven additional trials were begun in 1997–1998, and the ICTY was planning another eleven trials in 1998–1999.

Civil Suits against Karadzic in U.S. District Court

"The Courts of the United States provide a potential forum for claims of human rights violations in the Bosnian conflict. The United States 'has long recognized that an individual can both sue and be sued in federal courts for conduct in violation of international law.'"[87] Such a legal action against Radovan Karadzic may have an effect on his arrest and detention in the

Hague. Under a U.S. law promulgated in 1789 but rediscovered during the Carter administration by Drew Days III, the associate attorney general, Civil Rights Division, an alien can sue another person for injuries received anywhere in the world as a result of actions of the defendant in violation of international law. The 1789 Alien Tort Act states: "The [U.S.] district courts shall have original jurisdiction of any civil action by an alien for a tort only, committed in violation of the law of nations or a treaty of the United States."[88]

In the fall of 1993, Karadzic was in New York City to attend the UN General Session. While there, he was served with legal notice that he was being sued in U.S. district court for alleged human rights abuses. Once he was served, even though Karadzic left the United States, the federal court retained jurisdiction.

Early in 1994, two groups of Bosnian war victims went into federal district court in New York to bring Karadzic to trial on charges of genocide and atrocities committed by the Bosnian Serbs during the Bosnian war.[89] They grounded their lawsuits on the 1789 Alien Tort Act and the 1991 Torture Victim Protection Act.[90] They argued that Bosnian Serbs under Karadzic's command had committed a variety of atrocities, and they

> asserted causes of action for genocide, rape, forced prostitution and impregnation, torture and other cruel, inhuman, and degrading treatment, assault and battery, sex and ethnic inequality, summary execution, and wrongful death. They sought compensatory and punitive damages, attorney's fees, and, in one of the cases, injunctive relief.[91]

In the first suit, *S. K. v. Karadzic,* a class of plaintiffs sought to have the federal court award monetary damages and issue an injunction to stop the war crimes. It was brought by a woman, S. K., "who had one of her infant twin sons beheaded in her arms by one of Karadzic's soldiers and was subsequently gang-raped in an internment camp."[92] The second civil suit, *Doe v. Karadzic,* sought compensatory and punitive damages, along with lawyer's fees.

U.S. District Court Judge Peter K. Leisure dismissed both lawsuits on the grounds that the federal courts lacked subject matter jurisdiction.[93] On appeal to the U.S. Court of Appeals (Second Circuit), a three-judge panel unanimously reversed the trial court judgment dismissing the suits and remanded the cases back to the district court for trial on the merits. In the opinion, written by Chief Judge Jon O. Newman and announced in October 1995, the appeals court panel affirmed the plaintiffs' contentions "that foreign victims of torts that violate international law can sue their foreign oppressors in U.S. federal courts."[94]

The appellate panel examined the nature of the alleged violations and concluded that such allegations were "actionable" under the 1789 statute. Further, the panel noted that Karadzic was "a state actor" and was issuing commands in that capacity rather than as a private citizen. But even if he were acting as a private person, Karadzic would be subject to the court's jurisdiction. The appellate court noted that "the liability of private individuals for committing war crimes has been recognized since World War I and was confirmed at Nuremberg, after World War II."

The "nonjusticiability" argument put forward by Karadzic's attorney, Ramsey Clark, said that the suits addressed "acts of state" and "political questions," that is, foreign policy matters that were properly dealt with by the political agencies of government and were therefore outside the jurisdiction of federal courts. That argument was rejected by Judge Newman. Citing *Baker v. Carr*,[95] the appellate panel said that "not every case 'touching foreign relations' is non-justiciable."[96]

Karadzic appealed to the U.S. Supreme Court, but in mid-June 1996, the justices denied certiorari in the case.[97] The civil suit was then returned to the federal district court for further action. In early December 1997, the federal judge certified the case as a class action suit, which meant that if the plaintiffs won the suit against Karadzic, *all* other Bosnian Croat and Muslim survivors victimized by Karadzic's actions would be entitled to damages.

On December 16, 1997, Karadzic failed to answer the plaintiffs' complaint against him, which meant that he defaulted on the question of whether he was liable for the crimes he was accused of. Once a federal judge formally enters a default, hearings are held to assess civil, financial damages against the defendant. Clark indicated that Karadzic could not appear in his own defense because he would be arrested and flown to the Hague to stand trial for war crimes, crimes against humanity, and genocide. As of December 1998, the hearings to determine and assess civil damages against Karadzic had yet to take place.

The War in Kosovo Province: 1998

Kosovo province, a part of Serbia, is hallowed, religious-mythic ground for Serbs. In 1389, Prince Lazar led the Serbs into war against the infidels, the Turkish armies. The Serbs were defeated by the Turks, and Lazar, who was killed during the battle, became a Jesus-like icon. The loss led to the Ottoman

Empire's rule over the Serbs for five centuries. Serb nationalists from that time through the present argue that "Lazar's death represents the death of the Serb nation, which will not be resurrected until Lazar is raised from the dead and the descendents of Lazar's killers [Muslims] are purged from the Serbian people."[98]

Ten years after Slobodan Milosevic came to power in Yugoslavia, he was faced with rebellion in Kosovo. Milosevic believed that Kosovo province had to remain Serb. The province was, as he said again and again in the 1980s, "the cradle of the Serbs; its historical existence." In 1986, Milosevic accused the ethnic Albanians in Kosovo of being "neo-Fascists" who were conducting a reign of terror against the minority Serbs who lived in Kosovo. He cracked down hard on the ethnic Albanians. By March 1989, he "got the Serbian parliament to abolish Kosovo's political autonomy. He then removed its mainly Albanian leadership and replaced it with Serbs or 'honest' (read quisling) Albanians."[99] The province was not involved in the wars fought between 1991 and 1995. Local leaders were gravely concerned about the loss of autonomy, but they deferred raising the issue while Serbia and its surrogates were engaged in warfare against Croats and Muslims.

In 1998, a small band of ethnic Albanian Muslims, who constituted over 90 percent of the population of the once autonomous province, demanded the restoration of the rights they once had, angering Milosovic. Commencing in February 1998, Milosevic's JNA forces, including more than 10,000 troops and hundreds of jet fighters, tanks, and artillery pieces and another 10,000 "special police" and paramilitary units used for "ethnic cleansing," engaged about 2,000 ethnic Albanian forces (called the Kosovo Liberation Army) in Kosovo province after ethnic Albanian guerrillas attacked the Serb "occupiers."[100]

Hundreds of Muslims were killed in the initial JNA-Serb military response. These actions gravely concerned the Western powers, including the United States. As Holbrooke noted, American diplomats had "always viewed Kosovo as the most explosive tinderbox in the region. . . . An eruption in Kosovo . . . could trigger a wider war, involving Albania and Macedonia and perhaps even Greece."[101] In March 1998, the Western powers, led by the United States, imposed modest sanctions—diplomatic and economic—on Yugoslavia because of President Milosevic's "unacceptable use of force" against the ethnic Albanian majority in Kosovo.

Milosevic, unpersuaded, began a major campaign in June 1998 to wipe out the Kosovo Liberation Army rebels. JNA actions forced hundreds of thousands of ethnic Albanian Muslims to flee their towns, which were destroyed by bombings and shelling. Within two months, hundreds were killed, 10,000 refugees fled into Albania, and 80,000 ethnic Albanians became displaced persons.[102] (By August 1998, barely half a year after the fighting began, there were over 300,000 ethnic Albanian refugees, one-tenth of the population of Kosovo province.) To prevent flight into Albania, as well as to prevent the rebels from moving easily and safely back and forth across the border for arms and other supplies, in June 1998, Milosevic ordered the Yugoslav forces to use land mines to seal the Kosovo-Albania border, a stretch of seventy-five miles.

In April 1998, the United States sought to freeze Yugoslav assets held overseas and to institute a stiffer ban on trade with the Belgrade government, and it supported a British resolution in the UN authorizing NATO air strikes in Kosovo against Milosevic's military forces. In July 1998, Milosevic unleashed another series of heavy attacks against the Albanian separatists. Ominously, reporters witnessed, as in the earlier Bosnian wars, the horror of paramilitary units following the troops into small towns to kill ethnic Albanian civilian leaders.[103]

During the summer of 1998, JNA forces began firing on international aid workers bringing supplies to the refugees. In late August 1998, JNA artillery fire killed three Mother Teresa Relief Aid workers, all ethnic Albanians, who were riding on tractors pulling wagons loaded with food and clothing for refugees. The Serb attack was a deliberate one, occurring in an open field in the middle of the afternoon of a bright day.[104]

Incidents of terror, destruction, and ethnic cleansing regularly appeared in the media, including a small massacre featured on the first page of the *New York Times*. In a story entitled "New Massacres by Serb Forces in Kosovo Villages," Jane Perlez described in gruesome detail how fifteen women, children, and elderly members of the Deliaj family met their deaths outside their village of Gornji Obinje. The family's patriarch, Fazli Deliaj, ninety-five years old, was burned to death in his home by the Serb soldiers.[105]

These reports of atrocities, summary executions, kidnappings, and murders committed by the Serb police led the UN to plan contingency action. In late August 1998, the ICTY, noting its jurisdiction over conflicts in *all* of Yugoslavia, assembled UN investigators, including lawyers and military analysts, for fact-finding work in Kosovo. Over three dozen investigators have gone and will go to Kosovo to collect information, said the ICTY's deputy prosecutor, Graham Blewitt,

[to] examine accounts that numerous civilians, most of them ethnic Albanians, have been kidnapped and killed in circumstances that cannot

be defined as military combat, [and to] . . . assembl[e] cases and [draw] up plans for indictments [focusing on people of authority], the people who made things happen or who could prevent them from happening."[106]

However, Milosevic has remained undaunted in his efforts to destroy the moderates who demanded a return to the province's autonomous status, which had been taken away in 1989.

By late fall 1998, the situation in Kosovo had grown grim. Milosevic barred UN war crimes investigators, including Louise Arbour, the ICTY chief prosecutor, from looking into allegations of war crimes committed by Serb forces in Kosovo. As Milosevic stated in a communiqué to the ICTY, "the tribunal has no jurisdiction to conduct investigations in Kosovo and will no longer be allowed to do so."[107]

Nuremberg and the ICTY

The ICTY activities, especially after the tentative December 1995 closure of the Bosnian wars, did not lead to the outcry that arose after the Nuremberg and Tokyo war crimes trials: "victors' justice." Mostly Serbs, but also a scattering of Croats and Muslims, have been indicted by the ICTY since 1994. Nor have there been the legal justification complaints about the ex post facto nature of the Bosnian war crimes trials, for the international legal precedents and UN protocols and conventions that were created and signed in the years after Nuremberg formed the basis for the prosecution's indictments.

However, there are a number of problems confronting the ICTY that were not present after World War II. There are no written documentation trails, personal diaries, memos, or letters left behind by the Serbs in Bosnia, unlike post–World War II Germany with its mountains of written documents and film footage of atrocities taken and preserved by the Nazis, making the case against them quite easy. "There's no question that this is no Nuremberg," said an ICTY prosecuting attorney about the lack of documentary evidence.[108] Instead of documents, the ICTY prosecutors must rely on the testimony of witnesses at trial or by deposition, with all the problems entailed in using that type of evidence.

The pathological evidence is disappearing, and the ICTY investigators have had difficulty examining suspected grave sites and collecting the pathological evidence. As Cherif Bassiouni stated to a reporter, " 'You've got 174 bodies (in a mass grave near Vukovar, Croatia) in a country, torn by war, where you can't even get a plastic bag. What are you going to wrap the bodies in? Where will they be taken? How will you get them there? Who will perform tests?'"[109]

The ICTY prosecutors need the cooperation of Serbs and Croats, as well as an aggressive IFOR-NATO policy and practice of arresting those men charged with crimes who are still at large and sending them to the Hague. This is a particular problem with the Bosnian Serb paramilitary leaders at large in Republika Srpska.[110] At most, those who protect the indicted men "merely face Security Council sanctions; their leaders risk nothing worse than isolation."[111]

The ICTY prosecutors, in order to go beyond individual felonious charges, must show the planned nature of the crimes, that is, that the crimes of the paramilitary units were a strategic part of the creation of the Greater Serbia that Milosevic called for as early as 1986. There is also the continuing problem of realpolitik: Is there a "moral obligation for a civilized society to respect and enforce the laws it creates in the name of basic human rights and decency? Or should those who commit atrocities during war be allowed to extort amnesty in exchange for peace?"[112]

Under the ICTY's rules and procedures, there cannot be any trials in absentia; given the large number of indicted men who remain free, this can be a damaging blow to the ICTY. The hope expressed by the ICTY prosecutors was that the Tadic trial would be the first of many trials that would take the ICTY up the chain of "command responsibility" leading to Karadzic, Mladic, and Milosevic. Grant Niemann, the ICTY chief prosecutor in the Tadic case, said, "It'd be nice to have them lined up [after Tadic]."[113] Also, as William Horne suggests,

> The Tadic trial, beamed throughout the world by satellite, could send a message to the Serbs, Croats, and Bosnians—and for that matter, citizens of every country—that war crimes will not be tolerated, that whether it is next week or ten years from now, those who step over the bounds of acceptable behavior may end up being held accountable for their actions.[114]

The ICTY's actions in the Hague in the 1990s, legal actions that will continue into the next millennium, underscore a basic truism: "Despite a dim record in Bosnia, there is such a thing as an international community and even a civilized conscience [that] act[s] against atrocities that defy comprehension."[115] Although the major figures involved in the Bosnian tragedy, "Bosnian Serb thug-in-chief"[116] Radovan Karadzic and his general, Ratko Mladic, were still free in the spring of 1999, the probability grows that they will soon be facing trial at the Hague. But they are in hiding, fearful of capture or death at the hands of Croat or Muslim Bosnians or UN or NATO forces.[117] Clearly, in 1998, the "hunt" was on for these two Bosnian Serb leaders.[118] As Thomas Friedman wrote, "It's the right thing to do, and once [they're] gone maybe we can focus on our real choices [in Bosnia]."[119] Everyone knows that there must be closure regarding these two Republika Srpska leaders, for as Peter Galbraith, former ambassador to Croatia, said, "Justice isn't served unless they're dead or in the dock."[120]

While the Bosnian wars and the ICTY were winding down and flaring up in Kosovo, in Africa there was the continuation of bloody tribal warfare between the Tutsi and the Hutu in Rwanda. Eighteen months after the creation of the ICTY, the UN Security Council created the International Criminal Tribunal, Rwanda, to examine the horrors of primitive warfare in the jungles of Rwanda, where genocide took place with hoe, pickax, and machete. The news out of Rwanda shocked the world even more than that from Yugoslavia. In the four years of fighting in the former Yugoslavia, between 30,000 and 40,000 Muslims and Croats were massacred by the Serbs. In little more than *three months,* over 800,000 Rwandan civilians (Tutsi and moderate Hutu) were slaughtered.

6

MACHETE GENOCIDE IN RWANDA AND
THE INTERNATIONAL CRIMINAL TRIBUNAL

On March 24, 1998, U.S. president Bill Clinton arrived in Kigali, Rwanda's capital. When the Rwandan genocide began four years earlier, the Clinton administration's policy "was that the U.N. should get out of Rwanda completely, and the original force of 2,500 men was reduced to an ineffectual squad of 270. . . . [after receipt of urgent requests from the UN's military commander in Rwanda for additional military forces], the U.S. successfully obstructed the Security Council from heeding [the commander's] call."[1]

At the airport in 1998, Clinton spoke of the Rwandan genocide. It was "a systematic destruction of a people, . . . the most intensive slaughter in this blood-filled century we are about to leave." The Hutu killers, using machetes and clubs, for the most part, "did their work five times as fast as the mechanized chambers used by the Nazis." Then Clinton apologized for the failure of the West to respond to the genocide.

> The international community, together with nations in Africa, must bear its share of responsibility for this tragedy. . . . We did not act quickly enough after the killing began. We should not have allowed the refugee camps [in Zaire] to become safe haven for the killers. We did not immediately call these crimes by their rightful name: genocide. . . . All over the world there were people like me sitting in offices, day after day after day, who did not fully appreciate the depth and the speed with which you were being engulfed by this unimaginable terror.[2]

The "unimaginable terror" was the April–June 1994 Rwandan genocide, one that saw "Rwanda . . . largely destroyed."[3] Its consequences doubly astounded the world: the staggering numbers of children, men, and women executed by the special killing units, and the brutal, mind-numbing manner in which over 800,000 persons were killed by the *interahamwe* and their extremist militia colleagues the *impuzamugami*, the Rwandan government forces (RGF), and Hutu extremist peasants acting on orders from the Hutu regime in Kigali. During the 100 days of genocide, "an average of more than five Tutsi were murdered every minute in Rwanda."[4] In this bloodbath, the Tutsi population in Rwanda was reduced by over 50 percent.[5]

In Rwanda, as was the case in Nazi Germany, Japan, Cambodia, and the former Yugoslavia, "the enemy was demonized, made the incarnation of evil, and dealt with accordingly. . . . The killings were planned and orchestrated from above and owed little or nothing to a supposedly spontaneous outburst of anger from below." Continuing, Rene Lemarchand wrote that "as much as the appalling scale of the bloodletting, it is the element of planned annihilation that gives the Rwanda killings their genocidal quality."[6] For years prior to the formal start of the Rwandan genocide in 1994, there was careful organizational development for the eventual genocide by the leaders of the Hutu one-party dictatorship, known simply as "Hutu Power."[7]

Rwanda's Demographics

Called the "land of one thousand hills," Rwanda is a very rural land-locked sub-Saharan country about the size of Vermont, or approximately 26,000 square kilometers."[8] In 1991, there were more than 8 million Rwandan civilians, 95 percent of them living in rural areas.[9] Given Rwanda's small size, its population density was the highest in Africa. Rwanda is also considered the most Christianized of the African nations.[10] There are no railroads in Rwanda, and only eight airstrips (three of them paved). Rwanda is divided into eleven provinces or prefectures, each governed by a prefect. These eleven provinces are further broken down into communes, or towns, that are under the authority of mayors, called *bourgmestres*, who are appointed by the president of Rwanda and are loyal to the government in Kigali.

The ethnic makeup of Rwanda was estimated in 1994 to be about 85 percent Hutu (primarily farmers), 14 percent Tutsi (primarily cattle herders), and 1 percent Twa (Pygmy hunter-gatherers). The Hutu and the Tutsi shared the same language, Kinyarwanda; the same culture; the same clan names; and the same customs. For centuries there was intermarriage between Hutu and Tutsi, especially in southern Rwanda. Tragically, during the genocide, the children of these mixed marriages, called *Hutsi*, were treated as either Hutu or Tutsi, and if the latter, they were doomed.[11]

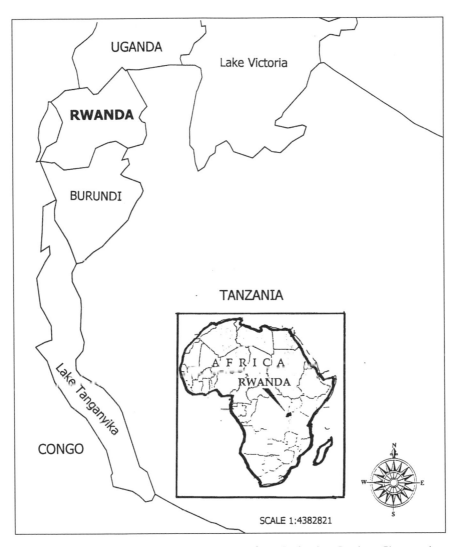

Rwanda, 1994. (UVM Geography Department: Professor Lesley Ann Dupigny-Giroux and Patrick Keane)

Inequality has been present in Rwanda for centuries, based on occupation and wealth. The Tutsi cattle herders were the traditional power holders, even though they were a minority. The Hutu peasant farmers, constituting the population majority, were at the "bottom of the heap, socially, economically, and politically."[12] The Belgian occupiers, in the interwar period, "provided the crucible within which ethnic identities were reshaped and mythologized.

The result was to drastically alter the norms and texture of traditional Rwanda society."[13]

Even though the Tutsi were and remain a minority in Rwanda, both the Germans (in 1890, Germany created German East Africa, consisting of present-day Rwanda and Burundi) and the Belgians (who governed the area after the 1919 Versailles Treaty was signed) "were quite smitten with the Tutsi" and allowed the Tutsi monarchy to continue to function.[14] Culturally and ethnically, the tall, light-skinned Tutsi, "often displaying sharp angular facial features,"[15] were seen by Europeans "as black Aryans, more noble than savage."[16]

The Hutu, who were shorter, more muscled, and darker than the Tutsi, were seen by the European occupiers as vastly inferior to the Tutsi. As the country grew under German, Belgian, League of Nations, and UN tutelage, the Tutsi were given coveted positions in the colonial government and administration, as well as in the education bureaucracy. The Belgian government, like its German predecessor, was closely aligned with the Tutsi through 1959, when it began to support the Hutu dictatorship. (France sent troops into Rwanda after Belgium pulled out its forces in 1990, and in May 1994 it was closely aligned with the RGF, which had been its ally for many years.)

By the time of the major genocide in Rwanda, the Hutu had endured centuries of racial discrimination by the German and then the Belgian colonial rulers and by the Tutsi. The Hutu were an extremely embittered majority in a colonial hierarchical framework—social, economic, and political—that had belittled them.

From Ruanda to Rwanda: 1919–1962

In 1919, the Treaty of Versailles placed German colonies in Africa under League of Nations auspices. Ruanda-Urundi (after independence, Rwanda and Burundi) was placed under Belgian jurisdiction. The areas were treated as separate colonies, and the Belgians appointed two different Tutsi monarchs. Ruanda was populated by two ethnic groups, the Tutsi and the Hutu. Both the Germans and the Belgians followed the policy of indirect rule, controlling Rwanda through the manipulation of Tutsi monarchs.

In 1933, the Belgians introduced a system of ethnic identity cards, referred to as "tribal cards," to be used for census and other administrative requirements. Ironically, this identification system was instituted just as the new Nazi dictatorship in Germany began stamping the identity cards of German Jews with a "J" (for "Juden"). The Belgian policy pushed forward the process of separating the two ethnic communities, for it "entrenched ethnicity as a major social divide."[17] It was a social division that, in both Nazi Germany and Rwanda, led to the "final solution" for Germany's Jews and Rwanda's Tutsi: extermination. (In 1994, the tribal cards provided the killing groups with a "ready made death list."[18] For Tutsi, their identity cards were quickly transmogrified into "death" cards.)

In 1957, the Hutu Party for the Emancipation of the Hutu (PARMEHUTU) was created in an effort to gain equality for the Hutu in the Tutsi-run monarchy. In 1959, the Tutsi monarch died, and Hutu extremists killed thousands of Tutsi and forced many tens of thousands to flee to surrounding countries, especially Burundi, Uganda, and Zaire. That year was the beginning of the end of Tutsi rule. In that year, the local infrastructure of the small country consisted mostly of Tutsi: 43 of 45 provincial chiefs and 549 of 559 of their subordinates in the towns were Tutsi.[19] Also in 1959, 61 percent of schoolchildren were Tutsi, although only 17 percent of the population was Tutsi.[20]

Three years later, in 1962, more than 200,000 Tutsi were in exile in Uganda, Burundi, and Zaire, and the prefects and *bourgmestres* across Rwanda were almost exclusively Hutu. (By 1990, the Tutsi population in Rwanda was less than 10 percent, but still 20 percent of the schoolchildren in Rwandan schools were Tutsi.)

A generation later, the sons of the 1959 Tutsi exiles would form the Rwandan Patriotic Front (RPF) in the (ultimately successful) effort to return to power in their Rwandan homeland. They frequently slipped across the Uganda border and killed Hutu military and civilians. The Hutu called the guerrillas *inyenzi*, cockroaches, because they came into Rwanda secretly and hid, waiting to attack the Hutu—the modus operandi of cockroaches living in Hutu huts.[21]

From Independence to the Beginning
of the Genocide: 1962–1994

In 1962, Ruanda, now called Rwanda, gained independence from Belgium. Fighting broke out between the majority Hutu and the Tutsi, resulting in Tutsi killings and flight to other nations. A Hutu one-party dictatorship was established, with the PARMEHUTU the central governing power.

Further massacres of Tutsi by Hutu occurred, beginning in 1963, in response to Tutsi-led attacks on Rwanda's armed forces, the Force Armee

Rwandese (FAR). In 1973, the Tutsi were forced out of universities and other government institutions, and the leader of Rwanda's one-party state, Juvenal Habyarimana, instituted an ethnic quota policy for public-service employment that restricted Tutsi to 9 percent of available jobs. New pogroms led to tens of thousands of Tutsi fleeing Rwanda to avoid the ethnic violence directed against them and their families. Habyarimana's party held the reins of power everywhere in Rwanda.

The enemies of the state were the Tutsi RPF and all the other Tutsi and moderate Hutu who supported the Tutsi army and opposed the Kigali dictatorship. There was intensive spying. Much like the spies in Nazi Germany and Cambodia, the Hutu spies carefully and secretly canvassed the cities and the rural areas, reporting the actions of opposition Hutu and Tutsi. "Every hill had its [party] cell, and party faithfuls, hoping for promotion and a professional boost, willingly spied on anybody they were told to spy on and on a few others as well."[22]

By the time of the 1994 genocide, there were over 4 million Tutsi refugees in neighboring states. Hutu pogroms against Tutsi led to four major movements of the Tutsi population out of Rwanda: 1959, 1963, 1966, and 1973. Over 600,000 Tutsi were killed by Hutu during this fourteen-year period. The "massive emigration" of the Tutsi from 1959 through 1994 left Zaire with 3 million Tutsi refugees, Uganda with almost 1 million, Burundi with over 120,000, and Tanzania with over 40,000.[23]

In 1986, thousands of exiled Tutsi in Uganda helped Yoweri Musaveni seize power from President Milton Obote. That year they formed the RPF, with an initial force of about 12,000 men (by 1994, there were about 23,000 RPF forces). The RPF included moderate Hutu concerned about the extremism of the ruling clique in Rwanda. Periodically the RPF crossed the border and attacked the FAR. They received financial support to buy arms and ammunition from Tutsi in the diaspora in Zaire, Belgium, and Tanzania, and especially from Tutsi living in Brussels and New York City. Young Tutsi living abroad, like the young men in the 1930s watching the civil war in Spain, joined their brothers in the jungles of Uganda as RPF military recruits.[24]

The FAR, consisting of about 20,000 men, received arms shipments from Egypt and South Africa but was a "minimally capable force, outmanned by and probably not as well trained as the RPF."[25] There were two exceptions: the FAR's Presidential Guard, an elite unit of trained military personnel whose sole task was to assist the *interahamwe* with Tutsi executions, and a secret organization of local militia, called the "Zero Network, which constituted a death squad on the Latin-American model."[26] The *interahamwe*, local militias and paramilitary organizations, were created, supplied, and trained by the FAR. They were ominously reminiscent of the Bosnian Serb "special forces" in the former Yugoslavia. These *interahamwe* ("those who stand together"), along with the *impuzamugami* ("those who have the same goal"), were, after 1990, in the forefront of the Tutsi massacres. The *interahamwe* were organized vertically, from the top down. In Kigali, there was a five-person National Executive and four national committees with their presidents. There were also presidents who controlled the *interahamwe* at the lower administrative levels: provinces, communes, and districts.[27] These paramilitary units, like their Nazi, Cambodian, and Yugoslav counterparts, were "slaughterhouse" support for the police, the local gendarmes, and the FAR. Almost 30,000 strong, they were armed with machetes, hunting rifles, modern assault rifles and grenades, and land mines. They led the local peasantry in the slaughter of Tutsi across Rwanda.

In 1990, as a result of world market downturns, Rwanda received aid from the West, in return for which Habyarimana was forced to accept the creation of a multiparty (Hutu and Tutsi) democracy in Rwanda. Strongly influenced by the French government (especially President Mitterand), which linked financial and economic aid with democratization in Rwanda, Habyarimana spoke out publicly about the importance of peace between Hutu and Tutsi and about the necessity of developing a multiparty political system in Rwanda.

That same year, the RPF invaded Rwanda from Uganda (in the north). On October 1, 1990, at 2:30 in the afternoon, a band of fifty RPF soldiers crossed the Uganda border to attack border-crossing FAR guards, killing one and forcing the other eight to flee for their lives. With that minor skirmish, "the civil war had begun."[28] With French and Zairian troops assisting, however, the RPF force was quickly repulsed and forced to flee back to Uganda's sanctuaries. However, the RPF action led to the execution of hundreds of Tutsi civilians in bloody reprisal for the abortive invasion. In November 1990, the RPF and the Rwandan government agreed to a cease-fire and monitoring of activity in that nation by Organization of African Unity (OAU) observers.

In July 1992, both the RPF and the FAR agreed to the stationing of neutral military observers between the two armies. Meanwhile, the battles and the reprisals continued, especially in northern Rwanda. By February 1993, the RPF was outside Kigali and controlled significant areas of Rwanda. It declared a unilateral cease-fire, quickly seconded by the FAR. In February 1993, both camps asked the UN to send observers into the country.

Marathon peace talks began in Arusha, Tanzania, in April 1992 and continued through August 1993. These lengthy negotiations only fed the rise of extremists in Habyarimana's party—men who feared the loss of power and funds if democratization and multipartyism were introduced in Rwanda. For them, the sole question was how to stop the peace process and, in so doing, preserve their power.[29]

Their worst fears came true when the peace treaty was signed in August 1993. It called for President Habyarimana to share power with the Tutsi minority and opposition Hutu through the establishment of a broad-based transitional government within thirty-seven days of the signing of the treaty. The transitional government was to exist for twenty-two months, at which time free elections would be held. The RPF was to be merged with the FAR, and the treaty requested the UN to send military personnel to maintain the peace in Rwanda. A protocol was signed that allowed for the repatriation of exiles, mostly Tutsi.

The Hutu extremists, who contolled the militia in the Zero Network as well as the *interahamwe*, were apoplectic when Habyarimana signed the peace accord. They immediately began to implement what they thought would end the peace process: the genocide of the Tutsi.

In June 1993, the UN Security Council passed a resolution establishing the United Nations Observer Mission Uganda-Rwanda (UNOMUR), involving observers and military stationed on the border between the two countries. In August 1993, the secretary-general of the UN requested deployment of a UN force of 2,500 men inside Rwanda to observe the implementation of the Arusha peace treaty. Formally called the United Nations Assistance Mission for Rwanda (UNAMIR), the Belgian, Bangladeshi, Ghanaian, and Zairian military personnel began arriving in Rwanda in October 1993 and were to serve until June 22, 1994.

The critical peace treaty agreements were not implemented at all. The FAR continued to train the special killing units, the *interahamwe*, for their brutal tasks, and radio stations loyal to the Hutu-led government continuously broadcast messages calling on Hutu to execute Tutsi. By the end of 1993, the hard-line Hutu leaders purged moderates from the government, executing many of them, and rejected—by their inaction—the stipulation in the peace accord that called for a broad-based transitional government. In January 1994, Habyarimana was sworn in as president of Rwanda. By this time, he was seen by the extremists as an ineffective, weak "has-been," someone who had become expendable.[30]

Although there had been pogroms targeting the Tutsi minority from the

time of Rwandan independence, the formal beginning of the machete genocide was April 6, 1994. President Habyarimana and President Cyprien
Ntaryamira of Burundi, returning from peace talks in Arusha, were killed by
disaffected Hutu extremist leaders who feared that their president was suc-
cumbing to Western pressures to form a multiparty democracy. Their plane
was shot down at 8:30 A.M. by two FAR rockets on its final landing approach
at Kigali's airport.

In less than an hour, at 9:15 A.M., the *interahamwe* killings began, initially
in Kigali. Within days, after the orders were delivered, the killings spread
throughout the country. Using the "death lists" that had been distributed
to the killing units months earlier, "organized bands of Hutu extremists
conduct[ed] house to house searches, set up roadblocks, and kill[ed] identified Hutu opposition, human rights advocates, and Tutsi. UN troops
[stood] by and follow[ed] their 'monitoring' mandate."[31] Within weeks, the
genocide was countrywide. The UN immediately withdrew the bulk of its
forces, leaving about 300 personnel in Kigali; they were frustrated soldiers
who could only stand by and watch as the horror of the genocide unfolded
before their eyes. Kigali became the "epicenter of genocide." Within days,
hundreds of thousands of Tutsi were murdered in their homes or stopped at
roadblocks and hacked to death.[32]

Sadly, tragically, the UN knew—in January 1994—about the existence of
the death lists and about the plans to exterminate Tutsi and moderate Hutu
but chose not to take action. The inaction of the UN led to the machete
genocide three months later. It was a genocide that could have been prevented had the UN Security Council chosen to approve the recommendations of its military commander in Rwanda, Canadian Major General Romeo
Dallaire.

In January 1994, Dallaire sent an urgent fax, labeled "most immediate,"
to New York. The general reported in great detail the planning by the Habyarimana dictatorship to exterminate the nation's Tutsi population. Someone in the government had informed Dallaire of these actions because the
informant was repulsed by them.[33] The informant, who was registering all
Tutsi in Kigali, preparing lists of Tutsi, and training the *interahamwe* to exterminate them, told Dallaire about the Hutu plan to "provoke a civil war,"
including a plan that forced Belgium to remove its troops. Dallaire's fax requested permission to raid an *interahamwe* arms cache in Kigali and asked
New York to evacuate the informant and his family from Rwanda. His requests were rejected by the UN. Three months later, the informant's warnings became reality. When the genocide began in April, General Dallaire

requested the UN to provide him with an additional 2,500 blue helmets to suppress the fighting and end the genocide. His request was rejected by the Security Council.[34]

The "hurricane of death" that began in April 1994 "crushed 80 percent of its victims in about six weeks, between the second week in April and the third week of May. [Given the death count, over 800,000 murdered in 100 days], the daily killing rate was at least five times that of the Nazi death camps."[35]

Machete Genocide: April 1994

The battle hymn of the *interahamwe,* sung as they rounded up and executed Tutsi in the spring of 1994, clearly defined their enemy:

> Is it a sin to kill a Tutsi? No. Let's exterminate them, exterminate them, kill them and bury them in the forests, let's chase them out of the forests and bury them in the caves, let's chase them out of the caves and massacre them. Stop so that we can kill you, don't cause problems because your god fell at Ruhengera, while he was on his way to the market to buy sweet potatoes. Don't even spare the babies, don't spare the old men, nor the old women.[36]

This goal of the Hutu, to make Rwanda "Tutsifrei," was described by a witness during one of the later trials: There was "the intention of completely wiping out the Tutsi from Rwanda so that—as they said on certain occasions—their children, later on, should not know what a Tutsi looked like, unless they referred to history books."[37] Clearly, this goal—"meticulously organized" by the Hutu Power leaders and the leaders of the National Executive of the *interahamwe* and their subordinates across Rwanda's eleven provinces—fell within the definition of genocide and crimes against humanity.

By 1992, the Hutu Power extremists had already put in place the apparatus for the 1994 genocide of the Tutsi. President Habyarimana and his clique planned the genocide because they "bitterly resented the prospect of power-sharing with the Tutsi minority" and believed that a civil war and the accompanying genocide would put an end to that prospect. For more than two years prior to the genocide, "Hutus were exposed to an ongoing and virulent campaign of anti-Tutsi brainwashing."[38] Most Hutu were illiterate and, given their authoritarian tradition, tended to believe what the authorities told them. And what they were told was quite fantastic.

The RPF Tutsi fighters were pictured as creatures from another world, with tails, horns, hooves, pointed ears and red eyes that shone in the dark. Anybody who could be their accomplice was bound also to be a very evil creature.[39]

Four distinct sets of events and actions were in place in 1992, awaiting the signal to begin the genocide. First, Habyarimana and his top staff and planners took up residence in the "little house" in Kigali. It was there that the president and the Hutu Power leaders organized and trained their extremist midlevel ideological cadres in the rural areas of Rwanda, the killers who were responsible for the genocide. Second, the prefects, all but one of them Hutu, knew their responsibilities when the orders came from Hutu Power. Third, the local militias, the *interahamwe* and the *impuzamugami,* about 50,000 men, were trained and waiting for the genocide to begin. Finally, the Presidential Guard, an elite group of 6,000 military personnel, were fully trained for their primary mission: assisting the *interahamwe* in the killing of Tutsi. All these killing units had secretly received copies of the death lists.

According to Dallaire, the UN's chief of staff assigned to Rwanda, "the rapid spread of violence just after the death of the president [on April 6, 1994] was primarily a 'political decapitation' of Hutu moderates and Tutsi in and around the capital. The killings, probably including that of the president, were directed by extremists with the deceased president's own party and were designed to disrupt the peace process permanently."[40]

The genocidal process followed by the killing units was similar to earlier genocides perpetrated by the Nazis, Cambodians, and Yugoslavs. The organizers of the genocide were a small group within the Hutu regime; they were "the political, military, and economic elite who had decided through a mixture of ideological and material motivation radically to resist political change which they perseived as threatening."[41]

The first victims of the genocide were the "selected" enemies: political opponents, moderate cabinet members, schoolteachers, intellectuals, newsmen, professional men and women and their families, and rural administrators. The exterminators selected their victims from the death lists developed by the Kigali leaders. After murdering the men and women of ideas, the killing units turned to the extermination of all other Tutsi in the towns and in the rural provinces. The goal: complete annihilation of that "racially alien" social group.[42]

The "main agents of the genocide were the ordinary [Hutu] peasants themselves."[43] The killers were the local militias and the local police. The

FAR was called into a rural province to assist in the genocide when the Tutsi were too numerous for the local killing squads to handle.

A common feature of the massacres "is that they were preceded by political meetings during which a 'sensibilization' process was carried out. These seemed to have been designed to put the local peasants 'in the mood,' to drum into them that the people they were soon to kill were *ibyitso*, i.e., actual or potential collaborators of the RPF arch-enemy. [After this] process had been carried out, the order would come sooner or later, . . . directly from the Ministry of the Interior."[44] When the orders did come from Kigali to the provinces, the local *bourgmestre* would call the local militia, and these Hutu peasants would search out and execute Tutsi and others on the local death list.

Euphemisms and metaphors were used by the local leaders, wrote Gerard Prunier, "as if the naked truth was too much to stomach." The killings were called *umuganda*, "collective work," while " 'bush clearing' [was the command to] chop up men, and 'pulling out the roots of the bad weeds' [meant] the slaughtering of women and children."[45]

The more fanatical Hutu did not need euphemisms to prepare them psychologically for the ensuing slaughter. The FAR, the Presidential Guard, the Zero Network local extremists, the *interahamwe,* and Hutu gendarmes set up roadblocks out of Kigali and other areas of Rwanda to round up moderate Hutu and Tutsi for execution. As in past genocides, the moderate civic, political, and religious leaders were targeted first. Anyone suspected of being sympathetic to the RPF was seen as a traitor and executed.[46] They were butchered by the local *interahamwe,* "the local police, neighbors, and even clergy."[47]

> Local political leaders, police, and the soldiers, with lists identifying those to be killed went from house to house. . . . [UN forces] were instructed . . . to protect themselves at all costs, even if that meant standing by while lightly armed, drunken thugs hacked women and children to death. Those who had cash could buy a quick death by firearm; those who could not received a less costly and less sophisticated execution by machete, stoning, or burning. . . . Within three months, between 500,000 and 800,000 Rwandans, mostly Tutsi, were dead; 500,000 Rwandans were replaced within the country; and over two million Rwandans had fled to surrounding countries. More human tragedy was compressed into three months in Rwanda than occurred in four years in the former Yugoslavia.[48]

The tools of death used in the Rwandan genocide were extremely primitive, unlike the technologically advanced mechanics of death used to implement the Nazis' final solution. A 1994 Physicians for Human Rights report noted:

> The *interahamwe* used the following methods of killing: machetes, massues (clubs studded with nails), small axes, knives, grenades, guns, fragmentation grenades, beatings to death, amputations with exsanguination, buried alive, drowned, or raped and killed later. Many victims had both their achilles tendons cut with machetes as they ran away, to immobilize them so that they could be finished off later.[49]

There was no safe haven for the ethnically distinct Tutsi to flee to. Churches, schools, and hospitals were "prime targets" for the killing units, and some of the massacres took place in these facilities. Indeed, in Rwanda's genocide, "more people [were] killed in churches and church compounds than in any other site."[50]

Hutu schoolteachers "commonly denounced their Tutsi pupils to the militia or even directly killed them themselves. [Said one Hutu teacher to a reporter]: "I killed some of the children. . . . We had eighty kids in the first year. There are twenty five left. All the others, we killed them or they ran away."[51]

Unlike the population demographics in the former Yugoslavia, where there were three distinct and largely separate ethnic concentrations, in Rwanda "the situation was much more homogeneous; both groups [Tutsi and Hutu] were evenly distributed throughout the country. Therefore the concept of safe havens was not as appropriate in Rwanda as in Bosnia."[52] As Prunier noted, both groups "lived side by side with each other without any 'Hutuland' or 'Tutsiland.'"[53]

Execution of Tutsi at the riverside was a common occurrence. "The river became an ideal carriageway for the disposal of evidence of Rwanda's genocide. People were routinely lined up beside the river for execution and then pushed into the flood. . . . Almost every river and lake in the country became dumping grounds for the dead. . . . When the dead finally reached Lake Victoria [by mid-May 1994, over 40,000 dead bodies had floated into the lake from Rwanda], Ugandian fishermen went out in their boats to recover them and gave them a decent burial [in Uganda]."[54]

The Hutu killers, much like earlier twentieth-century "killing units," did all they could to dehumanize the Tutsi victims. Like their predecessors, the

Rwanda. Rwandan Tutsi children who lost their parents in the genocide, 1994. (UN PHOTO 186799/J. Isaac 1059L)

interahamwe regularly forced members of Tutsi families to kill other members. A twenty-four-year-old Tutsi described the horror of being forced to kill his own brother or see the *interahamwe* kill his entire family:

> My brother [was not killed by Hutu peasants]. . . . The next day he came home and went straightway to a roadblock surrounded by *interahamwe*. He told them to kill him themselves and end the story there. [They] brought him back to the house. They told us that he had to be killed in order to prove that the whole family were not agents of the RPF. They left him in the house. . . . During this time messages were coming in every hour, urging our family to kill [my brother]. The whole family was threatened with death unless we killed [him]. He begged us to kill him. . . . After four days about 20 *interahamwe*, armed with machetes, hoes, spears and bows and arrows, came to the house. They stood over me and said: "kill him!" [My brother said to me]: "I fear being killed by a machete, so please go ahead and kill me but use a small hoe." He himself brought the hoe and handed it to me. I hit him on the head. I kept hitting him on the head but he would

not die. It was agonizing. Finally, I took the machete he dreaded in order to finish him off quickly.[55]

With the beginning of the slaughter, the RPF launched a military offensive aimed at linking its attacking forces with the 600 RPF military already in Kigali. (On July 4, 1994, the RPF captured Kigali and immediately established an interim government, dominated by the military leaders and including some moderate Hutu.) At the same time, the UN forces were reduced from 2,500 to 270 troops. In May 1994, after discussing the UN's response to the events in Rwanda, the Security Council adopted Resolution 918, authorizing the expansion (UNAMIR II) of military forces in Rwanda to 5,500 personnel to "provide protections to the displaced persons, refugees, and civilians at risk, while supporting relief efforts."[56]

During the height of the terror, only a handful of international agencies remained in Rwanda to provide humanitarian aid to the victims and the refugees, in particular the Medecins sans Frontieres and the International Committee of the Red Cross (ICRC). In 1994 alone, the ICRC spent over $130 million in a massive humanitarian aid program for Rwandan injured and refugees.

> Even before the assassination of the President [of Rwanda], the ICRC was providing food to over 600,000 displaced persons in Rwanda. . . . [As the UN did not take any action], the ICRC mounted its biggest world-wide relief in and around Rwanda. . . . The failure to get peacekeepers involved in protecting civilians put the burden on the ICRC. [After dealing with the food and medical problems], the ICRC found itself increasingly involved in prison work—restoring water supplies, registering 16,000 detainees, and providing blankets, soap, and utensils, . . . and in 1995, the ICRC actually participated in the construction of a prison.[57]

In May 1994, with the Tutsi population fleeing Rwanda for displaced person camps in surrounding countries, the *interahamwe* set up roadblocks along the escape routes, checked ethnic identity cards, culled targeted groups of Tutsi, and killed them in horrible fashion. The RPF, once it seized Kigali, declared a unilateral cease-fire and immediately formed a "government of national unity," including Hutu and Tutsi. Pasteur Bizimungo was chosen president of the Republic of Rwanda.

In an ironic twist of fate, after the RPF took power, the Hutu became refugees, and hundreds of thousands of Hutu fled Rwanda, many of them crossing the border to Zaire and Burundi. Once the civil war ended and the national unity government was formed, thousands of Hutu leaders and soldiers who had not fled quickly enough were arrested and held in prisons awaiting trial. In 1999 there were 150,000 Hutus awaiting trial in Rwanda.

However, much like in Kosovo, in Rwanda there is still bloody violence. Over 1.5 million Hutu crossed the border in a two-week period in early July 1994. Included in this mass exodus were the Hutu leaders of the genocide and most of the FAR generals. Since November 1996, rearmed by "France and Zaire, and to a lesser extent by South Africa, the Seychelles, and China,"[58] the FAR has come from Zaire (now the Congo Republic) and Burundi to raid Tutsi villages, continuing to execute Tutsi. These Hutu FAR have specifically targeted one group of Tutsi: those who went to Arusha to testify against the Hutu leaders charged with genocide and crimes against humanity. In August 1998, for example, the Hutu rebels, "armed with machetes and clubs, hacked to death at least 110 people in attacks northwest of Kigali."[59] International aid agencies such as the International Red Cross were thus "faced with a dilemma of feeding some Hutu who were responsible for the genocide and who were still committing genocide" and then returning to their safe havens in Zaire.[60]

Formation of the International Criminal Tribunal

For reasons associated with realpolitik, the major world powers and the international community did nothing to prevent the genocide. Although the general of UN forces in Rwanda had presented an action scenario that he believed would constrain the Hutu from committing genocide, his suggestions were rejected by the Security Council. Only after the magnitude of the genocide was revealed to the international community did the UN take any action.

In the summer of 1994, the UN sent a special rapporteur for Rwanda, Rene Degni-Segui, and then appointed a commission of experts to visit Rwanda and report back to the Security Council. In the fall of 1994, after visiting the genocide-ravished country and seeing mounds of dead bodies gnawed at by dogs and other animals, both the rapporteur and the commission reported finding clear evidence of genocide and crimes against humanity. Their recommendations called for the creation of an international criminal tribunal to hear cases and pronounce sentence on those found guilty of conspiring and/or committing these crimes.

Based on these recommendations and the request of the new government in Kigali, the International Criminal Tribunal, Rwanda (ICTR) was proposed by the UN Security Council in November 1994 (one year after the ICTY was established). The ICTR became the world's first "genocide court,"[61] with jurisdiction over crimes of genocide, other crimes against humanity, and actions in violation of Article III of the 1949 Geneva Conventions.[62] (Although some Bosnian Serbs had been indicted because they ordered genocidal acts by their subordinates, most of the ICTY charges were war crimes allegations.) On December 18, 1994, the Security Council passed Resolution 955 establishing the ICTR. Its charge was to

> prosecute persons responsible for genocide and other serious violations of international humanitarian law committed in the territory of Rwanda and Rwandan citizens responsible for genocide and other such violations committed in the territory of neighboring states between January 1st 1994 and December 31, 1994.

Another UN Security Council resolution, dated February 22, 1995, established the seat of the ICTR in Arusha, Tanzania. (A suboffice of the ICTR was established in Kigali, Rwanda.) The ICTR was not located in Rwanda to avoid the appearance of "victors' justice" by the new Tutsi-led Rwandan government.[63]

The initial trials of indicted defendants took place almost two years later, when Jean Paul Akayesu, a Hutu *bourgmestre,* was escorted into Trial Chamber One on January 9, 1997, to answer charges that he had committed genocide and other crimes against humanity.

Rwandan Opposition to Resolution 955

Ironically, the Rwandan delegation to the UN, sitting on the Security Council when the resolution proposing the ICTR was adopted on November 8, 1994, cast the sole vote against its creation. Even though they had requested the UN to respond to the genocide with the creation of an ad hoc criminal tribunal, Rwandan officials were sufficiently aroused by the perceived weaknesses of the tribunal to cast the sole negative vote.

There were several reasons for their vote. First, Rwanda objected to the time frame for ICTR prosecutions, January 1–December 31, 1994. Their argument was that the Hutu Power organizational planning for the genocide had begun in 1990 and that the UN resolution would not enable the ICTR to address those involved prior to 1994. Second, the statute gave the ICTR jurisdiction over "natural persons"; therefore, cases against groups, whether public or private, could not be instituted.

They also objected to the poor staffing of the ICTR. The ICTR statute "provided for so little personnel, both judicial and prosecutorial, that the ICTR could not possibly be expected to fulfill the monumental task set before it. Not only was the total number of judges very small (six trial judges and five appellate judges), but the appellate judges were to be shared with the ICTY. Moreover, the ICTR and ICTY were to share one prosecutor."[64]

Finally, Rwanda objected to the absence of the death penalty as a punishment for genocide. This, they argued, could lead to the Hutu leaders tried in the ICTR receiving prison terms while their subordinates in the provinces and communes, the men who had carried out the genocide, faced the death penalty if found guilty in Rwandan national courts.[65]

In a formal position paper to the UN entitled *The Position of the Government of the Republic of Rwanda on the International Criminal Tribunal for Rwanda (ICTR)*, the government enumerated its concerns about the international tribunal. It had "grave misgivings" about the structure and the functioning of the ICTR. In particular, the report focused on the following:

- The poor organization of the ICTR; for example, "the current prosecutor has centralized all decision making in the Hague. . . . Yugoslavia is the prime focus of the prosecutor's attention."
- The personnel problems of the ICTR, involving reporting lines and the competence of ICTR staff.
- The prosecution and investigation strategy; for example, "the office of the prosecutor has been the weakest link in the chain of organs that constitute the tribunal. . . . [The prosecutors] have never determined policy as to whom the tribunal should pursue. They have never indicated the kind of cases they wish to prosecute before the tribunal and those they expect to be tried by national courts. . . . They proceed on an *ad hoc* basis." Although some major defendants were still at large when the report was issued, the Rwandan government noted that "the Prosecutor has indicated both to her staff and to officials in the Ministry of Justice of the Republic of Rwanda that she does not in the foreseeable future plan to issue any new indictments and plans from now onwards to concentrate only on the prosecution of suspects who have so far been indicted."
- The ICTR conduct of investigations, which left "a lot to be desired." There had been no investigations of the regions "where some of the

worst atrocities took place." When they did visit the areas, the investigators were "discourteous"; they traveled in brightly marked UN vehicles, "clearly aggravating risks to the security of the potential witnesses."

- The prosecutor's interpretation of the ICTR mandate, which was "regrettab[ly] misconc[eived]. "She is on record . . . as saying that her objective is to render 'deluxe justice.' . . . Her actions are at variance with the spirit of Resolution 995 which seeks to promote national reconciliation and maintenance of peace in Rwanda by bringing to justice the perpetrators of genocide and other serious violations of international humanitarian law."

- The attitude of the Prosecutor's Office toward the Rwandan government and people, which was disgraceful. There was no sensitivity toward the survivors of the genocide; "on the contrary, personnel of the tribunal, specifically the prosecutor's office, have behaved with hostility, arrogance, and insensitivity that is difficult to explain."

The concluding segment contained the Rwandan recommendations for changing the ICTR. Kigali called for

an independent Prosecutor for the Rwandan tribunal;
moving the ICTR to Kigali, Rwanda;
strengthening the powers of the prosecutorial staff of the ICTR;
recruiting more qualified personnel for the ICTR; and,
improving cooperative actions with the Rwandan government and
legal authorities.[66]

These Rwandan recommendations have not been acted on by the Security Council, and the ICTR has functioned in accord with Resolution 955 since 1995.

As finally adopted, Resolution 955's annex spelled out the scope of the ICTR. Persons "responsible for serious violations of international humanitarian law [genocide and crimes against humanity, along with violations of Article III of the 1949 Geneva Convention] committed in the territory of Rwanda . . . between January 1 and December 31, 1994," were the sole targets of the ICTR prosecutors. The ICTR's jurisdiction extended to "natural persons" only, underscoring the principle of individual criminal responsibility that had emerged from the Nuremberg and Tokyo trials.

The organization of the ICTR mirrored that of the ICTY: the Chambers, the Prosecutor's Office, and the Registry. There was only one prosecutor for both ad hoc criminal courts, although deputy prosecutors were assigned to the two tribunals. In Arusha and Kigali, again mirroring the ICTY process, the prosecutor investigated charges and drew up indictments that were presented to the Chambers for approval by a judge. "If satisfied that a prima facie case has been established by the prosecutor, he or she shall confirm the indictment. If not so satisfied, the indictment shall be dismissed." After the indictment was confirmed, the ICTR issued "orders and warrants for the arrest, detention, surrender and transfer of persons . . . as may be required for the conduct of the trial."

The ICTR was responsible for conducting expeditious but fair and public trials of the defendants; Article XX, Rights of the Accused, laid out the protections that had to be accorded each defendant. Article XXI required the ICTR to protect victims and witnesses from harassment, including "the conduct of in camera proceedings and the protection of the victim's families." Judgment was by majority of the three-judge panel, and if found guilty, defendants faced penalties that "shall be limited to imprisonment." Final appeals were directed to the ICTR's Appeals Chamber, consisting of five ICTR judges.[67] UN member states were encouraged to cooperate with the ICTR regarding extradition of those indicted and with regard to human and other vitally needed resources.

The ICTR: A Weak Sister to the ICTY?

One writer noted that the ICTR "always seemed a shadow of its sister in the Hague, beset from its inception by a host of problems. [These difficulties involved] a lack of personnel, facilities for the trials, money mismanagement, and cronyism."[68]

Another huge problem was the location of the ICTR itself. The feeling in the UN Security Council was that the trials should take place in Africa, and after some discussion, the council selected Arusha, Tanzania (a city of 140,000 people), for largely symbolic and political reasons: it was the host city to the RPF–Rwanda government peace conferences and other African states' meetings. But the city is hard to get to. As the registrar for the ICTR, Agwu Ukiwe Okali, understated, Arusha is not a "global media station." Furthermore, "phone service, especially overseas, is spotty at best."[69]

Sara Darehshori, an ICTR prosecutor on loan from her law firm in New York City, was co-counsel in the trial of Jean-Paul Akayesu. Upon her arrival in Kigali, she found that the office she shared with about a dozen Dutch policemen lacked the most basic amenities. We created makeshift desks by removing doors from their hinges and placing them on crates. We fought over garbage cans, which we used as chairs. The one telephone line was erratic. [Although after three months we received] real desks and chairs, . . . we still didn't have pens, paper, or a dependable copy machine.[70]

Another deputy prosecutor from the United States, Brenda Sue Thornton, complained to the tribunal that trial transcripts of testimony given in October and November 1997 had not yet been received by either set of lawyers in the Clement Rayishema case as of mid-February 1998. She was informed by the Registry that the delay occurred because transcribing companies in Canada, the United States, and France were being used by the ICTR because of a "lack of staff."[71]

The existing infrastructure in Arusha was "not equipped to handle the technical needs of a staff that has now grown to 400 here and in Kigali." As a consequence of the city's remoteness and lack of amenities, the circumstances of the ICTR staff are "very difficult," said Alessandro Caldarone, the ICTR administrator responsible for the detention cells.[72] In May 1998, Registrar Okali told the UN that the ICTR needed "investigators, administrators, bilingual lawyers, interpreters, and court stenographers. . . . [Also needed were computers and computer experts, because] you can't just run down the street [in Arusha or Kigali] and buy computer parts." The ICTR had great difficulty finding these human resources. As Okali stated, "Arusha is four hours by road from Nairobi, Kenya, the nearest large international center. . . . In Arusha there is not even a cafeteria," he lamented.[73]

In spite of these difficulties—financial, human, and geographic—by the summer of 1998 the ICTR had indicted thirty-six individuals, with thirty-one of them in custody in Arusha detention cells. Most of those indicted were seized at the displaced persons camps in Zaire. Also, a number of nations, including Belgium, Cameroon, Zambia, and Kenya, turned people over to the ICTR.

In the United States, which passed domestic legislation in February 1996 to cooperate with the ICTR on the extradition of indicted persons, the government arrested a man on September 26, 1996, at the tribunal's request. He was a seventy-three-year-old Hutu religious leader, the former president of the Seventh Day Adventist Church in Rwanda, Elizaphan Ntakirutimana. He hired Ramsey Clark, former U.S. attorney general, as defense counsel. (Clark was also serving as Karadzic's defense attorney in civil proceedings in

U.S. federal court.) He unsuccessfully appealed his extradition from the United States to the ICTR. On August 5, 1998, United States District Court Judge John Rainey ordered the pastor "to be turned over to an international war crimes tribunal on the charge of genocide."[74] However, as of the end of 1998, Ntakirutimana was still in a Texas prison fighting extradition in the federal courts.

By mid-1998, the ICTR was conducting four trials, with others scheduled following this initial quartet of defendants. Unlike the ICTY, the defendants in Rwanda "include some of the highest-ranking officials [Jean Kambanda, the prime minister; Pauline Nyiramasuhuko, minister of family and social welfare;[75] and Colonel Theoneste Bagosora, head of the FAR during the genocide of the Hutu-dominated government whose officers and allied militia reportedly carried out the massacres, mainly of ethnic Tutsi, over three months in 1994."[76]

Because of poor funding and a perennial lack of staff, it took the ICTR over two years before the first indictments received from the prosecutor were approved by the judges. On December 15, 1995, the ICTR issued its first warrants for the arrest of eight men accused of genocide and crimes against humanity.[77] Legal proceedings opened against the first three men in May 1996, when their pleas were entered. The three were Georges Rutaganda, a radio station owner and a top official in the *interahamwe;* Jean-Paul Akayesu, a former *bourgmestre* of the Taba commune; and Clement Kayishema, a former prefect. The ICTR charged them with commission of genocide, crimes against humanity, and murder. All three pled not guilty. Immediately after the charges were read and the pleas entered, the court adjourned until December 1996, when the first trial began.

Rutaganda was one of the owners of Radio Television Libre de Mille Collins, which continually broadcast scurrilous attacks on the Tutsi and orders to kill them. He was also the second vice president of the National Committee of the *interahamwe*. The ICTR charged him with eight counts of genocide, crimes against humanity, and violations of Article III, carried out in the provinces of Kigali and Gitarama. He was arrested in Zambia in October 1995 and extradited to Arusha to stand trial. His trial began March 18, 1997, and as of the end of 1998, there had still been no judgment from the tribunal.

Kayishema was the prefect of Kibuye province and was charged with genocide. It was alleged that he and other Hutu leaders rounded up Tutsi and placed them in the local Catholic churches, which the Hutu claimed were "safe havens," and other public arenas. Then they executed the huddled, terrified Tutsi with machetes. Finally, the churches were burned to the ground with the Tutsi inside. He was arrested in Kenya in September 1996 and brought to Arusha. His trial began on April 11, 1997, and as of the end of 1998 was still ongoing. There were fifty-two witnesses for the prosecution and over 400 documents and depositions; all placed him at the center of the genocide, ordering the killings and taking part in them. One witness, NN, told the tribunal how Kayishema had murdered a baby: "'He took the baby, and then grabbed hold of one leg, giving the other to another soldier. Then he took a sword and cut the child in two vertically. Then he threw it to the ground.'"[78]

Akayesu, who had been extradited from Zambia on May 26, 1996, was also charged with genocide and crimes against humanity. The indictment alleged that he had encouraged the murder of Tutsi, directly ordered the killing of several persons near his office, and personally supervised the interrogation, beating, and execution of local residents of his commune.

The Jean-Paul Akayesu Trial: 1996–1998

The trial of Akayesu is a microscopic examination of the work of the ICTR. The evidence presented by both the prosecutors and the defense attorneys was primarily testimonial, and the tribunal gave great leeway in allowing hearsay and other statements that would have been excluded in an American criminal proceeding. These rulings from the bench angered civil rights groups such as Amnesty International, which argued that they did not measure up to minimal standards of procedural fairness.

Akayesu was formally indicted on February 13, 1996. The trial began on January 9, 1997, and testimony and final summaries were presented at the end of March 1998, at which time the panel took the case under advisement. Finally, on September 2, 1998, the three-judge tribunal handed down its judgment in the Akayesu case: guilty on nine of the fifteen counts. According to ICTR officials, a primary reason for its slowness was that it was the first genocide trial in history, and "every legal question had to be decided with no precedents" to guide the judges.[79]

In the case, known as *The Prosecutor of the Tribunal for Rwanda v. Jean-Paul Akayesu*, prosecutor Richard Goldstone charged Akayesu with twelve counts of genocide, crimes against humanity, and violations of Article III of the 1949 Geneva Conventions. On June 17, 1997, the new and energetic deputy prosecutor, Bernard Muna, responding to worldwide criticism from feminists and human rights groups, added three more counts of genocide and crimes against humanity. Akayesu was charged with ordering and condoning rape and sexual mutilation, followed by the killing of hundreds of Tutsi women who had sought sanctuary in the Taba commune civic center and found, instead, painful death.[80]

The prosecutor charged that Akayesu "had exclusive control over the communal police," that is, he had "command responsibility" over the inhabitants of Taba commune and was responsible for "the performance of executive functions and the maintenance of public order within his commune." At least 2,000 Tutsi were executed between the middle of April and the end of June 1994, during which time Akayesu "must have known about [the killings]" and "never attempted to prevent the killing of Tutsi."[81]

The prosecutors made their arguments and presented their witnesses to assist the tribunal in formulating its conception of genocide. The prosecutors clearly addressed legal questions and issues regarding the scope of the language in the 1948 Genocide Convention. In both the general allegations and the specific charges against Akayesu, the language of the 1948 convention was scrupulously used. "The victims in each paragraph charging genocide," the prosecutors wrote, "were members of a national, ethnic, racial, or religious group." Further, in each of the genocide counts, the defendant's "alleged acts or omissions were committed with intent to destroy, in whole or in part, a national, ethnical, or racial group." In the crimes against humanity charges against Akayesu, the prosecutor noted, consistent with the Nuremberg Principles, that the accused's alleged acts or omissions "were committed as a part of a widespread or systematic attack against a civilian population on national, political, ethnic, or racial grounds."

Akayesu was criminally responsible, the prosecutors argued, for four counts of genocide and "incitement to genocide" (three new genocide charges were added later). He was also charged with four counts of violation of Article III of the 1949 Geneva Convention and four counts of acting in violation of the Nuremberg Principles' prohibition against crimes against humanity.

The charges against Akayesu, at bottom, focused on his role, either directly or indirectly (through orders given to the militias), in the rapes and killings of Tutsi and his role in the destruction of property in the Taba commune. On the morning of April 19, 1994, the genocide came to Taba. Local Tutsi teachers were executed, and hundreds of local Tutsi were killed after a morning meeting in which Akayesu named at least three prominent Tutsi who had to be killed. House-to-house searches led to Akayesu's threatening the lives of captured Tutsi and allowing others to be executed in his presence.

He ordered and was present at the torturous interrogation of a number of Tutsi, he ordered and participated in the execution of three Tutsi brothers, and he ordered the deaths of eight Tutsi who had escaped from another commune.

Akayesu allegedly ordered the militia and the *interahamwe* to "kill intellectual and influential people (Tutsi), including five secondary school teachers." The five were "executed with machetes and agricultural tools" in front of Akayesu. Akayesu was charged with crimes against humanity because of the torture tactics, including horrible beatings, he had inflicted on Tutsi during interrogation. He was also alleged to have urged Hutu to

> ferret out Tutsi neighbors to kill them, even urging them to rip babies from mother's wombs. "He said the person who kills a rat never spares the one who is pregnant, you never spare a pregnant rat." At one point . . . Akayesu ordered all Tutsi children to be stripped and the boys killed. Later, children of both sexes were murdered on his orders.[82]

This behavior ended with the RPF assumption of power in late June 1994.

The trial lasted seventeen months, and the three judges—Laity Kama (Senegal), Lennart Aspegren (Sweden), and Havanethem Pilley (South Africa)—heard testimony from forty-two witnesses: thirty prosecution and twelve defense. The prosecution witnesses, acknowledged the tribunal, were extremely brave men and women who feared for their lives yet agreed to testify. Most of the prosecution witnesses were Tutsi who lived in majority Hutu towns in Rwanda, "where everybody knows everybody else." The ICTR could not protect the witnesses when they returned to Rwanda. Tragically, at least "two witnesses who testified against Mr. Akayesu were killed on their return to Rwanda."[83]

The proceedings generated over 4,000 pages of transcripts, and 125 documents were placed in evidence. The prosecutors presented dozens of witnesses who placed Akayesu at the sites of the killings, the interrogations, and the rape-executions of dozens of women from April 19 through the end of May 1994. They argued that Akayesu "succumbed to pressure from hardliners in the Hutu-led government and, after April 19, wholeheartedly joined the effort to exterminate Tutsi."[84]

Witnesses testified that they saw and heard him sanction the rape-executions of women. One witness, identified only as "P.P.," described in detail for almost an hour "how militiamen acting on Mr. Akayesu's orders raped and killed . . . three Tutsi women. . . . One of the women was pregnant

[and] was raped twice while several men held her down. Then she had a miscarriage. Finally, the militiamen beat her to death with clubs. 'They were tortured and they died but they continued to be beaten,' P.P. said. 'I don't know how many blows they received.' "[85]

Defense counsel for Akayesu presented witnesses to buttress the claim that Akayesu had first tried to protect the Tutsi in his commune but found that he could not control the militia and the *interahamwe* who did the killings. He was portrayed as a victim of "unfortunate circumstances, a decent man who continued to try to save Tutsi until he was forced himself to flee in May 1994. Akayesu had lost control of the town to Hutu killers and has been made the scapegoat for massacres he could not prevent."[86] In his testimony, Akayesu maintained,

> I tried to save some Tutsi and appeal for law and order. However, I was accused of supporting the RPF and my life was threatened. . . . [Even Radio Television Libre des Mille Collines broadcast allegations that] I was a tall and brown Tutsi who was supporting the RPF.[87]

On March 19, 1998, the prosecution presented its closing arguments in the case. The prosecutor maintained that

> Akayesu triggered, incited, and participated in the genocide in the commune of Taba where the population fell from 61,000 to 54,000 between April and June 1994. . . . He had the duty to protect the population, and the people looked up to him, but he betrayed them. . . . [After April 19, Akayesu was] transformed from protector of the people to a predator, . . . to an assassin, into a barracuda. . . . We have a duty to tell Mr. Akayesu that what he did was bad. We have a duty to tell the world that this should never happen again, and thus to help to prevent future genocides.[88]

On March 26, the defense delivered closing arguments. It maintained that Akayesu had tried to protect Tutsi until April 19, and that after that date, "Akayesu continued to save [Tutsi] lives in April–May 1994 until he finally fled Taba Commune." Defense counsel also argued that the prosecutor did not have the right to "speak in the name of the international community when the same community had not acted to stop the genocide. . . . The international community had lacked the political will to act." Finally, the defense challenged the prosecutors' claims that the elements of genocide, crimes against humanity, and other violations had been satisfied by the evidence presented.[89]

The tribunal ended its activities on that somber note. The prosecutors chose not to present arguments in rebuttal. The three judges adjourned to deliberate the question of guilt or innocence.

On September 2, 1998, the tribunal was reconvened to hear the judgment of the panel. In the 300-page decision, the judges pronounced Akayesu guilty of nine of the fifteen counts brought against him by the prosecution.[90] He was found guilty of genocide, direct and public incitement to commit genocide, and crimes against humanity (specifically, extermination, murder, torture, rape, and other inhumane acts). A number of nongovernmental organizations (NGOs) had insisted for years that rape by one group (Hutu) intent on destroying another group (Tutsi) was a genocidal act because its goal was to destroy, "in whole or in part," the raped group. The ICTR accepted that argument and ruled that rape could be considered, given the circumstances of the bloodbath in Rwanda, an act of genocide.[91]

The Akayesu trial was the first opportunity for an international tribunal to flesh out the meaning and the scope of the term *genocide*. It was clear to the three judges that the killing of Tutsi by Hutu was done "with the intent to wipe out the Tutsi group in its entirety, since even newborn babies were not spared."

In addition, adhering to the Nuremberg Principles, the tribunal emphatically concluded that Akayesu was individually responsible for his actions and for his failure to act. As *bourgmestre*, according to the ICTR's guidelines (Article VI, clause 3), Akayesu was "criminally responsible for the acts of subordinates if the Superior knew or had reason to know that the subordinate was about to commit such acts or had actually done so and yet failed to prevent or punish such acts."

The ICTR after Four Years: 1994–1998

There have been positive and negative actions during the first four years of the ICTR. Positively, on May 1, 1998, former prime minister Kambada, "settling accounts with his conscience,"[92] pled guilty to six counts of genocide. His plea was "the first time in history that anyone has pleaded guilty to the crime of genocide before an international war crimes tribunal."[93] Kambada admitted that he had led massacres in Rwanda during the genocide and had committed crimes against humanity and crimes of genocide.

He also indicated his willingess to work with the Prosecutor's Office by providing crucial evidence about the planning of genocide for use in other trials.

On September 4, 1998, two days after the Akayesu verdict was announced, the same three-judge panel sentenced Kambada to life imprisonment. After balancing the aggravating and mitigating factors related to the determination of Kambada's punishment, the tribunal concluded that the "heinous nature of the crime of genocide and its absolute prohibition" and Kambada's active participation in the genocide's planning and implementation outweighed the mitigating factors such as his plea of guilty, his remorse, and his previous and future cooperation with the Prosecutor's Office.

The sentence, the tribunal said, "must reflect the predominant standard of proportionality between the gravity of the crime and the degree of responsibility of the offender." The former prime minister's crimes, the judges concluded,

> carry an intrinsic gravity and their widespread, atrocious and systematic character was particularly shocking to the human conscience. [Kambada] committed the crimes knowingly and with premeditation. . . . On the basis of all the above, [we find] that the aggravating circumstances surrounding the crimes committed by Jean Kambada negate the mitigating circumstances, especially since Jean Kambada occupied a high ministerial post at the time he committed the said crimes.[94]

The judges then sentenced Kambada to life imprisonment.

Finally, given the demands for "quicker" justice in the genocide cases, in the spring of 1998, the ICTR Prosecutor's Office attempted to use a multiple joint trial. A "super-indictment" was prepared by the staff, charging twenty-nine Hutu defendants, including Theoneste Bagosora, with genocide and crimes against humanity. James Stewart, the senior trial attorney in the Prosecutor's Office, argued that the group trial was "the best and most efficient method of proceeding." However, the ICTR judge did not confirm the indictment, and in an ex parte hearing, the Prosecutor's Office appealed the rejection to the ICTR Appeals Chamber of five judges.[95]

The issue of group trials begins to address the negatives of the ICTR, which include a lack of funding and insufficient staff; the isolation of Arusha; problems raised by defense counsel (from not receiving prosecutorial data on witnesses or not having enough time to study new documents introduced by the prosecution, to not being able to cross-examine witnesses whose court appearances were in the form of written statements); clashes between the ICTR and the new Rwandan national government; and criticisms by NGOs, especially legal organizations and civil rights groups such as Amnesty International, about the quality of "justice" meted out by the ICTR and about its being "bogged down by procedural weaknesses."[96]

When the secretary-general of the UN, Kofi Annan, visited Arusha in May 1998, he experienced, firsthand, the tribunal struggling with these problems. He attended the trial of Colonol Anatole Nsengiumva, where he heard "defense counsel argue that the charges were imprecise, vaguely drawn and backed by documents turned over to his client too late. He asked for an adjournment."[97]

National Retribution: The Rwandan Genocide Trials

When the ICTR was established in November 1994, it was given concurrent jurisdiction with the national courts, but the ICTR had priority in the selection of Huto to indict and try. The new Tutsi Rwandan leaders, concerned about the effective functioning of the ICTR, decided to charge and try the Hutu leaders who had ordered the genocide and many of the followers who had carried out the orders. Tension therefore existed between the ICTR and the Rwandan government and its rebuilt judiciary.

By the middle of 1998, more than 135,000 alleged Hutu participants in the genocide had been caught and imprisoned since the RPF wrenched control from the Hutu Power in July 1994.[98] This created a terrible logistical problem, because the capacity of existing national detention centers was 18,000 persons. Since the end of the genocide, an additional five detention centers have been built (with room for 13,000 detainees), and another ten existing facilities were enlarged (to hold an additional 20,000 detainees) to provide secure holding areas for the nation's prisoners.

A host of problems faced the new coalition government in its efforts to punish those guilty of genocide. Chief among them was the fact that the civil war had "devastated . . . Rwanda's judicial structures. The great majority of judicial and law enforcement personnel had been killed or fled the country. Moreover, the basic resources needed to run a legal system—books, vehicles, even paper—were essentially unavailable."[99] Prior to April 7, 1994, there were over 750 judges in Rwanda; after the genocide, there were only 244 judges alive in Rwanda. There were 87 prosecutors prior to the genocide, but only 14 afterward. Investigators numbered 139 before but only 39 after the killings ended.[100]

Rwanda. Bodies of Tutsi dead awaiting burial, 1994. (UN PHOTO 186809/J. Isaac 1059L)

There were no statutes that addressed the country's nightmare of han-
dling over 130,000 potential genocide-related criminal cases with a judicial
infrastruture that was virtually nonexistent. On September 1, 1996, the
Rwandan Organic Law on the Organizations of Prosecutions for Offenses
Constituting the Crime of Genocide or Crimes against Humanity Committed since October 1, 1990, became effective. It was a unique law, because at
its core was the notion of plea bargaining. Rwanda's criminal justice system
was an inquisitorial one, as opposed to the accusatorial system in the United
States and Great Britain. Plea bargaining was unheard of in Rwanda until the
law was passed and implemented. However, given the sad state of the judicial infrastructure, the plea bargain was the only strategy that could be used
to reduce the number of trials in a stressed-out judiciary.

Under the Organic Law, suspects involved in the genocide fell into four
categories: (1) leaders and organizers of the genocide and perpetrators who
committed heinous murders and/or sexual torture (death was the punishment for those found guilty in this category), (2) all others who were found
guilty of murder, (3) those Hutu who were found to have committed "grave
assaults" that did not end with murder of the victim, and (4) all those who
committed property damages in connection with the genocide.[101]

The law also created, for these genocide cases only, a fundamental plea-bargaining arrangement for all persons indicted, except for those in category 1. Those who chose this arrangement were entitled to a reduced sentence. After the defendant confessed, entered a plea of guilty, and apologized to the victims' families, the reduced sentence was ordered. Category 2 defendants received a sentence of seven to eleven years in prison if the plea arrangement was made prior to beginning of the case (twelve to fifteen years if the arrangement was made after trial began) or a sentence of life imprisonment if the person was convicted at trial. Category 3 defendants, if they accepted the plea bargain, received one-third the prison sentence applicable to their crimes (half the penalty if they copped a plea after the trial began). All category 4 defendants convicted were to receive suspended sentences.[102]

These domestic trials for genocide and other crimes against humanity began in Kigali on December 27, 1996. More than eleven hundred defendants have been tried, and another hundred are ready for trial. There have been over four hundred death sentences, more than four hundred sentences of life imprisonment, other lesser prison sentences, and less than one hundred acquittals.

Almost two dozen of those sentenced to death were executed in April 1998. The news reports described these executions on page one in headlines that read: "As Crowds Vent Rage, Rwanda Executes 22 for '94 Massacres."[103] The convicted murderers were executed by firing squads. Tens of thousands witnessed the deaths of those convicted in the national courts of genocide and crimes against humanity in five cities and towns in Rwanda. In Kigali, four people were executed, including one woman; two were school administrators, one a prosecutor, and one a businessman. The executions proceeded even though the United States, the European Union, and Pope John Paul II appealed to the government for clemency for the condemned. The requests were categorically rejected. Foreign Minister Anastase Gasana stated that the executions served "an educational and pedagogical purpose." Another cabinet member, Patrick Mazimhaka, "rebuffed the Pope's call for mercy saying in 1994 'I didn't hear the Pope call for forgiveness then.'"[104]

A number of international human rights organizations, including the UN's human rights organization, argued against the executions. The defendants did not have adequate counsel (there were only sixteen defense lawyers in all of Rwanda at the end of 1997), and there was no guilt beyond a reasonable doubt, they maintained. "There is no such certainty of guilt" in these cases, stated Jose Luis Herrero, the UN organization's spokesperson.[105]

Amnesty International produced a report in January 1997 that claimed that the Rwandan trials lacked fundamental fairness. It called for Rwanda to adhere to "international standards of fairness," pointing out that defendants had "trials that lasted four hours. The defendants had no access to legal counsel either before or during their trial. They were neither given the opportunity to summon witnesses for their defense nor to cross-examine prosecution witnresses." There was bedlam in the courtroom; the defendants were booed and the prosecutors were cheered by the onlookers. The two men who were convicted and sentenced to death by the court "had two weeks in which to submit an appeal."[106]

Rwanda and Nuremberg

Unlike the Nuremberg and Tokyo tribunals, the ICTR, like its sister the ICTY, was an ad hoc court created "by a wide cross section of the international community represented in the UN." Unlike the ICTY, the Arusha tribunal dealt "exclusively with an internal conflict [a civil war] that did not cross national boundaries."[107] But the characteristics of the genocide in Rwanda were quite similar to the earlier genocides of the twentieth century.

There was the dehumanization, the demonizing, of the Tutsi enemy. They were described in less than human terms, from *inyenzi* (cockroaches) to "racially alien creatures from another world" with hooves, tails, and horns. None were spared from cruel, painful death. For the Hutu, as it was for the other perpetrators of genocide, the goal was elimination of the enemy; in the future, Rwandan children would not know what a Tutsi looked like unless they went to the history books.

Like the Nazis, the Khmer Rouge, and the Bosnian Serbs before them, the Hutu organized and successfully employed a brutal killing process. And like their genocidal predecessors' killing processes, the Hutu first prepared their killers for "clearing the bush." Then they methodically killed the political, civil, religious, and educational Tutsi leaders first, followed by the professionals, including the schoolteachers and their Tutsi students. Finally, all the others were killed by the killing squads.

In 100 days, almost a million Rwandan Tutsi were killed, more than half the Tutsi population. During those 100 days of genocide, the outside world was repulsed by the genocide but did nothing to end it. It ended only when the RPF forces captured Kigali, forcing hundreds of thousands of Hutu to become refugees, thereby ending the civil war and the mass genocide.

When UN Secretary-General Kofi Annan visited Kigali in May 1998, the reception for him was cold and strained. It reflected the bitterness felt by the Tutsi Rwandans toward the UN because of that organization's inaction during the genocide and its actions afterward surrounding the creation, funding, staffing, and location of the ICTR.

He was there to explain to the Rwandans why there had been inaction by the UN—but not to apologize. He confessed that the UN had done little to stop the 1994 genocide. "Instead of finding forgiveness, he received an outright hostile reception from Rwandan leaders." Rwanda's Foreign Minister Anastase Gasana accused the UN of not heeding warnings that the genocide was coming "and then lacking the political will to intervene once the massacres started. 'We are interested in knowing who was behind this lack of will.'" Annan knew the answer, for he had been the UN's head of peacekeeping in 1994. In the evening, Rwanda's three highest officials boycotted a reception in honor of Annan.[108]

The ICTR will continue to hold its trials in Arusha into the new millennium. In May 1998, the UN funded the building of a third court chamber as well as provided funds for more staff and an improved infrastructure. For the first time, the 1948 Genocide Convention, born in the days after the Nazi Holocaust, was used to charge persons with acting criminally toward others. Most of the major leaders of the genocide—the Kigali Hutu Power, the *interahamwe,* and the FAR—have been turned over to the ICTR to stand trial (unlike the ICTY, where many of those indicted are still free).

While the ICTR trials continued in Arusha, in the UN, discussions and debates began anew, after a forty-odd-year silence, about the costs and benefits of creating a permanent international criminal court, located in a major international city, that would have the facilities and the staff to handle the issuance of indictments and the conduct of trials for those accused of committing genocide, crimes against humanity, and other violations of the laws of war.

7

NUREMBERG'S LEGACY?
ADOPTION OF THE ROME STATUTE

Since the Nuremberg and Tokyo war crimes tribunals ended their work in 1948, "it's been a dream of international human rights advocates [to see created] a permanent world court that would try individuals for genocide, crimes against humanity, and crimes of war."[1] The unfinished legacy of those World War II ad hoc tribunals has been the creation of a permanent international criminal court (ICC) that could hear cases involving grave violations of the laws and customs of war—situations not addressed, for whatever reason, by national prosecutors.

Ironically, wrote T. R. Goldman in 1998, the "biggest impediment, say U.S. and international human rights groups, . . . is not rogue states like Libya, Nigeria, or Iraq [but the] government of the United States." Although President Bill Clinton was on record as supporting the creation of an ICC, the United States "has emerged as the main obstacle" to its creation.[2] The primary opposition to the Rome statute came from the Pentagon and some foreign policy planners in the White House.

U.S. Military Antipathy toward UN Peacekeeping and the ICC

In the last two years of the George Bush administration (1989–1993), the United States "jumped into peace enforcement [in Somalia and the Persian Gulf] with gusto."[3] Although there was a quick, somewhat successful, end to the UN's military action against Iraq, the deaths of scores of American soldiers in Somalia a few years later led to almost instant disenchantment with U.S. involvement in Somalia and with UN peacekeeping missions generally. American foreign policy, known for its "particular mix of generosity, power, and multiple personalities,"[4] took a bold right turn after Somalia and after Bill Clinton was elected president in 1992, defeating Bush.

When Clinton entered the White House, he was confronted by a military hierarchy that had little regard for the deployment of American military personnel in "dangerous" UN peacekeeping efforts. There was also the "warrior culture" in the Pentagon that initially disdained Clinton, the first post–World War II president. They did not appreciate his critical comments about Vietnam and his successful effort to evade the draft during that bloody, controversial war. They certainly did not like his view of gays and lesbians in the military and successfully thwarted the commander in chief's effort to liberalize military values and regulations regarding homosexual personnel.

The Pentagon leaders also did all they could to dampen Clinton's enthusiasm for U.S. participation in multinational UN peacekeeping efforts. Chairman of the Joint Chiefs of Staff General Colin Powell said in September 1993:

> Notwithstanding all of the changes that have occurred in the world, notwithstanding the new emphasis on peacekeeping, peace enforcement, peace engagement, preventive diplomacy, we have a value system and a culture system within the armed forces of the U.S. We have this mission: *to fight and win the nation's wars*. . . . Because we are able to fight and win the nation's wars, because we are warriors, we are also uniquely able to do some of these new missions that are coming along, . . . but we never want to do it in such a way that we lose sight of the focus of why you have armed forces—to fight and win the nation's wars.[5]

Anthony Lake, who was in the Clinton White House at the time, supported Powell's view and announced the Clinton turnaround on such UN activities: "Let us be clear: peacekeeping is not at the center of our foreign and defense policy. Our armed forces' primary mission is not to conduct peace operations but to win wars."[6]

Powell and others in the Pentagon took particular umbrage at a 1993 proposal for the creation of a UN rapid reaction force (RRF), essentially a standing UN multination military force that would be used to carry out the Security Council's peacekeeping responsibilities.[7] A Clinton transition team on foreign policy had enthusiastically supported the creation of the RRF, with the U.S. military forming part of it, but given the harsh criticism by his military experts, Clinton bowed to pressure from the Pentagon and the extremely popular Powell, then chairman of the Joint Chiefs of Staff.

Powell quashed the idea of committing American forces to fight in an unknown war, in an as-yet-undetermined land, for an unknown cause, led by a non–American general. His unequivocal rejection of what he believed was an outlandish proposal had an immediate impact. Clinton's UN delegation informed the secretary-general that although the RRF was needed, the United States was rejecting the creation of one "at this time."

> The U.S. does not plan to earmark forces or to assign troops to the UN Security Council permanently under Article 43 of the UN Charter.[8] Given the immediate challenges facing UN peacekeeping, these options are impractical at this time.[9]

Clearly, the military planners were concerned that the essential mission of America's armed forces, "to fight and win our nation's wars," would be jeopardized by U.S. membership in an RRF. Powell in the Pentagon and Lake in the White House emphatically rejected the idea of American participation in an RRF.

The military's anger at the RRF concept was repeated when the idea of an ICC became a serious issue in the early 1990s. The Pentagon was unalterably opposed to any institution that would place the lives and liberty of American men and women in jeopardy because of allegations that they had committed war crimes. This singular view was impressed on Clinton many times before and during the Rome meeting of 161 UN member states to discuss the creation of a permanent ICC.

The president and Secretary of State Madeleine Albright took the high road on the issue, repeatedly speaking positively about the need for such an international criminal law tribunal. He did so in Rwanda, barely four months before the convening of delegates in Rome, Italy. However, the Pentagon hard-liners—who, an observer wrote, "conducted [U.S. foreign policy] with the same brontosaurian finesse in vetoing U.S. accession to the UN convention against landmines"[10]—along with the State Department's delegation to the Rome conference, played hardball before and during the deliberations. The Pentagon never budged from its position, and the delegation in Rome only infrequently moved from predetermined positions on key issues—positions that went against the overwhelming majority of the delegations in Rome.

On March 3, 1997, more than a year before the Rome conference, nine women—all U.S. senators, liberal and conservative, Republican and Democrat[11]—wrote a letter to President Clinton. They welcomed his support for the "establishment of a permanent international institution for the prosecution of those who have committed war crimes. . . . It is critical that the international community take action to assure that war criminals not be allowed to continue to elude justice" with impunity. They implored the president to "aggressively exercise leadership in the international community to ensure that [violators] are brought to justice."

It is not known whether Clinton answered the solons. However, it has become evident that his administration, as well as leading figures in the U.S. Senate (which must give its advice and consent before a treaty becomes law), has come down hard on the ICC as proposed by the UN. A year after the president received the letter from the nine senators, the *New York Times* ran a story that illuminated the Clinton administration's view of the proposed ICC.

The article, "Pentagon Battles Plans for International War Crimes Tribunal," appeared in April 1998, just a few months before the UN-sponsored Rome conference was scheduled to begin. The story noted that "while President Clinton and Secretary of State Madeleine K. Albright have endorsed the idea of an [ICC], they have given their blessing to the Pentagon to become the attack dog in the United States' campaign to create a court more to Washington's liking."[12] The military's greatest fear, if an ICC were created, was "frivolous prosecutions of commanders and ordinary soldiers that are politically motivated by opposition to U.S. military actions."[13]

Military leaders in the Pentagon, as was the case in their opposition to the UN's RRF, were taking aggressive steps, including lobbying U.S. allies and many other nations, to reject the proposed ICC. These "scare campaign" tactics included the following:

- Briefings of over 100 foreign military attachés from embassies in Washington, D.C., about the "potential menace" to their troops posed by the ICC.
- Distribution of a three-page memo stating that "the U.S. is committed to the successful establishment of a court. But we are also intent on avoiding the creation of the wrong kind of court." Further on, the memo warned other nations about the threat posed to their military forces—and to their political and military leaders—by an ICC that gave "independent prosecutors unbridled discretion to start investigations. . . . We strongly recommend that you take an active interest in the negotiations regarding an international criminal court."
- The dispatch of a team of senior Pentagon officers to London, Paris,

Brussels, Rome, and Bonn, "impressing top military brass in each capital with the American arguments."

At about the same time, fifteen prominent lawyers, members of the Lawyers Committee for Human Rights (LCHR), wrote a letter to President Clinton.[14] They urged Clinton "to make certain that the United States leads the way in Rome for an independent ICC." They noted that "with only weeks until the nations of the world gather in Rome, the need for your leadership is more critical than ever."[15] Unfortunately for the LCHR, the president was already committed to a hard line on a score of critical, unresolved issues surrounding the birth of the ICC.

Essentially, the Pentagon's fear was that the ICC, as proposed by the UN drafting commission, could target for war crimes trials U.S. soldiers and their superiors, "particularly when they were acting as peacekeepers." Early on, the president was persuaded by the military that such a state of affairs must be rejected by the American delegation in Rome. Eric Schmitt's *New York Times* article concluded with a warning to the international community:

[T]he Pentagon has a key ally in the Senate, which must approve United States membership in the court. Senator Jesse Helms, the North Carolina Republican who heads the Senate Foreign Relations Committee, vowed last month that any international criminal court would be "dead on arrival" in the Senate unless Washington had veto power over it.[16]

During the Rome deliberations, a team of U.S. Senate Foreign Relations Committee members (the Subcommittee on International Operations) and staffers visited the conference, attending meetings and meeting delegates during their weeklong stay. At the end of their stay, they held a closed-door meeting with the American delegation. Marc Thiessen, a spokesperson for Helms, said that the group still "considers the ICC to be the most dangerous threat to national sovereignty since the League of Nations." American taxpayers, he concluded, "would not want to spend a single dollar for a Court that Washington does not support."[17] The head of the group, U.S. Senator Rod Grams (R-Minn.) told those in attendance that "this court is truly a monster, and it is a monster that must be slain."[18]

The message from the United States before the Rome deliberations even began in June 1998 was clarion: the United States would not support an ICC that could place Americans, civilian and military alike, in legal jeopardy.

The message was like other messages the Clinton administration had sent to the UN since 1993.

Molecular Movement toward Creation of the ICC: 1919–1998

The concept of a permanent ICC emerged in 1919 when the Allies crafted the Versailles Peace Treaty, signed reluctantly by Germany that year. One of the hundreds of articles in the treaty called for the creation of an international criminal tribunal to try Germans accused of committing war crimes in violation of the Hague Treaties of 1899 and 1907.[19] Given the unwillingness of the United States to implement that and other war crimes articles in the treaty (Articles 227–230), as well as the desire of the victorious Allies, "in the interest of regional stability and political agendas,"[20] to forgo its implementation, no international criminal tribunal was created.

These post-1919 events led one scholar to write that they "exemplified the sacrifice of justice on the altars of international and domestic politics of the Allies. . . . [The Allies] missed the opportunity to establish an international system of justice that would have functioned independently of political considerations to ensure uncompromised justice."[21] In 1926, a permanent ICC was again proposed in the League of Nations, but nothing came of it. During the interwar period, 1920–1937, nothing further was proposed by either the Allies or the League of Nations.

The horrors the world glimpsed at the end of the European (1939–1945) and Pacific (1937–1945) wars led the UN to reexamine the possibility of an ICC.[22] After the ad hoc Nuremberg and Tokyo war crimes trials ended, and with the adoption of the Convention on the Prevention and Punishment of the Crime of Genocide in 1948, there was renewed interest in the creation of a permanent ICC with jurisdiction over the actions of individuals that violated the Nuremberg Principles, the Genocide Convention, and the revised 1949 Geneva Protocols on the conduct of war on land and sea.

Article VI of the 1948 Genocide Convention was, in certain respects, a watershed section. It provided that persons charged with genocide "shall be tried by a competent tribunal of the State in the territory of which the act was committed *or by such international penal tribunal as may have jurisdiction.*" This language introduced the world community to the concept of *complementarity* in international law. A national authority has first crack at bringing to justice persons who commit war crimes, genocide, or crimes against humanity. Another consequence of the 1948 convention was the notion that crimes against humanity and genocide were so universally abominable that an offender could be tried in the domestic criminal court of any nation. The brutal actions were considered "crimes of *universal jurisdiction,* meaning that all who commit them can be tried in any court, even if the court has no connection with the crime." Complementarity and universal jurisdiction underscore the precedential point that if "national authorities are 'unwilling or unable' to carry out a genuine investigation and prosecution," then a regional or an international penal tribunal has jurisdiction to investigate and, if appropriate, to prosecute.[23]

The General Assembly, in the 1948 Convention, also invited the creation of a UN committee "to study the desirability and possibility of establishing an international judicial organ for the trial of persons charged with genocide." The UN mandated that the International Law Commission (ILC), a UN General Assembly body created to implement Article XIII of the UN Charter,[24] codify the Nuremberg Principles and prepare a draft statute for the establishment of a permanent ICC. Draft statutes were submitted in 1951 and 1953, but no further action was taken. In 1948, with the onset of the cold war between the United States and its allies and the Soviet Union and its "captive" socialist nations, interest in the creation of an ICC "ebbed because of the fear that a powerful court could be manipulated for political ends."[25]

With the collapse of the Soviet Union's "evil empire" in 1989, along with the "freedom" revolutions that took place across Eastern Europe, the idea of a permanent ICC was renewed. In that year, the Trinidad and Tobago delegate, speaking for a group of sixteen Caribbean and Latin American countries in the General Assembly, called for the establishment of an international court to prosecute international drug traffickers. On November 25, 1992, the General Assembly passed a resolution requesting the ILC to prepare a draft statute for a permanent ICC.

In 1993 and 1994, the UN Security Council created the ad hoc war crimes tribunals for the former Yugoslavia and Rwanda, respectively. Viewing the negatives of these ICTs—the slow start-up, the personnel problems, the management and financial inefficiencies, and the inordinate delays in getting to trial—as well as the positives—the eventual incarceration of some of those indicted, followed by trials and convictions of war criminals and those who committed genocide—many nations insisted that the UN encourage the creation of a permanent ICC.

In November 1994, the ILC presented a draft treaty to the UN General Assembly, and on December 9, 1994, that body created an ad hoc committee to review the seminal issues in the draft treaty. In 1995, the ad hoc committee recommended the establishment of a UN preparatory committee (Prep-Com) that would hold a series of meetings to refine and redraft the ILC proposal.

PrepCom was established and given the task of examining the ILC work, making changes in the draft statute, and recommending further action by the UN on the question of the establishment of a permanent ICC. Its chairperson was Adriaan Bos (Netherlands). All member states of the UN were permitted to send delegates to the PrepCom sessions (as well as members of specialized agencies and members of the International Atomic Energy Agency).

There were six committee sessions between 1996 and early 1998, as well as a drafting committee meeting in the Netherlands in January 1998. To manage the complex issues associated with the establishment of an ICC, the PrepCom was divided into eight smaller working groups, including the Working Group on Definitions and Elements of Crimes, the Working Group on General Principles of International Law, the Working Group on Procedural Matters, the Working Group on International Cooperation and Judicial Assistance, and the Working Group on Penalties.

The first session was held in New York on March 25–April 12, 1996. The agenda focused on the jurisdiction of the ICC, definitions of the core crimes that would fall under its jurisdiction, trigger mechanisms (an extremely contentious issue then and now), and general principles of international criminal law. Alternative drafts of the ICC statute were the outcome of the meeting.

Between August 12 and 30, 1996, PrepCom, meeting again in New York, turned its attention to procedural questions, issues of fair trials and rights of defendants, organizational questions, and the relationship of the proposed ICC to the Security Council and to the UN. In December 1996, the General Assembly scheduled a diplomatic conference on the establishment of a permanent ICC, to be held in 1998. Italy immediately offered to host the meeting in Rome.

The third meeting of PrepCom, February 11–12, 1997, saw the delegates begin redrafting the ILC statute, which would be the basis of deliberations in Rome. They focused on the definitions of core crimes that fell under the new court's jurisdiction (genocide, war crimes, aggression, and crimes against humanity), as well as the general principles of international law and penalties for those found guilty of committing one or more of the core crimes. At this session, no fewer than six draft statutes were reviewed by the delegates.

A fourth meeting of PrepCom, held on August 4–15, 1997, examined the contentious "trigger mechanism," that is, the manner by which ICC proceedings would be initiated, and, equally contentious, the issue of "complementariness," that is, the relationship between the ICC and national jurisdiction. At the fifth meeting, held December 1–12, 1997, PrepCom continued discussions on international cooperation, extradition, and penalties and general principles of international criminal law. The sixth meeting, held in New York City on March 16–April 3, 1998, focused on preparation of the draft statute's text for consideration by the delegates in Rome.

After the sixth meeting, a draft statute was adopted and presented to Kofi Annan, the UN's new secretary-general. The draft statute was 167 pages long, with 13 parts, 116 articles, and 478 bracketed passages indicating words that were disputed by one or more states.[26] It was the foundation for the debates and bargaining at the Diplomatic Conference on the Establishment of an ICC. PrepCom had done a great deal of work since 1996: the ILC draft statute had contained only sixty articles, half the number contained in the final draft.[27]

Participants at the Rome Conference on the Establishment of a Permanent ICC: June–July 1998

Of the 185 member states of the UN, 161 sent represesatives to Rome for the conference, officially called the United Nations Diplomatic Conference of Plenipotentiaries on the Establishment of an International Criminal Court. There were 235 accredited NGOs in attendance at the Rome deliberations that began on June 15, 1998, and ended on July 17, 1998. These NGOs were all under one organizational roof: the Coalition for an Independent Criminal Court (CICC). Workers for the CICC were vital to the final actions of the conferees. The CICC continually lobbied for the strongest, most independent ICC that could be created. Additionally, the CICC served as the circulator of information to the delegates in Rome.

A list of some of the CICC groups illustrates the representational breadth of this important cohort, with its many hundreds of professional and volunteer workers who monitored every committee and subcommittee session during the four and a half weeks of deliberation:

American Bar Association
Amnesty International
Association Internationale de Droit Penal

Baha'i International Community
B'nai B'rith International
Carter Center
Center for the Development of International Law
Coordinating Board of Jewish Organizations
DePaul Institute for Human Rights
European Law Students Association
Equality NOW
FN-Forbundet
Global Policy Forum
Human Rights Watch
Instituto Superiore Internazionale de Scienze Criminali
International Commission of Jurists
International Human Rights Law Group
Lawyers Committee for Human Rights
No Peace without Justice
Parliamentarians for Global Action
Quaker UN Office
Transnational Radical Party
United Nations Association–USA
War and Peace Foundation
World Federalist Movement
World Order Models Project

As one observer in attendance at the Rome deliberations wrote:

> The Coalition . . . monitored all of the working committees of the
> Conference, and provided vital head counts of the countries that had
> declared themselves for or against the many contentious issues facing
> the delegations. Delegations from smaller countries lacked the person-
> nel to keep in touch with the many simultaneous meetings. . . . In the
> end, the CICC also helped to strengthen the resolve of the "like-
> minded" countries to resist the pressure applied by the United
> States.[28]

These NGOs and their staffers were joined by the diplomatic plenipotentiaries from 161 nations. Fifty years after the Nuremberg and Tokyo trials
ended, fifty years after the Genocide Convention and the Universal Declaration of Human Rights were adopted by the UN,[29] the 50th UN General

Assembly placed on its agenda the establishment of a permanent ICC. However, the draft treaty that was the basis of the Rome sessions contained almost 500 disputed options that the delegates had to resolve. Further confounding the dynamics of the Rome conference were the concerns of the United States and other major powers about the emergent ICC. As the London *Economist* editorialized:

> After nearly four years of intense negotiations among some 120 countries, the effort to set up the world criminal court has run smack into the ambivalence that has always been felt by the world's biggest powers about international law: they are keen to have it apply to others in the name of world order, but loath to submit to restrictions on their own sovereignty.[30]

Three Major Unresolved Issues

When the representatives arrived in Rome, there were three major questions left open by PrepCom for the delegates to answer: (1) What would be the relationship of the ICC and the UN Security Council? (2) Was there to be the creation of a truly independent Prosecutor's Office? and (3) What were the core crimes that made up the jurisdiction of the ICC? The "heart of the debate" before and during the Rome conference was "the scope of the UN's Security Council involvement in deciding whether or not the ICC takes up a particular case." Could a permanent member of the Security Council veto the ICC's ability to investigate and to prosecute war criminals?[31]

The PrepCom draft that the representatives brought with them to Rome had hundreds of options available for answering these difficult issues and others. For example, Section 23 (1) of the draft treaty stated that only states party to the treaty and the UN Security Council could refer "situations" to the prosecutor for investigation and prosecution. However, a fundamental option discussed in Rome was whether the Prosecutor's Office could or should institute proceedings on its own authority.

A number of states, especially the United States, fought against that option, fearing an overzealous, politically motivated prosecutor, but to no avail. Many delegations maintained that the draft treaty did have constraints on the prosecutor: impeachment, "complementariness," and Article 23 (3), stating that the Security Council had the power to prescribe the actions of the prosecutor in a situation that was "being handled" by the Security Council.

The "core crimes" jurisdiction of the ICC was generally accepted by the delegates: genocide, crimes against humanity, and substantive war crimes. Jurisdictional options presented in the draft treaty included wars of "aggression," terrorism, and treaty-based crimes.

Opposing the American positions on accountability, prosecutorial independence, and the relationship of the ICC to the Security Council were the great majority of the nations present. In the center of the opposition was a group of forty-two nations (ultimately over eighty nations were in the group) led by Great Britain, Canada, and Argentina, called the "Like-Minded Group."[32] This group of delegates, working with the 264 NGOs and human rights associations that were in Rome to observe and to lobby for a strong ICC, pushed for the selection of options for the final treaty that would create a truly independent ICC, free of Security Council (read U.S.) control.

Elisa Massimino, with LCHR–USA, said of her government's position: "[a veto power in the Security Council] would eviscerate the court's effectiveness." The NGOs and the human rights groups, especially those from the United States, saw Rome "as a classic opportunity for President Clinton to assert what they consider a moral prerogative: to craft a treaty which creates an ICC with enough safeguards to avoid frivolous pursuits, but enough independence to investigate the major powers, if it must."[33]

President Clinton, obviously overwhelmed by the ongoing investigation of his sex life by an aggressive independent prosecutor, and accepting the Pentagon's arguments about the weaknesses of the treaty, did not rise to the occasion.[34]

U.S. Concerns

The problem faced by the national representatives and NGOs at the Rome conference was that the U.S. delegation, as a matter of principle and policy, was unwilling to compromise on its insistence of a veto power for the five permanent members of the Security Council. Since PrepCom began meeting in 1996, the U.S. position had been unvarying: actions of U.S. citizens, especially the U.S. military, "will always remain beyond the conceivable reach of such an [international criminal] court."[35] David Scheffer, head of the U.S. delegation, said, the "Security Council needs to be a very significant player in the operation of this court."[36] The major areas of concern for the Clinton administration were as follows:

1. *How cases come to the ICC.* The U.S. view was that there must be limits on prosecutorial powers. The ICC's ability to hear cases must be determined

by the Security Council, either through referral or though a Security Council veto of proposed ICC action, and by states that refer cases to the ICC.

2. *National court versus ICC action.* The U.S. position on this issue was that "complementariness" must limit the scope of the ICC only to "grave" situations in which a nation's criminal justice system did not, could not, or would not take action against persons within its jurisdiction who were accused of genocide. The ICC could not substitute for a national prosecution of alleged war criminals.

3. *Definition of criminal procedures and guarantees for the protection of sovereign states.*[37] The U.S. position, expressed by its ambassador, was that the rights of governments that refused to cooperate with ICC investigations and trials had to be ensured by the Security Council. From the time deliberations surrounding the creation of an ICC became serious, Washington was and "remains strongly opposed to giving an international prosecutor the right to initiate cases."[38]

The U.S. delegation was also unwilling to compromise on its view that the ICC had substantive limitations on its jurisdiction. The Americans insisted, both before and during the Rome meetings, that the ICC, before it could begin an investigation, must secure the consent of any state that had an "interest" in the case. For one of the American delegates, the U.S. unwillingness to compromise on this issue was America's "nuclear bomb" in the tense negotiations.[39]

This attitude of the Americans was not unusual. From its refusal to join the League of Nations in 1919 to the crises over U.S. membership in the UN (1945) and acceptance of the World Court's jurisdiction, the United States continually opted for the primacy of national sovereignty. It took four decades for the United States to ratify, with substantive reservations, the 1948 Genocide Convention. And just a few years prior to the Rome conference, the United States refused to sign a treaty banning the use of land mines that had been signed by over 100 other nations.[40]

The majority of delegations blocked efforts by the United States, France, and China to delay the creation of the ICC. Further, the majority added language that automatically extended the jurisdiction of the ICC to cover genocide, crimes against humanity, and war crimes. The polar view of the majority in Rome was that the American "position in the ICC negotiations would compromise the court's independence and credibility by politicizing the most crucial decisions—namely, determining which cases the ICC will be able to consider."[41]

The United States was not happy, for example, with the Singapore compromise proposal, proffered before the Rome conference even began. It proposed that the Security Council could opt to take action to delay or forestall ICC investigations and prosecutions. It would take the veto action of one of the five permanent members to halt the ICC's actions—if there was agreement from the other four and a majority vote of the entire Security Council. Prior to Rome, only Great Britain endorsed the proposal. There was also an American unwillingness to compromise on the role of the Prosecutor's Office, which the United States believed should be circumscribed and limited.

U.S. Arguments against Ratification of the Rome Statute

The United States' concerns about the direction the conference was taking were both practical and legal, said Scheffer.

On the practical side, no other nation matches the extent of U.S. overseas military commitments through alliances and special missions such as current peacekeeping commitments in the former Yugoslavia. . . . We don't have the luxury of not considering those factors. [On the legal side], the proposed treaty violates a fundamental principle of international law that a treaty cannot be applied to a state that is not a party to it.

With the withering away of the Soviet Empire in 1989, the United States was the world's only superpower, providing the bulk of finances and military personnel for the various peacekeeping actions of the UN. As Scheffer said in another sharp statement: "We constantly have troops serving abroad on humanitarian missions, rescue operations, or missions to destroy weapons of mass destruction. . . . Someone out there isn't going to like it, but we're the ones who do it. [And U.S. personnel must be protected from the possibility of politically inspired legal actions in the ICC.]"[42]

Because of their presence in Asia, Europe, the Middle East, and the Pacific, American personnel were potentially vulnerable to charges that they had committed grave crimes that fell under the ICC's jurisdiction. The bottom line for the Pentagon and hence for the United States was: "It is in our collective interest that the personnel of our militaries and civilian commands be able to fulfill their many legitimate responsibilities without *unjustified* exposure to criminal legal proceedings."[43]

Scheffer also focused on the principle of national sovereignty, an extremely powerful concept defended by most members of the House of Representatives and the Senate. He said, months before Rome, that "the . . . bedrock of international law [was the] threshold of [national] sovereignty."[46] For the Americans, the commitment to the vitality of national sovereignty, in the face of growing demands for international agencies that preempted national law, had to be firm and unyielding. If not, the United States would confront two choices: remain committed to treaties that involved U.S. forces (thereby subjecting them to the jurisdiction of the ICC), or pull its military troops out of these missions to avoid the possibility of a zealous prosecutor investigating and indicting U.S. military leaders for allegedly committing war crimes.

On June 17, 1998, Ambassador Bill Richardson presented the U.S. policy on the question of nation-state and international law to the assembled delgates and NGOs. It contained basic principles of American policy, as well as using the categorical word "must" six times in the following excerpt regarding the establishment of the ICC. His country's views remained seriously at odds with the views of almost all those in attendance:

> We *must* recognize the reality of the international system today. . . .
> [The ICC] will not act in a political vacuum. Experience teaches us
> that we *must* carefully distinguish between what looks good on paper
> and what works in the real world. . . . The ICC cannot stand alone. . . .
> The U.S. believes that the Security Council *must* play an important
> role in the work of a permanent court. . . . [Furthermore], the ICC
> *must* work in coordination, not in conflict, with states. The Court
> *must* complement national jurisdiction and encourage national state
> action wherever possible. . . . We *must* not turn the ICC—or its Pros-
> ecutor—into a human rights ombudsman, open to, and responsible for
> responding to, any and all complaints from any source. . . . An ICC
> will succeed only if governments draft a treaty that melds effectively
> the proper roles of individual states, their national judicial systems, the
> Security Council, and the UN itself. The U.S., which has been so in-
> strumental in establishing [ad hoc] international tribunals from
> Nuremberg to Arusha, will continue to seek actively the achievement
> of this important objective.

The United States established, in statements such as the above, *de minimus* lines beyond which it would not go. In the end, although there was U.S. agreement on some changes to the language of the ICC treaty, especially the concept of complementarity, the delegation did not go beyond the line drawn by the Pentagon and the president.

Domestic Woes for the President and U.S. Opposition to the ICC

Early in the PrepCom work on the ICC draft statute, on October 31, 1996, U.S. ambassador to the UN Bill Richardson spoke in the General Assembly. In the relatively brief speech, although supporting the concept of a permanent ICC, he warned the UN about his country's serious problems with the proposed ICC. The gravest concerns for the Americans were the "trigger mechanism" issue and the need for "checks and balances with respect to the powers and the decisions of a single Prosecutor."

> There are some who argue that the Security Council will politicize the work of the Court, that it will undermine the Court's independence. [Regarding the perception that] the Security Council is a political body, and its actions are therefore wholly suspect, . . . while individual governments and individual Tribunal staff are objective, non political, and reliable, [that is an incorrect view]. . . . The Security Council transcends the individual political views and agendas of each specific member. It is an institution with checks and balances and an essential, objective mission to fulfill. . . .
>
> There is also a need for checks and balances with respect to the decisions of a single Prosecutor, who in theory also could be influenced by *personal and political considerations.* If the Prosecutor has sole discretion to initiate investigations and file complaints—as some delegations have sought under the rubric of "inherent jurisdiction"—*the results could be more idiosyncratic, possibly even more political, than the decisions of the Security Council* [emphasis added].

Richardson's words about the ICC prosecutor possibly being "influenced by personal and political considerations" went to the heart of one set of American objections to the Rome statute. Michael Sharf's reactions to the ambassador's speech are appropriate: "There's a fear the ICC's prosecutor will become an independent counsel for the universe. The actions of Independent Prosecutor Kennth Starr," he continued, have "fueled anxiety about an ICC prosecutor untrammeled by Security Council oversight."[45] The Clinton administration, in small part, continually pushed for Security Council control of the ICC's Prosecutor's Office because of its real fear of a prosecutor "running wild." This fear of an independent prosecutor intruding into the domestic life of a sovereign nation-state has been expressed throughout the twentieth century. It led the United States to reject the call for an international tribunal to bring the kaiser to justice after the First World War, to defeat President Wilson's efforts to get America to join the League of Nations, and to take four decades to ratify the Genocide Convention. In the Clinton administration, that "evil" person had a face and a name. The Clinton White House had a vision of an international Kenneth Starr.[46]

For the Americans, there was and remains a fundamental unwillingness to surrender national sovereignty to an international prosecutor with the ideological drive and political agenda of a Ken Starr. Therefore, in a basic way the ICC "must" be answerable to the world's major powers, the five permanent members of the Security Council (the United States, Russia, China, France, and Great Britain).

The Americans were accused by the other delegations of erecting a "serious roadblock" to consensus about the ICC. The American view, "that it must be able to veto any effort [by the Prosecutor's Office] to investigate and prosecute,"[47] was pronounced daily at the Rome deliberations, much to the anger and chagrin of a number of its allies as well as third-world delegations. Among the five permanent Security Council members, only Great Britain categorically rejected the American views. President Clinton and his representatives at Rome wanted "to see a court emerge, as long as it was a court they can control," said Richard Dicker, the spokesperson for Human Rights Watch, one of the NGOs present at the deliberations in Rome.[48]

Critics of the U.S. position on the ICC's jurisdiction and independence referred to it as a "neocolonial" policy. The United States was also seen as an uncomfortable member of a very small group of strange bedfellows that included Libya, Iraq, and China. Louise Arbour, the Canadian prosecutor for the Bosnian and Rwandan ICTs, along with the rest of her Canadian cohort, repeatedly called for the creation of an ICC "with considerable independent prosecutorial power. . . . [This independence] was crucial to the success of a permanent tribunal," she said. Furthermore,

> an organization should not be constructed on the assumption that it will be run by incompetent people, acting in bad faith, for improper purposes. It's better to equip the prosecution well but to keep him or her under some kind of institutional leash by some kind of impeachment process.[49]

Lloyd Axworthy, the Canadian foreign minister, admonished the United States about its hard-and-fast position on the relationship between the ICC and the Security Council. He said, "You need to have a court with teeth even if you have to sacrifice some participation."[50]

The Americans professed "dismay" over the extreme idealism of most of the supporters of an ICC that would give substantive powers to the prosecutor and have a broad-based jurisdiction. Said Scheffer, "That's unrealistic: these things (ICC) work when governments such as the U.S. use their clout to make it work."[51]

The Rome Statute Emerges: Specifics

The PrepCom draft statute that the Rome deliberations were based on was 167 pages long; it was divided into 13 parts and contained 116 articles. Only 2 of the 13 part titles (3 and 8) were changed—very slightly—in the final draft of the ICC, approved by 120 nations at the end of the Rome conference in July 1998. The numbering of the articles also changed as a consequence of the deliberations, because articles were added; the final Rome statute contained 128 articles. The section headings for the 13 parts of the PrepCom draft suggest the agenda for those in working in Rome:

Part 1. Establishment of the Court (Articles 1–4), including general observations about its relationship with the UN.

Part 2. Jurisdiction, Admissibility, and Applicable Law (Articles 5–20). This part contained many options for the delegates to discuss and choose among, regarding controversial issues such as the ICC's jurisdiction, core crimes, the trigger mechanism, the role of the prosecutor, complementarity, and the law to be applied by the ICC in deciding cases.

Part 3. General Principles of International Law (Articles 21–34), called *General Principles of Criminal Law* in the final draft. Individual responsibility for genocide and other war crimes, recognized at Nuremberg, was a conceptual anchor in this part of the draft statute. Draft Article 23 (final treaty Article 25) held that such individuals were individually responsible and liable for punishment for their crimes. Article 31 (in both versions) laid out exceptions to individual responsibility: mental illness, intoxication, and threats to one's life.

Part 4. Composition and Administration of the Court (Articles 35–53). This part essentially replicated the composition and administration of the two ad hoc tribunals of the 1990s: Yugoslavia and Rwanda. Articles in this section, borrowing from the two ICTs, discussed the role and functions of the Presidency, the Appeals Chamber, the Office of the Prosecutor, and the Registry and the qualifications of ICC judges.

Part 5. Investigation and Prosecution (Articles 54–61). This section dealt with investigational and prosecutorial aspects of the international criminal justice process, including due process for those suspected of committing genocide and other crimes.

Part 6. The Trial (Articles 62–74). These articles addressed the various aspects of the trial proceedings, including the rights of the accused, the protection of witnesses and victims, and the issue of reparation for victims.

Part 7. Penalties (Articles 75–79). The segment limited punishment to imprisonment. The absence of the death penalty led to heated discussions in Rome.

Part 8. Appeal and Review (Articles 80–84), called *Appeal and Revision* in the final draft. This part addressed issues relating to the appeal and review of judicial decisions.

Part 9. International Cooperation and Judicial Assistance (Articles 85–92).

Part 10. Enforcement (Articles 93–101). States that were party to the treaty had to enforce the judgments of the ICC by providing, at their discretion, prison facilities for convicted defendants.

Part 11. Assembly of States Parties (Article 102) dealt with the oversight of the ICC divisions by states that ratified the Rome treaty.

Part 12. Financing of the Court (Articles 103–107).

Part 13. Final Clauses (Articles 108–116) created parameters for states to file reservations and amendments to the ICC statute, for review of the statute, and for its ratification and entry into force.

The Rome conference began with four days of speech making and public celebrations. The size of the national delegations ranged from one person (Nicaragua) to the fifty delegates representing the host nation, Italy. The five permanent members of the Security Council had large delegations: United States, forty; France, forty; Great Britain, twenty-one; China, fifteen; and Russia, eleven.

Divergent views were expressed by the delegates in the opening speeches, especially "concerning the relationship between the Court and the Security Council and the power of the Prosecutor to initiate investigations."[52] These were huge political decisions that had to be made if there was to be an ICC statute. Their difficulty made the Rome meeting a "lengthy, tense, and divided conference."[53] The delegates began tackling the major unresolved issues, which were intensely political in nature, and the politics of bargaining and compromise took place in the daily informal meetings in Rome.

UN ICC Conference, Rome, Italy. Secretary-General Kofi Annan, 1998. (UN/DPI Photo by G. Diana)

There were, as one onlooker wrote, several levels of work at Rome. There were plenary sessions at the beginning and end of the convention. The Committee of the Whole, chaired by Canadian Phillipe Kirsch, delegated the work of revising the PrepCom draft treaty to eight smaller working groups. Once the deliberations began, given the time line for concluding the treaty drafting process, there were daily, lengthy sessions of the working groups, often as long as fifteen hours.

There were two types of daily meetings, an observer noted. The daily public work sessions consisted of delegates speaking for hours on end on the agenda items for that working group. There was no debate, just speeches translated into a number of languages by UN translators. The second type was referred to as "informals," the daily off-the-record meetings of "serious players" trying to resolve hotly debated differences on specific issues within the domain of that working group. The "real negotiations took place elsewhere, either bilaterally, or in delegations that met together, but outside the format of the Conference itself."[54]

On July 8, Kirsch addressed the group. He presented a set of ten basic questions that had to be answered if there was to be closure. Six of the unresolved issues involved the complex problem of defining the scope of "serious crimes," and the other four focused on the ICC's powers. The two most contentious issues remaining at the Rome conference were the questions of automatic jurisdiciton of the ICC and whether the prosecutor would be an independent officer of the ICC.

The first set of questions dealt with the definition of "aggression," whether "treaty crimes" would be included in the treaty, and whether war crimes and genocide that occurred during internal armed strife fell within the jurisdiction of the statute. The four jurisdictional questions Kirsch raised were: What was the jurisdiction of the ICC? What were the trigger mechanisms (i.e., was there to be automatic jurisdiction)? Should the prosecutor be independent (i.e., with *propio motu* power [power on his own initiative])?[55] What was the role of the Security Council regarding jurisdiction and an independent prosecutor?

The U.S. delegation's response to the working agenda presented by Kirsch was quick and unchanged: the new court must not have automatic jurisdiction over cases involving war crimes and crimes against humanity. Automatic jurisdiction of the ICC should apply only to genocide, the U.S. statement concluded. States must give their consent before the ICC could proceed with an investigation involving other charges. The response on the part of the opposing delegations was to essentially write off the United States as a substantive participant in the negotiations. In exasperation, the associate counsel of Human Rights Watch said to reporters in Rome that "on some key issues of the court's jurisdiction [the U.S.] position is closer to that of Iraq and Pakistan than such close allies as Britain and Canada."[56] Kirsch did not include the U.S. position paper on these issues because it was "so indefensible."[57]

The head of the LCHR, Jelena Pejic, issued a statement maintaining that

> such U.S. inflexibility at this late date sharply increases the chances that the U.S. is simply going to be left behind by this conference. . . . The U.S. approach would create a court that the Pol Pots of the world could laugh at. The U.S. is in effect saying that you should ask Pol Pot's permission before you can bring him before the court. It would gut the court.[58]

Over the next week, these and other controversial questions were hammered out in the "informals." American delegates were in attendance in all of them, and their position was the losing one. In the last two days of the Rome conference, another tough speech by Scheffer and a potent rumor swept across the conference that further eroded the U.S. position on the issues and isolated the U.S. delegation. At a press conference on July 15, 1998, Scheffer said that the world stands "on the eve of the conference's conclusion without having found a solution. We fear that governments *whose nations make up at least two thirds of the world's population* will find the emerging text unacceptable. The world desperately needs this mechanism for international justice, but it must be a community, not a club" (emphasis added). The immediate response of the LCHR was one of "dismay." The head of the LCHR said:

> The U.S. is saying "our way or no way." It is making a thinly veiled threat to get what it wants in the ICC package "or else." We can just imagine what the "or else" might be. . . . President Clinton has not backed up his words [about the necessity of an ICC] with deeds at this conference. This Court is squarely in the U.S. national interest, but President Clinton is pandering to the lobby of fear.[59]

On July 16, 1998, the *International Herald Tribune* carried a story confirming a rumor that had spread like wildfire the previous day. The rumor "at the Conference was that the U.S. was threatening poor nations with a loss of aid and its NATO allies with the reduction of U.S. military support."[60] The *Tribune* story quoted "talking points" prepared for U.S. Secretary of Defense William Cohen, including the following: "If Germany succeeded in lobbying for 'universal jurisdiction' for the court, the U.S. might retaliate by removing its overseas troops, including those in Europe."[61]

The Rome conference required, for passage of the treaty, a two-thirds vote of the 161 delegations. The minimum number required was 107; in the end, 120 voted in favor of the draft treaty. On the final day of the Rome conference, July 17, 1998, the U.S. delegation requested a roll-call vote on the treaty. Three permanent Security Council members, Russia, France, and Great Britain, voted for the statute; the United States and China voted against it. Five other nations also opposed the treaty—Israel,[62] Libya, Iraq, Qatar, and Yemen—"leaving the U.S. in unfamiliar—and no doubt unwelcome—company."[63]

Some saw the U.S. negative vote as a strategic blunder as well. By not signing the Rome statute, "a largely nonbinding gesture," the United States could not participate in the follow-up meetings of PrepCom "in drafting

UN ICC Conference. Rome, Italy, 1998. (UN/DPI Photo by Evan Schneider)

procedural rules, defining elements of crimes, financing arrangements and other matters [including] the preliminary selection of a prosecutor and judges."[64]

The treaty is open for nations to sign until December 31, 2000. It will enter into force when ratified by at least sixty nations. By mid-September 1998, about sixty nations had signed the treaty, including France, Greece, the Netherlands, Spain, and Switzerland. Ratification comes after the initial signing of the document.

The week after the Rome conference ended, Michael Posner, the executive director of LCHR, gave a briefing in the U.S. State Department. He argued that supporting the ICC would lessen the need for U.S. forces to be sent to crises around the globe: "Once established, such a Court will deter gross abuses, such as genocide, that may otherwise require U.S. military involvement." Added Jerry Fowler, the LCHR's legislative counsel: "An effective Court also will deter the commission of war crimes against U.S. military personnel when they are deployed overseas. It will help break the impunity of those who commit genocide, crimes against humanity, and war crimes."[65]

Part 2 of the Rome Statute: Addressing the Major Issues

Part 2 was the centrally important—and very controversial, from the U.S. perspective—"Jurisdiction, Admissibility, and Applicable Law" section of the Rome statute. It contained sixteen articles (5–20), some of which were included after some bitter clashes between the United States and the majority of states participating in the conference.

Article 5 focused on the threshold for ICC jurisdiction: The ICC "shall be limited to the most serious crimes of concern to the international community as a whole (genocide, war crimes, crimes against humanity, and the crime of aggression [when it was defined at a subsequent time, but no sooner than seven years after the Rome statute comes into force])." At least 73 percent of the nations participating in the discussion, sixty-four states, voted for automatic ICC jurisidction for all three core crimes, whereas the United States and twenty others voted for automatic jurisdiction for crimes of genocide only, with an (extremely unlikely) "opt in" by an affected state for the other core crimes.

There was no disagreement on the definition of genocide. Article 6 was taken from the 1948 Genocide Convention. Article 7, "Crimes against Humanity," covered actions committed by either official or nongovernmental actors in either peacetime or time of armed conflict. Further, the article authorized the ICC to prosecute forcible transfers of population, severe deprivation of physical liberty, rape, sexual slavery, enforced prostitution, forced pregnancy, and persecution on political, racial, national, ethnic, cultural, religious, gender, or other grounds that are universally recognized as impermissible under international law. The language used to enumerate these core crimes was, to American delegates and others, too amorphous and general. Many of the criminal acts were ill defined. For example, the statute used such phrases as "mental harm" and "committing outrages on personal dignity."

Article 8 (1), agreed on by 80 percent of the nations voting (thirty-nine), stated that there was ICC jurisdiction "in particular, when" war crimes were committed as part of a plan or conspiracy. The losing position, argued by the United States and eight other nations, was that there should be ICC jurisdiction "only when" war crimes were committed as part of a plan or conspiracy. Article 8 (2) provided the ICC with jurisdiction over war crimes committed in both international and noninternational (internal) armed conflict.

Article 12 (1) provided for automatic jurisdiction by the ICC over all three core crimes. (To obtain French agreement to the Rome statute, a "transitional provision," Article 124, was added. It allowed a nation that was party to the treaty to "opt out" of court jurisdiction for alleged war crimes for a period of seven years following the "entry into force of the Statute for the Party concerned.") However, Article 12 (2) did not provide "universal jurisdiction" to accompany the automatic jurisdiction. Absent a referral by the Security Council, the ICC can take up a case *only* when submitted to it by a state party *or* initiated by the prosecutor when either the state on whose territory the crime was committed or the state of the accused's nationality is a state party or has accepted the ICC's jurisdiction over the crime on an ad hoc basis. (Article 12 [2] is a limitation on the ICC until all states are parties to the statute, thereby making it universal.)

There emerged, as a result, the Article 12 paradox. Even if the United States, for example, did not ratify the Rome statute, its military and civilian forces would be subject to ICC jurisdiction so long as the nation in which the alleged war crimes took place had ratified the statute and could not or would not try the American soldiers charged with war crimes or other crimes of universal jurisdiction. In contrast, the opt-out clause in Article 12 enabled nation-states that had committed war crimes and were party to the Rome statute not to be exposed to ICC jurisdiction, for at least seven years, and possibly for decades.

The controversial issue of whether the Prosecutor's Office had independent power was addressed in Article 15(1) of the Rome treaty. The U.S. position was convincingly rejected by 83 percent of the nations participating. By a vote of sixty-three to thirteen, the delegates adopted language that gave the prosecutor independent power to investigate and to initiate prosecutions. In addition, as noted in Article 13(b) and (c), cases could be referred to the Prosecutor's Office by the Security Council or by a state that was party to the treaty. To dampen concern on the part of some states about the discretionary powers of the prosecutor in initiating investigations, Articles 15(3)(4) and 18 were grafted onto this part of the statute. The former requires the prosecutor to obtain judicial approval by the Chambers at an early stage of the ICC actions. Article 18 enables an "interested party" to challenge the admissibility of a case at an early stage in the ICC proceedings.

The Singapore compromise, allowing the Security Council to defer a case for one year, was included in the final Rome statute as Article 16. It enabled the Security Council, when necessary for "peacekeeping" purposes, to halt ICC actions for one year: "No investigation or prosecution may be commenced or proceeded with under this statute for a period of 12 months after the Security Council, in a resolution adopted under Chapter VII of the Charter of the UN,[66] has requested the Court to that effect; the request may be renewed by the Council under the same conditions." Fifty-three nations opted for the one-year deferral; the United States and four other nations voted for the "unspecified number of years" deferral option.

The ICC: Political Expediency over Justice?

In addition to the Pentagon, foreign policy personnel in the White House, and U.S. senators such as Jesse Helms,[67] there were others who harshly condemned the creation of the permanent ICC as an idealistic, utopian project that had no hope of being actualized in practice. Given the primacy of the nation-state system and the foreign policy agendas of major powers such as the United States, it was nonsense to think about an effective supranational criminal court.

There was "unwarranted enthusiasm for the ICC," wrote critics after the Rome meetings ended in July 1998.[68] The events that had transpired in Rome were an acknowledgment of the reality that the world is "facing moral and political challenges posed by the world of genocide and 'ethnic cleansing' in which we find ourselves." And law, wrote David Rieff, "cannot rescue us from situations from which politics and statecraft have failed to deliver us."[69]

The ICC was too weak—basically without universal jurisdiction, for example—to deal with internal civil wars and the accompanying genocide, but just strong enough to impinge on the sovereignty of individual states. The prosecutor's powers and the ICC's jurisdiction were limited in the treaty: there is no jurisdiction over genocide, crimes against humanity, and war crimes committed in an internal armed conflict by states that have not signed the treaty—unless a Pol Pot–type leader "opts in" to the Rome statute.

At bottom, the critics are pessimistic about human nature: world behavior has not changed since Nuremberg and Tokyo. Nations are lawless and understand only force, not the abstractions of international law. Hubert Vedrine, the French foreign minister, noted that the "world . . . isn't getting any stronger, with 25 regional conflicts involving 40 countries."[70] These wars, the majority of them internal conflicts, continue unabated as the world approaches the millennium, occasionally involving Security Council peacekeeping action in light of Article 24 of the UN Charter.

Criminals, they claim, are not deterred by international laws and customs of war. Armed force, as proposed by General Dallaire in Rwanda in January 1994, not law, can prevent genocide and other crimes against humanity. So long as there is the cruel Hobbesian state of nature, where life is short and brutish, these critics maintain that force is needed and an ICC-type of justice is doomed to failure. "Law proceeds out of civilizational change; it can never prefigure it."[71]

Yale Law School professor Ruth Wedgwood was another critic of an independent ICC. Although "we often set ourselves up as Alamo holdouts,[72] and are criticized as the indispensable country with indefensible positions," the U.S. position on the criticality of Security Council referral (and veto) power to the ICC was the correct stance. To "disregard the Security Council is unrealistic."[73]

UN Secretary-General Kofi Annan had a view light-years distant from that of the critics.[74] In his opening statement to the delegates in Rome, he said:

> There can be no global justice unless the worst of crimes—crimes against humanity—are subject to the law. In this age more than ever we recognize that the crime of genocide against one people truly is an assault on us all—a crime against humanity. The establishment of an ICC will ensure that humanity's response will be swift and will be just.[75]

"Justice" was the central concept for those supporting the creation of the ICC. Without the reality of perpetrators of horrible crimes being indicted, tried, and punished if found guilty—either by a national court of justice or by the ICC if domestic law is not enforced—hatred between groups will fester, and there will be no realistic peace and rapprochement in the community after the fighting ends. Said Sadako Ogata, the UN's High Commissioner for Refugees, "Is it fair and realistic to expect the survivors to forgive and to cooperate if there is not justice? In the absence of justice, private revenge may prevail, which will spread fear and undermine the possibility of reconciliation."[76]

"There is a delicate balance between peace and justice," a study group concluded. "Some degree of justice is increasingly a precondition of peace and reconciliation." If war criminals are immunized from prosecution, as was the case in Cambodia, that inaction "corrodes the fabric of society."[77] Richard Dicker, associate counsel for Human Rights Watch, said that "any notion of international peace and security at the end of the 20th Century that subordinates justice and bringing individuals accused of genocide . . . before the ICC for the sake of a peace agreement, is a violation of the permanent members' fiduciary duties."[78]

ICTY judge Gabrielle Kirk McDonald, one of the judges in the *Tadic* trial at the Hague and presently president of the ICTY Chambers, recently gave a speech to members of the U.S. Judge Advocate General's School in Charlottesville, Virginia. Part of her talk focused on what she called "the cycle of impunity."

The twentieth century is best described as one of split personality: as-piration and actuality. The reality is that this century has been the bloodiest period in history. As improvements in communications and weapons technology have increased, the frequency and barbarity of systematic uses of fundamental rights have likewise escalated, yet little has been done to address such abuses. . . . In the prospect of an ICC lies the promise of universal justice.[79]

"*Impunity,*" she said, "is not a new phenomenon. However, the crystalliza-tion of the cycle of impunity is very much a twentieth century concept: per-petrators of massive human rights violations[80] have often been supported, rather than held accountable, by the international community. . . . With few, but notable exceptions, there has been no reckoning for the great majority of mass violations of human rights throughout this century; perpetrators have ei-ther not been identified, or have not been required to account for their crimes. *The prevalence of such impunity has placed expediency above both principle and pragmatism,*" she concluded. She closed her observations with a somber warning to the audience: "*there will be no lasting peace without justice.*"[81]

The Rome statute's preamble states, in part, that the world community is "conscious" of the "grave crimes" committed in war and in peace, and that it is "determined to put an end to *impunity* for the perpetrators of these crimes." Norman Dorsen, a civil liberties advocate and board member of the LCHR attending the Rome conference, fervently supported the preamble's concepts. He echoed the judge's concern about the evil of impunity for al-leged war criminals: "the ICC treaty is an historic step toward ending im-punity for serious human rights violations."[82]

After fifty years, the global community has finally structured a permanent international criminal court. There was, in the end, a great deal of unanim-ity on the fundamentals of a working ICC: jurisdiction, definition of the major crimes (genocide, crimes against humanity, and war crimes), an inde-pendent Prosecutor's Office to investigate possible "grave violations" of in-ternational law, and the ICC's relationship to the UN Security Council. In the end, only seven nations voted against the Rome statute's adoption.

A review of the activities, the bargaining, and the negotiations involving many of the 160 nations attending the Rome meeting shows a lessened re-liance on the once-steel reality of nationalism and its corollary, realpolitik, national political expediency. Judge McDonald observed that because "the international community has clung passionately, politically, to the immov-able rock of State sovereignty that keeps alive and keeps dominant archaic perceptions of warfare, the pace of the [international] law has been far slower than the pace of the war."[83]

However, at the Rome conference, nations opted to give the notion of international criminal justice some form of operational status. They did so by delegating a very small number of once-sovereign national rights and powers in the area of criminal justice to the new international creation, the ICC. However, given the principle of complementarity in the treaty, the nation-state still has the initial opportunity to try war criminals and others who have committed crimes against humanity or genocide. Only if such action does not take place can the ICC take jurisdiction to investigate and, if appropriate, charge the offender with violations of the human rights conventions.

The United States drew a *de minimus* line on this crucial issue, and in the end, the delegation did not cross it. Instead, isolated and with a small number of unusual "friends," it voted against the ICC and vowed to "actively oppose" its final ratification. This negative foreign policy of the United States (probably shared by most of the Security Council's permanent members), if "actively" implemented, can cause serious problems for the ICC. That tribunal needs international "marshals," i.e., law-enforcement personnel, to enforce its orders.

Persons indicted must be apprehended. Apprehension today is not what it was in Germany and Japan after their "unconditional" surrender in 1945. Fugitives seek refuge in "friendly" states, protected by their own forces and those of the host nation. If they are not tried in a national court for their alleged war crimes, and if they are not captured and brought to the Hague (selected as the permanent site of the ICC) to stand trial for grave war crimes, then the reputation—and power—of the ICC suffers immeasurably, and the alleged war criminals continue to act with impunity.

In the end, the success of the ICC depends on the willingness of powerful nation-states, chief among them the United States, to support and to assist the ICC in these matters. Initially, there must be a commitment in domestic policy and law to act against persons charged with committing these violent, universally condemned, actions. If a nation-state will not or cannot provide a fair trial for the defendant, ICC jurisdiction enables the independent prosecutor to initiate action in the Hague. If it is to succeed, the ICC must reflect a balancing of international idealism with the realpolitik of the nation-state system, epitomized by the United States' "multiple personalities" in the foreign policy arena.

8

FULFILLING THE LEGACY:
PROBLEMS AND PROSPECTS

The paradox of the twentieth century is that although it has been prolific in terms of producing international treaties that define and codify war crimes, crimes against humanity, and genocide, it has evidenced a kind of brutality never before experienced in the violent history of the world. The treaties were efforts to diminish the evils of civil, regional, and world wars. Yet the bestiality evidenced in the wars of the twentieth century absolutely stunned, again and again, the world's conscience. The post–World War II war crimes trials at Nuremberg and Tokyo were an international response to the genocides discovered by the victors.

Does the adoption and certain ratification of the Rome statute of the ICC by at least sixty nation-states by December 31, 2000, close the circle that began with the creation of the Nuremberg IMT? Without major power support, the question is whether it will be an *effective* international criminal tribunal. And an answer will be forthcoming the next time a Hitler or a Karadzic or a Milosevic or a Pol Pot emerges from the depths and seizes power.

Is the unfinished legacy of the World War II trials of Nazi Germany's and Japan's major war criminals finally finished? After the war ended in 1945, the victorious Allies vowed that the unimaginable atrocities committed by the Nazis and the Japanese would never occur again. "Even in war, there are limits as to what governments may use as means of killing and what they may do even to their own citizens."[1]

Individual responsibility for planning and implementing "final solutions" for Jews, Gypsies, Russians, Chinese, and other targeted "demonized" groups was acknowledged in international law in 1945. Generals, admirals, and government leaders were brought to the dock of justice to face allegations that they were involved in unhuman and criminal actions. The concepts of "sovereign immunity," "military necessity," and "following a superior's

217

orders" were of little help to the defendants in the post–World War II trials. Tyranny and savage behavior were on trial, and they lost. In the end, the individual was held responsible in international law for his actions against others, either in peacetime or during war.

Two Obstacles to an Effective ICC

The hope after Nuremberg and Tokyo was that the international criminal laws that emerged from the ashes of the killing centers would become effective deterrents against any new Hitlers that might emerge. The unfulfilled hope, after these trials, was that there would be a permanent court and an independent prosecutor that would effectively act against the world's new tyrants, apprehending, trying, and punishing them in a permanent ICC.

The world is on the verge of seeing such a permanent ICC become a reality. However, its success is problematic for two basic reasons. One of the essential questions is whether it will ever get off the ground, given the opposition by the United States (and other major world powers). Can the ICC be an effective deterrent without the most powerful nation in the world prepared to use its influence and its military power to ensure the court's success? An ICC *must* be supported—at least financially and militarily—by the major powers sitting on the Security Council. (As seen with the ICTY and the ICTR, finding the human resources to staff and support the prosecutor's office and the court bureaucracy is going to be an immense problem, and it will be almost impossible if funding from the major powers is not forthcoming.)

The second question begging for an answer is, What can an international criminal tribunal possibly do to lessen the wanton, unbelievable cruelty the world's population has seen inflicted on tens of millions of civilians in the twentieth century? Can the ICC punish those who commit such horrendous crimes, and will its actions deter future genocides?

Explaining the Cruelty

Scholars, political leaders, military leaders, ethicists, and religious leaders, among others, have struggled to explain the cruelty exhibited by one group against another group: the Hutu genocide of Tutsi, the Khmer Rouge annihilation of the Buddhists, the genocide committed by Bosnian Serbs against their erstwile friends and neighbors the Bosnian Muslims, the Nazi slaughter of Jews, and so on. Since Nuremberg and Tokyo, there have been at least fifteen major genocides:

USSR, 1943–1947 (ethnic minorities)

China, 1950–1951 (landlords)

Tibet, 1951– (Buddhists)

Sudan, 1955–1972 (nationalists)

Indonesia, 1965–1966 (Communists)

China, 1966–1975 (Cultural Revolution victims)

Uganda, 1971–1979 (opponents of Idi Amin)

Pakistan, 1971 (Bengali nationalists)

Cambodia, 1975–1979 ("new people" and ethnic and religious minorities)

Afghanistan, 1978–1989 (political opponents)

Sudan, 1983–1998 (nationalists)

Iraq, 1984–1991 (Kurds)

Yugoslavia, 1991–1995 (Bosnian Muslims and Croats); 1998– (Kosovars)

Burundi, 1993–1998 (Tutsi)

Rwanda, 1994 (Tutsi)

Approximately 15 million persons, mostly civilian, were massacred during these incidents.[2] Chile, under military dictator Pinochet (1973–1990), was another nation where thousands of persons, including Spanish and French citizens residing in Chile, "disappeared," never to be seen alive again. Such disappearances also happened in Argentina and in Guatemala, where indigenous villages were destroyed with the accompanying murders of over 200,000 innocent Guatemalan men, women, and children.

As contemporary essayist Lance Morrow wrote recently:

> The genocidal impulses that led the Hutu to slaughter one million Tutsi in 1994 are identical to the tribal bloodlusts at work in the Balkans. Eerily the same: the neighbors who suddenly turn a killing fury upon neighbors, the roving bands fueled round the clock on alcohol, the strange, dull light in the murderers' eyes, the sudden civic duty to exterminate the Other.[3]

How could "ordinary men,"[4] persons who had lived with and alongside those they massacred, commit such unimaginable crimes? How could they, using the euphemisms of genocide, "clear the brush," engage in "ethnic cleansing," engage in "collective work," or implement the "final solution"?

How could they come to believe and then to say to their enemy, before killing her, that she was:

to be murdered because "to allow you to live is no benefit, to destroy you is no loss" (Cambodia)

an "undesirable parasite" (Bosnia)

a rodent, or vermin, or a disease carrier (all)

"less valuable than a pig, because a pig is edible" (Japan)

"a sleazy cockroach" (Rwanda–Hutu Power)

"unworthy of life" (Nazi Germany)

"dog food" (Turkey)

wearing glasses (Cambodia)

"less than nothing" (Nazi Germany)

the people's "vampire" (Nazi Germany)

a creature not of this world, with horns and tails (Rwanda–Hutu Power)

subhuman, and her murder "would create no greater moral weight than squashing a bug or butchering a hog" (Japan)

The answer to why ordinary men kill innocent civilians so barbarically is a multifaceted one. Genocide is, in part, one's response to the brutalization of war, or deference to authority, or obedience to orders, or just plain racism. For Christopher Browning, two factors stand apart from the rest: ideological indoctrination and propaganda, and the concept of "distancing," a corollary of the first.

Indoctrination of the ordinary men and women who committed the crimes against humanity began before the genocide began, whether in Nazi Germany, Japan, Cambodia, Bosnia, or Rwanda. In all these genocidal societies, there were training programs to imbue the cadres and the ordinary people with racist hatred of the Jew or the Chinese, of the bourgeoisie in Cambodia or the Muslims and Croats in Bosnia, of the Tutsi in Rwanda. And ordinary men, for the most part, went along with the racist propaganda because they needed to conform to the norms of the group (of killers) and of the state.

The second factor that explains the killing fields since 1915 is the dehumanization, the demonization, of selected groups—political, religious, ethnic—that the regime wanted to disappear from the face of the earth. In a perversion of Aristotle's "equals treated equally; unequals treated un- equally," the racial ideology of the regime, presented to ordinary men in the press, in posters, on the radio, and in film and plays, created a demon— without any human characteristics—in the minds of the loyal, conforming citizens. (With all this, however, alcohol was used "to break down the nor- mal inhibitions of [some of] the young men [Germans, Bosnian Serbs, Khmer Rouge, and *interahamwe*]" who were given the final task: killing the victims.[5])

John Dower wrote that the "dehumanization of the Other contributed immeasurably to the psychological distancing that facilitated killing."[6] This dehumanization "was achieved through a variety of methods."

> Captives would be held for months in extremely cramped quarters, without toilets or sanitary facilities. Women spoke of the shame of being forced to wear clothes stained with menstrual blood. Weeks of starvation, diet, lack of water, and lack of hygiene would turn captives into filthy, emaciated shadows of the persons they had once been.[7]

Browning also maintains, after studying a group of over 100 middle-aged men from Hanover, Germany, who were used by the Nazis to kill Jews rounded up in Poland, that the "distancing [factor] is one of the keys to ex- plaining why ordinary men kill."[8]

When an enemy is successfully denied humanity (through the propaganda and indoctrination of the ordinary men and women of the regime), he be- comes what the labels say he is: less than human. When members of the tar- geted group are called *untermenschen* or cockroach again and again, ordinary men eventually come to regard them as worthless. Recall the Khmer Rouge soldier who told a few professionals that "to save you is no benefit, to kill you is no loss to Angkar."

For most of these soldiers and killing units, there was no problem in doing away with, murdering, these innocent people. Jews, Buddhist monks, and Tutsi were not the equal of Hitler's SS, the Khmer Rouge, or the Hutu killing units. Noted historian Raul Hilberg observed that the Nazi destruc- tion of Jews was based on three premises: (1) no Jew was overlooked in the effort to destroy the whole cohort, (2) "the complex relationship between Jews and non-Jews was to be severed with least harm to individual Germans and to the economy as a whole," and (3) "the killings had to be conducted in a manner that would limit psychological repercussions in the ranks of the perpetrators, prevent unrest among the victims, and preclude anxiety or protest in the non-Jewish population."[9] This pattern of behavior was seen in Bosnia, Rwanda, and Cambodia and in the Kosovo madness.

In all these genocides, there was the specter of "unrepentant participation" by the overwhelming majority of ordinary men and women.[10] In light of this reality, what can international law do to minimize such behavior on the part of the leaders as well as the rank-and-file killers of innocent civilians who have been demonized, dehumanized, and damned with the label "the Other"? Can anything be done by international organizations such as the ICC to address this problem, thereby deterring future genocides? This question is almost impossible to answer. The answer, ultimately, rests with society's leaders.

A Comparison: Nuremberg and the ICC

What do the Nuremberg IMT and the ICC have in common? Did the Nuremberg trial address the demonization issue? Will the ICC be able to apprehend, arrest, try, and convict those who have committed genocide?

First of all, the ICC is a permanent criminal court, with jurisdiction to hear cases involving grievous acts including war crimes, crimes against humanity, genocide, and carrying on an aggressive war. The Nuremberg IMT was an ad hoc tribunal and ceased to exist after the judgment and verdicts were read in 1946. Also, the ICC's Chamber will consist of judges elected by all the member nations in the UN General Assembly that have ratified the Rome statute. The Nuremberg tribunal consisted of judges from the four victorious Allies.

For some, such as John R. Bolton, former assistant secretary of state for international organizational affairs, there is no analogy. Nuremberg was a "victors' tribunal," where the probable defendants were in custody and the "whole of the German archives was available and was seized by the victorious allies upon the total surrender of the Nazis and Japanese." Alfred P. Rubin, international law professor at the Fletcher School of Law and Diplomacy at Tufts University, supports Bolton's contentions.[11]

Furthermore, the defeated Axis powers were occupied by the victorious armies of the United Nations. Thousands of Nazis (and Japanese) leaders and followers who were alleged to have committed war crimes and crimes against humanity were apprehended and brought to trial before Allied judges—French, British, Russian, and American jurists assigned to preside over these lesser-known trials that took place in the four occupied zones of Berlin and in Allied courts in the Pacific Rim. The major war criminals were sent to Nuremberg to stand trial for their war crimes.

In both the Nuremberg and the Tokyo war crimes tribunals, there was clear evidence of the bureaucratization of genocide. In Cambodia, Bosnia, and Rwanda, there was a decision-making entity, called Angkar or Hutu Power or Milosevic, that issued general orders to kill the enemy and gave the killers free rein regarding the manner of massacre. Most of the killers lived next to or knew the innocents they killed. It was common to hear horrible tales from survivors of the mass killings; for example, that two of the many men who had raped a victim were her high school teachers.[12] However, although friends and neighbors of the victims did much of the killing, there was also the presence of a bureaucracy that informed and directed the killers. Wole Soyinka recalled one such example of bureaucratic genocide in Rwanda:

[A Hutu *bourgmestre*] felt personally indicted after a visit from a Government official, who accused the citizenry of being lax in the task of "bush clearing"—one of the many euphemisms for the task of eliminating the Tutsi. A day after the official departed, the [mayor], whose wife was a Tutsi, called a meeting of the villagers for some soul-searching. He took his four sons with him. He began his address by revealing that, having taken to heart the rebuke from their visitor, he had decided to set an example, and thus slaughtered his Tutsi wife before leaving home. But that was only the first step, he said. It was not enough to kill all Tutsi, they must eliminate every vestige of Tutsi blood that contaminated the purity of the breed. . . . And with one stroke of his machete, he lopped off the head of his eldest son. One by one, three other sons were led out of the hut in which he kept them, and slaughtered. And with that, another village that, until then, had withstood the hate rhetoric of the *interahamwe* dived headfirst into the sump of bloodletting.[13]

The ICTY and the ICTR, unlike the Nuremberg and Tokyo trials, were the right deeds done for the wrong reason, according to Aryeh Neier. As pointed out earlier, these tribunals were created as "substitutes for effective action [by the UN and the major powers] to halt Serb [and Hutu] depredations in BiH [and Rwanda]."[14] The major powers, especially the United States, shamefully evaded action to prevent and then to end the genocides in Bosnia and Rwanda. "Madeleine Albright, who was Clinton's ambassador to the UN, temporized as the death toll in Rwanda climbed into the hundreds of thousands. It was 'the absolute low point of her career as a statesperson.'"[15] Even after the Dayton Peace Accord was signed, albeit reluctantly by the Bosnian

Serbs, the NATO powers and the UN put the minimum number of troops into the region and developed operational plans that avoided potential hot spots where fighting could take place between IFOR soldiers and Bosnian Serb fighters.

In Yugoslavia, where 60,000 NATO and UN troops have been patrolling BiH since 1996, Karadzic and Mladic, the two major leaders of the Bosnian Serbs, are still fugitives from the ICTY. (General Mladic retired comfortably in Belgrade, Serbia, on his army pension; Karadzic is somewhere in Republika Srpska, moving regularly to avoid capture by NATO forces patrolling BiH.) There has been little effort to apprehend such fugitives because of fears of bloodshed.

In Rwanda, many of the Hutu military leaders have found safe haven in bordering nation-states. From these locations, they have led military raids into Rwanda, killing tens of thousands of Tutsi and moderate Hutu.

This suggests another basic difference between the 1945 and the 1998 tribunals: in 1945, the defendants were in custody; today, there is no mechanism for searching for and seizing persons who have been indicted. If a nation's military plays the role of bounty hunter, the fear is that there will be military attacks on the troops trying to apprehend those indicted by the ICC.

The Justice of the Matter

Justice for victims of genocide and other war crimes is achieved when the alleged war criminal is in the dock or, preferably, dead. Can there be a stable peace in Rwanda, Bosnia, Cambodia, and other countries that have experienced genocide and crimes against humanity if the perpetrators do not stand trial? Can there be peace without that type of justice?

There is a delicate balance that must be struck between peace and justice. Clearly, in world politics, as seen most recently in the 1995 Dayton Peace Accord, realpolitik dictates that peace is, on balance, more valuable than providing justice for the victims of war crimes and genocide. At Dayton, the idea of using IFOR troops to hunt for defendants, arrest them, and transport them to the Hague for trial was rejected. At Dayton, Slobodan Milosevic, the major architect of the "ethnic cleansing" program, as well as the supplier of arms and equipment to the Bosnian Serbs, sat around the conference table with other national leaders.

There are others who argue that providing justice will ease the way to peace in a nation devastated by war. Trying war criminals furthers the goal of justice in three ways. In a trial before an ICC:

1. There is the assignment of specific, individual guilt, thereby avoiding collective guilt.
2. There is the acknowledgment of the victims of the genocide.
3. There is established "an accurate historical record of the nature of and responsibility for the crimes committed."[16]

For many, the last justification is the most important one. Roger Rosenblatt wrote that the struggle of men against power is the struggle of memory over forgetting. If there are no ICC trials of alleged war criminals, there will be no accurate memory. Without the thousands of pages of documents and tribunal judgments, the victims' suffering and the horrid deeds of the killers will in part rest in the hands of the "revisionists," persons who say that the Jewish Holocaust never occurred. And the perpetrators will have accomplished one of their goals: to erase all memory of the victims.

There is also an urgent need for justice for the hundreds of thousands of civilians in Cambodia, BiH, Rwanda, and Kosovo who have become reluctant displaced persons. For many, the most urgent agenda for the UN and the NATO powers is the return home "of refugees and getting international assistance to them."[17] Although NGOs have been involved in the humanitarian effort to care for the survivors of war crimes and genocide, principally the ICRC, and emergency aid has been sent to these regions by the major powers, the people of Bosnia and Kosovo need massive aid.

The More Things Change, the More They Remain the Same

Since Secretary of State Robert Lansing objected to the creation of a permanent international criminal court to try the kaiser and other German military and civilian leaders for war crimes at Versailles in 1919, U.S. policy has remained the same. The U.S. government has objected to and voted against any international organization that would weaken the concept of sovereign immunity. Examination of Ambassador Bill Richardson's speeches, or the comments of David Scheffer, head of the U.S. delegation to the Rome conference, places the observer in a time warp back to 1919.

For the Americans and others at Versailles and at Rome, the twentieth century was a century of nation-state dominance. There would never be acceptance of an international treaty that threatened American citizens, especially U.S. military forces. From the record at Rome and a number of speeches given by American policy makers and military leaders afterward, as well as the loud outbursts of defiance from Senator Jesse Helms, it seems that either the Rome statute must be amended or the United States must eventually sign the protocol, with its reservations noted as a matter of international law.

The ICC and Human Nature

A parable in the Midrash is illustrative:[18] Rabbi Shimon said that when God was creating man—when God was about to create Adam—the ministering angels split into two camps. One camp said, "'Yes, let Adam be created!" and the other said, "Let Adam not be created!" Lovingkindness said, "Let Adam be created, for human beings do acts of lovingkindness." Truth said: "Do not create human beings, for they will be false." Righteousness said: "Let human beings be created, for they will do righteous deeds." Peace said, "Do not create human beings, for they will never cease quarreling."[19] The next sentence in the Midrash is in dispute. It read: "Chesed Va Amech Nifgawsu Zedek V'Shalom Nasawku." One psalmist interpreted it to mean: "Lovingkindness and truth have *collided,* righteousness and peace *engaged in a clash*" (Psalm 85:11). However, a more common understanding of Psalm 85:11 is put forward by the rabbis and has a very different message: "Lovingkindness and truth *meet,* righteousness and peace *kiss.*" Which is the correct interpretation? It depends on one's view of human nature.

This choice is seen as well in the actions surrounding the creation of a permanent ICC. Can belligerents be constrained by the rule of law in their actions on the battlefield and toward civilians in occupied territory? If not, then the presence of an ICC is necessary to deny impunity to the killers. Is human nature affected by international conventions such as the Nuremberg Principles and the Genocide Convention? Will these international laws serve as deterrents to the commission of war crimes and genocide in the future? Or are they, as Hermann Göring cynically said, "mere toilet paper"?

In the movement toward a permanent ICC that began eight decades ago, there are also two opposing camps. Both base their comments about the effectiveness of an ICC on different views of human nature. One group, the realist school of foreign policy, denies the efficacy of international law and, by implication, places limits on the effectiveness of both domestic and international law. Thise argument is premised on a negative, base view of human nature. Adherents argue, like Truth and Peace argued before God, that human beings are false, ever quarreling, and warlike and readily use force and extreme cruelty against their enemies to achieve domestic and foreign policy goals. International legal restraints on their behavior hardly matter; the only restraint that is effective in deterring genocidal behavior is the use of force against them. And the only effective military force, at the end of the twentieth century, is the armed might of a small number of powerful nation-states.

If international systems are anarchic, if nation-states are the primary actors on the international stage, then the "functions of international organizations are primarily and disproportionately determined by the organization's dominant power(s)."[20] Looking at the recent genocides in Cambodia, Bosnia, and Rwanda, it was clear that the "[national] politics of opportunism that forever seeks scapegoats provided the motor for the murderous ideology of 'ethnic cleansing,' of 'Hutu Power,' that translated into—no other expression—the Final Solution."[21] And the only actors on the international stage who could have prevented the genocides, or at least minimized the number of victims, were nation-states such as the United States. But they chose not to respond to the very visible genocides, for fear of becoming entangled in military clashes that would inevitably involve the deaths of their young soldiers.

Critics of the ICC created in Rome in July 1998, including members of the Clinton administration, have proffered this realistic (read cynical) view of human nature. The Security Council, argued the U.S. delegates, must play a substantive role in the activities of a succcessful ICC because it has the ability to use force to buttress ICC opinions. This position also gives the five permanent members of the Security Council a veto power over possible ICC actions.

Without such involvement by the major world powers, the ICC would be impotent. To alienate a world power such as the United States at the Rome conference was to possibly minimize its role as military enforcer of ICC orders and judgments. And without the use of force by the UN in its peacekeeping operations, there is no peace.

Furthermore, the realists claim that law has little or no impact on human behavior. As President Dwight D. Eisenhower cynically said at a press conference after the U.S. Supreme Court handed down its watershed race relations opinion, *Brown v. Board of Education of Topeka, Kansas*, in May 1954: No opinion of the Court standing alone can change the beliefs and attitudes of the publics who believe in the correctness of racial inequality. (In 1957, Eisenhower was forced to use military troops to enforce a federal court order that called for the racial integration of Little Rock's Central High School.)

The other camp has a less pessimistic view of human nature. Like Lovingkindness and Righteousness, they maintain that law can have an impact on humans because they are capable of doing righteous deeds and will do acts of loving-kindness for other less fortunate human beings. In their view, law is a "lodestar," a target that fallible human beings hope to reach someday. Brightly lighting up the sky and showing humans the proper direction for both individual and community actions, this notion of law implies that human nature can be positively impacted by treaties and their messages about the limits of human behavior. Unlike the realists, they see nation-states sharing common interests, such as punishing those who commit genocide, that are advanced through the creation of international organizations such as the ICC.[22]

Adherents of this view believe that national leaders are capable of giving up some sovereignty to the ICC; they see human nature as being more than Hobbesian. They are willing to surrender some national sovereignty because they believe that the rule of law can modify, or at the very least restrain, unwarranted and unwanted human behavior in the relations between nations and between groups within a nation.

These supporters of the independent ICC, nations such as Canada, Italy, Costa Rica, Sweden, and Norway, believe that the awesome terrors of genocide, crimes against humanity, and egregious war crimes are crimes of universal jurisdiction. They have had an effect on human societies, and the time has come for such an ICC. In their view, shared by the author, there is a civilized universal conscience, referred to in the Martens clause of 1907. When touched by injustice, human beings support international acts against the perpetrators of atrocities that defy comprehension.

Balancing Realpolitik with the Need for Justice

Some observers sadly note that realpolitik "most likely will prevent the ICC from being a truly effective organ of justice."[23] A noted liberal advocate, Aryeh Neier, wrote that "the heart says civilized men and women with respect for the rule of law cannot permit these kinds of [war] crimes to happen again. The mind, sadly, sends a different kind of message."[24]

At some point, however, and the 1998 Rome convention is such a watershed, the world community has to say, enough killing! Even if it means the possible surrender of some national sovereignty, the killing has to stop. Sooner rather than later, nation-states must accept the concept of national submission (with adequate protections) to international authority with respect to jurisdiction over war crimes, crimes against humanity, and genocide.

The language of the Martens clause in the 1907 Hague Convention is appropriate: those who violate "the rule of law as used among civilized peoples, [or who violate] laws of humanity and the dictates of the public conscience," must be punished, *even though the specific criminal action is not enumerated in the treaty.* As Jackson said at Nuremberg in 1945: "Murder, torture, and enslavement are crimes recognized by all [civilized] human beings." They must be punished lest other genocidal leaders think that they have impunity for their evil plans, orders, and acts. Clearly, the humanity of the issue must be addressed by the opponents of the ICC. There is, I believe, an international civilized conscience that categorically rejects the continuation of genocidal warfare and that demands that the international community take substantive steps—quickly, without debates and filibusters in the Security Council—to end the horrible consequences of such crimes.

The world community must deny the perpetrators of genocide, war crimes, and crimes against humanity safe haven and impunity from punishment. The peoples of the world are ahead of their political leaders on this matter. Without the interference of realpolitik, they understand that those men and women who commit grave, grievous crimes against others, especially women, children, and the elderly, must be punished.

There must be a balancing of the two contending concepts—realpolitik and the need to provide justice for the victims of genocide and a complete trial record for posterity. If there is no resolution of the dynamic tension between them, the world community will enter the twenty-first century without a legal mechanism to punish such criminals. If that is the case, one must note the lack of moral commitment to the concepts of equity and justice for men and women.

As an idealist without illusions, I believe that the United States will sooner rather than forty years later support the ICC, either individually or through its participation in NATO. There are enough checks in place in the Rome statute to convince reasonable Americans that a runaway special prosecutor would be controlled or removed by the ICC Chambers. With a growing trust in the integrity of the ICC, especially its independent prosecutor, there will come a greater willingness to accept the organizational and jurisdictional structure and work to change it, if necessary, once the statute is ratified. If the powerful nation-states do not support the ICC, there will be no data on whether it is a successful deterrent to crime. Risky though it may be for America's public policy makers and military leaders to overcome their fears about the loss of sovereignty, it is a risk that must be taken.

President Bill Clinton was publicly chastised at the Washington, D.C., ceremony opening the United States Holocaust Museum on April 22, 1993, by the dedication speaker, Nazi Holocaust survivor and author Elie Wiesel, for not acting against the genocide taking place in Bosnia-Herzegovina. Turning to the president, Wiesel, who had recently returned from a visit to a Serb prison camp, said:

> Mr. President, I cannot not tell you something. I have been in the former Yugoslavia last fall. I cannot sleep since for what I have seen. As a Jew I am saying that we must do something to stop the bloodshed in that country. People fight each other and children die. Why? Something, anything must be done![25]

There was thunderous silence: Clinton did not respond to Wiesel. However, there must be more than silence in the face of war crimes, torture, crimes against humanity, and genocide. The world cannot tolerate these heinous crimes going unpunished, with the butchers of innocents given impunity by the silence of the powerful nations. The international community must move beyond silence to action.

Pinochet's Arrest: The Beginning of Justice without Borders?

In October 1998, the concept of sovereign immunity was exhumed in a strange case involving eighty-three-year-old General Augusto Pinochet, Chile's military dictator from 1973 to 1990. For seventeen years, Chile was controlled by an "iron-fisted, right-wing military [clique]" led by Pinochet. His dictatorship "was blamed for the death or disappearance of 3,400 suspected communists and leftists, not to mention the torture of thousands of others."[26] When he arrived in London, the governments of Spain, France, Switzerland, and Belgium asked England to extradite him.

In a London hospital for surgery on a herniated disc, the former dictator and, after 1990, Chilean senator-for-life was arrested on October 16, 1998, by the British police. A Spanish judge had requested Pinochet's extradition to Spain to face trial for violating human rights. (The Spanish request was the first of four extradition requests received by the British courts.) Judge Baltasar Garzon,[27] citing no fewer than nine human rights conventions, charged Pinochet with torture, genocide, and terrorism against ninety-four Spanish citizens and thousands of other persons. The charges were filed on behalf of Spanish citizens living in Chile during Pinochet's rule who disappeared and are presumed to be among the almost 4,000 persons liquidated by Pinochet's military minions.[28]

The major argument advanced on behalf of the former dictator, ignoring the precedents in international law created since Nuremberg, was sovereign immunity. His lawyer argued that Pinochet, as a former head of state, has total immunity for any actions taken while in office. The British advocate for the Spanish judge countered by stating that Pinochet had practiced a form of genocide: he had set out "to destroy a national group—Chilean nationals who did not share his ideological values."[29]

The case went to the High Court of Justice, which ruled on October 28, 1998, that Pinochet was immune from such actions. "The applicant is entitled to immunity as a former sovereign from criminal and civil process in the English courts." English law, the judges concluded, "grants immunity . . . to heads of state who committed crimes 'in the course of exercising public functions.' "[30]

This judgment was immediately appealed to England's highest court, the Law Lords, a five-judge panel of the House of Lords. On November 25, 1998, that court rejected Pinochet's claim of sovereign immunity by a vote of three to two and "committed him to remain in custody [in England] while Spain seeks his extradition on charges of mass murder and terrorism."[31] The dissenters maintained that

> in [their] opinion, the respondent was entitled to claim immunity as a former head of state from arrest and extradition proceedings in the United Kingdom in respect of official acts committed by him whilst he was Head of State.

The majority concluded that "universal" crimes against humanity and genocide are not protected by the concept of sovereign immunity:

> International law has made plain that certain types of conduct . . . are not acceptable conduct on the part of anyone. This applies as much to heads of state, or even more so, as it does to everyone else. The contrary conclusion would make a mockery of international law. . . . Acts of torture and hostage taking, outlawed as they are by international law, cannot be attributed to the state to the exclusion of personal liability. It is not consistent with the existence of these crimes that former officials, however senior, should be immune from prosecution outside their own jurisdictions.

The judges clearly established a watershed precedent in international criminal law. Sovereign immunity does not extend to actions taken by a leader that are violations of legal and ethical principles of "universal justice" that have been drafted and confirmed by the world's civilized societies since 1899.

The practical legal issue then shifted to the Labour government's home secretary, Jack Straw, Britain's law-enforcement minister, acting in his "quasi-judicial" capacity.[32] By December 11, 1998 (he received an additional nine days to prepare his response), in a hearing conducted by Chief Magistrate Graham Parkinson and with General Pinochet present in the courtroom, Straw had to decide whether, on compassionate grounds, Pinochet could return to Chile or whether the Spanish government's petition for extradition should go forward. Immediately, Straw was besieged by important political friends and foes of Pinochet attempting to influence his judgment. He refused to meet with the Chilean ambassador and other political types and would only read "written briefs from advocates on both sides."[33]

On December 9, 1998, Straw turned down Pinochet's request to be freed and return to Chile. Straw ruled that the Spanish extradition case against Pinochet could go forward in British courts. The military dictator was not entitled to the protections offered by sovereign immunity because the alleged crimes he had committed were crimes of universal jurisdiction. The British government, he noted in his short order, had "obligations under the European Convention on Extradition to extradite Senator Pinochet to Spain" that outweighed Pinochet's arguments.

The legal implications of the Pinochet case on international criminal law are breathtaking. *El Mundo,* a Spanish news daily, editorialized about the Law Lords' judgment: "It is a decision without precedent. The basis is beginning to be set for what can and should be justice without borders."[34]

Another observer wrote that "the legal precedent thus established must send cold shivers down the spines of other dictators and torturers—retired or still up to their elbows in blood—and should, at the very least, discourage them from certain forms of indulgent tourism, like General Pinochet's shopping trips to Burberrys and teas with Baroness Thatcher in London."[35]

In a final judgment, the Law Lords, England's highest court, on March 24, 1999, ruled that Pinochet had to remain in British custody to face possible extradition to Spain. In the 6:1 decision, however, the court concluded that Pinochet could not be extradited for alleged crimes committed prior to 1988 (the year Great Britain, in the Criminal Justice Act, made torture committed in another nation a crime punishable in Britain). As most of his alleged tortures and execution of political opponents occurred prior to 1988, the Law Lords suggested that Home Secretary Jack Straw consider whether he wanted to go forward with the extradition. Critically important was the legal position of the Law Lords on the matter of impunity and sovereign immunity for alleged war criminals: the "head of state immunity" argument was rejected by six of the seven judges. It does not immunize leaders such as Pinochet, who allegedly commit war crimes and other crimes against humanity from facing their accusers in a court of law—either domestic or international.

The "universal jurisdiction" crimes such as torture, genocide, and crimes against humanity, the judges said, "do not qualify as legitimate acts of a head of state" and subject the defendant to jeopardy in a criminal justice action in either a domestic court or the ICC. Although there are many, including the U.S. military and political leadership, who look on in dismay at the actions of the Spanish judge, there are many more who believe that impunity must be denied to those who massacre innocents. One cannot really balance the inviolability of diplomatic passports against the horror of genocide and crimes against humanity. The latter must take precedence over the former.

Unlike the Pol Pot story, where no nation called for his extradition to face charges of genocide and crimes against humanity, four European nations— Spain, France, Switzerland, and Belgium—sought Pinochet's extradition. Their argument is that he has allegedly committed crimes against humanity and genocide, violations of human rights conventions passed since Nuremberg. And for the first time, nations appear willing to extradite former dictators such as Pinochet to face trial in another nation's criminal court.

Louise Arbour, the chief prosecutor of the ICTY and ICTR, recently summed up the importance of the Pinochet incident for international law.

> It seems to me that . . . with the apprehension of Pinochet, the 120 countries in Rome who signed the text of the treaty are also domestically starting to reflect on the need to break this culture of *impunity* in the international scene. [The Pinochet situation] fits exactly within the spirit of the Rome Treaty—that domestic courts will take the initiative and that only when they are unwilling or unable to carry out these prosecutions will the international forum be activated. . . . We are starting to sense a willingness, particularly in judicial circles, to turn to methods of enforcement of the grossest violations of human rights.[36]

As if to underscore her views about the emergent message in the Pinochet incident, in late November 1998, two French human rights groups, the International Federation of Human Rights Leagues and the French League for the Defense of Human Rights, requested the French government to begin criminal proceedings against President Laurent Kabila of the Congo on charges of torture and crimes against humanity. (He was one of thirty-four African government leaders invited to attend a French-African summit meeting in Paris when the request was made.) Not surprisingly, in the rapidly unfolding post-Pinochet era, Kabila sent an advance party to Belgium, the first stop on his European trip. Its task: "to seek assurances that there would be no nasty surprises waiting—an arrest warrant, for example."[37]

The French government turned down the request for action against Kabila. Charles Josselin, the French minister in charge of African relations, explained that, unlike Pinochet, Kabila "was invited as the chief of state of Democratic Congo. In this capacity, he benefits from the immunity accorded chiefs of state *while in office*, a big difference with General Pinochet, who no longer was [in office]."[38] Given that France was one of four nations that requested the extradition of Pinochet, the French are not opposed to trying alleged former leaders who are accused of violating human rights in French courts.

Looking at the two incidents, Pinochet and Kabila, it seems clear that foundations are being developed regarding domestic trials of those who have allegedly committed crimes against humanity, torture, or genocide beyond the borders of the nation conducting the criminal trial. The French, and perhaps the European, view is that if Pinochet were still the Chilean head of state, immunity would attach. Once Pinochet, or Kabila, or some other leader accused of crimes against humanity leaves office, there is no immunity from a domestic criminal trial. When Kabila is deposed and travels anywhere in Europe, he would place himself in jeopardy of detention and criminal prosecution in a domestic court for crimes against humanity.

Clearly, these two incidents are encouraging portents of the world's evolving policy of denying impunity to perpetrators of crimes against humanity, torture, or genocide. As prosecutor Arbour said: "We are starting to sense a willingness, particularly in judicial circles, to turn to methods of enforcement of the grossest violations of human rights."[39]

Postscript: Kosovo, Fall–Winter, 1998–1999

This book opened with the horrors of genocide in Kosovo. It is fitting that it ends in Kosovo, but on a more optimistic note. NATO members[40] in mid-October 1998 took a watershed action, with U.S. participation, that fundamentally changed NATO's original mission (providing for collective

Kosovo. Serb war crimes. The bodies of Hafir Elshani (left), 35, and Miliam Bugari (right), 29, found near the town of Vranic in Kosovo. Elshani was found dead with his nose cut off. Bugari appeared to have been shot at close range. (Peter Bouckaert for Human Rights Watch)

self-defense against the Soviet bloc). The original mandate of the organization was "to safeguard the freedom and security of all its members by political and military means in accordance with the principles of the UN Charter."[41]

Its new mandate is to unilaterally, without UN participation, "extend freedom, human rights, and the Rule of Law in Europe." U.S. Secretary of State Madeleine Albright justified NATO's new attention to individual rights. She said at a NATO conference in Brussels, Belgium, that "NATO was our institution of choice [for] defending Western values on the continent."[42] Said another Western diplomat: "The humanitarian question was decisive. In the end, faced with tens of thousands of evicted [Kosovars] dying this Winter and doing something, the decision was pretty clear." Dominique Moisi, deputy director of the French Institute for International Relations, said that now NATO "has become the fireman for an enlarged Europe, a stabilizer for all seasons. That is a critical role, one that should be carried out within the context of the law."[43]

NATO ministers justified the new mission by turning to one of the international treaties that address the crimes committed against innocent civilians in Kosovo. The 1949 Geneva Peace Conventions, specifically Article 3 of the Fourth Geneva Convention, states that, in conflicts "not of an international character,"

> people taking no active part in the hostilities [shall always] be treated humanely, without any adverse distinction founded on race, color, religion or faith, birth or wealth; . . . humiliating and degrading treatment [is prohibited as is] violence to life and person, in particular, murder of all kinds, mutilation, cruel treatment and torture.

The first application of the new mandate was Kosovo in March 1999. Earlier, NATO had issued an "activation order" for military aircraft to stand ready to bomb Serbia if human rights violations by Serbs against ethnic Albanian civilians in Kosovo (such as Rexhap Bislimi, who was beaten to death by Serb special police) continued. One commentator writing about the change said that "it appears that NATO has decided it must sometimes have the courage to act to uphold a moral standard, one that the laws of war have long, but often vainly, identified."[44]

This determined threat by NATO, with aggressive diplomacy practiced by the experienced and successful American envoy Richard Holbrooke, forced Milosevic to agree, on October 13, 1998, to pull half of his forces out of Kosovo and to allow the presence of 2,000 civilian monitors selected by the regional Organization for Security and Cooperation in Europe (OSCE). The monitors' task was to monitor the cease-fire in Kosovo and to work for a political settlement that would give Kosovo more autonomy. Almost 2,000 NATO troops, including American soldiers, were based in neighboring Macedonia in order to "rush to the aid of the civilian monitors if necessary."[45]

Since then, Milosevic has become, in the eyes of some of his longtime associates, "increasingly insecure, even paranoid." Kosovo is out of his control, with a movement toward independence as the third republic within Yugoslavia probable (the two existing republics are powerful Serbia and the smaller Montenegro, whose president has been critical of Milosevic's policies). The Serb economy remains battered due to the sanctions against Serbia, bans on loans from the World Bank and the International Monetary Fund, and NATO bombings.

In late November 1998, Milosevic conducted an "extraordinary purge of his innermost circle" of military, intelligence, and political associates, including "one of his most trusted political commissars." He also dismissed General Momcilo Perisic, Milosevic's long-serving army chief of staff "and an architect of the war in Bosnia." An American diplomat in Serbia said: "The regime is brittle. It will crack. It will break."[46]

In the months before NATO military action against Milosevic, he was "waging war" on his civilian opposition, particularly press and television reporting. By March, Serb courts had ruled in at least six separate cases against a free press. This "drastic escalation of the ongoing wave of repression against the media in Serbia"[47] was documented by the U.S. State Department in its 1998 Report on Serbian Human Rights Violations and Belgrade's own Association of Independent Electronic Media.

These events came as a consequence of the NATO policy shift. By the time representatives of the ethnic Albanians and the Serbs met in France in February 1999, a NATO proposal had been cobbled together by the leading powers (the six-nation Contact Group) for acceptance by the warring forces. It called for a NATO peacekeeping force of 28,000 troops, including 4,000 American GIs. Within three months of the signing, 50 percent of the 18,000-person Yugoslavian army's forces in Kosovo would withdraw; within four months, 80 percent of the 12,500 Serb police and "special" forces would be withdrawn and the KLA disarmed by the NATO forces. Six months after the signing, the entire Yugoslavian army would be withdrawn from Kosovo and, finally, at the end of three years, there would be a final determination of the status of Kosovo. The Kosovars rejected the proposal because it did not have a referendum vote at the end of three years while the Serbs rejected the proposal because allowing NATO forces on Serb territory infringed Yugoslavian sovereignty.

The first round of peace talks ended without any resolution of the dilemma, and the second round took place in mid-March 1999. Determined to succeed in the new round of talks, President Clinton appointed former U.S. Senator Robert Dole (R-Kans.) to meet with the ethnic Albanians and get their signatures on the proposal. This finally accomplished, Ambassador Richard Holbrooke, who brokered the Bosnian peace agreement at Dayton in 1995, made an eleventh-hour visit to Belgrade to pressure Slobodan Milosevic to agree to the proposal. There was an adamant refusal, and on March 23, 1999, the nineteen NATO members initiated bombing raids on Serbia and Kosovo. Clearly, as Friedman has noted, the scenario reflects the reality, in 1999, of "a soft partition (Orthodox Serbs and Muslim ethnic Albanians continuing to share the same territory) with a hard fist (NATO forces implementing the peace)."[48]

President Clinton addressed the American nation the following day to explain the reasons for the bombing raids. After talking about the scenes of "innocent people taken from their homes, forced to kneel in the dirt and sprayed with bullets; Kosovar men dragged from their families, fathers and sons together lined up and shot in cold blood," Clinton concluded that

Kosovo. Serb war crimes. The body of Ali Koludra, sixty-two. Ali Koludra was executed by Serbian police with an axe. He lies in an open field in the village of Gornje Obrijne, Kosovo, still clutching his cane. His wife was found murdered only meters away. (Peter Bouckaert for Human Rights Watch)

"ending this tragedy is a moral imperative. NATO forces acted, for the first time to "restore the peace."

> Our mission is clear: to demonstrate the seriousness of NATO's purpose so that the Serbian leaders understand the imperative of reversing course; to deter an even bloodier offensive against innocent civilians in Kosovo; and, if necessary, to seriously damage the Serbian military's capacity to harm the people of Kosovo. In short, if President Milosevic will not make peace, we will limit his ability to make war.

On March 24, 1999, to "limit Milosevic's ability to make war" and force his army out of Kosovo, NATO commenced daily strategic bombing of sites in Serbia and Kosovo. In its new mission as "regional policeman," the 50-year-old alliance acted to roll back Serb ethnic cleansing in the province. It was "a mission of human rights and trying to preserve human values," said NATO's Secretary General Javier Solara.[49]

In the next eight weeks, however, almost one million Kosovars, about 90 percent of the ethnic Albanian population in Kosovo, were forced to flee for their lives. With the forced exodus came new accounts of the horror of war crimes, rape, and crimes against humanity committed by the Serbs against innocent ethnic Albanian Kosovars. The 1998–1999 horror stories were carbon copies of the genocidal strategy of the Serb and Bosnian Serb crimes against the ethnic Muslims in BiH committed between 1991 and 1995. Some of the Kosovo terrors were captured on video recorders smuggled out by the refugees and broadcast to a horrified world.

In mid-May 1999, U.S. President Clinton spoke to a veterans' group on the importance of NATO actions in Kosovo. Noting that Bosnia and Kosovo were brutal examples of a "systematic ethnic cleansing and slaughter of people because of their religious or ethnic background," Clinton, echoing former IMTY prosecutor Richard Goldstone, blamed Milosevic as the person responsible for the crimes against humanity in the Balkans. "The real enemy in the Balkans is a poisonous hatred unleashed by cynical leaders based on a distorted view of what constitutes real national greatness." Like Hitler and Pol Pot before him, Milosevic was the evil catalyst. "Ethnic conflicts do not explode on their own"; leaders trigger the genocide and crimes against humanity and Milosevic is a prime example.[50]

> You do not have systematic slaughter in an effort to eradicate the religion, the culture, the heritage, the very record of presence of the people in any area, unless some politician thinks it is in his interest to foment that sort of hatred. That's how [Bosnia and Kosovo] happen. People [Milosevic] with organized political and military power decide it is in their interest that they get something out of convincing the people they control or they influence to go kill other people and uproot them and dehumanize them. . . . The cycle of violence has to end. It is the morally right thing for [NATO and for] America.

The more than one million ethnic Albanians *must* be able to go back to their villages in Kosovo. For this to happen, "the Serb forces must leave [and] an international security force with NATO at its core" must be placed in Kosovo in order "to make peace work."[51]

I believe that with the change in the agendas of major political and military entities such as NATO, the ICTY's indictment of Yugoslav President Slobodan Milosevic for ordering or failing to prevent "war crimes on a massive scale" (the first ever international tribunal indictment of a sitting national leader), as well as national reexamination of domestic policy toward bringing to justice those who have committed crimes of "universal jurisdiction," the world community's quest for an effective enforcement response to these horrendous crimes will be realized sooner than later and that the twenty-first century will be the initial millennium where justice for victims of human rights abuses, genocide, torture, war crimes, and crimes against humanity becomes the norm rather than the exception.

NOTES

Introduction

1. Seth Mydans, "Two Khmer Rouge Leaders Spend Beach Holiday in Shadow of Past," *New York Times*, January 1, 1999, p. A1.

2. Quoted in AP, "Senators Urge Clinton to Seek Deal to Remove Yugoslav Leader," *New York Times*, December 30, 1998.

3. Seth Mydans, "Revenge or Justice? Cambodians Confront the Past," *New York Times*, December 31, 1998, pp. A1, A8.

4. Serbia and Macedonia are the two regional entities that make up present-day Yugoslavia, after the creation of the independent nation-states of Slovenia, Croatia, and Bosnia-Herzegovina. The former Yugoslavia began on a path of self-destruction in 1980 with the death of Tito, the nation's Communist Party leader. By 1992, Bosnia-Herzegovina, Slovenia, and Croatia had broken away from Yugoslavia and declared independence, and they were recognized by many nation-states soon thereafter. The bloody war between Serbia and its Bosnian Serb surrogates and the Croats and Bosnian Muslims began in 1991. In this book, for all practical purposes—politically, economically, and militarily—Yugoslavia is Serbia.

5. Philip Shenon, "U.S. Appears to Be Undecided on Kosovo Crisis," *New York Times*, September 16, 1998, p. A1.

6. Ibid.

7. The information and the quotations in this section come from Jane Perlez, "In Kosovo Death Chronicles, Serb Tactic Revealed," *New York Times*, September 27, 1998, p. A14.

8. "U.S. Envoy Issues a Stern Warning on Kosovo," *New York Times*, September 27, 1998, p. A14.

9. Samuel Totten and William S. Parsons, introduction to *Century of Genocide*, ed. Samuel Totten, William S. Parsons, and Israel Charney (New York: Garland, 1997), p. xxi.

10. Quoted in Seth Mydans, "Cambodia's Leader Says Top Khmer Rouge Defectors Will Be Spared," *New York Times*, December 29, 1998.

11. Martha Minow, *Between Vengeance and Forgiveness: Facing History after Genocide and Mass Violence* (Boston: Beacon Press, 1998).

12. Mydans, "Cambodia's Leader Says."

13. John R. Bolton, "The Global Prosecutors: Hunting War Criminals in the Name of Utopia," *Foreign Affairs* 78, no. 1 (January/February 1999): 161.

241

14. On New Year's Day 1999, however, Hun Sen changed his message. He publicly announced that trials for the Khmer Rouge leaders were a "fait accompli." The only question for the prime minister is whether the trial will be a national trial, with assistance from Western lawyers, or an international criminal trial similar to the UN's ICTY and ICTR. He stated that he supported such legal inquiry "into the genocidal regime of Pol Pot, which must be punished." Seth Mydans, "Cambodian Denies He Opposed Trial for Khmer Rouge," *New York Times*, January 2, 1999, p. A1.

15. After World War I, because most of the Young Turks were not punished for their genocidal orders regarding ethnic Armenians, many of the leaders were assassinated by Armenian radicals.

16. M. Cherif Bassiouni, "Symposium: Nuremberg and the Rule of Law: A Fifty Year Verdict," *Military Law Review* (summer 1995): 56.

17. "Interview with Nuremberg Trial Prosecutor Drexel Sprecher," www.courttv.nuremberg.com, December 1995, pp. 15–16.

18. Corell, in ibid., p. 100. Another participant, Graham T. Blewitt (who served on the prosecution team at the International Criminal Tribunal for the Former Yugoslavia in the Hague), observed that war crimes and genocides such as those that took place in the former Yugoslavia occur "due to the lack of an effective deterrent for gross criminal behavior at the nation state level. This pattern of violence and criminal behavior will continue until a strong deterrent is in place to prevent or limit the commission of such crimes" ("Symposium," p. 103).

19. Bolton, "Global Prosecutors," p. 158.

20. Ibid., p. 159.

1. War Crimes and Genocide, 1899–1939

1. See Michael Howard, George J. Andreopoulos, and Mark R. Shulman, eds., *The Laws of War: Constraints on Warfare in the Western World* (New Haven, Conn.: Yale University Press, 1994), pp. vii–viii.

2. Ibid., pp. 2, 8.

3. Note, "The Iraqi Conflict: An Assessment of Possible War Crimes and the Call for Adoption of an International Criminal Code and Permanent International Criminal Tribunal," 14 *New York Law School Journal of International and Comparative Law* 81 (1993).

4. The International Committee of the Red Cross (ICRC), the National Red Cross and Red Crescent Societies, and the International Red Cross and Crescent Societies were joined in 1929. Non-European nations were sought out by the ICRC in the late 1860s, shortly after the Red Cross was founded. In 1868 the Ottoman (Turkey) Society was founded; in 1876 it adopted the red crescent symbol. See, generally, Nicholas O. Berry, *War and the Red Cross: The Unspoken Mission* (New York: St. Martin's Press, 1997), pp. 9–15, passim.

5. Howard et al., *Laws of War*, pp. 4, 6.

6. Michael Akehurst, *A Modern Introduction to International Law* (London: Allen and Unwin, 1977), p. 27.

7. Quoted in Berry, *War and the Red Cross*, p. 8.

8. Ibid., pp. 8, 9.

9. Quoted in Howard et al., *Laws of War*, pp. 6–7.

10. Fred L. Morrison, "The Significance of Nuremberg for Modern International Law," in "Symposium: Nuremberg and the Rule of Law: A Fifty Year Verdict," 149 *Military Law Review* 209 (summer 1995); hereafter "Symposium."

11. Note, "Iraqi Conflict," p. 81.

12. M. Cherif Bassiouni and Ved P. Nanda, eds., *A Treatise on International Criminal Law,* vol. 1, *Crimes and Punishment* (Springfield, Ill.: Charles C. Thomas, 1973), p. 104.

13. Hague I, July 29, 1899, Article XVI.

14. Note, "Iraqi Conflict," p. 104.

15. Hague IV, October 18, 1907, preamble; emphasis added.

16. See Articles 23–28 of the 1907 Hague Annex.

17. Note, "Iraqi Conflict," p. 90.

18. Comment, "Security Council Resolution 808: A Step toward a Permanent International Court for the Prosecution of International Crimes and Human Rights Violations," 25 *Golden Gate University Law Review* 443 (1996).

19. Ibid.

20. Generally, until the First World War, the primary goal of belligerent forces was to destroy the opposing nation's military capabilities; consequently, war had a limited effect on the private citizen. This began to change in 1914 and by the 1930s, as seen in the Spanish civil war and then the Second World War, "collateral damage" became a significant war crimes matter (Note, "Iraqi Conflict," p. 90).

21. Comment, "Security Council Resolution 808," p. 447.

22. See, generally, James F. Willis, *Prologue to Nuremberg: The Politics and Diplomacy of Punishing War Criminals of the First World War* (Westport, Conn.: Greenwood Press, 1982), p. 15ff.

23. Ibid., p. 442.

24. David Armstrong, Lorna Lloyd, and John Redmond, *From Versailles to Maastricht: International Organization in the Twentieth Century* (New York: St. Martin's Press, 1996), p. 18.

25. Ibid.

26. Ibid., pp. 75–76.

27. Comment, "Security Council Resolution 808," p. 442.

28. Willis, *Prologue,* p. 65.

29. Ibid., p. 68.

30. Ibid.

31. Vahakn N. Dadrian, *The History of the Armenian Genocide: Ethnic Conflict from the Balkans to Anatolia to the Caucasians* (Providence, R.I.: Berghahn Books, 1995, 1997), p. 392.

32. Willis, *Prologue,* p. 138ff.

33. M. Cherif Bassiouni, in "Symposium," p. 55.

34. Monroe Leigh, in "Symposium," p. 114.

35. Willis, *Prologue,* pp. 83–84.

36. See, generally, John Campbell, *The Experience of World War II* (New York: Oxford University Press, 1989), p. 8ff.

37. Roger Smith, "Human Destructiveness and Politics," in *Genocide and the Modern Age,* ed. Isidor Walliman and Michael Dobkowski (Westport, Conn.: Greenwood Press, 1987); Israel W. Charney, "The Study of Genocide," in *Genocide: A Critical Bibliographic Review,* ed. Israel W. Charney (New York: Facts on File, 1988), p. 7; Samuel Totten, William S. Parsons, Israel Charney, eds., *Century of Genocide* (New York: Garland, 1997), p. xxii.

38. Leo Kuper, *The Prevention of Genocide* (New Haven, Conn.: Yale University Press, 1985), p. 9.

39. Raphael Lemkin, *Axis Rule in Occupied Europe: Laws of Occupation, Analysis of Government, and Proposals for Redress* (Washington, D.C.: Carnegie Foundation for International Peace, 1944), p. 79.

40. For twenty years preceding the 1904 native rebellion, "German settlers moving inland had been stealing land and cattle, raping women, lynching men with impunity and calling them 'baboons' to their faces." The Herero attack killed all the male settlers but allowed women and children to live. Kaiser Wilhelm II ordered German troops to counterattack, which led to the slaughter of most of the Hereros by the poisoning of waterholes and the bayoneting of all men, women, and children who survived. See Donald G. McNeil, Jr., "Its Past on Its Sleeve, Tribe Seeks Bonn Apology," *New York Times,* May 31, 1998, p. A3.

41. Richard Bernstein, "Books of the Times," review of *To End a War,* by Richard Holbrooke, *New York Times,* May 20, 1998.

42. Dadrian, *History of the Armenian Genocide,* p. xviii.

43. Totten et al., *Century of Genocide,* p. 41.

44. Quoted in Dadrian, *History of the Armenian Genocide,* p. 159.

45. Ibid., pp. 203–207, passim.

46. Leo Kuper, *Genocide: Its Political Use in the Twentieth Century* (New Haven, Conn.: Yale University Press, 1981), pp. 108–113, passim.

47. Quoted in Dadrian, *History of the Armenian Genocide,* p. 209 n. 8.

48. Henry Morganthau, *Ambassador Morganthau's Story* (New York: Doubleday, 1918), p. 302.

49. Arnold J. Toynbee, *The Treatment of the Armenians in the Ottoman Empire, 1915–1916* (London: HMSO, 1918), p. 291.

50. Quoted in Dadrian, *History of the Armenian Genocide,* p. 225.

51. Ibid., p. 236ff.

52. Ibid., p. 211 n. 19.

53. Ibid., p. 232 n. 27.

54. Ibid., p. 216; emphasis added.

55. Gary J. Bass, "Due Processes," *New Republic,* March 30, 1998, p. 16.

56. Quoted in K. Bardakjian, *Hitler and the Armenian Genocide* (Cambridge: Harvard University Press, 1985), p. 76.

57. Jay Winter and Blaine Baggett, *The Great War and the Shaping of the 20th Century* (New York: Penguin Books, 1996), p. 153.

58. Article I, paragraph 1, League of Nations Covenant, 1919.

59. Armstrong et al., *From Versailles,* p. 7.

60. Quoted in ibid., p. 15.

61. Part I, Articles 1–26, Versailles Treaty, 1919.

62. See the excellent book by Ron Rosenbaum, *Explaining Hitler* (New York: Random House, 1998), for an examination of the many ways scholars have tried to explain the Nazi dictator.

63. Robert S. Wistrich, *Weekend in Munich: Art, Propaganda, and Terror in the Third Reich* (London: Pavillion, 1995), p. 27.

64. Akehurst, *Modern Introduction to International Law,* p. 26.

65. Howard et al., *Laws of War,* p. 8.

66. Armstrong et al., *From Versailles,* p. 36.

67. Note, "Iraqi Conflict," p. 81

68. Campbell, *Experience of World War II,* p. 8.

2. WORLD WAR II IN EUROPE AND THE NUREMBERG TRIBUNAL

1. M. Cherif Bassiouni and Ved P. Nanda, eds., *A Treatise on International Criminal Law,* vol. 1, *Crimes and Punishment* (Springfield, Ill.: Charles C. Thomas, 1973), p. 159.

2. See John Campbell, *The Experience of World War II* (New York: Oxford University Press, 1989), p. 12.

3. See *Korematsu v. United States*, 323 U.S. 214 (1944), dissenting opinion of Justice Owen Roberts.

4. A.W. Brian Simpson, *In the Highest Degree Odious: Detention without Trial: Wartime Detention in Britain* (New York: Oxford University Press, 1994).

5. See Robert F. Nelson, *Revolution and Genocide: On the Origins of the Armenian Genocide and the Holocaust* (Chicago: University of Chicago Press, 1992), p. 208ff.

6. Quoted in ibid., p. 207.

7. See Raul Hilberg, *Perpetrators, Victims, Bystanders: The Jewish Catastrophe, 1933–1945* (New York: HarperCollins, 1992), pp. 12–14.

8. United States Holocaust Memorial Museum, *Historical Atlas of the Holocaust* (New York: Macmillan, 1996), p. 14.

9. Victor Klemperer, "Personal History: The Klemperer Diaries," *New Yorker,* April 27/May 6, 1998, p. 125.

10. Robert S. Wistrich, *Weekend in Munich: Art, Propaganda, and Terror in the Third Reich* (London: Pavillion Books, 1995), p. 27. By war's end, the Nazi dictatorship had established over 100 major concentration camps across Germany and other occupied countries of Europe. See David Scrase and Wolfgang Mieder, eds., *The Holocaust: Introductory Essays* (Burlington, Vt: Center for Holocaust Studies at UVM, 1996), pp. 5, 24, 240.

11. Hilberg, *Perpetrators,* p. 15.

12. Klemperer, "Diaries," p. 125.

13. Wistrich, *Weekend,* p. 27.

14. See, generally, James M. Glass, *"Life Unworthy of Life:" Racial Phobia and Mass Murder in Hitler's Germany* (New York: Basic Books, 1997).

15. U.S. Holocaust Memorial Museum, *Historical Atlas,* pp. 51–53. See also Samuel Totten, William S. Parsons, and Israel Charney, eds., *Century of Genocide* (New York.: Garland, 1997), p. 137.

16. Quoted in G. M. Gilbert, *Nuremberg Diary* (New York: DaCapo Press, 1995), pp. 113–114.

17. Scrase and Mieder, *Holocaust,* pp. 241, 247; U.S. Holocaust Memorial Museum, *Historical Atlas,* p. 77. Auschwitz and Majdenek were also slave labor concentration camps. When arrivals got off the transports, medical doctors made decisions regarding the fate of the Jews: immediate death in the gas chambers, or a slower death working as slave laborers in industrial plants adjacent to the camp. Totten et al., *Century of Genocide,* pp. 138ff.

18. Quoted in Joseph E. Persico, *Nuremberg: Infamy on Trial* (New York: Penguin Books, 1992), p. 338.

19. Quoted in ibid., p. 171.

20. See, for example, ibid., p. 69ff.

21. Bassiouni and Nanda, *Treatise,* p. 583.

22. Telford Taylor, *The Anatomy of the Nuremberg Trials: A Personal Memoir* (New York: A. A. Knopf, 1992), p. 28.

23. Quoted in Richard H. Minear, *Victors' Justice: The Tokyo War Crimes Trial* (Princeton, N.J.: Princeton University Press, 1971), pp. 8–9.

24. Persico, *Nuremberg,* p. 15.

25. Ibid.

26. Bradley F. Smith, *The Road to Nuremberg* (New York: Basic Books, 1981), pp. 20–21.

27. Taylor, *Anatomy,* p. 31.

28. Persico, *Nuremberg*, p. 15.

29. Smith, *Road to Nuremberg*, p. 22.

30. Ibid., pp. 45, 28ff.

31. Ibid., p. 76.

32. Taylor, *Anatomy*, pp. 35–36.

33. Smith, *Road to Nuremberg*, p. 51ff.; Taylor, *Anatomy*, p. 36ff.

34. Persico, *Nuremberg*, p. 18.

35. United Nations War Crimes Commission, *Law Reports of Trials of War Criminals: Four Genocide Trials* (New York: Fertig, 1992), p. 45.

36. Persico, *Nuremberg*, p. 17.

37. Smith, *Road to Nuremberg*, p. 114. After the war, in a trial held in the American sector of Germany, seventy-seven Waffen SS soldiers were convicted of the murders of the American military prisoners; forty-three were hung for their crimes. Persico, *Nuremberg*, p. 332.

38. Quoted in Smith, *Road to Nuremberg*, p. 116.

39. Quoted in Minear, *Victors' Justice*, pp. 9–10.

40. Smith, *Road to Nuremberg*, p. 152ff.

41. Samuel I. Rosenman, Roosevelt's special envoy to the British, noted that in 1947, Churchill told him: "I think the President was right [about conducting a trial] and I was wrong." Samuel I. Rosenman, *Working with Roosevelt* (New York: Harper, 1952), p. 545.

42. Persico, *Nuremberg*, p. 78.

43. See, for example, Minear, *Victors' Justice*.

44. Quoted in Persico, *Nuremberg*, p. 83.

45. Quoted ibid., pp. 33–34. In a note to Roosevelt that touched on this issue of victors' justice, Jackson wrote: "We can save ourselves from those pitfalls if our test of what legally is crime gives recognition to those things which fundamentally outraged the conscience of the American people and brought them finally to the conviction that their own liberty and civilization could not persist in the same world with the Nazi power. . . . I believe that these instincts of the American people were right and that they should guide us as the fundamental tests of criminality." Quoted in Minear, *Victors' Justice*, p. 16.

46. See Viscount Maugham, *U.N.O. and War Crimes* (Westport, Conn.: Greenwood Press, 1975), p. 17.

47. Quoted in Taylor, *Anatomy*, p. 59.

48. Gilbert, *Nuremberg Diary*, pp. 7, 37.

49. Persico, *Nuremberg*, p. 27.

50. Ibid., p. 176.

51. United States Holocaust Memorial Museum, *In Pursuit of Justice: Examining the Evidence of the Holocaust* (Washington, D.C.: U.S. Holocaust Memorial Council, 1996), pp. 237, 253, 254.

52. Quoted in Gilbert, *Nuremberg Diary*, p. 123.

53. Quoted in ibid., p. 135.

54. U.S. Holocaust Memorial Museum, *Historical Atlas*, p. 31.

55. Campbell, *Experience of World War II*, p. 217.

56. See Gilbert, *Nuremberg Diary*, pp. 148ff, 407ff.

57. Quoted in ibid., p. 351.

58. Persico, *Nuremberg*, p. 329.

59. Quoted in ibid., p. 365.

60. Quoted in Gilbert, *Nuremberg Diary*, pp. 415, 420.

3. WORLD WAR II IN ASIA, THE FAR EAST TRIBUNAL, AND POSTWAR DEVELOPMENT IN INTERNATIONAL LAW

1. Gavan Daws, *Prisoners of the Japanese: POWs of World War II in the Pacific* (New York: William Morrow, 1994), p. 17.

2. Iris Chang, in her important book on the Rape of Nanking in December 1937, indicates that between 6 million and 19 million Chinese—all but 400,000 of them civilians—were killed by the Japanese occupiers in this period of time. See Iris Chang, *The Rape of Nanking: The Forgotten Holocaust of World War II* (New York: Basic Books, 1997).

3. See, for example, Donald Knox, *Death March: The Survivors of Bataan* (New York: Harcourt, Brace, Jovanovic, 1981).

4. Chang, *Rape of Nanking*, p. 218.

5. Ibid., p. 55.

6. Quoted in ibid., p. 59.

7. John L. Ginn, *Sugamo Prison, Tokyo* (London: McFarland, 1992), p. 16.

8. See, generally, John Campbell, *The Experience of World War II* (New York: Oxford University Press, 1989), pp. 8–9.

9. Ibid., p. 24.

10. Quoted in ibid., p. 26.

11. See, for example, Chang, *Rape of Nanking*, pp. 20ff.

12. Stanley L. Falk, introduction to Knox, *Death March*, pp. xxiii–xxiv.

13. Daws, *Prisoners of the Japanese*, p. 18.

14. Quoted in Kevin Uhrich, "The Other Holocaust," *Los Angeles Reader*, July 1, 1994.

15. Quoted in Chang, *Rape of Nanking*, p. 52.

16. Falk, introduction to Knox, *Death March*, p. xxiv.

17. Quoted in Daws, *Prisoners of the Japanese*, p. 82.

18. Ginn, *Sugamo Prison*, p. 137; see also Peter Williams and David Wallace, *Unit 731: Japan's Secret Biological Warfare in World War II* (New York: Free Press, 1989).

19. Arnold C. Brackman, *The Other Nuremberg: The Untold Story of the Tokyo War Crimes Trial* (New York: William Morrow, 1987), p. 17.

20. Testimony of Tanisuga Shizuo, soldier, Japanese army, Tokyo, IMTFE, 1948. See Haruko Coon, ed., *Japan at War: Selected Essays* (New York: New Press, 1992).

21. Knox, *Death March*, pp. 337–338.

22. See Chang, *Rape of Nanking*.

23. Ginn, *Sugamo Prison*, p. 138.

24. Quoted in Richard L. Lael, *The Yamashita Precedent: War Crimes and Command Responsibility* (Wilmington, Del.: Scholarly Resources, 1982), p. 40.

25. Brackman, *The Other Nuremberg*, p. 40. One wonders how much longer the trial would have run if these files had not been destroyed. As it was, the Tokyo tribunal conducted business for two years and ninety-eight days.

26. Quoted in ibid., p. 41.

27. Quoted in ibid., p. 44.

28. Quoted in ibid., p. 26.

29. See Douglas MacArthur, *Reminiscences* (New York: McGraw-Hill, 1964), pp. 287–288.

30. Mark Osiel, *Mass Atrocity, Collective Memory, and the Law* (London: Transaction Publishers, 1997), p. 138.

31. See Richard H. Minear, *Victors' Justice: The Tokyo War Crime Trial* (Princeton,

N.J.: Princeton University Press, 1971), p. 243ff.; C. Hosoya, N. Ando, Y. Onuma, and R. Minear, eds., *The Tokyo War Crimes Trial: An International Symposium* (Tokyo: Kodansha, 1986), p. 18ff.

32. Lael, *Yamashita Precedent*, p. xi. The charge read as follows: Yamashita "unlawfully discharged or failed to discharge his duty as commander to control the operations of the members of his command, permitting them to commit brutal atrocities and other high crimes." Quoted in majority opinion, *In Re Yamashita*, 327 U.S. 1 (1946).

33. *In Re Yamashita*, 327 U.S. 1 (1946).

34. *Homma v. Patterson*, 327 US 759 (1946).

35. See Chang, *Rape of Nanking*, pp. 170–172.

36. Brackman, *The Other Nuremberg*, p. 51ff.

37. Minear, *Victors' Justice*, p. 6.

38. Brackman, *The Other Nuremberg*, p. 19.

39. Osiel, *Mass Atrocity*, p. 138. Osiel argues that the strategy proved "counterproductive," because placing the blame on just a few major war criminals and not implicating Hirohito at all "impeded the awakening of the Japanese people's own historical consciousness. Many would find it difficult to believe that they had been accomplices in aggression and murder on a near-genocidal scale when the Emperor whom they had served so loyally never had to bear any responsibility for his own speech and actions." Japan's postwar legislature enacted legislation that exonerated the people of Japan: "War responsibility should not extend to ordinary people who, after the declaration of war, dedicated themselves to duty in a lawful manner in order to conduct the war, obediently following the orders of the state" (p. 187).

40. Ginn, *Sugamo Prison*, p. 242.

41. The five crimes were (1) planning, (2) preparing for, (3) initiating, and (4) waging aggressive wars and (5) participating in a common plan or conspiracy to dominate Asia. The first two, involving dozens of counts, were dropped by the tribunal because the fifth crime included planning and preparing for an aggressive war.

42. Phillip Piccigallo, *The Japanese on Trial* (Austin: University of Texas Press, 1979), p. 7.

43. Brackman, *The Other Nuremberg*, p. 85.

44. Minear, *Victors' Justice*, p. 22.

45. See ibid., pp. 32–33.

46. See Brackman, *The Other Nuremberg*, pp. 122–160, passim.

47. Ibid., p. 187.

48. Ibid., p. 286. Chang (*Rape of Nanking*, p. 174) notes that "the evdience presented [by the prosecution] overwhelmed the Japanese defense [attorneys]."

49. Quoted in Brackman, *The Other Nuremberg*, pp. 289, 291.

50. Quoted in ibid., p. 312.

51. Daws points out that the American death rate was 34 percent, the Australian death rate 33 percent, and the British death rate 32 percent. Dutch POWs brought the overall death rate down to 27 percent for only (!) 20 percent of the Dutch POWs died while in captivity. Daws, *Prisoners of the Japanese*, p. 360.

52. Chang, *Rape of Nanking*, p. 173.

53. Brackman, *The Other Nuremberg*, pp. 406–441.

54. *Hirota, Dohihara, Kido v. General MacArthur*, 338 U.S. 197 (1949). Justice Jackson voted to grant certiorari in the case because the Court was deadlocked. Four justices—Chief Justice Vinson and Justices Frankfurter, Reed, and Burton—were of the opinion that the Court lacked jurisdiction. Four others—Justices Black, Douglas,

Murphy, and Rutledge—believed that the Court should hear arguments. Since "neither side in good grace can retreat," Jackson reluctantly participated in the initial vote to grant the petitioners a hearing. He did not participate in the final vote on the merits.

55. "Japanese Emperor Jeered in England," *New York Times,* May 26, 1998.

56. Osiel, *Mass Atrocity,* p. 134.

57. James F. Willis, *Prologue to Nuremberg: The Politics and Diplomacy of Punishng War Criminals of the First World War* (Westport, Conn.: Greenwood Press, 1982), p. xi.

58. Lawrence J. LeBlanc, *The United States and the Genocide Convention* (Durham, N.C.: Duke University Press, 1981), p. 22.

59. Quoted in ibid., pp. 22–23.

60. Quoted in M. Cherif Bassiouni and Ved P. Nanda, eds., *Treatise on International Criminal Law,* vol. 1, *Crimes and Punishment* (Springfield, Ill.: Charles C. Thomas, 1973), pp. 524ff; emphasis added.

61. See, generally, Bassiouni and Nanda, *Treatise,* p. 531ff.

62. Leo Kuper, *The Prevention of Genocide* (New Haven, Conn.: Yale University Press, 1985), p. 9.

63. See, generally, LeBlanc, *The United States and the Genocide Convention,* for an examination of the politics of ratification of the convention in the United States.

64. Ibid., p. 368ff.

65. Torture Convention, Article 1, paragraph 1.

66. "Survey of Human Rights Law," *The Economist,* December 5, 1998, pp. 3–16.

67. Reed Brody, "Bringing Tyrants to Trial," *Legal Times,* December 7, 1998, p. 28.

68. Quoted in "Prosecutor to the World," www.courttv.casefiles.com (interviewer, Terry Moran), 1996, pp. 3–4.

69. A. Mark Weisburd, *Use of Force: The Practice of States since World War Two* (University Park: Pennsylvania State University Press, 1997).

70. M. Cherif Bassiouni, "Symposium: Nuremberg and the Rule of Law: A Fifty Year Verdict," 149 *Military Law Review* (summer 1995): 56.

71. LeBlanc, *The United States and the Genocide Convention,* pp. 2–3.

72. Quoted in Willis, *Prologue,* p. 173; emphasis added.

73. In 1998, there were plans to bring Pol Pot, the communist leader responsible for the genocide in Camboida, to trial. However, he died in the Cambodian jungles before he could be seized. See, for example, Philip Shenon and Eric Schmitt, "U.S. Is Planning a Move to Seize Pol Pot for Trial," *New York Times,* April 9, 1998, pp. A1, A8.

4. THE CAMBODIAN GENOCIDE

1. See Terry McCarthy, "The Butcher of Cambodia, Pol Pot Is Dead," *Time,* April 27, 1998, pp. 40–41.

2. Ibid., p. 41.

3. Roger Rosenblatt, "Memories of Pol Pot," *Time,* August 18, 1998, p. 26.

4. Stephen J. Morris, "Pol Pot's Lingering Influence," *New York Times,* April 19, 1998.

5. Seth Mydans, "Pol Pot, Brutal Dictator Who Forced Cambodians to Killing Fields, Dies at 73," *New York Times,* April 17, 1998, p. A14.

6. Ibid., p. A14.

7. Seth Mydans, "Faces from Beyond the Grave," review of *The Killing Fields,* by Chris Riley and Douglas Niven, *New York Times Book Review,* October 1998, p. 21.

8. Morris, "Pol Pot's Lingering Influence."

9. McCarthy, "Butcher of Cambodia," p. 41.

10. Rosenblatt, "Memories of Pol Pot," p. 26.

11. See, generally, Henry Kamm, *Cambodia: Report from a Stricken Land* (New York: Arcade, 1998), pp. xiii–xxiv.

12. Ibid., pp. xiii–xv, passim.

13. Editorial, "Justice for Cambodia," *Asiaweek,* April 21, 1998. Kiernan observed that "Pol Pot's revolution would not have won power without United States economic and military destabilization of Cambodia, which began in 1966." Ben Kiernan, *The Pol Pot Regime: Race, Power, and Genocide in Cambodia under the Khmer Rouge, 1975–1979* (New Haven, Conn.: Yale University Press, 1996), p. 16ff.

14. Mydans, "Pol Pot, Brutal Dictator," p. A14.

15. Violating the agreement, President Nixon continued the bombing of Cambodia. Finally, in late June 1973, the U.S. Congress ordered a halt to American bombing by August 1973. Kamm, *Cambodia,* p. xviii.

16. Mydans, "Pol Pot, Brutal Dictator," p. A14.

17. Kiernan, *Pol Pot Regime,* p. 16.

18. Kamm, *Cambodia,* p. 130.

19. Quoted in Seth Mydans, "Phantoms Rule in Former Khmer Stronghold," *New York Times,* April 14, 1998.

20. David P. Chandler, *The Tragedy of Cambodian History: Politics, War, and Revolution since 1945* (New Haven, Conn.: Yale University Press, 1991), p. 236.

21. Ibid., p. 238.

22. Kiernan, *Pol Pot Regime,* p. 55ff.

23. Ibid., p. 164.

24. Philip Gourevitch, "Pol Pot's Children," *New Yorker,* August 10, 1998, pp. 41–42.

25. Kiernan, *Pol Pot Regime,* pp. 8, 9.

26. Kim DePaul, ed., *Children of Cambodia's Killing Fields: Memoirs by Survivors* (New Haven, Conn.: Yale University Press, 1998), p. 13.

27. Sydney Schanberg, participant in the symposium "Continuing Unrest," *PBS Newshour,* June 18, 1997.

28. Kamm, *Cambodia,* p. 127.

29. DePaul, editor, *Children of Cambodia's Killing Fields,* p. 131.

30. Elizabeth Becker, *When the War Was Over: The Voices of Cambodia's Revolution and Its People* (New York: Simon and Schuster, 1986), p. 269.

31. DePaul, *Children of Cambodia's Killing Fields,* p. 22.

32. See Mydans, "Pol Pot, Brutal Dictator, p. A14.

33. Becker, *When the War Was Over,* p. 257.

34. Kamm, *Cambodia,* pp. 131, 135.

35. Becker, *When the War Was Over,* p. 266.

36. Quoted in McCarthy, "Butcher of Cambodia," p. 41.

37. Quoted in ibid.

38. See Kiernan, *Pol Pot Regime,* p. 458.

39. The seven zones were further divided into regions, then into many dozens of numbered districts, then into subdistricts, and finally into villages or hamlets consisting of between 200 and 300 persons. Every one of these geographic and political

divisions had Khmer Rouge leaders who took their orders from Pol Pot and his Angkar.

40. Kiernan, *Pol Pot Regime*, p. 5.

41. Becker, *When the War Was Over*, p. 223.

42. DePaul, *Children of Cambodia's Killing Fields*, p. xi.

43. Ibid., p. 14.

44. Ibid., p. 167.

45. Becker, *When the War Was Over*, p. 257.

46. Kamm, *Cambodia*, pp. 126–127.

47. Becker, *When the War Was Over*, p. 264.

48. Quoted in Ben Kiernan, "The Cambodian Genocide, 1975–1979," in *Century of Genocide*, ed. Samuel Totten, William S. Parsons, and Israel Charney (New York: Garland, 1997), p. 340.

49. Chandler, *Tragedy of Cambodian History*, p. 241.

50. Kamm, *Cambodia*, p. 128.

51. DePaul, *Children of Cambodia's Killing Fields*, p. 78. Another survivor recalled: "Every night when I went to sleep I heard gunshots. Every night many families were being killed by Pol Pot's soldiers because they were accused of being Chinese, Vietnamese, or in Lon Nol's former army. Pol Pot killed my mom's friend and her whole family after accusing them of being Chinese" (ibid., p. 112).

52. Mydans, "Pol Pot, Brutal Dictator."

53. DePaul, *Children of Cambodia's Killing Fields*, p. 70.

54. Becker, *When the War Was Over*, p. 259.

55. Gourevitch, "Pol Pot's Children," p. 46.

56. Kamm, *Cambodia*, p. 128.

57. Quoted in Mydans, "Phantoms Rule," p. A5.

58. DePaul, *Children of Cambodia's Killing Fields*, p. 32.

59. Some estimate that 40 percent of the population, about 3.1 million Cambodians, died or were killed by the Khmer Rouge in this period. Whereas the U.S. Central Intelligence Agency demographic analyses place the number killed between 1 million and 2 million, other analyses place the number between 1.5 million and 1.7 million. "The Khmer Rouge Regime," *Yale University Documentation Center*, p. 1. Craig Etcheson, a research associate in the Yale Cambodian Genocide Program, indicated that "new evidence suggests that the death toll might be closer to 2 million." Reuters, "'Killing Fields' Toll May Be 2 Million," *Washington Post*, January 26, 1997, p. A6.

60. Quoted in Paul Malamud, "New Documents Shed Light on Khmer Rouge Genocide," *United States Information Agency Electronic Journal* 1, no. 3 (May 1996): 1.

61. DePaul, *Children of Cambodia's Killing Fields*, p. 12.

62. Reuters, "'Killing Fields,'" p. 1.

63. Ben Kiernan, quoted in Malamud, "New Documents," p. 3.

64. Kiernan, *Pol Pot Regime*, p. 5.

65. Becker, *When the War Was Over*, p. 253.

66. Ibid.

67. Quoted in ibid.

68. Kiernan, "Cambodian Genocide," pp. 340–341.

69. Becker, *When the War Was Over*, pp. 260–264, passim; Kiernan, "Cambodian Genocide," p. 342.

70. Kiernan, *Pol Pot Regime*, table 4, p. 458.

71. Ibid., p. 314.

72. Quoted in McCarthy, "Butcher of Cambodia," p. 41.

73. Ben Kiernan, "Cambodian Genocide," pp. 337–338.

74. Becker, *When the War Was Over*, pp. 271, 296–297. See also Gourevitch, "Pol Pot's Children," p. 45.

75. Kamm, *Cambodia*, p. 141.

76. Quoted in Kiernan, *Pol Pot Regime*, p. 357.

77. Kamm, *Cambodia*, p. xx.

78. Quoted in Elizabeth Becker, "Pol Pot's End Won't Stop U.S. Pursuit of His Circle," *New York Times*, April 17, 1998, p. A17.

79. Gourevitch, "Pol Pot's Children," p. 45.

80. Quoted in ibid.

81. Mydans, "Pol Pot, Brutal Dictator," p. A14.

82. See, generally, Kamm, *Cambodia*.

83. Mydans, "Pol Pot, Brutal Dictator," p. A14.

84. Quoted in Becker, "Pol Pot's End," p. A15.

85. Quoted in *New York Times*, October 24, 1991, p. A16; emphasis added.

86. Seth Mydans, "The Demons of a Despot," *New York Times*, April 17, 1998, p. A1.

87. 22 U.S.C. 2656, part D, sections 571–574, 1994.

88. Quoted in Malamud, "New Documents," p. 2.

89. Press briefing, UN Secretary-General's Special Representatives for Human Rights in Cambodia, Internally Displaced Persons," November 13, 1997, p. 1.

90. Becker, "Pol Pot's End," p. A17.

91. Quoted in ibid.

92. Quoted in ibid.

93. Rosenblatt, "Memories of Pol Pot," p. 26.

94. Kiernan, "Cambodian Genocide," p. 396.

95. Quoted in Robert D. McFadden, "Survivor of Killing Fields Is Resolute in Quest of Justice," *New York Times*, April 17, 1998.

96. AP, "Local Trial for Khmer Rouge Leader," *New York Times*, March 9, 1999, p. A1.

5. "Ethnic Cleansing" in the Balkans

1. The information in the following paragraphs comes from Mihailo Crnobrnja, *The Yugoslav Drama* (Quebec: McGill-Queens University Press, 1996), pp. 15–33, passim.

2. Ibid., p. 19.

3. Peter Maas, *Love Thy Neighbor: A Story of War* (New York: A. A. Knopf, 1996), p. 27. Given that the Bosnian Muslims are Slavic, not Arabic, "a man with blond hair and blue eyes in Bosnia is just as likely to be a Muslim as a Serb or Croat" (ibid., p. 69).

4. See Zoran Paji, "The Conflict in Bosnia-Herzegovina," Occasional Paper No. 2, in *Violation of Fundamental Rights in the Former Yugoslavia* (n.p.: David Davies Memorial Institute of International Studies, February 1993), p. 2. Muslims lived in urban areas such as Sarajevo, and Serbs generally lived in the countryside, which meant that at the start of warfare in 1992, Serbs controlled about 55 percent of Bosnia-Herzegovina.

5. See Michael P. Scharf, *Balkan Justice* (Durham, N.C.: Carolina Academic Press, 1997), p. 23ff.

6. Both quoted in ibid., p. 23.

7. A. M. Rosenthal, "Back from the Grave," *New York Times,* April 15, 1997, p. A13.

8. For an examination of the major support role played by the Roman Catholic Church during the Ustasha regime's genocide (1941–1945), see Vladimir Dedijer, *The Yugoslav Auschwitz and the Vatican: The Croatian Massacre of the Serbs during World War Two* (Buffalo, N.Y.: Prometheus Books, 1992).

9. Aleksa Djilas, "A Collective Madness," *New York Times Book Review,* October 18, 1998, p. 17.

10. Scharf, *Balkan Justice,* p. 24ff.

11. Kosovo was a largely autonomous province in Serbia with an over 90 percent ethnic Albanian population and a very small Serb minority that was feeling discriminated against by the majority. The plight of the Serb minority in Kosovo was the "rallying cry" for Serb nationalism in 1989–1990. Crnobrnja, *Yugoslav Drama,* p. 104.

12. Crnobrnja, *Yugoslav Drama,* pp. 97–105, passim.

13. Anthony Lewis, "War Crimes," in *The Black Book of Bosnia: The Consequences of Appeasement,* ed. Nader Mousavizadeh (New York: Basic Books, 1996), p. 58.

14. Scharf, *Balkan Justice,* p. 24.

15. See Richard Holbrooke, *To End a War* (New York: Random House, 1998), p. 27.

16. Ibid., pp. 21–28, passim.

17. Arkan's real name was Zeljko Raznatovic; he lived in Belgrade, ran a popular restaurant, and was married to a rock star. He was also "one of the most notorious men in the Balkans," wrote Holbrooke. "Even in the former Yugoslavia, Arkan was something special, a freelance murderer who roamed across Bosnia and eastern Slavonia with his black-shirted men, terrorizing Muslims and Croats. . . . Many Serbs regarded him as a hero. His private army, the Tigers, had committed some of the war's worst atrocities, carrying out summary executions and virtually inventing ethnic cleansing in 1991–1992" (Holbrooke, *To End a War,* p. 189).

18. "'Do you know the best way to interrogate prisoners,' he asked. 'You burn them and pour vinegar on the wounds, mostly on the genitals and the eyes. Then there is a field telephone that can be plugged into a Serb. It is a direct current, but it does not kill them'" (Chris Hedges, "Croatian's Confession Describes Torture and Killing on a Vast Scale," *New York Times,* September 5, 1997, p. A1).

19. Hedges, "Croatian's Confession," p. A4; emphasis added.

20. Jan Willem Honig and Norbert Both, *Srebrenica: Record of a War Crime* (New York: Penguin Books, 1996), pp. 73–74.

21. Honig and Both, *Srebrenica,* pp. 75–76.

22. Or they were shot "by Serbian paramilitary units, secretly enlisted by the Serb leadership (Milosevic) in Belgrade" (Johanna McCreary, "Face to Face with Evil," *Time,* May 13, 1996, p. 49).

23. Maas, *Love Thy Neighbor,* p. 39. The May 1994 UN report to the Security Council observed that "the main objective of the concentration camps . . . seems to have been to eliminate the non-Serbian leadership. Political leaders, officials from the Courts and administration, academic and other intellectuals, religious leaders, key business people and artists—the backbone of the Muslim and Croatian communities—were removed, apparently with the intention that the removal be permanent."

24. Crnobrnja, *Yugoslav Drama,* p. 141.

25. Ibid., p. 178.

26. Maas, *Love Thy Neighbor;* Laura Silber and Allan Little, *Yugoslavia: Death of a Nation* (New York: Penguin USA, 1996); Roy Gutman, *Witness to Genocide* (New York: Macmillan, 1993); Edward Vulliamy, *Seasons in Hell: Understanding Bosnia's War* (London: Simon and Schuster, 1994); Thomas Cushman and Stjepan G. Mestrovi, eds., *This Time We Knew: Western Responses to Genocide in Bosnia* (New York: New York University Press, 1996); Scharf, *Balkan Justice;* Crnobrnja, *Yugoslav Drama;* Holbrooke, *To End a War;* Amnesty International, *Report on Bosnia-Herzegovina* (London: Amnesty International, January 1994). See also Roger Cohen, *Hearts Grown Brutal* (New York: Random House, 1998); Chuck Sudetic, *Blood and Vengeance* (New York: Norton, 1998); Aryeh Neier, *War Crimes: Brutality, Genocide, Terror, and the Struggle for Justice* (New York: Times Books, 1998).

27. Nedzib Sacirbey, "The Genesis of Genocide: Reflections on the Yugoslav Conflict," *Brown Journal of World Affairs* 3, no. 1 (winter/spring 1996): 341.

28. Quoted in Anthony Lewis, "No Peace without Justice," *New York Times,* November 20, 1995.

29. Graham Blewitt, an Australian serving as deputy prosecutor of the ICTY, had been investigating Nazi war crimes for a number of years and argued that the phrase "'ethnic cleansing,' had been used by the Nazi-backed Croats in their vicious campaign against Serbs during World War II" (in William W. Horne, "The Real Trial of the Century," *The American Lawyer,* June 1997).

30. Holbrooke, *To End a War,* p. 34.

31. Maas, *Love Thy Neighbor,* p. 5.

32. Silber and Little, *Yugoslavia,* p. 244. "To assume that the [Bosnian Muslim] refugees would be able to return after the fighting had ended was to miss the whole point of the war, *which was being waged deliberately to ensure that they would never return*" (p. 247; emphasis added).

33. Quoted in Honig and Both, *Srebrenica,* pp. 71, 72.

34. Quoted in Sacirbey, "Genesis of Genocide," p. 345.

35. Quoted in Silber and Little, *Yugoslavia,* p. 215.

36. Testimony of James Gow, ICTY, Hague, May 9, 1996, reported on *Court TV,* May 14, 1996.

37. Maas, *Love Thy Neighbor,* p. 27.

38. Ibid., p. 33.

39. Sacirbey, "Genesis of Genocide," p. 347.

40. McCreary, "Face to Face with Evil," *Time,* p. 49.

41. Maas, *Love Thy Neighbor,* pp. 50–51.

42. UN Document S/1994/674–27, May 1994, part III B.

43. Honig and Both, *Srebrenica,* p. 80ff.

44. Zlata Filipovic, *Zlata's Diary: A Child's Life in Sarajevo* (New York: Viking Press, 1994), pp. 51–52, 54–55, 56–57, 199–200, 170.

45. Honig and Both, *Srebrenica,* p. 178ff.

46. Ibid., p. 62.

47. Ibid., p. 65. In July 1998, the Red Cross reported that the number of Muslims missing had climbed to 7,300, with only 1,000 bodies found and only fifteen bodies identified. David Rohde, "In Bosnian Town Where Thousands Died, Ethnic Hate Overwhelms Small Kindnesses," *New York Times,* July 25, 1998, p. A3.

48. Quoted in Honig and Both, *Srebrenica,* p. 37.

49. Richard Holbrooke, "Why Are We in Bosnia?" *New Yorker,* May 18, 1998, p. 43.

50. Ted Zimmerman, "A Chilly Peace in Bosnia," *U.S. News and World Report,*

December 4, 1995, p. 26. See also Holbrooke's account of the negotiations in *To End a War*.

51. Quoted in Zimmerman, "A Chilly Peace," p. 27.

52. For example, the U.S. State Department's 1994 *Report on Bosnia and Herzegovina Human Rights Practices,* dated February 1995, documents the existence of concentration camps and gives detailed accounts of ethnic cleansing. Included in the report were sections covering political and other extrajudicial killing; disappearances; torture and other cruel, inhumane, or degrading treatment or punishment; arbitrary arrest, detention, or exile; denial of fair, public trial; arbitrary interference with privacy, family, home, or correspondence; and use of excessive force and violations of humanitarian law in internal conflicts. One section of the report cited denial of civil liberties, including freedom of speech and the press, freedom of peaceful assembly and association, freedom of religion, and freedom of movement. Other segments of the report examined the denial of political rights and general discrimination based on race, sex, religion, disability, language, or social status.

53. Elaine Sciolino, "Fate of Bosnian Serb Chiefs Snag Talks," *New York Times,* November 17, 1995, p. A4. Holbrooke wrote that "Milosevic remained adamant; he could not, and would not, deliver [Karadzic and Mladic] to an international tribunal" (Holbrooke, *To End a War,* p. 320).

54. Quoted in Lewis, "No Peace without Justice," p. A25.

55. Roger Cohen, "When the Price of Peace Is Injustice," *New York Times,* November 19, 1995, p. 4.

56. Chris Hedges, "Fallen Serb on the Run, Hotly Pursued by NATO," *New York Times,* May 31, 1998, p. A6.

57. Ibid.

58. Ibid.

59. The Statute of the International Tribunal, May 25, 1993, UN Document S/RES/827 (1993).

60. Cohen, "When the Price of Peace Is Injustice," p. 4.

61. See, for example, McCreary, "Face to Face with Evil," pp. 46–52.

62. Zimmerman, "A Chilly Peace," p. 26.

63. Cohen, "When the Price of Peace Is Injustice."

64. See UN Document S/24365 (1992).

65. UN Document E/CN.4/1992/S-1/9, at pp. 2–3.

66. UN Document S/RES/827 (1993). Resolution 827, adopted by the Security Council at its 3,217th meeting, May 25, 1993.

67. Resolution 827, p. 1.

68. Holbrooke, *To End a War,* p. 190.

69. Ibid.

70. The U.S. investigators included attorneys from the Justice Department and the FBI. Some U.S. federal judges took leaves of absence to serve in the Chambers and in the Prosecutor's Office.

71. Horne, "The Real Trial of the Century."

72. Ibid.

73. There are 101 rules of procedure and evidence; see UN Document IT/32/Rev. 7 (1996).

74. In addition, the UN created a second tribunal to hear cases involving alleged war crimes in Rwanda.

75. The eleven nations that have offered prison facilities are Denmark, Finland, Germany, Iran, Italy, the Netherlands, Norway, Pakistan, Muslim-controlled Bosnia,

Spain, and Sweden. As of 1998, only Italy and Finland had formally agreed to accept convicted persons.

76. Fouad Ajami, "On War Crimes: Why Bosnia Needs a Nuremberg," *U.S. News & World Report,* February 19, 1996, p. 67. See also Lewis, "No Peace without Justice," and Cohen, "When the Price of Peace Is Injustice."

77. Quoted in Neil A. Lewis, "Nuremberg Isn't Repeating Itself," *New York Times,* November 19, 1995.

78. Lewis, "No Peace without Justice," p. 18.

79. Ajami, "On War Crimes," p. 67.

80. These two Bosnian Serb leaders were indicted twice by the ICTY. One indictment was for their "command responsibility" for the "systematic" commission of genocide and crimes against humanity "arising from atrocities perpetrated against the civilian population throughout Bosnia-Herzegovina, including Tuzla and Srebrenica. The other indictment was for their responsibility for the three-year-long shelling and sniping campaign against civilians in Sarajevo, and for the taking of U.N. peacekeepers as hostages and their use as human shields." See Mary Williams Walsh, "Tribunal Indicts Serb Leaders for War Crimes," *Los Angeles Times,* July 26, 1995. Goldstone charged them with genocide because the Bosnian Serbs acted "'with intent to destroy, in whole or in part, a national, ethnic, or religious group.'"

81. Marlise Simons, "Controversy over Death of a Serb War Crime Suspect," *New York Times,* August 18, 1998.

82. See Tina Rosenberg's essay about Kovacevic, "Defending the Indefensible," *New York Times Sunday Magazine,* April 19, 1998, pp. 46–56, 69, for the details of his alleged crimes against humanity and genocide, discovered by reporters in August 1992.

83. At Trnpolje, hundreds of Muslim women were tortured and raped by Bosnian Serb special forces and local policemen. See Marlise Simons, "First Genocide Trial of a Bosnian Serb Opens in the Hague," *New York Times,* July 7, 1998.

84. Third Annual Report, ICTY, 31 July 1995–31 July 1996, *UN Documents,* the Hague, Netherlands, 1997.

85. Although Tadic's was the first trial, the first person to be convicted was an ethnic Croat soldier, Drazen Erdemovic, who pled guilty to crimes against humanity for his part in the massacre of thousands of Muslims after Srebrenica was captured by the Serbs in July 1996. Although he confessed to participating in the killing of more than seventy Muslim men in the village of Pilica, he told the court, "I had to do this. If I had refused, I would have been killed together with the victims. When I refused, they told me, 'If you are sorry for them, line up with them and we will kill you too'" (quoted in *New York Times,* June 1, 1996, p. A4). In November 1996, he was sentenced to ten years in prison for his crimes. His lawyers have appealed the sentence.

86. Annexure "MK 1" to Application for Deferral, *Declaration,* p. 2; emphasis added.

87. Beth Ann Isenberg, "Comment: Genocide, Rape, and Crimes against Humanity: An Affirmation of Individual Accountability in the Former Yugoslavia in the Karadzic Actions," 60 *Albany Law Review* 1051, 1056 (1997).

88. 28 U.S.C. section 1350 (1789, 1988).

89. The two suits are *S. K., on her own behalf and on behalf of her infant sons Benjamin and Ognjen, Internationalna Iniciativa Zena Bosne I Hercegovine "Biser," and Zene Bosne I Hercvine, Plaintiffs-Appellants, v. Radovan Karadzic, Defendant-Appellee,* and *Jane Doe I, on behalf of herself and all others similarly situated; and Jane Doe II, on behalf of herself and as administratrix of the estate of her deceased mother,*

and on behalf of all other similarly situated, Plaintiffs-Appellants, v. Radovan Karadzic, Defendant-Appellee, Nos. 1541, 1544, August Term, 1994, Docket Nos. 94-9035, 94-9069.

90. This 1991 statute, Chief Judge Newman wrote, "is not a jurisdictional one but permits the appellants to pursue their claims of official torture under the jurisdiction conferred by the Alien Tort Act." The law provides a cause of action for official torture and extrajudicial killing: "Any individual who, under actual or apparent authority, or color of law, of any foreign nation (1) subjects an individual to torture shall, in a civil action be liable for damages to that individual, or (2) subjects an individual to extrajudicial killing shall, in a civil action, be liable for damages to the individual's legal representative, or to any person who may be a claimant in an action for wrongful death."

91. *S. K. v. Karadzic; Doe v. Karadzic,* Newman opinion, at p. 3.

92. Thomas Scheffey, "U.S. Court Opens Doors to Victims of Bosnian War," *Legal Times,* November 13, 1995, pp. 2, 14. According to Catharine A. MacKinnon, a highly respected feminist legal scholar who brought suit on behalf of S. K., the woman was raped every day, ten times a day, for three weeks.

93. 866 Fed. Supp. 734 (1994).

94. Scheffey, "U.S. Court Opens Doors," p. 2.

95. 369 U.S. 186 (1962), at 211.

96. Newman, *S. K. v. Karadzic; Doe v. Karadzic* (1995), at p. 14.

97. *Kadic v. Karadzic,* 116 S.Ct. 2524 (1996).

98. Michael A. Sells, *The Bridge Betrayed: Religion and Genocide in Bosnia* (Berkeley: University of California Press, 1998), p. 31.

99. Warren Zimmerman, "The Demons of Kosovo," *National Interest* 52 (spring 1998), p. 6.

100. See Steven Lee Myers, "NATO Action in Kosovo Would Face New Pitfalls," *New York Times,* June 12, 1998, p. A10.

101. Holbrooke, *To End a War,* p. 357.

102. Steven Erlanger, "Milosevic Agrees to Let Observers into Kosovo," *New York Times,* June 8, 1998.

103. See "Serb Forces Said to Abduct and Kill Civilians," *New York Times,* July 17, 1998.

104. Mike O'Connor, "Serbian Cannon Fire Kills Three Mother Teresa Aid Workers," *New York Times,* August 26, 1998, p. A1.

105. Jane Perlez, "New Massacres by Serb Forces in Kosovo Villages," *New York Times,* September 20, 1998, p. A1.

106. Marlise Simons, "U.N. War Crimes Panel Steps Up Kosovo Inquiry," *New York Times,* August 26, 1998, p. A1.

107. Marlise Simons, "Belgrade Bars UN War-Crimes Investigators, *New York Times,* October 8, 1998.

108. Minna Schrag, quoted in Horne, "The Real Trial of the Century."

109. See Rosmarie Buchanan, "Battling the Crimes of War," *Student Law,* May 1993, pp. 14–15.

110. See, for example, Jane Perlez, "War Crimes Tribunal on Bosnia Is Hampered by Basic Problems," *New York Times,* January 28, 1996, pp. A1, A6.

111. Gary J. Bass, "Courting Disaster: The U.N. Goes Soft on Bosnia Again," *New Republic,* September 6, 1993, p. 49.

112. Aryeh Neier, "Watching Rights: War Crimes," *The Nation* (1993), p. 825.

113. Quoted in Horne, "The Real Trial of the Century."

114. Ibid.

115. Walter Goodman, "Sorting Out War Crimes and Tangles of History," *New York Times,* May 13, 1996, p. C14.

116. Thomas L. Friedman, "Wishing Away Bosnia," *New York Times,* September 8, 1997, p. A23.

117. In August 1998, a report surfaced that "undercover French troops literally had Mladic and Karadzic in their crosshairs on several occasions but did not fire because there was never an official green light." Thomas Sancton and Gilles Delafon, "The Hunt for Karadzic," *Time,* August 10, 1998, pp. 68–69.

118. On July 26, 1998, a page-one *New York Times* story headlined: "U.S. Cancels Plans for Raid on Bosnia to Capture 2 Serbs." Evidently, over $100 million was spent preparing missions, training commandos, and gathering intelligence for a clandestine raid to seize Karadzic and Mladic, only to have the mission "scuttled by American commanders who fear[ed] a blood bath." The code name of the perilous operation was Amber Star and personnel included FBI agents, U.S. marshals, the CIA, and British intelligence. See Tom Weiner, "U.S. Cancels Plans for Raid on Bosnia to Capture 2 Serbs," *New York Times,* July 26, 1998, p. A1.

119. Friedman, "Wishing Away Bosnia."

120. Weiner, "U.S. Cancels Plans," p. A1.

6. MACHETE GENOCIDE IN RWANDA AND THE
INTERNATIONAL CRIMINAL TRIBUNAL

1. Philip Gourevitch, "The Genocide Fax," *New Yorker,* May 18, 1998, p. 46. See his book, *We Wish to Inform You that Tomorrow We Will Be Killed with Our Families: Stories from Rwanda* (New York: Farrar Strauss and Giroux, 1998).

2. Speech, President Bill Clinton, Kigali, Rwanda, March 24, 1998. Four years earlier, Kofi Annan, then the vice secretary-general of the UN, spoke to the lack of international response to the genocide: "Nobody should feel he has a clear conscience in this business. If the pictures of tens of thousands of human bodies rotting and gnawed on by the dogs . . . do not wake us up out of our apathy, I don't know what will" (*Le Monde,* May 25, 1994).

3. Madeline H. Morris, *The Case of Rwanda.* www.americandiplomacy.com, December 1997, p. 1.

4. Gourevitch, "The Genocide Fax," p. 42.

5. Andrew Bell-Falkoff, *Ethnic Cleansing* (New York: St. Martins Press, 1996), p. 181.

6. Rene Lemarchand, "The Rwanda Genocide," in *Century of Genocide,* ed. Samuel Totten, William S. Parsons, and Israel Charney (New York: Garland, 1997), p. 408. Helen Fein wrote of genocide that it is preventable "because it is usually a rational act; that is, the perpetrators calculate the likelihood of success, given their values and objectives" (quoted in ibid., p. 409).

7. One newsman spoke for many when he wrote that the "idea that the madness might have been planned, that it was the direct result of political scheming, was far from my thoughts" (Fergal Keane, *Season of Blood: A Rwandan Journey* [New York: Viking Press, 1995], pp. 6, 108).

8. Ibid., p. 109.

9. More than 11 percent of all sexually active Rwandans are infected with the human immunodeficiency virus (HIV), the precursor to acquired immunodeficiency syndrome (AIDS). A *New York Times* story noted that the prevalence of HIV "is a

sign of things to come in rural Rwanda, where people are facing a new catastrophe, after living through civil war, massacres, and a refugee crisis of monumental proportions. . . . The [AIDS] epidemic will take the life of 1 person out of 10 in the next decade" (James C. McKinley, Jr., "AIDS Brings Another Scourge to War-Devastated Rwanda," *New York Times,* May 28, 1998, p. A1).

10. Clorrine Vanderwerff, *Kill Thy Neighbor* (Boisie, Idaho: Pacific Press, 1996), p. 8.

11. Vanderwerff, *Kill Thy Neighbor,* p. 16.

12. Lemarchand, "Rwanda Genocide," p. 409.

13. Ibid., p. 410.

14. Gerard Prunier, *The Rwanda Crisis: History of a Genocide* (New York: Columbia University Press, 1995), p. 6.

15. Ibid., p. 5.

16. Keane, *Season of Blood,* p. 13. Prunier noted that, to the Europeans, the Tutsi "were too fine to be 'negroes'" (*Rwanda Crisis,* p. 6).

17. Bell-Falkoff, *Ethnic Cleansing,* p. 184.

18. Keane, *Season of Blood,* p. 86.

19. Prunier, *Rwanda Crisis,* p. 27.

20. Bell-Falkoff, *Ethnic Cleansing,* p. 185.

21. Vanderwerff, *Kill Thy Neighbor,* pp. 25–26.

22. Prunier, *Rwanda Crisis,* pp. 76–77.

23. Bell-Falkoff, *Ethnic Cleansing,* pp. 181–186, passim.

24. Prunier, *Rwanda Crisis,* pp. 116–117. One consequence was that the volunteers, all educated and many with university degrees, made the RPF the most educated military group the world had ever seen.

25. Scott R. Feil, "Preventing Genocide: How the Early Use of Force Might Have Succeeded in Rwanda," in *A Report to the Carnegie Commission on Preventing Deadly Conflict* (Washington, D.C.: April 1998), p. 17.

26. Prunier, *Rwanda Crisis,* p. 168.

27. *Ubutabera,* no. 33 (March 30, 1998), p. 7. This biweekly, funded by the European Community, is the newsletter for the staff of the ICTR. It contains personnel movements and trial information, including segments of actual testimony. The word *Ubutabera* means "justice" in Kinyarwanda.

28. Prunier, *Rwanda Crisis,* p. 93.

29. Ibid., pp. 166–170, passim.

30. Ibid., p. 203.

31. Feil, "Preventing Genocide," p. 48.

32. Keane, *Season of Blood,* p. 121.

33. Gourevitch, "The Genocide Fax," p. 42.

34. See Nicholas O. Berry, *War and the Red Cross: The Unspoken Mission* (New York: St. Martin's Press, 1997), p. 76ff. Berry noted that the International Committee of the Red Cross delegate to the UN, Daniel Augstburger, "was screaming at the Security Council for its failure to move" (p. 77).

35. Prunier, *Rwandan Crisis,* p. 261.

36. *Ubutabera,* no. 30 (February 16, 1998), p. 9.

37. The witness was Alison DesForges, a historian, testifying in *Prosecutor v. Akayesu,* ICTR-96-4-T, quoted by the tribunal in its judgment, September 2, 1998, p. 3.

38. Keane, *Season of Blood,* p. 8.

39. Prunier, *Rwandan Crisis,* p. 142.

40. Feil, "Preventing Genocide," p. 6.

41. Prunier, *Rwandan Crisis,* p. 241–242.

42. Ibid., p. 238.

43. Ibid., p. 347.

44. Ibid., pp. 137–138.

45. Ibid., pp. 141–142.

46. Lemarchand, "Rwanda Genocide," p. 415.

47. Feil, "Preventing Genocide," p. 7.

48. Ibid., p. 2.

49. Physicians for Human Rights, www.phr.com, 1994, p. 11.

50. Keane writes about a Hutu massacre of over 800 Tutsi who had taken refuge in Zasa parish, "the site of one of the oldest and most prestigious Roman Catholic missions in Rwanda. The people who fled there doubtless believed that, as one of the places of origin for the Christian religion in Rwanda, it would be a sanctuary." They were wrong. Keane, *Season of Blood,* p. 154. See also Prunier, *Rwanda Crisis,* p. 253ff.

51. Prunier, *Rwanda Crisis,* pp. 254–255.

52. Feil, "Preventing Genocide," p. 9.

53. Prunier, *Rwanda Crisis,* p. 5.

54. Keane, *Season of Blood,* pp. 74–75. See also Prunier, *Rwanda Crisis,* p. 255.

55. Quoted in African Rights, *Rwanda: Death, Despair, and Defiance,* www.un. rwanda.com, 1994, pp. 344–345.

56. Feil, "Preventing Genocide," p. 48.

57. Berry, *War and the Red Cross,* pp. 79–80.

58. Krishna Kumar, ed., *Rebuilding Societies after Civil War* (Boulder, Colo.: Rienner, 1997), p. 67.

59. AP, "Rwandan Rebels Massacre at Least 110," August 3, 1998.

60. Feil, "Preventing Genocide," p. 49.

61. Kingsley Chiedu Moghalu, "A Shared Duty to Justice," *Legal Times,* August 17, 1998, p. 29.

62. Article III deals with the treatment of prisoners of war, prohibiting "willful killing, torture, or inhuman treatment, including biological experiments, willfully causing great suffering or serious injury to body or health, . . . or willfully depriving a prisoner of war of the rights of fair and regular trial."

63. Vantage Conference, 1997, "Post-Conflict Justice: The Role of the International Community," Stanley Foundation, Queenstown, Md., 1997, p. 19.

64. Morris, "Case of Rwanda," pp. 1–5.

65. See, generally, "Open Letter Regarding the Need to Expand the Jurisdiction of the International Tribunal for Rwanda," Attorneys without Borders, May 18, 1995, pp. 1–2.

66. *Position of the Government of the Republic of Rwanda on the ICTR,* April 21, 1998, pp. 1–9.

67. See UN Security Council Resolution 955 (1994), S/RES/955, adopted on November 8, 1994.

68. Steven Lee Myers, "In East Africa, Panel Tackles War Crimes, and Its Own Misdemeanors," *New York Times,* September 14, 1997, p. A6.

69. UN press release, March 25, 1998, p. 1.

70. Sara Darehshori, "Inching toward Justice in Rwanda," *New York Times,* September 8, 1998.

71. *Ubutabera,* no. 30 (February 16, 1998), pp. 7–8.

72. Myers, "In East Africa," p. A6.

73. Barbara Crossette, "UN Told a Tribunal Needs Help," *New York Times*, May 23, 1998, p. A8.

74. Moghalu, "Shared Duty," p. 29. The pastor was charged with ordering the death of hundreds of frightened Tutsi who had sought safe haven in his church. He had offered them refuge, and after the Tutsi were inside, he brought a truckload of *interahamwe* to the church and ordered them to begin the killings. AP, "Rwandan Pastor Arrested, Charged with Genocide," September 28, 1996.

75. She is the first woman to be indicted by a war crimes tribunal.

76. Myers, "In East Africa," p. A6.

77. UN press release/L2841, December 15, 1995, p. 1.

78. Quoted in *Ubutabera,* no. 32 (March 16, 1998), p. 12.

79. James C. McKinley, Jr., "UN Court Issues First Guilty Verdict for Genocide," *New York Times,* September 3, 1988, p. A7.

80. James C. McKinley, Jr., "Rwanda Blood Bath: Justice Is Slow," *New York Times,* November 21, 1997, p. A1.

81. United Nations, case no. ICTR 96-4-1, *The Prosecutor of the Tribunal against Jean Paul Akayesu,* p. 3. Quotes in succeeding paragraphs are from the indictment, unless otherwise noted.

82. McKinley, "UN Court Issues," p. A1.

83. McKinley, "Rwanda Blood Bath," p. A8.

84. McKinley, "UN Court Issues," p. A7.

85. McKinley, "On 1994 Blood Bath," p. A8.

86. McKinley, "UN Court Issues," p. A1.

87. Quoted in *Africa News,* March 18, 1998, pp. 1–2.

88. Quoted in *Africa News,* March 19, 1998, p. 3.

89. Quoted in "Closing Arguments in the Trial of Jean-Paul Akayesu," *Africa News,* March 26, 1998, p. 1.

90. Akayesu was found not guilty on count 2 (complicity in genocide). He was charged with genocide for the same incident, and the tribunal noted that one could not be both the principal perpetrator and an accomplice at the same time. He was also not guilty on counts 6, 8, 10, 12, and 15 (violation of Article III of the 1949 Geneva Conventions). The tribunal noted that although the Rwandan civil war itself fell within the contours of these international conventions that punished war crimes, the prosecution "failed to show beyond a reasonable doubt that Akayesu was a member of the armed forces and that he was duly mandated, in his capacity as a public official or agent or person otherwise vested with public authority of a *de facto* representative of the government, to support and carry out the war effort" (judgment, *Prosecutor v. Akayesu,* ICTR-96-4-T, September 2, 1998).

91. ICTR/INFO-9-2-138 Document. The tribunal defined the crime of rape for the first time in international law. "The Chamber defines rape as a physical invasion of a sexual nature, committed on a person under circumstances which are coercive. Sexual violence, including rape, is not limited to physical invasion of the human body and may include such acts which do not involve penetration or even physical contact." These actions constitute genocide "as long as they were committed with intent to destroy a particular group targeted as such. The rape of Tutsi women was systematic and was perpetrated against all Tutsi women and solely against them. Furthermore, these rapes were accompanied by a proven intent to kill their victims."

92. Quoted in Stephen Buckley, "Ex-Leader in Rwanda Admits to Genocide," *Washington Post,* May 2, 1998, p. A1.

93. Moghalu, "Shared Duty," p. 30.

94. Judgment, ICTR, September 4, 1998. UN press release, AFR 95/L/2898.

95. *Ututabera*, no. 4 (April 13, 1998), p. 4.

96. Barbara Crossette, "UN Chief Visits Rwanda Tribunal in Tanzania," *New York Times*, May 6, 1998, p. A1.

97. Ibid.

98. Aryeh Neier, *War Crimes: Brutality, Genocide, Terror, and the Struggle for Justice* (New York: Times Books, 1998), p. 220. A little more than one year earlier, there were about 66,000 prisoners held by the Rwandan government.

99. Morris, "Case of Rwanda," p. 1.

100. "The Judicial System in Rwanda: A Report on Justice," April 21, 1998, pp. 1–2. Between 1996 and 1998, the Rwandan government provided training for 450 new judges, 150 new prosecutors, and 450 new investigators (ibid., p. 4).

101. Morris, "Case of Rwanda," pp. 6–7.

102. Ibid., pp. 7–8.

103. James C. McKinley, Jr., "As Crowds Vent Rage," *New York Times*, April 25, 1998, p. A1.

104. Ibid., p. A7.

105. Quoted in *New York Times*, April 23, 1998, p. A1.

106. "Rwanda: First Defendants Faced Unfair Trials," *Amnesty News*, January 14, 1997, pp. 1–2. The Amnesty International Report, AFR 47/08/97, entitled "Rwanda Unfair Trials: Justice Denied" (April 8, 1997) presented a host of details illuminating the charge that the defendants in the national trials had been denied due process of law by the Rwandan government.

107. Moghalu, "Shared Duty," pp. 29–30.

108. James C. McKinley, Jr., "UN Leader Gets Chilly Reception in Rwanda," *New York Times*, May 8, 1998, p. A1.

7. NUREMBERG'S LEGACY? ADOPTION OF THE ROME STATUTE

1. T. R. Goldman, "A World Apart? U.S. Stance on a New ICC Concerns Rights Groups," *Legal Times*, June 8, 1998, p. 1.

2. Ibid.

3. William J. Durch, "Keeping the Peace," in *UN Peacemaking, American Policy, and the Uncivil Wars of the 1990s*, ed. William J. Durch (New York: St. Martin's Press, 1996), p. 12.

4. Ibid.

5. Testimony before U.S. Congress, House Committee on Foreign Affairs, *U.S. Participation in UN Peacekeeping Activities*, 1993, pp. 31–59.

6. Anthony Lake, "The Limits of Peacekeeping," *New York Times*, February 6, 1994, p. D17.

7. In Article 24 of the UN Charter, which entered into force on October 24, 1945, the UN Security Council was given "primary responsibility for the maintenance of international peace and security." There emerged four types of peacekeeping activities since 1945: (1) traditional peacekeeping, with a UN force between the belligerents, often for decades; (2) multidimensional peacekeeping, which involves the presence of UN Blue Helmets between the belligerents and assistance in the implementation of peace accords, as in the former Yugoslavia after the Dayton Peace Treaty was signed; (3) humanitarian intervention by the UN to relieve the suffering of innocent civilians trapped in the midst of civil war; and (4) peace enforcement, the use of UN Blue Hel-

mets to suppress conflict before war crimes, genocide, and crimes against humanity have an opportunity to occur. See Durch, "Keeping the Peace," pp. 3–7, passim.

8. Article 43 of the UN Charter calls for "all members of the UN . . . [to] undertake [and] to make available to the Security Council, on its call and in accordance with a special agreement or agreements, armed forces, assistance, and facilities, including rights of passage, necessary for the purpose of maintaining international peace and security."

9. Frank Wisner, statement before U.S. Congress, Senate Committee on Armed Forces, *International Peacekeeping and Peace Enforcement*, 1993, p. 69.

10. Ian Williams, "Criminal Neglect," *The Nation*, August 10, 1998.

11. The senators were Barbara Boxer (D-Calif.), Susan M. Collins (R-Me.), Dianne Feinstein (D-Calif.), Kay Bailey Hutchison (R-Tex.), Mary L. Landrieu (D-La.), Barbara A. Mikulski (D-Md.), Carol Mosely Braun (D-Ill.), Patty Murray (D-Wash.), and Olympia J. Snowe (R-Me.).

12. Eric Schmitt, "Pentagon Battles Plans for International War Crimes Tribunal, *New York Times*, April 14, 1998, p. 7.

13. Thomas Omestad, "The Brief for a World Court," *U.S. News and World Report*, October 6, 1997, p. 53.

14. Among the fifteen lawyers were former U.S. attorney general Benjamin R. Civiletti, former federal court of appeals judge A. Leon Higginbotham, Jr., American Civil Liberties Union leader Norman Dorsen, and others, including three former American Bar Association presidents.

15. Letter, Lawyers Committee for Human Rights (LCHR) to President William J. Clinton, May 15, 1998, published in *Media Alert*, May 15, 1998, p. 1.

16. Quoted in Schmitt, "Pentagon Battles Plans," p. A 7. In his March 26, 1998, letter to Secretary of State Albright, Helms rejected any ICC compromise that placed Americans in any prosecutorial jeopardy.

17. Quoted in Donald W. Jackson, "Creating a World Criminal Court Is Like Making Sausage—Except It Takes Longer," *Texas Observer*, June 30, 1998, pp. 7–8.

18. James Podgers, "War Crimes Court under Fire," 84 *American Bar Association Journal* 64 (September 1998).

19. Article 227 stated: "A special tribunal will be constituted to try the accused [Wilhelm II]. . . . [The special tribunal] will be composed of five judges, one appointed by each of the following Powers: namely, the United States of America, Great Britain, France, Italy, and Japan. . . . In its decision the tribunal will be guided by the highest motives of international policy, with a view to vindicating the solemn obligations of international undertakings and the validity of international morality. It will be its duty to fix the punishment which it considers should be imposed."

20. Barrett Prinz, "The Treaty of Versailles to Rwanda: How the International Community Deals with War Crimes," 6 *Tulane Journal of International and Comparative Law* 553 (spring 1998).

21. M. Cherif Bassiouni, "From Versailles to Rwanda in Seventy Five Years: The Need to Establish a Permanent International Criminal Court," *Harvard Human Rights Journal* 10:11, 20–21 (1997).

22. Also created was the International Court of Justice (ICJ), which was a dispute resolver in cases involving states party to the ICJ treaty, with their consent.

23. Kenneth Roth, "The Court the U.S. Does Not Want," *New York Review of Books*, November 10, 1998, p. 45.

24. The ILC was created to encourage the development of international law. Article XIII states that "the General Assembly shall initiate studies and make recom-

mendations for the purpose of encouraging the progressive development of international law and its codification."

25. Omestad, "Brief for a World Court," p. 52.

26. Jackson, "Creating a World Criminal Court," p. 4.

27. An earlier draft by PrepCom contained ninety-nine articles.

28. Donald W. Jackson and Ralph G. Carter, "Public International Law and the Politics of Judicial Creation: The Permanent International Criminal Court and American Foreign Policy," paper presented at the 1998 American Political Science Association National Convention, Boston, August 30–September 3, 1998, p. 24.

29. The Genocide Convention was finally adopted by the United States, with reservations, in the late 1980s, four decades after it was ratified by the UN. The UN's Universal Declaration of Human Rights was adopted by the General Assembly in 1948 and contained thirty articles "which are mainly concerned with setting out traditional civil and political rights such as equality before the law, freedom from arbitrary rights and freedom of peaceful assembly." David Armstrong, Lorna Lloyd, and John Redmond, *From Versailles to Maastricht: International Organization in the Twentieth Century* (New York: St. Martin's Press, 1996), p. 265. Article 1 states: "All human beings are born free and equal in dignity and rights."

30. Editorial, "A New World Court," *Economist,* June 13–19, 1998, p. 16.

31. See Goldman, "A World Apart?" p. 16. Aryeh Neier wrote that the "most contentious issues" were the independence (or lack of independence) of the ICC and what would be the "trigger mechanisms" for launching an ICC investigation into possible war crimes, crimes against humanity, and/or genocide (*War Crimes: Brutality, Genocide, Terror, and the Struggle for Justice* [New York: Times Books, 1998], p. 257).

32. By the fourth week of the Rome conference, the number of nations in the "Like-Minded Group" had almost doubled, to eighty.

33. Quoted in Goldman, "A World Apart?" pp. 16, 17.

34. See, for example, John N. Broder and Don Van Netter, Jr., "Clinton and Starr, a Mutual Admonition Society," *New York Times,* September 20, 1998, pp. A1, 35.

35. Joe Stork, "The ICC in focus," *International Criminal Court* 3, no. 4 (1998): 1.

36. Quoted in Goldman, "A World Apart?" p. 16.

37. Barbara Crossette, "World Criminal Court Having a Painful Birth," *New York Times,* August 13, 1997, p. A7.

38. Barbara Crossette, "U.S. Budges at UN Talks on a Permanent War Crimes Tribunal," *New York Times,* March 18, 1998, p. A1.

39. Quoted in Stork, "ICC in Focus," p. 5.

40. See Jackson and Carter, "Public International Law," pp. 13–17, passim.

41. Stork, "ICC in Focus," p. 2.

42. Quoted in Alessandra Stanley, "U.S. Specifies Terms for War Crimes Court," *New York Times,* July 10, 1998, p. A1.

43. Podgers, "War Crimes Court under Fire," p. 65; emphasis added.

44. David Frum, "The International Criminal Court Must Die," *Weekly Standard,* August 10, 17, 1998, p. 27.

45. Quoted in Goldman, "A World Apart?" p. 17.

46. Kenneth Starr, a Republican lawyer who served as U.S. solicitor general during the Bush administration (1989–1992), was appointed by a panel of three federal judges to examine possible criminal actions of President and Mrs. Clinton involving, initially, land deals in Arkansas while he was governor. In December 1997, Starr was given approval by the federal panel and U.S. Attorney General Janet Reno to examine

possible obstruction of justice, perjury, and abuse of power by President Clinton in his efforts to cover up a sexual affair he had with White House intern Monica Lewinsky.

47. Norman Dorsen and Morton H. Halperin, "Justice after Genocide," *Washington Post*, May 13, 1998, p. A17.

48. Quoted in Alessandra Stanley, "UN Conference to Consider Establishing Court for Crimes against Humanity," *New York Times*, June 15, 1998, p. A1.

49. Barbara Crossette, "UN Prosecutor Urges New Criminal Court," *New York Times*, December 9, 1997, p. A8.

50. Quoted in Goldman, "A World Apart?" p. 17.

51. Quoted in Stanley, "UN Conference," p. A1.

52. UN press release, *Daily Summary*, June 18, 1998, p. 1.

53. Alessandra Stanley, "U.S. Dissents but Accord is Reached on War-Crimes Court," *New York Times*, July 18, 1998, p. A7.

54. See Jackson, "Creating a World Criminal Court," p. 4.

55. See ibid., pp. 10–11.

56. Quoted in Stanley, "UN Conference," p. A1. Canadian Foreign Minister Lloyd Axworthy said to the reporter that the Clinton policy was "specious—an exercise in realpolitik."

57. Quoted in *Media Alert*, July 9, 1998, p. 1.

58. LCHR, "Lawyers Committee Labels U.S. Statement on ICC 'A Major Disappointment,'" *Media Alert*, July 9, 1998, p. 1.

59. LCHR, "Lawyers Committee Expresses Dismay at U.S. Statement," *Media Alert*, July 15, 1998, p. 1.

60. Jackson, "Creating a World Criminal Court," p. 19.

61. Quoted in ibid., p. 18.

62. Israel voted against the draft treaty because the omnibus war crimes definition in Article 8 (2) (b) (viii) included "the transfer, directly or indirectly, by the Occupying Power of parts of its own civilian population into the territory it occupies, or the deportation or transfer of all or parts of the population of the occupied territory within or outside this territory." The Israeli delegation viewed this as a pro–Palestine Liberation Organization (PLO) section.

63. Jackson and Carter, "Public International Law," p. 24.

64. Podgers, "War Crimes Court under Fire," p. 65.

65. LCHR, "Lawyers Committee Urges U.S. Government to Support ICC," *Media Alert*, July 21, 1998, p. 1.

66. Section VII is a critical definition of the role of the UN Security Council. Entitled "Action with Respect to Threats to the Peace, Breaches of the Peace, and Acts of Aggression," its thirteen articles (39–51) provide guidelines for the Security Council to take necessary steps to restore the peace, including the use of military force.

67. In April 1998, Helms, the chair of the Senate Foreign Relations Committee, sent Secretary of State Madeleine Albright a letter. In it, he said that any ICC treaty "without a clear U.S. veto" of an ICC investigation will be "'dead on arrival' when it reaches the Foreign Relations Panel" (quoted in Goldman, "A World Apart?" p. 17).

68. David Rieff, "Court of Dreams," *New Republic*, September 7, 1998, p. 16.

69. Ibid.

70. Quoted in R. W. Apple, "Deep Concern in the World over Weakened Clinton," *New York Times*, September 25, 1998, p. A1.

71. Rieff, "Court of Dreams," pp. 16–17.

72. The United States, Russia, and China were among a handful of nations that did not ratify the Anti-Landmines Treaty of 1997.

73. Ruth Wedgwood, "The Pitfalls of Global Justice," *New York Times,* June 10, 1998, p. A24.

74. Annan was, in January 1994, an undersecretary at the UN, head of the Department of Peacekeeping Operations. He worked with the commanders of UN peacekeeping missions. It was Annan who received General Dallaire's warnings about Hutu extremist plans for a Tutsi genocide and the general's request for a few thousand more UN Blue Helmets. Dallaire argued, unsuccessfully, that with only 5,000 soldiers he could prevent the genocide he knew was about to occur in Rwanda. Annan rejected the proposal, as did the Security Council. The genocide began three months later, in April 1994.

75. Speech, Rome, Italy, June 15, 1998.

76. Speech, Rome, Italy, June 18, 1998.

77. "The UN Security Council and the ICC: How Should They Relate?" Stanley Foundation, Arden House, N.Y., February 20–22, 1998, p. 11.

78. Quoted in "Press Briefing of the NGO Coalition for an International Criminal Court," Lawyers Committee for Human Rights, New York, August 4, 1997, p. 5.

79. Gabrielle Kirk McDonald, "The Changing Nature of the Laws of War," 156 *Military Law Journal* 30, 32–33 (June 1998).

80. She noted that "scholars estimate that over 175 million non-combatants have been killed in episodes of mass killings in the twentieth century. A further 40 million combatants have died in conflicts. That is a total of over 210 million people, or one in every 25 persons alive today—truly a figure that defies imagination" (McDonald, "Changing Nature of the Laws of War," p. 34).

81. McDonald, "Changing Nature of the Laws of War," p. 33; emphasis added.

82. Norman Dorsen, "The United States and the War Crimes Court: A Glass Half Full," *Lakeville, Florida Journal,* July 30, 1998, p. 1.

83. McDonald, "Changing Nature of the Laws of War," p. 51.

8. Fulfilling the Legacy: Problems and Prospects

1. Neil A. Lewis, "Nuremberg Isn't Repeating Itself," *New York Times,* November 19, 1995, p. 5.

2. Barbera Huff, "Victims of the State: Genocide, Politicide, and Group Repression since 1945," *International Review of Victimology* 1 (1989): 23–41.

3. Lance Morrow, "Rwandan Tragedy, Lewinsky Farce," *Time,* October 12, 1998, p. 126.

4. See Christopher R. Browning, *Ordinary Men: Reserve Police Battalion 101 and the Final Solution in Poland* (New York: Harper, 1992).

5. Michael A. Sells, *The Bridge Betrayed: Religion and Genocide in Bosnia* (Berkeley: University of California Press, 1998), p. 75.

6. John Dower, *War without Mercy: Race and Power in the Pacific War* (New York: Pantheon, 1986), p. 11.

7. Sells, *The Bridge Betrayed,* p. 75.

8. Browning, *Ordinary Men,* p. 162; see also Daniel J. Goldhagen, *Hitler's Willing Executioners: Ordinary Germans and the Holocaust* (New York: A. A. Knopf, 1996).

9. Raul Hilberg, *Perpetrators, Victims, Bystanders* (New York: HarperCollins Perennial, 1993), pp. 20–21.

10. Wole Soyinka, review of *We Wish to Inform You that Tomorrow We Will Be Killed with Our Families,* by Philip Gourevitch, *New York Times Book Review,* October 4, 1998, p. 11.

11. Gary Dempsey, "The Permanent War Crimes Tribunal," *Insight on the News,* September 7, 1998, p. 25.

12. Aryeh Neier, *War Crimes: Brutality, Genocide, Terror, and the Struggle for Justice* (New York: Times Books, 1998), p. 17.

13. Soyinka, review of *We Wish to Inform You,* p. 11.

14. Neier, *War Crimes,* p. 112.

15. Morrow, "Rwandan Tragedy," p. 126.

16. Marshall Harris, R. Bruce Hitchner, Michael P. Scharf, and Paul R. Williams, "Bringing War Criminals to Justice," in *Making Justice Work* (New York: Century Foundation Press, 1998), p. 27.

17. Editorial, "The Urgent Agenda in Kosovo," *New York Times,* October 8, 1998, p. A30.

18. The Midrash is an extensive set of tracts containing biblical exegesis by rabbis and other students of the Torah. In contemporary times, the term has been expanded to mean personal interpretations of the Torah. See Harold Bloom, review of *Kaddish,* by Leon Wieseltier, *New York Times Book Section,* October 4, 1998, p. 10.

19. And what did God do? According to the parable, "God took Truth, which had said 'don't create human beings for they will be false'—God took Truth and cast it into the ground" (Bereshit Rabbah, 8:5).

20. Richard E. Rupp, "The Western Powers and the Balkan State: Clashing Security Interests and Institutional Paralysis," *Southwestern Political Review* 26 no. 3 (September, 1998): 612–613.

21. Soyinka, review of *We Wish to Inform You.*

22. Rupp, "The Western Powers and the Balkan State," pp. 613–614.

23. Lewis, "Nuremberg Isn't Repeating Itself," p. 5.

24. Neier, *War Crimes,* p. xiv.

25. Quoted in Peter Maas, *Love Thy Neighbor: A Story of War* (New York: A. A. Knopf, 1996), p. 243.

26. Tim Padgett, "A Knocking at Midnight," *Time,* October 26, 1998.

27. Judge Garzon was also investigating rights abuses against Spanish citizens by other South American dictators including Argentina's Admiral Emilio E. Massera, chief ideologue of the military junta that took power in 1976. Clifford Krauss, "Spanish Judge Investigating Rights Abuses in Argentina," *New York Times,* November 29, 1998, p. A4.

28. Tim Golden, "Arresting a Dictator Is One Thing: Then It Gets Tough," *New York Times,* October 25, 1998, p. 5.

29. Quoted in Marlise Simons, "New Actions on Pinochet Begin in Paris and Geneva," *New York Times,* October 27, 1998.

30. Editorial, "Augusto Pinochet's Escape Route," *New York Times,* October 29, 1998.

31. Warren Hoge, "British Court Rules against Pinochet: Government Must Decide on Extradition," *New York Times,* November 26, 1998, p. A1.

32. Warren Hoge, "Britain Postpones Pinochet Hearing as Minister Meets with Chilean Envoys," *New York Times,* November 28, 1998.

33. T. R. Reid, "Briton Besieged on Pinochet Ruling," *Boston Globe,* November 27, 1998, p. A2. In late November, it was reported by two reputable English newspapers, the *Sunday Telegraph* and the *Observer,* that Tony Blair's Labour government was close to reaching a compromise that would return Pinochet to Chile to stand trial for human rights abuses that occurred during his dictatorship. Robert Barr, "Britain Nears Deal on Pinochet," *Burlington Free Press,* November 29, 1998, p. A2.

34. Barbara Crossette, "Dictators (and Some Lawyers) Tremble," *New York Times,* November 29, 1998, sec. 4, p. 1.

35. Quoted in "U.N. Prosecutor Applauds 'Innovations,'" *National Law Journal,* November 16, 1998, p. A11.

36. Quoted in Crossette, "Dictators Tremble," p. 1.

37. Craig R. Whitney, "France Rejects Calls to Try Congo Leader for Torture," *New York Times,* November 28, 1998.

38. Ibid.

39. One month after the Law Lords' decision was announced in November 1998, the House of Lords took the extraordinary step of setting aside the three-to-two judgment against the ex-dictator. Pinochet's lawyers successfully maintained that one of the judges, Lord Hoffmann, had close ties to Amnesty International, a major NGO that had lobbied for Pinochet's extradition. On January 18, 1999, a second panel of seven Law Lords (including three holdovers from the first trial) began hearings to determine whether Pinochet should be extradited to Spain to face charges of torture and genocide.

40. Member states of NATO are Belgium, Canada, Czech Republic, Denmark, France, Germany, Greece, Hungary, Iceland, Italy, Luxembourg, the Netherlands, Norway, Poland, Portugal, Spain, Turkey, the United Kingdom, and the United States.

41. NATO, *The NATO Handbook: Partnership and Cooperation* (Brussels: NATO Office of Information and Press, 1995), p. 17.

42. Quoted in Roger Cohen, "NATO Shatters Old Limits in the Name of Preventing Evil," *New York Times,* October 18, 1998, p. 3

43. Quoted in Cohen, "NATO Shatters."

44. Cohen, "NATO Shatters."

45. Steven Erlanger, "Bosnian Serb General Is Arrested by Allied Force in Genocide Case," *New York Times,* December 3, 1998, p. A4.

46. Jane Perlez, "Purges Hint Beginning of the End for Milosevic," *New York Times,* November 29, 1998, p. A1. On December 11, 1998, a *New York Times* story filed by Steven Erlanger quoted senior U.S. diplomats as stating that U.S. policy in Yugoslavia "is moving to undermine President Slobodan Milosevic's tight control over Yugoslavia. . . . 'There is a generalized feeling now throughout the Administration that Milosevic is the problem in the Balkans, and less vital for the solution,' a senior American official said. . . . James P. Rubin, spokesman for Secretary of State Madeleine Albright said last week: 'He is not simply part of the problem—Milosevic is the problem.'"

47. Editorial, "Serbia's Other Crackdown," *Washington Post,* March 18, 1999, p. A20.

48. Thomas L. Friedman, "Is Kosovo Worth It?" *New York Times,* March 2, 1999.

49. Jane Perlez, "NATO Confronts a New Role: Regional Policeman," *New York Times,* April 22, 1999. Article V of the NATO Charter addressed the central purpose of the organization for 50 years, from 1949–1999: "*Collective defense against armed attack*" by the Soviet Union and its allies. Kosovo is the first of NATO's non–Article V missions in Europe (my emphasis).

50. See Tina Rosenberg, "Keeping Ethnic Tension from Turning Violent," *New York Times,* April 22, 1999.

51. "Clinton's Remarks in Defense of Military Intervention in Balkans," *New York Times,* May 14, 1999, p. A1.

BIBLIOGRAPHY

African Rights. *Rwanda: Death, Despair, and Defiance.* www.un.rwanda.com, 1994.

Ajami, Fouad. "On War Crimes: Why Bosnia Needs a Nuremberg." *U.S. News & World Report,* February 19, 1996.

Akehurst, Michael. *A Modern Introduction to International Law.* London: Allen and Unwin, 1977.

Amnesty International. *Report on Bosnia-Herzegovina.* London: Amnesty International, January 1994.

Amnesty News. "Rwanda: First Defendants Faced Unfair Trials," January 14, 1997.

Analysis. "Serb Forces Said to Abduct and Kill Civilians." *New York Times,* July 17, 1998.

Apple, R. W. "Deep Concern in the World over Weakened Clinton." *New York Times,* September 25, 1998.

Armstrong, David, Lorna Lloyd, and John Redmond. *From Versailles to Maastricht: International Organization in the Twentieth Century.* New York: St. Martin's Press, 1996.

Bardakjian, K. *Hitler and the Armenian Genocide.* Cambridge: Harvard University Press, 1985.

Barr, Robert. "Britain Nears Deal on Pinochet." *Burlington Free Press,* November 29, 1998.

Bass, Gary J. "Courting Disaster: The U.N. Goes Soft on Bosnia Again." *New Republic,* September 6, 1993.

———. "Due Processes." *New Republic,* March 30, 1998.

Bassiouni, M. Cherif, "From Versailles to Rwanda in Seventy Five Years: The Need to Establish a Permanent International Criminal Court." *Harvard Human Rights Journal* 10 (1997).

———. "Symposium: Nuremberg and the Rule of Law: A Fifty Year Verdict." 149 *Military Law Review* (summer 1995).

Bassiouni, M. Cherif, and Ved P. Nanda, eds. *A Treatise on International Criminal Law,* Vol. 1. *Crimes and Punishment.* Springfield, Ill.: Charles C. Thomas, 1973.

Becker, Elizabeth. "Pol Pot's End Won't Stop U.S. Pursuit of His Circle." *New York Times,* April 17, 1998.

———. *When the War Was Over: The Voices of Cambodia's Revolution and Its People.* New York: Simon and Schuster, 1986.

Bell-Falkoff, Andrew. *Ethnic Cleansing.* New York: St. Martin's Press, 1996.

Bernstein, Richard, "Books of the Times." Review of *To End a War,* by Richard Holbrooke. *New York Times,* May 20, 1998.

Berry, Nicholas O. *War and the Red Cross: The Unspoken Mission.* New York: St. Martin's Press, 1997.

Bloom, Harold. Review of *Kaddish,* by Leon Wieseltier. *New York Times Book Section,* October 4, 1998.

Bolton, John R. "The Global Prosecutors: Hunting War Criminals in the Name of Utopia." *Foreign Affairs* 78, no. 1 (January/February 1999): 1–24.

Brackman, Arnold C. *The Other Nuremberg: The Untold Story of the Tokyo War Crimes Trials.* New York: William Morrow, 1987.

Broder, John N., and Don Van Netter, Jr. "Clinton and Starr, a Mutual Admonition Society," *New York Times,* September 20, 1998.

Brody, Reed. "Bringing Tyrants to Trial." *Legal Times,* December 7, 1998.

Browning, Christopher R. *Ordinary Men: Reserve Police Battalion 101 and the Final Solution in Poland.* New York: Harper, 1992.

Buchanan, Rosmarie. "Battling the Crimes of War." *Student Law,* May 1993.

Buckley, Stephen. "Ex-Leader in Rwanda Admits to Genocide." *Washington Post,* May 2, 1998.

Campbell, John. *The Experience of World War II.* New York: Oxford University Press, 1989.

Chandler, David P. *The Tragedy of Cambodian History: Politics, War, and Revolution since 1945.* New Haven, Conn.: Yale University Press, 1991.

Chang, Iris. *The Rape of Nanking: The Forgotten Holocaust of World War II.* New York: Basic Books, 1997.

Charney, Israel W. "The Study of Genocide." in *Genocide: A Critical Bibliographic Review,* ed. Israel W. Charney. New York: Facts on File, 1988.

Cohen, Roger. *Hearts Grown Brutal.* New York: Random House, 1998.

——. "NATO Shatters Old Limits in the Name of Preventing Evil." *New York Times,* October 18, 1998.

——. "When the Price of Peace Is Injustice." *New York Times,* November 19, 1995.

Comment. "Security Council Resolution 808: A Step toward a Permanent International Court for the Prosecution of International Crimes and Human Rights Violations." 25 *Golden Gate University Law Review* (1996).

Coon, Haruko, ed. *Japan at War: Selected Essays.* New York: New Press, 1992.

Crnobrnja, Mihailo. *The Yugoslav Drama.* Quebec: McGill-Queens University Press, 1996.

Crossette, Barbara. "Dictators (and Some Lawyers) Tremble." *New York Times,* November 29, 1998.

——. "UN Chief Visits Rwanda Tribunal in Tanzania." *New York Times,* May 6, 1998.

——. "UN Prosecutor Urges New Criminal Court." *New York Times,* December 9, 1997.

——. "UN Told a Tribunal Needs Help." *New York Times,* May 23, 1998.

——. "U.S. Budges at UN Talks on a Permanent War Crimes Tribunal." *New York Times,* March 18, 1998.

——. "World Criminal Court Having a Painful Birth." *New York Times,* August 13, 1997.

Cushman, Thomas, and Stjepan G. Mestrovi, eds. *This Time We Knew: Western Responses to Genocide in Bosnia.* New York: New York University Press, 1996.

Dadrian, Vahakn N. *The History of the Armenian Genocide: Ethnic Conflict from the Balkans to Anatolia to the Caucasians.* Providence, R.I.: Berghahn Books, 1995, 1997.

Darehshori, Sara. "Inching toward Justice in Rwanda." *New York Times,* September 8, 1998.

Daws, Gavan. *Prisoners of the Japanese: POWs of World War II in the Pacific.* New York: William Morrow 1994.

Dedijer, Vladimir, *The Yugoslav Auschwitz and the Vatican: The Croatian Massacre of the Serbs during World War Two.* Buffalo, N.Y.: Prometheus Books, 1992.

Dempsey, Gary. "The Permanent War Crimes Tribunal." *Insight on the News,* September 7, 1998.

DePaul, Kim, ed. *Children of Cambodia's Killing Fields: Memoirs by Survivors.* New Haven, Conn.: Yale University Press, 1998.

Djilas, Aleksa. "A Collective Madness." *New York Times Book Review,* October 18, 1998.

Dorsen, Norman. "The United States and the War Crimes Court: A Glass Half Full." *Lakeville, Florida Journal,* July 30, 1998.

Dorsen, Norman, and Morton H. Halperin. "Justice after Genocide." *Washington Post,* May 13, 1998.

Dower, John. *War without Mercy: Race and Power in the Pacific War.* New York: Pantheon, 1986.

Durch, William J. "Keeping the Peace." In *UN Peacemaking, American Policy, and the Uncivil Wars of the 1990s,* ed. William J. Durch. New York: St. Martin's Press, 1996.

Editorial. "Augusto Pinochet's Escape Route." *New York Times,* October 29, 1998.

Editorial. "Justice for Cambodia." *AsiaWeek,* April 21, 1998.

Editorial, "A New World Court." *Economist,* June 13–19, 1998.

Editorial. "The Urgent Agenda in Kosovo." *New York Times,* October 8, 1998.

Erlanger, Steven. "Bosnian Serb General Is Arrested by Allied Force in Genocide Case." *New York Times,* December 3, 1998.

———. "Milosevic Agrees to Let Observers into Kosovo." *New York Times,* June 8, 1998.

Feil, Scott R.. "Preventing Genocide: How the Early Use of Force Might Have Succeeded in Rwanda." *A Report to the Carnegie Commission on Preventing Deadly Conflict.* Washington, D.C.: April 1998.

Filipovic, Zlata. *Zlata's Diary: A Child's Life in Sarajevo.* New York: Viking Press, 1994.

Friedman, Thomas L. "Wishing away Bosnia." *New York Times,* September 8, 1997.

Frum, David. "The International Criminal Court Must Die." *Weekly Standard,* August 10, 17, 1998.

Gilbert, G. M.. *Nuremberg Diary.* New York.: DaCapo Press, 1995.

Ginn, John L. *Sugamo Prison, Tokyo.* London: McFarland, 1992.

Glass, James M. *"Life Unworthy of Life:" Racial Phobia and Mass Murder in Hitler's Germany.* New York: Basic Books, 1997.

Glenny, Misha. "Motives for a Massacre." *New York Times,* January 20, 1999.

Golden, Tim. "Arresting a Dictator Is One Thing: Then It Gets Tough." *New York Times,* October 25, 1998.

Goldhagen, Daniel J. *Hitler's Willing Executioners: Ordinary Germans and the Holocaust.* New York: A. A. Knopf, 1996.

Goldman, T. R. "A World Apart? U.S. Stance on a New ICC Concerns Rights Groups." *Legal Times,* June 8, 1998.
Goodman, Walter. "Sorting out War Crimes and Tangles of History." *New York Times,* May 13, 1996.
Gourevitch, Philip. "The Genocide Fax." *New Yorker,* May 18, 1998.
———. "Pol Pot's Children." *New Yorker,* August 10, 1998.
———. *We Wish to Inform You that Tomorrow We Will Be Killed with Our Families: Stories from Rwanda.* New York: Farrar Straus Giroux, 1998.
Gutman, Roy. *Witness to Genocide.* New York: Macmillan, 1993.
Harris, Marshall, R. Bruce Hitchner, Michael P. Scharf, and Paul R. Williams. "Bringing War Criminals to Justice." In *Making Justice Work.* New York: Century Foundation Press, 1998.
Hedges, Chris. "Croatian's Confession Describes Torture and Killing on a Vast Scale." *New York Times,* September 5, 1997.
———. "Fallen Serb on the Run, Hotly Pursued by NATO." *New York Times,* May 31, 1998.
Hilberg, Raul. *Perpetrators, Victims, Bystanders: The Jewish Catastrophe, 1933–1945.* New York: HarperCollins, 1992; HarperCollins Perennial, 1993.
Hoge, Warren. "Britain Postpones Pinochet Hearing as Minister Meets with Chilean Envoys." *New York Times,* November 28, 1998.
———. "British Court Rules against Pinochet: Government Must Decide on Extradition." *New York Times,* November 26, 1998.
Holbrooke, Richard. *To End a War.* New York: Random House, 1998.
———. "Why Are We in Bosnia?" *New Yorker,* May 18, 1998.
Honig, Jan Willem, and Norbert Both. *Srebrenica: Record of a War Crime.* New York: Penguin Books, 1996.
Horne, William W. "The Real Trial of the Century." *American Lawyer,* June 1997.
Hosoya, C., N. Ando, Y. Onuma, and R. Minear, eds. *The Tokyo War Crimes Trial: An International Symposium.* Tokyo: Kodansha, 1986.
Howard, Michael, George J. Andreopoulos, and Mark R. Shulman, eds. *The Laws of War: Constraints on Warfare in the Western World.* New Haven, Conn.: Yale University Press, 1994.
Huff, Barbera. "Victims of the State: Genocide, Politicide, and Group Repression since 1945." *International Review of Victimology* 1 (1989).
Isenberg, Beth Ann. "Comment: Genocide, Rape, and Crimes against Humanity: An Affirmation of Individual Accountability in the Former Yugoslavia in the Karadzic Actions." 60 *Albany Law Review* (1997).
Jackson, Donald W. "Creating a World Criminal Court Is Like Making Sausage— Except It Takes Longer." *The Texas Observer,* June 30, 1998.
Jackson, Donald W., and Ralph G. Carter. "Public International Law and the Politics of Judicial Creation: The Permanent International Criminal Court and American Foreign Policy." Paper presented at the 1998 American Political Science Association National Convention, Boston, August 30–September 3, 1998.
Kamm, Henry. *Cambodia: Report from a Stricken Land.* New York: Arcade, 1998.
Keane, Fergal. *Season of Blood: A Rwandan Journey.* New York: Viking Press, 1995.
Kiernan, Ben. "The Cambodian Genocide, 1975–1979." In *Century of Genocide,* ed. Samuel Totten, William S. Parsons, and Israel Charney. New York: Garland, 1997.
———. *The Pol Pot Regime: Race, Power, and Genocide in Cambodia under the Khmer Rouge, 1975–1979.* New Haven, Conn.: Yale University Press, 1996.

Klemperer, Victor. "Personal History: The Klemperer Diaries." *New Yorker*, April 27/May 6, 1998.

Knox, Donald. *Death March: The Survivors of Bataan*. New York: Harcourt, Brace, Jovanovich, 1981.

Krauss, Clifford. "Spanish Judge Investigating Rights Abuses in Argentina." *New York Times*, November 29, 1998.

Kumar, Krishna, ed. *Rebuilding Societies after Civil War*. Boulder, Colo.: Rienner, 1997.

Kuper, Leo. *Genocide: Its Political Use in the Twentieth Century*. New Haven, Conn.: Yale University Press, 1981.

———. *The Prevention of Genocide*. New Haven, Conn.: Yale University Press, 1985.

Lael, Richard L. *The Yamashita Precedent: War Crimes and Command Responsibility*. Wilmington, Del.: Scholarly Resources, 1982.

Lake, Anthony. "The Limits of Peacekeeping." *New York Times*, February 6, 1994.

Lawyers Committee for Human Rights. "Lawyers Committee Labels U.S. Statement on ICC 'A Major Disappointment.'" *Media Alert*, July 9, 1998.

———. "Lawyers Committee Urges U.S Government to Support ICC." *Media Alert*, July 21, 1998.

LeBlanc, Lawrence J. *The United States and the Genocide Convention*. Durham, N.C.: Duke University Press, 1981.

Lemarchand, Rene. "The Rwanda Genocide." In *Century of Genocide*, ed. Samuel Totten, William S. Parsons, and Israel Charney. New York: Garland, 1997.

Lemkin, Raphael. *Axis Rule in Occupied Europe: Laws of Occupation, Analysis of Government, and Proposals for Redress*. Washington, D.C.: Carnegie Foundation for International Peace, 1944.

Lewis, Anthony. "No Peace without Justice." *New York Times*, November 20, 1995.

———. "War Crimes." In *The Black Book of Bosnia: the Consequences of Appeasement*, New York: Basic Books, 1996.

Lewis, Neil A. "Nuremberg Isn't Repeating Itself." *New York Times*, November 19, 1995.

Maas, Peter. *Love Thy Neighbor: A Story of War*. New York: A. A. Knopf, 1996.

MacArthur, Douglas. *Reminiscences*. New York: McGraw-Hill, 1964.

Malamud, Paul. "New Documents Shed Light on Khmer Rouge Genocide." *United States Information Agency Electronic Journal* 1, no. 3 (May 1996).

McCarthy, Terry. "The Butcher of Cambodia, Pol Pot Is Dead." *Time*, April 27, 1998.

McCreary, Johanna. "Face to Face with Evil." *Time*, May 13, 1996.

McDonald, Gabrielle Kirk. "The Changing Nature of the Laws of War." 156 *Military Law Journal* (June 1998).

McFadden, Robert D. "Survivor of Killing Fields Is Resolute in Quest of Justice." *New York Times*, April 17, 1998.

McGeary, Johanna. "Face to Face with Evil: Many Men Suspected of Unspeakable War Crimes Remain at Large in the Balkans." *Time*, May 13, 1996.

McKinley, James C., Jr. "AIDS Brings Another Scourge to War-Devastated Rwanda." *New York Times*, May 28, 1998.

———."As Crowds Vent Rage." *New York Times*, April 25, 1998.

———. "Rwanda Blood Bath: Justice Is Slow." *New York Times*, November 21, 1997.

———. "UN Court Issues First Guilty Verdict for Genocide." *New York Times*, September 3, 1998.

———. "UN Leader Gets Chilly Reception in Rwanda." *New York Times*, May 8, 1998.

McNeil, Donald G., Jr. "Its Past on Its Sleeve, Tribe Seeks Bonn Apology." *New York Times,* May 31, 1998.

Minear, Richard H. *Victors' Justice: The Tokyo War Crime Trial.* Princeton, N.J.: Princeton University Press, 1971.

Minow, Martha. *Between Vengeance and Forgiveness: Facing History after Genocide and Mass Violence.* Boston: Beacon Press, 1998.

Moghalu, Kingsley Chiedu. "A Shared Duty to Justice." *Legal Times,* August 17, 1998.

Morganthau, Henry. *Ambassador Morganthau's Story.* New York: Doubleday, 1918.

Morris, Madeline H. *The Case of Rwanda.* www.americandiplomacy.com, December 1997.

Morris, Stephen J. "Pol Pot's Lingering Influence." *New York Times,* April 19, 1998.

Morrison, Fred L. "The Significance of Nuremberg for Modern International Law." In "Symposium: Nuremberg and the Rule of Law: A Fifty Year Verdict." 149 *Military Law Review* (summer 1995).

Morrow, Lance. "Rwandan Tragedy, Lewinsky Farce." *Time,* October 12, 1998.

Mydans, Seth. "Cambodian Denies He Opposed Trial for Khmer Rouge." *New York Times,* January 2, 1999.

———. "Cambodia's Leader Says Top Khmer Rouge Defectors Will Be Spared." *New York Times,* December 29, 1998.

———. "The Demons of a Despot." *New York Times,* April 17, 1998.

———. "Faces from Beyond the Grave." Review of *The Killing Fields,* by Chris Riley and Douglas Niven. *New York Times Book Review,* October 1998.

———. "Phantoms Rule in Former Khmer Stronghold." *New York Times,* April 14, 1998.

———. "Pol Pot, Brutal Dictator Who Forced Cambodians to Killing Fields, Dies at 73." *New York Times,* April 17, 1998.

———. "Revenge or Justice? Cambodians Confront Past." *New York Times,* December 31, 1998.

———. "Two Khmer Rouge Leaders Spend Beach Holiday in Shadow of Past." *New York Times,* January 1, 1999.

Myers, Steven Lee. "In East Africa, Panel Tackles War Crimes, and Its Own Misdemeanors." *New York Times,* September 14, 1997.

———. "NATO Action in Kosovo Would Face New Pitfalls." *New York Times,* June 12, 1998.

NATO. *The NATO Handbook: Partnership and Cooperation.* Brussels: NATO Office of Information and Press, 1995.

Neier, Aryeh. *War Crimes: Brutality, Genocide, Terror, and the Struggle for Justice.* New York: Times Books, 1998,

———. "Watching Rights: War Crimes." *The Nation* (1993).

Nelson, Robert F. *Revolution and Genocide: On the Origins of the Armenian Genocide and the Holocaust.* Chicago: University of Chicago Press, 1992.

Note. "The Iraqi Conflict: An Assessment of Possible War Crimes and the Call for Adoption of an International Criminal Code and Permanent International Criminal Tribunal." 14 *New York Law School Journal of International and Comparative Law* (1993).

Note. "The Khmer Rouge Regime." *Yale University Documentation Center,* vol. 1. 1997.

Note. "U.S. Envoy Issues a Stern Warning on Kosovo." *New York Times,* September 27, 1998.

O'Connor, Mike. "Serbian Cannon Fire Kills Three Mother Teresa Aid Workers." *New York Times,* August 26, 1998.

Omestad, Thomas. "The Brief for a World Court." *U.S. News and World Report,* October 6, 1997.

Osiel, Mark. *Mass Atrocity, Collective Memory, and the Law.* London: Transaction Publishers, 1997.

Padgett, Tim. "A Knocking at Midnight." *Time,* October 26, 1998.

Paji, Zoran. "The Conflict in Bosnia-Herzegovina." Occasional Paper no. 2. In *Violation of Fundamental Rights in the Former Yugoslavia.* N.p.: David Davies Memorial Institute of International Studies, February 1993.

Perlez, Jane. "In Kosovo Death Chronicles, Serb Tactic Revealed." *New York Times,* September 27, 1998.

———. "New Massacres by Serb Forces in Kosovo Villages." *New York Times,* September 20, 1998.

———. "Purges Hint Beginning of the End for Milosevic." *New York Times,* November 29, 1998.

———. "War Crimes Tribunal on Bosnia Is Hampered by Basic Problems." *New York Times,* January 28, 1996.

Persico, Joseph E. *Nuremberg: Infamy on Trial,* New York: Penguin Books, 1992.

Piccigallo, Phillip. *The Japanese on Trial.* Austin: University of Texas Press, 1979.

Podgers, James. "War Crimes Court under Fire." 84 *American Bar Association Journal* (September 1998).

Prinz, Barrett. "The Treaty of Versailles to Rwanda: How the International Community Deals with War Crimes." 6 *Tulane Journal of International and Comparative Law* (spring 1998).

Prunier, Gerard. *The Rwanda Crisis: History of a Genocide.* New York: Columbia University Press, 1995.

Reid, T. R. "Briton Besieged on Pinochet Ruling." *Boston Globe,* November 27, 1998.

Reuters. "'Killing Fields' Toll May Be 2 Million." *Washington Post,* January 26, 1997.

Rieff, David. "Court of Dreams." *New Republic,* September 7, 1998.

Rohde, David. "In Bosnian Town Where Thousands Died, Ethnic Hate Overwhelms Small Kindnesses." *New York Times,* July 25, 1998.

Rosenbaum, Ron. *Explaining Hitler.* New York: Random House, 1998.

Rosenberg, Tina. "Defending the Indefensible." *New York Times Sunday Magazine,* April 19, 1998.

Rosenblatt, Roger. "Memories of Pol Pot." *Time,* August 18, 1998.

Rosenman, Samuel I. *Working with Roosevelt.* New York: Harper, 1952.

Rosenthal, A. M. "Back from the Grave." *New York Times,* April 15, 1997.

Roth, Kenneth. "The Court the U.S. Does Not Want." *New York Review of Books,* November 10, 1998.

Rupp, Richard E. "The Western Powers and the Balkan State: Clashing Security Interests and Institutional Paralysis." *Southwestern Political Review* 26, no. 3 (September 1998).

Sacirbey, Nedzib. "The Genesis of Genocide: Reflections on the Yugoslav Conflict." *Brown Journal of World Affairs* 3, no. 1 (winter/spring 1996).

Sancton, Thomas, and Gilles Delafon. "The Hunt for Karadzic." *Time,* August 10, 1998.

Scharf, Michael P. *Balkan Justice.* Durham, N.C.: Carolina Academic Press, 1997.

Scheffey, Thomas. "U.S. Court Opens Doors to Victims of Bosnian War." *Legal Times,* November 13, 1995.

Schmitt, Eric. "Pentagon Battles Plans for International War Crimes Tribunal." *New York Times,* April 14, 1998.

Sciolino, Elaine. "Fate of Bosnian Serb Chiefs Snag Talks." *New York Times,* November 17, 1995.

Scrase, David, and Wolfgang Mieder, eds. *The Holocaust: Introductory Essays.* Burlington, Vt.: Center for Holocaust Studies at UVM, 1996.

Sells, Michael A. *The Bridge Betrayed: Religion and Genocide in Bosnia.* Berkeley: University of California Press, 1998.

Shenon, Philip. "U.S. Appears to Be Undecided on Kosovo Crisis." *New York Times,* September 16, 1998.

Shenon, Philip, and Eric Schmitt. "U.S. Is Planning a Move to Seize Pol Pot for Trial." *New York Times,* April 9, 1988.

Silber, Laura, and Allan Little. *Yugoslavia: Death of a Nation.* New York: Penguin USA, 1996.

Simons, Marlise. "Belgrade Bars UN War-Crimes Investigators." *New York Times,* October 8, 1998.

———. "Controversy over Death of a Serb War Crime Suspect." *New York Times,* August 18, 1998.

———. "First Genocide Trial of a Bosnian Serb Opens in the Hague." *New York Times,* July 7, 1998.

———. "New Actions on Pinochet Begin in Paris and Geneva." *New York Times,* October 27, 1998.

———. "U.N. War Crimes Panel Steps up Kosovo Inquiry." *New York Times,* August 26, 1998.

Simpson, A. W. Brian. *In the Highest Degree Odious: Detention without Trial: Wartime Detention in Britain.* New York: Oxford University Press, 1994.

Smith, Bradley F. *The Road to Nuremberg.* New York: Basic Books, 1981.

Smith, Roger. "Human Destructiveness and Politics." In *Genocide and the Modern Age,* ed. Isidor Walliman and Michael Dobkowski. Westport, Conn.: Greenwood Press, 1987.

Soyinka, Wole. Review of *We Wish to Inform You that Tomorrow We Will Be Killed with Our Families,* by Philip Gourevitch. *New York Times Book Review,* October 4, 1998.

Stanley, Alessandra. "UN Conference to Consider Establishing Court for Crimes against Humanity." *New York Times,* June 15, 1998.

———. "U.S. Dissents but Accord Is Reached on War-Crimes Court." *New York Times,* July 18, 1998.

———. "U.S. Specifies Terms for War Crimes Court." *New York Times,* July 10, 1998.

Stanley Foundation. "The UN Security Council and the ICC: How Should They Relate?" Arden House, N.Y.: Stanley Foundation, 1998.

Stork, Joe. "The ICC in Focus." *International Criminal Court* 3, no. 4 (1998).

Sudetic, Chuck. *Blood and Vengeance.* New York: Norton, 1998,

Taylor, Telford. *The Anatomy of the Nuremberg Trials: A Personal Memoir.* New York: A. A. Knopf, 1992.

Totten, Samuel, William S. Parsons, and Israel Charney, eds. *Century of Genocide.* New York: Garland, 1997.

Toynbee, Arnold J. *The Treatment of the Armenians in the Ottoman Empire, 1915–1916*. London: HMSO, 1918.

Uhrich, Kevin. "The Other Holocaust." *Los Angeles Reader,* July 1, 1994.

UN Document. *Position of the Government of the Republic of Rwanda on the ICTR.* April 21, 1998.

United Nations War Crimes Commission. *Law Reports of Trials of War Criminals: Four Genocide Trials.* New York: Fertig, 1992.

United States Holocaust Memorial Museum. *Historical Atlas of the Holocaust.* New York: Macmillan, 1996.

———. *In Pursuit of Justice: Examining the Evidence of the Holocaust.* Washington, D.C.: U.S. Holocaust Memorial Council, 1996.

U.S. State Department. *1994 Report on Bosnia and Herzegovina Human Rights Practices.* February 1995.

Vanderwerff, Clorrine. *Kill Thy Neighbor.* Boise, Idaho: Pacific Press, 1996.

Vantage Conference, 1997. "Post-Conflict Justice: The Role of the International Community." Queenstown, Md.: Stanley Foundation, 1997.

Viscount Maugham. *U.N.O. and War Crimes.* Westport, Conn.: Greenwood Press, 1975.

Vulliamy, Edward. *Seasons in Hell: Understanding Bosnia's War.* London: Simon and Schuster, 1994.

Walsh, Mary Williams. "Tribunal Indicts Serb Leaders for War Crimes." *Los Angeles Times,* July 26, 1995.

Wedgwood, Ruth. "The Pitfalls of Global Justice." *New York Times,* June 10, 1998.

Weiner, Tom. "U.S. Cancels Plans for Raid on Bosnia to Capture 2 Serbs." *New York Times,* July 26, 1998.

Weisburd, Mark A. *Use of Force: The Practice of States since World War Two.* University Park: Pennsylvania State University Press, 1997.

Whitney, Craig R. "France Rejects Calls to Try Congo Leader for Torture." *New York Times,* November 28, 1998.

Williams, Ian. "Criminal Neglect." *Nation,* August 10, 1998.

Williams, Peter, and David Wallace. *Unit 731: Japan's Secret Biological Warfare in World War II.* New York: Free Press, 1989.

Willis, James F. *Prologue to Nuremberg: The Politics and Diplomacy of Punishing War Criminals of the First World War.* Westport, Conn.: Greenwood Press, 1982.

Winter, Jay, and Blaine Baggett. *The Great War and the Shaping of the 20th Century.* New York: Penguin Books, 1996.

Wisner, Frank. Statement before U.S. Congress, Senate Committee on Armed Forces, *International Peacekeeping and Peace Enforcement,* 1993.

Wistrich, Robert S. *Weekend in Munich: Art, Propaganda, and Terror in the Third Reich.* London: Pavillion Books, 1995.

Zimmerman, Ted. "A Chilly Peace in Bosnia." *U.S. News and World Report,* December 4, 1995.

Zimmerman, Warren. "The Demons of Kosovo." *The National Interest* 52 (spring 1998).

INDEX